A SHOW OF HANDS

The story of a daring
rescue mission in Iraq

Joseph Agris, M.D.
"The Crazy Texan"

A-to-Z Publishing • Houston, Texas

ISBN 978-0-9994855-1-4 (hardcover)
ISBN 978-0-9994855-2-1 (paperback)
ISBN 978-0-9994855-4-5 (e-book)

Library of Congress Cataloguing In Publication Information: Pending

Printed in the United States of America on acid-free paper
First Edition, May 2023

A-to-Z Publishing offers a wide range of topics for speaking events.
To find out more, or to inquire about permission
to use material from this book
(other than fair-use purposes such as quoting passages for reviews),
please contact Dr. Joseph Agris at 713-705-6625 or email
TerryAgris@Att.net

A portion of the proceeds from the sale of this publication goes to
the Agris-Zindler Children's Foundation (Children's Fund)
to provide medical and surgical care for children with burns,
cleft lip and palate, post-war injuries,
and everyday medical emergencies and injuries
occurring at home or on the farm.

Literary collaboration and book & cover design provided by
Schmidt Kaye & Company Professional Literary Services
Ron Kaye & Connie L. Schmidt
schmidtkaye.com

To my beautiful wife, Terry Bodkin Agris:
soul mate, muse, and cherished travel partner in the journey of life.
Thank you for your unwavering
love and support throughout the years,
especially during my extended time in the Middle East.
God and thoughts of you got me home safely.

And to Len Rokaw – "Dad" – on your 101st birthday.

In Loving Memory Of Don North
War correspondent, documentarian, teacher,
author, advocate, friend

Donald George North, born in a small town in British Columbia, Canada in 1938, passed away at the age of 80 on January 7, 2019. He wore many hats in his long life: award-winning journalist, cameraman, film and video producer, and author, in addition to being a teacher, spokesperson, humanitarian, and fearless adventurer. Don was best known as a war correspondent, often working as an embedded journalist and covering numerous conflicts over more than half a century for radio, television, and print. He worked both as a freelancer and, at various times, for the Canadian Broadcasting Corporation (CBC), as well as ABC News and NBC News. And he produced numerous documentaries through his own video production company, Northstar Productions, Inc.

After earning a degree in advanced international journalism at the Columbia University graduate school in New York, Don began his career as a reporter, working for the CBC for a while and later accepting a position with the *Hong Kong China Mail* in the early 1960s. In 1964 he took his tape recorder, video camera, two 35mm Nikons, and a pen and notepad, and set off to cover the Vietnam war as a one-man media outlet, freelancing for a wide variety of news outlets. Years later he would describe the conflict in Vietnam as an unwinnable war, but he also said he was grateful to have been there, and he counted his coverage of that war as some of his finest work as a journalist. Over the course of his career, Don also covered wars in places such as Borneo, Cambodia, Afghanistan, Egypt, Israel, the Persian Gulf, Central America, Bosnia, Kosovo, Nigeria, and of course Iraq.

Don said on more than one occasion that he hated war, but loved the job of covering it. He felt that his reporting, whether in print, on video, or via still photography, would help educate people on the horror and futility of war, and he was a big believer in the power of photographs in particular to motivate people to right wrongs. Don also believed that journalism is an honorable profession which benefits humanity, but only if it is practiced vigorously and honestly. Regarding Iraq, in 2015 he told an interviewer that he felt the Western allies were poorly served by journalists who did not question the wisdom of attacking that country.

Most important to the focus of this book is the simple fact that without Don North, the dramatic story of the "seven brothers" – the Iraqi men whose right hands were amputated by order of Saddam Hussein and who were later given a second chance at life with new myoelectric hands – would never have happened. It was Don who first heard about their plight, and who ultimately set the wheels in motion to find these men, bring them to the United States, and restore them to wholeness.

During the course of my involvement with this mission, I became good friends with Don, and it was one of my most cherished friendships. When we lost Don, we lost not only a stellar journalist, but a profoundly good man.

Thank you, Don, for everything.

Note: The "seven brothers" were the topic of hundreds of national and international media stories. Many of these stories listed some or all of the men by name, and there were numerous inconsistencies in the spelling of these names. For *A Show Of Hands,* I have adopted the spelling used in Don North's award-winning documentary about the seven men, *Remembering Saddam*.

A Special Dedication To Our Armed Forces

When the United States formed the Coalition and entered the war in Iraq, many young Americans were asked for extraordinary service and willingness to make the ultimate sacrifice. These service members met the highest of military expectations; some would never come home, and those who did come home were changed in ways that perhaps they never could have imagined. In a way, this is their story as well.

Years have passed, and many of these brave men and women have put their uniforms aside and returned to civilian life – to home, to families, to work. They did their job and many were proud of their accomplishments, but they rarely discuss their experience in Iraq with each other, much less their families and friends. Some still do not really know why they were sent to fight there.

Unfortunately, I felt it was also necessary to depict those who failed to measure up to their sworn oath. But taken as a whole, the young men and women of the military undertook their job respectfully and not only met but exceeded all expectations, not because of but in spite of the officers and the politicians who had sent them to Iraq.

God bless them, and God bless America.

Contents

FOREWORD

Nestled in Iraq in the heart of the so-called Sunni triangle, located between the cities of Baghdad and Ramadi, lies the small town of Abu Ghraib. To most Westerners, awareness of the town's existence first came with media outlets posting "breaking news" about American guards allegedly abusing inmates being held in the infamous Abu Ghraib prison. To residents of the town, however, stories of abuse in the prison were anything but "breaking." They were a part of everyday life.

Inside this compound, built by Saddam Hussein and his ruthless regime, prisoners had been brutally tortured for decades, and barbaric executions had long since become commonplace. My late friend Don North referred to Abu Ghraib prison as "The Iraqi Gulag," and that was no exaggeration.

Tens of thousands of prisoners were hanged or otherwise executed during the Saddam regime; bodies were later found buried in cemeteries and mass unmarked graves throughout all regions of Iraq. The Iraqi people lived in a constant state of fear.

That Saddam was a monster is a point with which few people will disagree. But he was a monster that United States policy helped to create, and that the U.S. enabled for many years. With the overthrow of Saddam's regime in 2003, under the administration of George W. Bush, the U.S. military took over the prison and used it to house and interrogate prisoners captured by the American-led coalition. Unfortunately, it was in some ways a case of, "Meet the new boss, same as the old boss." Some members of the United States Army and the Central Intelligence Agency (the latter also known in Iraq as the "OGA (Other Government Agency)" guys, whom you'll unfortunately meet in this book) seemed determined to carry on the tradition of vicious treatment of prisoners.

But that is not the whole story – far from it. The brutality at Abu Ghraib under the occupying forces was real and it made international news, and I will not attempt to sugar-coat it. Nor will I attempt to underplay the atrocities committed by Saddam. But some good ultimately emerged, inspired in great part by this long legacy of cruelty, and that's the story I intend to tell in this book. I was pleased to be part of a team that helped, in its own small way, to undo some of the damage done by

1

Saddam Hussein, and, I believe, helped heal the deep wounds to America's reputation that happened because of a few bad apples in the immediate post-Saddam era.

In these pages, I hope to take you on a journey through Iraq in general, and Abu Ghraib prison specifically. More importantly, this is the story of seven "brothers" from different mothers: respectable businessmen who became political prisoners ostensibly for dealing in foreign currency – U.S. dollars –- but who were actually imprisoned for no other reason than publicly and repeatedly voicing opinions critical of the Saddam Hussein regime. For that "crime," they were not only incarcerated but they also suffered a form of torture that would haunt them for the rest of their lives: each of these men was subjected to the surgical amputation of his right hand – and then charged $50.00 for the "surgery."

To literally add insult to injury, the surgeon who cut the men's hands off tattooed an "X" of shame into their foreheads. This was a common practice following these punitive amputations, and removing the marks was strictly forbidden. Doctors who attempted to do so would be punished by having their own foreheads similarly tattooed.

As indicated above, however, atrocities at Abu Ghraib prison didn't stop once Saddam was gone. Having spent years as an officer in the Navy and as a Lieutenant Commander in the United States Public Health Service Commissioned Corps (USPHS), I was deeply upset by the mere suggestion that my fellow service men and women were engaging in Saddam-esque acts. The images and videos that served as documentation of such misconduct enraged me. Our own U.S. service members serving within the prison were clearly involved in a scandal that shocked America and impugned the honor of all our armed forces.

You probably remember seeing the photographs and videos that were leaked from the prison to the U.S. press corps, and perhaps you read the associated stories that were never fully explained to the American public and world. Many of us wondered what really happened behind these prison walls, not only during the Saddam Hussein regime, but also after American troops took control of the facility. The subject has been well covered in the years since then, but my hope is that this book will add insight and context.

I became involved through the friend I mentioned earlier, Don North, an author, reporter, and veteran TV news and documentary producer who had been embedded with the troops in this and many other conflicts over the span of many years. Don had heard about the seven men from Iraqi contacts, who told him that Saddam had insisted on videotaping the men's amputations, and, indeed, on taping the atrocities committed on countless other prisoners in Abu Ghraib. Later on we would discover that there was an entire macabre library of videotaped atrocities deep in the prison's underbelly, but even the limited information Don initially had was enough to inspire him to seek out the "brothers" in order to make a documentary about their plight, and to get help for them.

It was in a café in Baghdad that he met an oil engineer from Houston named Roger Brown, who overheard North talking about the men. Brown suggested that Don get in touch with Marvin Zindler of KTRK-TV – Channel 13, the ABC affiliate – in Houston, Texas. Marvin, who passed away in 2007, had a well-deserved reputation for delivering help to desperate people all over the world, while drawing attention, through his reporting, to the larger social, economic, and political issues behind these people's suffering.

Almost immediately, Don contacted Marvin, who in turn scheduled a meeting with me. Marvin and I had a long history together; initially I was his cosmetic surgeon, but over the years we had become close friends. We had traveled the world on numerous medical and goodwill missions, and had even founded a charity together to help deliver medical care to children and adults in some of the poorest and most dangerous parts of the world. So it was only natural that Marvin would call on me.

From both a news and human-interest angle, Marvin and his writer-programmer, Lori Reingold, were attracted to this story. Being the consummate showman Marvin was, he latched onto an angle that he knew would appeal to the American public and put a new and more positive twist on the Abu Ghraib narrative, as well as the larger narrative about America's involvement in Iraq. He decided that with my help and additional support from the world-famous Texas Medical Center in Houston, he would bring the seven Iraqi brothers to the United States.

Once the brothers were settled in, we would perform the necessary revision surgery on their amputated right hands, and provide them with the state-of-the-art myoelectric prosthetic arms that functioned almost as well as the patients' hands and fingers had prior to being amputated.

The material felt like human skin, and the prostheses would be dyed to closely match each man's skin tone. Upon completion of the subsequent post-revision therapy and training, the patients would be able to perform previously impossible tasks with the myoelectric hands, such as tying a shoelace and buttoning a shirt.

As I was gathering the support we would need from the surgeons and staff at the Texas Medical Center, Lori Reingold quickly contacted the United States Army, the Department of Defense, and the State Department. Before all was said and done, our idea had gone all the way to the White House.

Within twenty-four hours, the idea was approved. Everyone liked it, but there was one catch: all aspects of the operation would have to be funded and orchestrated privately. The United States government would have no direct involvement. And despite the relatively rapid approval of the project, actually putting all of the pieces in place turned out to be a long and complex process. But that didn't discourage us.

I, along with hand surgeon Dr. Fred Kestler, would perform the surgical procedures at no cost. The myoelectric prostheses themselves would be supplied by the German-American prosthetic company Otto Bock, also at no cost. The hospital stay would be covered by The Methodist Hospital in Houston. The post-operative care would be provided free of charge by the renowned Texas Institute for Rehabilitation and Research, or TIRR. Afterwards, housing for · the patients would be provided by myself and others in the Houston area.

Houston is a very patriotic and giving city, whose residents were just as upset as anyone else by the various films, photos, and news reports coming in of the atrocities being committed at Abu Ghraib prison. Many viewers were on board to put a stop to such barbaric acts and help the men whose story had captured their hearts.

My own motivations stemmed not only from being a surgeon and physician, but also from holding the rank of Lieutenant Commander. I felt personally tarnished by the reports of atrocities committed by my fellow countrymen, and to the extent that I was able, I wanted to help put an end to these cruel practices. I hoped that I would be able to do so.

Within a few days, Marvin, Lori Reingold, and I were ready to proceed, as was Don North, who would meet up with me in Iraq. And before the week was out, we received an overnight FedEx with an executive memo from the White House Oval Office – a letter that would prove invaluable to my part of the mission. I now had what we needed to find these men with Don's help, and to bring them back to Houston and the Texas Medical Center. But there were still a lot of preparations to be completed, and red tape to navigate.

Ultimately our plan succeeded beyond our wildest imagination, and upon their arrival, the seven brothers became overnight celebrities in Houston. Before long they were national celebrities as well.

Getting to that point, however, was anything but easy. In these pages you'll read about the adventures and misadventures of a determined group of Western doctors and journalists in their quest to help seven innocent men who had suffered vile injustice under Saddam Hussein. We'll also explore some of the historical, social, and foreign-policy matters that give a larger context to the story. I think that's important because even though the rescue and restoration of the "seven brothers" took place in the early 2000s, those larger issues are still pertinent today, perhaps even more so than ever.

When I first thought about writing this book, I was thinking in terms of straight reporting about my own experiences in Iraq and at Abu Ghraib prison, as well as the participation of Don North, about whom I cannot say enough good things, and who as I noted above is really the one who put the ball in motion. I envisioned a book that would provide an interesting, informative, and historic account, while giving the reader the opportunity to better understand the truth of life in a war-torn region.

I also wanted this book to be more personal than a straight historical report or journalistic account could be. That's only fitting, for I am neither a historian nor a journalist. But more importantly, even I was surprised by the extent to which I became personally involved – not only in the plight of the "seven brothers" but in that of the Iraqi people, as well as some of the marginalized ethnic and religious groups in the region.

I was most immediately concerned with the seven brothers, of course, but for me it was a life-changing experience to visit the towns and cities that had been destroyed in Iraq, and especially to learn about the genocide of groups such as the Yazidis and Kurds in the north, and the Marsh Arabs of the south. We'll explore these issues in more depth in the pages of this book.

What struck me was that so many of these people were fighting for their lives with minimal resources and equipment, and living hand to mouth in the most deplorable conditions possible, facing seemingly impossible odds across this bloody landscape. Entire generations had come of age in a country where economic despair and hardship hovered over the land like a plague. Many families would go hungry; they would lose their businesses, farms, and jobs, with all of their hopes for a better life being shattered. It was heartbreaking to see what had been done to them, and I was determined not to let their plight be worsened and ignored or forgotten.

And yet I saw over and over again that regardless of the crushing challenges they experienced every day, most of them had stayed true to their values of personal responsibility, love of beauty, and their faith. They were not embittered by the cruelties that they saw all around them, and they were not defeated by the brutality that they had experienced themselves; instead they remained strong and quietly proud of what they had endured, and they looked forward to a brighter future for themselves and their families.

To say that I was deeply moved by what I had seen and what I had learned would be an egregious understatement and an unforgivable slight to their courage and endurance. They simply deserved better.

The stories of the seven brothers, and of countless other suffering Iraqis, did not come easily. I had to keep asking questions. Sometimes I was blunt and brash and, well… a little bit pushy, as I have a tendency to be when I get impatient. But sometimes a more subtle touch was needed. In particular my experiences at Abu Ghraib prison taught me the necessity of taking a step back and waiting for people to provide me with the information I sought, rather than push them to give me what I wanted. My efforts and patience were rewarded whenever someone would share with me their stories of the inhumane treatment under the Saddam Hussein regime or, unfortunately, under the subsequent "interrogation techniques" carried out by the U.S.

The men and women caged in Abu Ghraib prison had an overpowering determination to survive their conditions. They described going through alternating stages of rage and later calm. (And understandably, there was a prolonged period when the almost nightly mortar attacks only added to their stress.)

Speaking with these detainees, I learned something about fighting for what you believe in. The Iraqi population is large and diverse, contrary to what many Westerners may think, and so was the population at Abu Ghraib – and yet the conditions under which they had lived for so many years had created a common ethos. I remain in awe of them and feel privileged to have been a witness to their lives and their sacrifices. I am grateful that I am able to tell their stories and that of the Iraqi people in general.

One of the most profound lessons I learned from my experience with the seven brothers was how much they loved each other, their families, their countries, and life – and how unashamed they were to express this love. And yet, as I keep saying, there are so many others like them, people whom Don North and I met whose stories of suffering and resilience could have been told in this book. Some of those stories are in these pages, but I wish I could have included them all.

In any case I hope that this book will in some small way pay tribute not only to the seven brothers, but also to the many others throughout Iraq who underwent similar terrible experiences, and in all too many cases who gave their lives.

In the years since the events in this narrative occurred, I've wondered more than once whether anyone could honestly say that the U.S. has "won" the war in Iraq. Events over the past couple of decades would seem to render the question ludicrous. We surely have failed to democratize Iraq or any of the Middle Eastern countries or those in the surrounding region, and we have paid an enormous price in our young American lives as well as our treasury. I would love to say that we finally learned our lesson – the hard way – and that we will never repeat our mistakes. But I am neither that idealistic nor that naive.

Truth be told, even the narrative of the seven brothers does not have a completely happy ending. Although their story was a public relations triumph for the Bush administration while the men were in the United States, in the years after they returned to Iraq they faced varying degrees of harassment, threats, and violence from insurgents and terrorists because of their well-publicized association with Americans. Some wanted to escape Iraq, and felt that the U.S. government was indifferent to their plight.

Despite all of this, several of the men retained warm feelings for the United States and particularly for Houston, where they had spent most of their time. And most of them ultimately ended up relocating to the States.

As for me, even knowing all that I know as I navigate my eighth decade, I can honestly say that if I had my life to live over again, I would do everything the same way – including and especially my trips to Iraq and my involvement with the seven brothers. I studied engineering, then dentistry and medicine. I spent six years in general surgery and two years in plastic and reconstructive surgery. It was the type of education that opened the world to me, and I have used this background to travel on missions to countries around the world where people had a desperate need for medical care and humanitarian assistance.

My experiences also inspired me to start my Children's Foundation decades ago. You will find more information about that at the back of this book.

As I traveled through war-torn countries, I have been extensively exposed to inhumanity. I have seen the dark world of war: the death, injuries, and universal cruelty. But nothing in medical school or during my internship, residency, years of practice, and even decades of travel, had quite prepared me for the primal struggles that I witnessed in Iraq. Don North and I saw more suffering and death there than most doctors see in a lifetime of practice.

Yet the entire experience was one of the highlights of my life, on both a personal and professional level. I found myself with a renewed sense of mission for the people of Iraq and the detainees within Abu Ghraib prison.

This narrative is not intended to be pure reporting – not only because as noted earlier I wanted to make it more personal than that, but also because for the sake of flow and reader engagement, I have taken some liberties in places with dialogue and the description of some events. I have also changed some names. The basics of the story, however, are accurate.

But it is the core message that is personally most important to me: that despite the seemingly endless negative stories – those involving the mercilessness of tyrants, the atrocious misbehavior of some military and intelligence personnel, the cynicism and bumbling of politicians, and the continued (and increasing) unrest in America as well as in the Middle East and the world over – there are positive stories too. Everywhere there are decent people who see a wrong and want to right it, and who will do whatever it takes to help those who can't help themselves.

I've seen firsthand that America is full of such altruistic people. We may not always be the proverbial shining city upon a hill, but it is my hope that this book will serve as a reminder that our light still burns brightly, and will continue to do so as long as we have people who feel a calling to make life better for their fellow human beings.

It is also my hope that you will take away something good about the human spirit from the story of the seven brothers. That good exists in every one of us, if we will just give it space to flourish.

~ Joseph Agris, M.D.

Hell, emptied: Abu Ghraib prison is vacant now, but during the decades-long regime of Saddam Hussein, and even after Saddam, the prison was home to many thousands of prisoners who were abused, tortured, or killed.
The "seven brothers" were among thousands of Iraqis who were subjected to cruel amputations by order of Saddam Hussein.

PROLOGUE

The reality – and illusion – of the Iraq war

After the horror of 9/11, there was a lot of pressure for a global push to combat the war on terrorism, and the United States seemed chosen for this task. While there had been many terrorist attacks around the world, the attacks on the Twin Towers and Pentagon had been particularly heinous, with thousands of casualties counted, and many more that might never be found and identified. A multi-national coalition was formed, its objectives being to disarm Iraq and free its people. The American public was led to believe this war would serve two purposes: to protect the Iraqi people, who had suffered for years under the brutal Saddam; and to find and remove Saddam's alleged store of weapons of mass destruction (WMDs). (Spoiler: No WMDs were ever found.)

According to public announcements, the U.S. Army's Fifth Corps would rapidly sweep into Iraq with the goal of finding and taking possession of WMDs. Primary on their list of objectives was rapid execution, completing the advance across Iraq as quickly as possible. The poorly trained Iraqi Army retreated and ran, and within three weeks, the American forces entered the capital city of Baghdad.

The international news media showed the statue of Saddam Hussein being pulled down and the American flag being raised. Commentators on radio and television news programs were declaring that the Iraqi people were euphoric at what was happening. In the wake of these events, President George W. Bush's airplane landed on the U.S.S. Lincoln aircraft carrier, where Bush, standing under a "Mission Accomplished" banner, all but announced that the war was over. Those of us who had been through situations like this in our lifetime – and particularly those who had been to Iraq – said, "There's no way that it's over." We all felt this was just the beginning. Indeed, Bush himself would be haunted by that speech in the years to come. Even though he did say that the danger was not completely over, the nuances of his message were drowned out by that big "Mission Accomplished" banner. He later said the White House had nothing to do with the banner, but the fact remains that he consented to stand under it for his speech.

The effects of the collapse of Saddam's central government and the governing elements were seen not only in Baghdad but throughout the other major Iraqi cities as well. There was no more electric power grid, and water supplies dried out as pumping stations stopped.

Transportation and the shipping of food and other necessities halted. In short, the country of Iraq ground to a halt. Gangs formed in the cities, looting was common, and crimes, including murder, increased.

The U.S. Army seemed helpless and did nothing to stop it. Bush's top people, including Vice President Dick Cheney and Defense Secretary Donald Rumsfeld, just wanted to pull the American troops and get out. They had pushed for the war in the first place, and pushed hard, but now they wanted to get out. On the other side of the table were then-national security adviser Condoleezza Rice and her supporters, who said that we needed to stay in Iraq and "make it right." Two big questions remained: Who would now secure the peace in Iraq; and who would start a new government for the country?

Meanwhile, the looting continued unabated, and it became increasingly obvious that it was impossible to stop. Following the invasion, Lieutenant General Jay Garner had been appointed by President Bush as Director of the Office for Reconstruction and Humanitarian Assistance for Iraq. His job was to lead the post-war reconstruction efforts, to "make it right." But Garner was soon removed from that position, to be replaced by Ambassador Paul Bremer. It was a monumental task for which Bremer was given full authority. Unfortunately, he didn't understand the tribal, religious, and cultural situations in Iraq, between the Shiites, Ba'athists, Sunnis, and others.

Equally unfortunately, Bremer's first order was to paralyze the Ba'athist Party – the very people who had been keeping the country running. The Ba'athists were outlawed and removed from their jobs. Next, in an even bigger mistake, Bremer disbanded what remained of the Iraq Army, whose remaining members had been acting as a local force to keep the peace and prevent at least some of the looting. Now they were gone too, and the country's basic systems – the power grid, water supplies, and the economy in general – were essentially nonexistent. Still, President Bush stood by Bremer, thus solidifying the error and setting the stage for years if not decades of chaos and civil wars.

All that had been accomplished was to set Iraq spinning completely out of control. Vigilante groups and tribal factions took over, now armed with the weapons left behind by the fleeing Iraqi army. These well-armed, well-organized insurgents, many of them former members of the Iraqi military, began to ambush the American and coalition forces, resulting in the wounding and deaths of many U.S. and coalition troops. The U.S. and coalition forces were now hip deep in a guerilla war – so much for "Mission Accomplished."

I and others who have been to Iraq and understood the politics of tribal forces and religions knew that while the United States had initially "won" the war, we had lost the peace. But President Bush was determined that the people of Iraq should form a government and run their own country. He was driven by an almost religious faith in the Iraqi people and their abilities. And while I deeply admire the Iraqi people myself, I think that Bush had an overly optimistic, almost naïve, view of human goodness and competence. His cabinet members, however, were not so encumbered.

The sad and uncomfortable truth was that Iraq as a country only worked because the Iraq people were under the rigid control of Saddam Hussein and his army. The U.S. and the rest of the world didn't have to like it, but as I said, President Bush believed in the good of people, and decided American troops were not going to leave Iraq until a national government was formed and took full charge. I also suspect that he had underestimated the resolve and agendas of his vice president and the most hawkish of his cabinet members, who favored an expanding and long-term Western military presence in Iraq.

I still remember President Bush responding to Iraqi insurgents' threats to attack U.S. and coalition forces with a bellicose, "Bring it on." He was definitely picking for a fight when he made that statement, which had been popularized in a few high-school cheerleader competition movies of the period. None of us knew with any certainty whether the taunt would be answered with more American and coalition deaths. At best, we felt it was an irresponsible thing for any commander, much less Commander in Chief, to say.

Even so, for the most part Bush left Iraq up to the American military and turned his interest elsewhere, to other issues, such as fighting the pandemic of AIDS as HIV continued to spread throughout the world. He undertook a humanitarian assault on an AIDS pandemic in Africa. My only question was, "Why? Is it America's role in the world to be both policemen and physicians to the world?"

Meanwhile, the search for WMDs continued. Another outsider, David Kay, was brought in to deal with that problem. Kay had been Chief Weapons Inspector for the United Nations following the first Gulf War in the early 1990s. The official line from the White House, and continued statements in the American press, proclaimed that the weapons of mass destruction had been well hidden, but that our military in Iraq would ultimately find them. Kay had his own little army of 1,500 people working under him to find the WMDs.

Vice President Dick Cheney and his chief of staff Scooter Libby were closely monitoring David Kay's search for WMDs. Articles began appearing in the U.S. press accusing President Bush of taking the U.S. into a war with Iraq that was based upon the false premise of nonexistent WMDs, since after many months of searching, no such weapons had yet been found. This raised the question: Was the *threat* of WMDs presented to mislead the American public and the U.S. Congress so that Vice President Cheney, Donald Rumsfeld, or President Bush could justify going to war with Iraq?

In January 2004, the U.S. Intelligence Service reported their findings, which can be summed up as: "No WMDs." Unfortunately, President Bush would not accept this report. He would not admit it had been a mistake. Bush took it personally – not a wise or productive stance in American politics.

I'll never argue with the statement that Saddam Hussein and his two sons, Qusay and especially Uday, were psychopaths, sociopaths, and in simple terms, bad people. My experience at Abu Ghraib prison gave clear credence to such a determination. The "seven brothers" who had their right hands amputated were graphic examples of Saddam's cruelty, and there were untold thousands of other instances of innocent Iraqis being maimed, tortured, or killed by Saddam and sons But demonstrating compassion for the suffering of these people was not high on the list of the U.S.'s justifications for going to war with Iraq, if it was even on the list at all.

While our leaders were arguing over policy, guerilla groups continued to move throughout Iraq, attacking U.S. and coalition forces with hit-and-run tactics, and they were even able to fire mortars into the Abu Ghraib prison facility every few nights. Another group of insurgents attacked the U.S. military base in Fallujah, burned it, and also hung Americans on the bridge. With that, President Bush ordered a large scale attack on the city of Fallujah. The coalition forces were now falling apart as the British forces pulled out, and some of the men who had been appointed by the U.S. as interim Iraqi leaders quit and walked away. The Shiite religious cleric and militia leader, Muqtada al-Sadr, now took over

Baghdad and the surrounding area. To make it worse, Al Qaeda was now operating freely in Iraq, wounding and killing Americans at will.

The American troops on the ground, as well as the American interrogators, were under a lot of pressure to get as much information as they could from the detainees at Abu Ghraib and other prisons. This was the rationale for the so-called "enhanced interrogation" techniques. The OGA (CIA) interrogators vowed to get the information in any way possible, Geneva Conference rules and supposed American values be damned. Yet we had President Bush insisting at press conferences and in TV interviews that, "We are a country of laws."

Unfortunately, in early 2004, photographs taken in Abu Ghraib prison were made public. Dozens of explosive photos were circulated not only in the U.S., but worldwide. They say a photo is worth a thousand words, but these prison torture photos showed how far the OGA and various private contractors and interrogators had strayed from our American ideals. I want to make it clear that this should not reflect on the majority of the men and women in the armed forces, who were working diligently at their jobs and were in danger every day in Iraq. The OGA did this on their own, and the brutal techniques they used were their way of getting the information in any way possible – even if those being interrogated died in the process.

In 2006, Secretary of Defense Rumsfeld resigned, despite President Bush having declared that he would not accept Rumsfeld's resignation. Many were outraged by the fact that Rumsfeld had apparently escaped accountability for the brutal interrogation techniques, when in fact, no one was held responsible other than some of the low-level interrogators themselves, who had actually done the brutalizing. The official statement was that these procedures were safe and lawful, but there were at least 34 deaths in Abu Ghraib prison that I am aware of (and likely many more) as a direct result of the torture. What made it worse was that these techniques were not of any value, made obvious when they didn't produce any information that was helpful.

But back in 2004, even more grisly photos with terrifying images from Abu Ghraib prison were reaching the American press. The White House and Cabinet were under mounting pressure when these photos were released. The press was now asking, "How could President Bush have handled this better?"

Clearly a more sensitive occupation in Iraq was needed. The kill or-be-killed attitude toward torture had to end, particularly because it accomplished nothing except to antagonize the Iraqi population and make the American forces seem no better than Saddam Hussein's regime. It was time for a new kind of story to emerge, a story that would show America in a better light than what the daily news reports were telling our own people and the rest of the world.

But before we get to that story, let's take a closer look at the chief antagonist (or villain) in the larger narrative: Saddam Hussein.

The butcher of Baghdad

Saddam Hussein was born in 1937 to a peasant family in a village near the city of Tikrit, in the northern part of Iraq – one of the poorest areas in the country. Saddam grew up in poverty, his father having died of cancer before he was born. His immediate family was illiterate and uneducated, and, as is so often the case, his limited education left him vulnerable to a narrow view of the world, leading to his adoption of extreme nationalistic tendencies.

In 1957 Saddam joined the Ba'athist Party, and in 1959 he became involved in an unsuccessful assassination attempt upon the Iraqi prime minister. Wounded, he fled to Syria and then later to Egypt, where he attended law school for a year.

In 1963 the Ba'athists took power in Iraq, and Saddam returned to his home country. After that he very rarely left Iraq, certainly not enough to develop a realistic perspective on the world outside its borders. He married his first wife, who also happened to be his first cousin. He dabbled at being an author and also continued his law studies – none of which came to anything.

Later in 1963, the Ba'athists lost power, and Saddam spent several years in a prison in Iraq. Eventually he escaped and became a leader of the Ba'athist Party, participating in the coup that finally brought the party back to power in 1968. He shared power with the Iraqi head of state, President Ahmad Hasan al-Bakr, and was instrumental in nationalizing Iraq's oil industry in 1972.

Saddam surrounded himself with those who had similar political ideals and aspirations, and advanced himself politically. Regardless of their denomination, Saddam very openly worked with Kurds, Shiites, and even Christians. However, even those with whom he closely worked were summarily eliminated should they dare to challenge him or otherwise find fault with his policies. Kurds, and later the Yazidis, Marsh Arabs, and even Shiite clerics were murdered if they were not fully supportive of his programs.

As Saddam's power grew, so did his wealth. Ultimately the Ba'athist party and Hussein's Ba'athist cronies came to control the entire country of Iraq and its military.

The Iraqi public despised him, but were placated by his establishment of excellent education and healthcare systems. Using money from oil reserves, he provided comprehensive healthcare and first-rate hospitals, airports, and hydro-electric facilities. However, the fact that he never really ventured beyond Iraq's borders and culture left him with little understanding of events and agendas in the world at large.

Growing up in poverty without a father, and surrounded by illiteracy, Saddam had developed many insecurities. He seemed to have a deep-seated need for everything in his life – relationships, material possessions, power, and acclaim – to be bigger and better than what anyone else had. And he wanted the Arab world and the greater world to see what he had done and could still do. He arrogantly believed he could form a Ba'athist-led Arab unity.

Saddam had been through a war with Iran without any real consideration of the possible consequences. But one consequence of that war was that in only one year, despite more than 40,000 Iraqi troops having been captured, Iraq became the aggressor in the eyes of the world.

During this time the United States remained more or less neutral, but then came the Reagan administration. At that time, Reagan felt that the Arab war would cause a "significant imbalance" in the Middle East, so naturally, the U.S. intervened, providing Saddam with support from the CIA, who in turn were given a station in Baghdad.

Unfortunately, and against a ruling by the United Nations prohibiting the use of chemical weapons in any war, the Iraqi military and Ba'athist party used nerve gases and mustard gases, both on the battlefield and internally against dissenters, and they did not even bother trying to conceal these violations. In fact, Iraq was the first country to have used such weapons since the first World War. As a result, the United States Department of State rebuked Saddam Hussein, despite the fact that the forbidden weapons materials and technology had earlier been sold to Iraq by the United States and European countries.

The Kurds in Northern Iraq occupied lands rich in oil, and wanted to form their own country, Kurdistan. They had a close relationship with the Yazidis, whom Saddam considered to be "not Muslim enough" and devil worshippers. Saddam assaulted them with mustard gas, sarin, and other nerve gases. It was genocide at its worst, and a grave violation of the Geneva Convention. Dealing with Iraq's aggression on one hand, and accepting Iraqi funds in exchange for weapons technology on the other, stood as a clear example of opportunistic breach of international laws and foreign policies by both Saddam's Iraq and Western coalition countries. This gave rise to a precarious relationship between the United States and Iraq's Ba'athist Party.

Saddam wanted to achieve a victory over his opponents in Iraq and his Kurdish neighbors. A sociopathic rebel, he became a new force as leader of the Ba'athist Party, set to take on the entire Middle East and extend brutal Ba'athist policy across the region and beyond.

Iraqi state-sponsored terrorism was also rearing its ugly head. With what was happening with the Kurds and Yazidis in Northern Iraq, and the Marsh Arabs in the South, the United Nations was looking into human rights violations. The Iraq-Iran war was just one of the Saddam administration's many blunders.

Saddam, willfully ignorant of the objectives, agendas, and cultures of countries other than the Iraq in which he had spent virtually his entire life, continued to ignore any significant international pressure to rein in his brutality. This probably was as much the result of his small-town provincial education as it was his own megalomania.

In his communications with the U.S. ambassador, he claimed that he hated communists, yet all the while he was acquiring the latest in Soviet military hardware for his army. This was hardly an effective path toward building alliances, but did prove to be somewhat effective at broadening his internal power base.

Saddam knew that Israeli aircraft had destroyed Iraq's nuclear reactor, and he felt that the American Zionist movement would pressure the U.S. and Israel to attack Iraq more broadly. Still, he continued to stockpile his chemical weapons. The U.S. and its allies feared that Saddam Hussein could launch an unprovoked attack against Israel itself. Iraq, in short, remained a threat.

In short order, Saddam Hussein became the bully of the Middle East. His two sons, Uday and Qusay, were as psychopathic as their father, and as was the case with their father, people who disagreed with the sons or failed to honor their "requests" ended up dead.

Saddam became even more of a bully as he and his Ba'athist regime began feeling increased pressure from within and without Iraq. In order to exert effective but non-military pressure on Saddam, the Gulf States sustained exceptionally large production quotas that drove down the global price of oil and choked off the oil revenues upon which Saddam was so dependent to hold onto power. Iraq became economically depressed without the oil revenues, especially given how much the war with Iran was costing, not to mention his need to remain current on repayment of the loans that were rapidly becoming the sole source of his barbaric regime's economic support.

In order to reverse Iraq's economic situation, Saddam turned to Kuwait's Rumaila oil field, claiming that Kuwait was actually a part of Iraq, and that the British who had long controlled this territory did not have the right to form a separate state. In Saddam's mind, the U.K. and the United States were interfering in his country's rights by permitting the Kuwaitis to flood the oil market with cheap oil, thus exacerbating Iraq's economic hardships. He vowed that he would not allow this to occur. The United States and Britain wanted to stay out of any Arab-to-Arab conflicts, and when Saddam issued a complaint to the American ambassador, the ambassador stated that the U.S. government had no interest in Iraq's "border disputes," essentially giving Saddam tacit approval for attacking Kuwait. Then in August of 1990, Iraq's elite Republican Guard invaded Kuwait.

The United States and the world responded with several weeks of aerial bombardments, followed by an invasion with a multi-country coalition of troops that, in a short period of four days, destroyed Saddam Hussein's army, which at that time was the fourth largest army in the world.

Kuwait was effectively liberated, and the threat posed by Saddam Hussein's poorly thought-out invasion was felt to be eliminated. Thousands of Iraqi soldiers fled back to their home country. Saddam Hussein and his sons survived to remain in power, which was at best a huge blunder on the part of the U.S. With Operation Desert Storm over, Iraq formally surrendered, but of course that was not the end of the problem by any means.

The United Nations was given the job of entering Iraq and looking for weapons of mass destruction (WMDs), a task that would involve many years of investigation, with little or no cooperation from Saddam Hussein and his Ba'athist party.

Iraq had no choice but to let the United Nations inspectors come in, but Saddam showed them as little as possible of the weapons he had. He claimed that what weapons were found were only for defense purposes, and repeatedly insisted that he did not have WMDs.

In what should have come as a surprise to nobody, Saddam's declared inventories were never accurate. They were revised every few months to satisfy the United Nations inspectors, and Iraq claimed that what nuclear programs they possessed were for peaceful purposes only.

Facilities, equipment, and ammunition were all hidden from the inspectors, and Iraq continued with one denial after another, claiming that they had little to no chemical weapons stockpiles or biological weapons. But discrepancies were repeatedly found by the U.N., and Iraq was caught in more lies. Through the United Nations, the U.S. insisted that Saddam Hussein and his administration had a lot of explaining to do.

The Ba'athist regime definitely had many things to hide, and deceptions continued during the United Nation investigations. Virtually everyone concerned felt that Iraq still had substantial hidden weapon stockpiles, but inspectors were stymied in their quest to find a "smoking gun" that would prove their suspicions to be true. Finally the U.N. grew fed up with being stiff-armed by Saddam and his cronies, and accordingly passed and enforced sanctions that withheld basic goods from the Iraqi population. The hope was that this would force Saddam's regime to provide accurate information about weapons of mass destruction. The sanctions accomplished little, however, other than making the populace suffer even more.

In January of 1998, Saddam Hussein had finally had enough of playing this cat-and-mouse game with the inspectors, and he declared there would be no further inspections in Iraq by U.N. observers. After that, he did not allow any U.N. inspectors to return to his country, and a shroud of darkness fell over Iraq and its population. Prisons such as Abu Ghraib were again filled to overflowing.

Iraq's infrastructure was severely crippled in its capacity, due to its multiple wars and a severe shortage of funds. Saddam's elite Republican Guard and other military were a mere fraction of their pre-war strength. The reality was that Iraq had now become almost totally dysfunctional as a country, yet Saddam and his Ba'athist party managed to keep this secret from the outside world, and frightened the populace into staying silent.

Notwithstanding the many challenges Saddam Hussein faced, however, by the year 2000 he had rebuilt his country and restored his military to pre-war levels. Saddam was a skilled politician, and he developed good relations with other leaders in the Arab world, which enhanced his elite status in the Middle East. Over the next couple of years, Saddam and the Ba'athist party made significant connections in all areas of Iraq. Saddam was a ruthless and brutal dictator, but all things considered, Iraq's recovery from its former economically depressed state was quite remarkable.

In 1998, during the time that Saddam was working so hard to build Iraq, the United States had been engaging in its usual high-minded play on words – or, more accurately, doublespeak – regarding "the Middle East problem." Congress did what it is known for doing best, and passed the Iraq Liberation Act, declaring that the United States believed that a regime change was needed in Iraq, beginning with the removal of Saddam Hussein from power. Although in reality there were no teeth in the legislation, it was used a few years later as a justification to authorize military force against Iraq.

I actually had the dubious privilege of meeting Saddam Hussein, as well as his two psychopathic sons, in person, a few years before my involvement with the seven brothers. I was on a trip to the Middle East with my medical team, along with Marvin Zindler and some other members of the ABC-TV Channel 13 news team. We were making stops in Egypt, Syria, and Jordan. I and my group of American physicians and surgeons were giving lectures, teaching students, interns, and residents at the universities, and participating in surgical procedures. We were teaching them about the latest in techniques and equipment.

We were honored by having the King of Jordan and his wife visit us on that mission. At the end of the week, we toured some of the historic sites in the countries we visited. Some of these sites were little known to Westerners, being located deep in the desert, and thus rarely visited by tourists. The medical team and I very much enjoyed the trips and the chances to photograph these rarely seen sights. Despite my own history of extensive travel across the region on medical mission trips, I was unaware even of the existence of many of these historically and culturally significant sites. They were exquisite, having been built by the Romans when they conquered this part of the world.

I am saddened by the fact that later on, ISIS and Al Qaeda, who considered these sites to be built by idol worshippers and pagans, took it upon themselves to destroy many of these historical treasures, blowing them up and returning them to the sands of the desert. It just didn't make any sense to me to blow them up. I often found myself wondering why so many senseless acts have been and continue to be perpetrated in the name of "religion." But I feel fortunate to have seen these wonderful cities of antiquity. They will always remain in my memory, and I am so grateful that I had the chance to photograph some of them before they were destroyed. Unfortunately, it is impossible to capture the sheer beauty of so many of these sites in photographs, and oftentimes, the photographs themselves only serve to deepen the sadness that the destruction of such important relics causes.

After our tours, the medical team and I returned to continue our work in Jordan and later in Syria. One afternoon, I was sitting in a hospital lunchroom after having just finished a teaching session in the operating room, which had been so crowded that we were elbow to elbow at the operating tableside.

I was discussing the procedures with several young doctors when an excited young man, also a doctor, joined us. He loudly proclaimed that there was going to be a big celebration in Iraq by Saddam Hussein – the biggest ever! Actually Saddam had been throwing big birthday celebrations for himself every year since 1985, but apparently this was to be the most spectacular bash ever.

Marvin Zindler and his photographer and producer, as well as several Channel 13 writers, were in the room. They had been following my surgical team across the Middle East on this medical mission, which was to be the subject of a future documentary. There were various other press members in the room as well, and they all perked up at the young doctor's excited proclamation of this grand event, which was to take place the following weekend in Iraq. "There will be parties and dances and parades throughout Baghdad, magnificent beyond anyone's imagination!" he said.

This young man had no idea what he had just started. It was like a ball rolling down a steep hill, going faster and faster. An announcement like that in front of the American press was an invitation to pandemonium.

Several members of the press who were in the lunchroom with me got on their satellite phones. Some of the others started researching with their computers. Within minutes, they confirmed that such a celebration was indeed scheduled to take place in Iraq.

One of the Channel 13 writers said, "This is a once in a lifetime news story. We need to cover this. We need to get to Iraq. No other American TV station will have this."

Our cameraman, Bob Dows, said, "I can't wait to get this on film. Videoing this display could win me an Emmy. We might be the only American news team there."

The members of the TV news teams were all talking at once. When the excitement seemed to slow, I reminded the Channel 13 team that we were here as physicians and educators, and that even though attending and recording this big celebration sounded very exciting, this was not our goal or main purpose. Also, we did not have travel papers, or visas to enter Iraq, which was particularly risky as that country had become considerably more volatile in recent years..

Bob Dows almost cut me off in mid-sentence in his excitement, saying, "You don't operate on the weekends. We could do a short tour next weekend and go to this event, Why don't we just do it?"

I raised my hands in surrender and replied, "Look, I'm going back to the operating room with the students and faculty. You people work it out and give me a report tonight, and we will consider it then. Remember: we don't have any travel papers to allow us to travel into Iraq. We do not have any visas, and they've been known to shoot people at the border for attempting to cross illegally."

The room went quiet for a few moments; then from the far corner a female voice said, "We have our press cards. They won't shoot us!" Everyone in the room began to laugh. On that note, I went back to the operating room.

That day, I had been in the OR for sixteen hours. The children we were taking care of were the poorest of the poor; if our American medical team had not been there, they would have received no care at all. The students, residents, and faculty that joined us learned more that week than they would have in six months of study. To a person, the medical team felt an exhilaration and a wonderful feeling of accomplishment. I can attest to the fact that those good feelings don't diminish on subsequent missions. Every mission is an entity unto itself, and even (or especially) the trips that present the greatest challenges leave us all with that sense of accomplishment.

I enjoyed a dinner of delicious local cuisine at about 10:00 that night. The entire team was exhausted, and we didn't hear any more about the big event in Iraq. It was a bit of a relief to me, especially since I felt strongly that our medical mission, with its compelling human-interest angle, was the real story. During the day, the television team had been taking notes and doing interviews with our patients and their families, and Bob Dows was even allowed to do some photography in the operating room.

Despite the fact that we all had plenty to keep our minds busy, however, the buzz about Saddam Hussein's mega event didn't go away. In subsequent days, I heard whispers about this function, and more about my press companions' plans to attend. At the end of the week, the press corps and Marvin Zindler cornered me – and a weary surgical team – with a written proposal on how they planned to travel to and attend the big bash. Of course, I was invited.

They said that they would be able to rent a large van that would accommodate all those who wished to go, as well as their equipment, food, and water. The Channel 13 team had also acquired a driver who spoke several Middle Eastern languages and dialects. As well, they had sent emails and a fax to the Iraqi government, but as yet had not received a reply.

At this point, my press buddies still had not obtained travel papers or visas. They were hoping only to use their press identification cards to get across the Iraq border and into Saddam Hussein's function. In other words, they – or, if I consented to go, we – would be party crashers.

I can't stress enough that in those days, Iraq was not a country you could enter lightly. It was a place where many people were never heard from again, a place notorious for prisons such as Abu Ghraib and others throughout Iraq: in short, for all too many people, a one-way ticket to oblivion for all too many people.

Nevertheless, Marvin Zindler and the gang were determined to attend Saddam's event. They told us that they had acquired four five-gallon gas cans, which would be strapped to the side of the vehicle. They had also made arrangements for two cases of bottled water and a chest with ice. The trip would be ten to twelve hours across the desert on a road that was considered to be closed at night. This meant that we would have to be up with the sunrise and on our way promptly.

My friends told me that they had extra photo and television recording equipment in the van. They said the equipment was hidden in the floor of the van, just in case Bob's personal camera and audio-video equipment and lights were confiscated.

I continued my questioning for a few minutes, but then returned to the word, "equipment." I said, as casually and calmly as I could, "Explain this 'equipment' to me. What else is there besides audio and video equipment?"

One of the most vocal advocates of the trip spoke up. "Guns."

Trying to remain calm, I responded, "We are going to cross the Iraq border with guns? I can't think of anything that would be more likely to get us detained or killed."

By way of explaining, Lori Reingold said, "There are warring tribes and other groups that might try to rob us in the desert."

Abandoning my effort to remain cool and collected, I yelled, "No guns! No guns!"

"We can use them to trade," someone said.

Again, I screamed, "No guns! Traveling as a humanitarian medical team with guns is a no go."

"We *are* a humanitarian team, but traveling armed is the safest approach. And isn't safety what we're all about?" someone else said.

I then got up and left the room. I had said my piece, I had vented, and now I needed to be alone to think about it some more.

You can probably guess how this part of the story ended: I ultimately agreed to our going as a humanitarian medical team that had been working and teaching in Egypt, Syria, and Jordan... and now, we were simply going to go to this event in Iraq. As humanitarian medical personnel, of course. With no guns.

Once this was decided, though, several members of the medical team said they were not up to a twelve-hour trip across the desert in 120 degrees or higher temperatures. They said they would stay to do the post-op follow-ups and dressing changes, and await our return before performing more surgeries.

That meant that I would be the only physician going on this trip, so that night I put together a chest of basic medical supplies and equipment, as well as an overnight bag. I couldn't stop the flow of anxious thoughts, however. What would they do to me? Torture me? Shoot me? I doubted that. After all, we were a humanitarian medical team. But still...

The next morning at sunup, the driver helped me load my heavy chest of medical supplies and equipment into the van. I had also decided to bring my two Nikon cameras with the telephoto lens; I certainly wasn't going to miss an opportunity to shoot some pictures. The television crew had loaded all their equipment the night before, and the only thing remaining was the chest with the ice, water, and food. I checked, and as promised there were four five-gallon gas cans strapped to the vehicle as well.

Our driver, Qassim, was fluent in five languages, including English, and had worked with the U.S. military as an interpreter. After speaking with him for about ten minutes, I was comfortable with him as our driver.

He said the air conditioning system in the van was good, but if temperatures reached 120 to 130 degrees, it would still get quite warm in the vehicle. No air conditioning system could compete with those temperatures. It was a good thing that we had plenty of water to prevent dehydration.

It would be several hours before the sun would reach its zenith, so we started our trip cool and comfortable. I was still worried about this undertaking, but I have to admit that I was also very excited about going to Iraq and attending this gala event.

I had brought with me several albums of Polaroid photos showing the before and after photos of our surgical patients, pictures that would help confirm that we had been taking care of these children in Egypt, Syria, and Jordan. I reasoned that the photos would help substantiate that we were a humanitarian medical and surgical team, and that the press was there to document the facts and to do a story for American and possibly international television. It's said that a picture is worth a thousand words, and I was hoping that would be true in this case, especially since I knew so few actual words in the native languages and regional dialects.

The road across the desert was a one-lane blacktop in each direction, and once we left the confines of the city there was no other automobile traffic. We passed a small caravan of camels, possibly nomads on the move with their animals seeking water and grazing land. There was an occasional oasis with fig palm trees and some mud huts... and then nothing, for as far as the eye could see. The burning hot sun was now overhead. Ahead of us, mirages looking like ponds stretching across the road were common. There were no animals in evidence, not even a bird in the sky. *A sane person does not do something like this,* I thought to myself.

After a few hours the van indeed became quite uncomfortable, as Qaasim had warned. Droplets of perspiration appeared around my forehead, and my sweat-soaked shirt was sticking to me. I kept thinking to myself, *What if we arrive at the Iraqi border and they turn us away? Will they at least be kind enough to fill up our gas tank so we can return safely, and supply us with water and food for our return journey?*

I didn't have a press card. I did have my passport, but it had no visa for Iraq, and thinking about that set off a whole new round of worries. But my worries dissipated as my eyes closed and I drifted off into an uneasy sleep. Sixteen hours or more a day in the operating room for the past week had finally caught up with me.

I don't know how long I had been asleep, but when I awoke the press team was eating sandwiches and crunching on chips while drinking water or colas. As I looked around, I could see that most of the men had removed their shoes and shirts, and were sitting in slacks. But clearly they were still uncomfortably hot.

I moved forward to the front of the van and asked Qassim how much longer it would be.

"I don't want to overheat the engine," he replied, adding that we could go 80 to 90 miles an hour, but he felt that would be too much strain on the engine. I had yet to see any other traffic on the road, so I knew that 80 to 90 mph would not be a dangerous speed, but I agreed with him and told him to keep a steady pace of 50 to 60 mph. He assured me that this was what he had been doing, and that so far, the engine and all the gauges showed everything was fine.

I asked him if he would like a cola or a bottle of water.

Qassim said, "I have been drinking water and have a bottle right next to me."

I went back to my seat in the van and opened my backpack, taking out my diary and a pen. Then I moved forward again to the shotgun seat and strapped myself in. With the big windows up front the light was the best for writing in my diary.

The road was smooth, and I had no trouble writing. I had kept a diary for many years, and today there are probably about 120 diaries on my library shelf. I had been documenting this trip, recording what people had said, and what we were hoping to accomplish, as well as what we were praying to avoid. After a couple more hours I looked up and turned to Qassim, asking him, "Are those buildings in the distance?"

He said, "Yes, we are approaching the border."

The border crossing site was unremarkable. There were some concrete buildings, and steel posts with a heavy chain stretched across them. One of the concrete buildings looked like a guardhouse, and there were several larger buildings on the other side of the border, about fifty yards away. Yet there was really nothing on our side of the border to indicate that we were leaving one country and entering another. I was grateful to have a driver who knew where we were, and presumably also knew what we needed to do.

As we got closer, I could see there were several well-armed border guards. Bob immediately went to the back of the van, grabbed his TV camera from its case, and turned facing forward. I turned and grabbed him by the shoulder, warning him, "This is not the time and place. Put that away or you might get us shot."

He looked at me with a scowl, but I pushed on his shoulder and he turned and replaced the camera in its case in the back of the van. Qaasim stopped and said something in Arabic to one of the border guards, who removed the chain and allowed us to pass, but then signaled him to stop the vehicle.

I told Qassim to tell them we were guests at Saddam Hussein's event. "Let them know that we have come a long way to film the event, which will then be shown on American television and possibly even in Europe," I added, and then I whispered into his ear, "This should please Saddam Hussein immensely, and show the strength and beauty of a new Iraq to the world."

Qassim translated my statements, apparently including the one I had whispered, to the border guard, who seemed very pleased with this. He said he would have to fill out forms for anything we had to declare. I said that I was a doctor and had some medical equipment with me, but other than that, we had only our cameras and some food and water in the van, and nothing else. We had Qassim tell him that he was welcome to enter the vehicle and verify what we had said, but asked him to please be careful with the equipment.

A military man then called out to the van and asked that we follow him to one of the buildings, because he wanted to check our passports. I walked with him while Qassim kept up a congenial conversation with the border personnel. I had one of the photo albums tucked up under my arm to help verify what I was doing in Egypt, Syria, and Jordan. I intended to make it clear that I would offer the same medical care to Iraq's children.

The border guard, who was apparently the commanding officer, sat us down at a metal table with folding chairs and indicated that we were to fill out forms while he put in the data from our passports. I understood that and I handed him our passports and the American press paperwork, which he took to another room. All I could do was pray that we would get everything back.

The guard soon returned with a well-dressed gentleman who I assumed was the chief of the station. He didn't look very pleased with us. He went through each of the passports and pointed out that we didn't have any Iraqi visas to enter the country. He asked if we had any other paperwork to support our entrance into Iraq.

Bob Dows took out his press identification card, and pulled off the chain he had been wearing around his neck. The chain had a plastic emblem that had the word, PRESS, along with his photo.

He handed these items to the station chief, who seemed marginally more pleased with the additional information. He disappeared into the back room and a few minutes later, he came back out, beckoning Bob to accompany him. Looking a bit uneasy, Bob rose to go, and I told Qassim to go with him to help him interpret.

They were gone for almost an hour, and when they returned, Bob said that he had been verbally strip-searched, and the same questions were asked of him again and again. He said he repeated the same answers over and over. Clearly exhausted, he added, "They were not pleased with me."

I turned to him and said, "You did your best; let's just see where this will go."

The station chief, who now had two other armed men with him, approached me next. With what little Arabic I knew I introduced myself, made a fist and swung my right arm across my chest over my heart. With a big smile, I said, *"As-salaam 'alykum,"* which means, "Peace be upon you." He responded appropriately and in a pleasant manner, with a smile on his face – the first time we had seen him smile.

I asked if he spoke any English and he said, "A little."

I told Qassim to tell him I was the doctor for the group and to present him with the album and an explanation of what we were doing in Egypt, Syria, and Jordan. Then I took a few steps backwards.

An intense conversation took place between Qassim and the station chief. I was thinking to myself that this was a good sign. Finally the chief asked me to follow him to the back room. The two armed men were now at my side, and I asked Qassim to come with us. Fortunately, they allowed it, as they had with Bob.

Once in the back room, the station chief asked me if I would empty my pockets. I had nothing to speak of – just a pen, some paper, and a rubber band around a few hundred dollars of American currency. The chief began to count the bills out very carefully, after which he replaced the rubber band around them.

Qassim told him there was a trunk of medical supplies and equipment in the van and that it belonged to me. I instructed Qassim to tell him that we would be happy to donate all of it to one of their hospitals as a gift. At that the station chief smiled again, even more warmly than he had when I had greeted him in Arabic.

I began to replace the contents of my pockets, and the station chief asked me to remain seated. He stayed with me, but everyone else left the room, Qassim included.

We sat there for what seemed like an inordinate amount of time, saying little. It was at least an hour, but may have been longer. Finally Qassim came back into the room and said, "Do not worry. Good things are happening." I trusted Qassim, but I was still worried. The suspense was stressful, and it was beginning to get to me. Then everything changed.

Other men began arriving, and finally a man who apparently was actually in charge entered the dismal room. He was dressed in a beautiful blue pin-striped suit, a cotton button-down white shirt and tie, and what looked like black calfskin loafers. His hair was cut short and he had a short, well-trimmed beard, and his fingernails were perfectly manicured. His face was lit up with a broad smile as he introduced himself, shook my hand firmly, and then said, "I apologize for any inconvenience."

He went on to say that he was the Minister of Communications, and that we were the only American television team to have come to Iraq for this three-day event. Then he apologized again and asked if we needed any food or water.

The station chief then entered and handed me back my album, which I presented to the Minister of Communications. He quickly flipped through the photos, saying things such as, "This is wonderful, this is beautiful, you do good things, we are pleased to have you here in Iraq for this upcoming auspicious event."

Then I said, "We are very glad to be here. We do not have any hotel reservations, but we can sleep in our van if need be."

He replied, "No, no. I have suites for you at our finest hotel. You are our honored guests! You will attend the VIP reception and dinner tonight. You will have VIP identification so you can attend all the events. I have arranged for two limos and drivers that you can use to tour Baghdad.

"And you, doctor, will be allowed to photograph whatever you wish. We would like to show you our newest hospitals and medical facilities, and you are welcome to photograph there as well."

I could hardly believe what I just heard. Our gamble had actually paid off.

To myself I thought, *Congratulations to Marvin Zindler and the Channel 13 news team. You have an exclusive! We're not going to go to prison. We're not going to be shot. We are going to suites in a five-star hotel!*

After I had taken a moment to recover from the tremendous feeling of relief that we would not be thrown in jail, or worse, but instead were to be treated like honored guests, I began to think in more practical terms. If we were going to attend a VIP reception and dinner, it would most likely be formal dress. I said to the Minister of Communications, "We'd be delighted to be your guests at tonight's gathering, but all I have is a dark suit. I didn't bring any formal clothing."

He smiled. "That would be more than adequate, but those of you who wish it can have a tailor come to your hotel room and have a more formal suit made, if desired, in just hours. Just let the front desk know when you check in, and the tailors will meet you in your rooms."

I thanked him and asked, "How far is the hotel from here, sir?"

"It's about twenty minutes away," he replied.

Just to make sure that I had all of the bases covered, I said, "Our camera man, Bob Dows, has brought his own equipment. We also have our writer and producer, Lori Reingold, with us."

The Minister of Communications nodded, and then he and I left the back room and returned to the front lobby, where members of my team had been given some water and sandwiches. But they were still looking very grim. I introduced the Minister of Communications to them, then I told them about the cars and hotel reservations that had been set aside for them, as well as letting them know that they could even have tailor-made suits if they desired.

It was like turning on a light switch. Their attitudes changed in an instant, reflected in the broad smiles on their faces. They were all very well aware that this was going to be a once in a lifetime trip, and that this story was going to be an exclusive; they would be the only TV station in the United States with this material. They could forward it to their stations in Europe as well.

The Minister of Communications said there were major events at several of the hotels and at the palace, and that we would be their honored guests at all events. There would be a reception line, and I would be meeting with Saddam Hussein and other members of the Iraqi administration that evening.

Then we were given back our passports, and told that we were cleared to enter Iraq and that tonight other government officials would come to our rooms at the hotel with paperwork. This paperwork would grant us something akin to diplomatic status, but actually even better, for the duration of our stay in Iraq.

The Minister of Communications said that we would get a VIP pass to all the events on a diplomatic level and that the members of the press would be given special press cards that would allow them into all the events as well as the ability to photograph what they wished. It was basically the same news he had given me earlier, but with a little more detail.

Once again, I was nearly overwhelmed as the significance of his words hit me. I could see that this man very much wanted our small group to bring this elaborate event to the United States and TV affiliates in Europe. The reason seemed clear: it would take the event far beyond the Arab world. Our participation could be very important to Iraq's Office of Communications.

That was fine with me. I was not being detained in a jail cell and better yet, I was not being shot. I was, however, wondering if our willful and even enthusiastic participation would be spun by the Iraqi propaganda machine as an endorsement of Saddam, even though Marvin and I and the news crew would absolutely never endorse brutality and authoritarianism. But I knew it would be foolish to openly address the incongruity at this point and risk losing the opportunity our access would provide.

I think I've always been very clear about my abhorrence of brutality, and I stressed with our crew that we didn't want to appear as if we cared more about being on camera than about human rights. We discussed whether failing to directly address the issue might make it seem that way. Yet we acknowledged that we needed to walk a fine line here, because drawing too much attention to the issue, especially while we were on Saddam's home turf, would very likely open a can of worms, causing our access to information to dry up, and possibly resulting in our learning first-hand more about Saddam's brutality than we had bargained for. So we all agreed that we would be there merely as guests, observers, and reporters, recording events without injecting commentary or opinions until we were again safe at home in Houston.

Within the hour, both interpreters and our transportation arrived, and took us to the hotel, which looked more like a palace to me. As we checked in, those of us desiring tailors made arrangements, and as promised by the Minister of Communications, the tailors were awaiting us in our rooms. Measuring and fitting only took about twenty minutes, with the assurance that our evening wear would be ready for us when we returned from the tour we'd been promised.

Then we were taken on a short tour of Baghdad, passing through Firdos Square, towered over by the now-infamous statute of Saddam Hussein, so the TV news crew could photograph it. We had no way of knowing it then, of course, but in 2003, television screens across the world would show footage of this very statue, toppled through the cooperative effort of Iraqi civilians and American soldiers. Many media reports about the toppling of the statue were in some ways exaggerated and distorted, and years later, one of the Iraqi civilians who had struck the statue with a sledgehammer actually said that he wished Saddam were back, because Iraq had become a hotbed for extremism and terrorism. Nevertheless, the footage of the statue's destruction became a powerful symbol of the regime's fall. But that was still in the future.

We also drove under the arch of crossed swords, known as the Victory Arch, which had been constructed in the late 1980s to commemorate the Iran-Iraq War. It's quite impressive, and is one of Baghdad's most photographed monuments.

After the Baghdad tour, we were returned to our hotel, where we all got a hot shower and changed into the tailored evening wear that, as promised, awaited us in our rooms. Talk about good service! As we emerged from our rooms, the cars and drivers were waiting to take us to the facilities where all of the activities were taking place. We were told again that Saddam Hussein would be present, as well as many other dignitaries from Arab countries.

Upon our arrival, we were escorted to our seats near the front and then to the reception line to meet with Saddam Hussein and his two sons,

Uday and Qusay. Entering the reception line, I turned left and stopped, captivated by the sight of dignitaries from many of the Arab countries and their parties. They were dressed in typical Middle Eastern formal wear, with very colorful tunics and gowns.

As I stood there my gaze kept returning to one man in particular, who was wearing white robes and a headpiece with gold braids. I took a few steps forward to get a better look at him. Then our eyes met, and as his lit up with recognition, I smiled at him. I continued a few steps more and stopped, because this first row was roped off with a red velvet chain. I rested my hands on the velvet barrier and as I did so, two well-dressed gentlemen who had been sitting to either side of the man in the white robes abruptly stood. It was clear that they were bodyguards.

One of these men was now focused on me. He strode forward to the barrier, smiled, and said, "This is His Highness, the King of Saudi Arabia, Fahd bin Abdulaziz Al Saud, Defender of the Faith, protector of Mecca and Medina."

As it happened, I knew exactly who His Highness was, because he had been my patient, spending seven weeks under my care in Houston a couple of years earlier. King Fahd had even visited me at my home for dinner on several occasions.

Suddenly, the king came forward and lifted the barrier, giving me a big bear hug and kissing me on both cheeks. The room in which we stood had became very silent, and all eyes were on us now. Even Saddam Hussein, who was on the reception line, had stopped and was looking our way.

Then King Fahd motioned to his bodyguards to remove the barrier altogether. He put his arm into mine, and arm and arm we walked back to where he was sitting. The king had another chair brought over and placed it to the right of his. It seemed like an excessively long time before people resumed talking and the reception line continued moving again.

Before long King Fahd and I were like two old friends, conversing about our families. The king remembered that I had horses and other animals on my property in Texas, and he asked how they were and whether I had added to my menagerie. For my part, I reminded him even though he might feel fine right now, he needed a follow-up medical exam. I added, "I look forward to seeing you at The Methodist Hospital again in Houston for that examination,"

Laughing, he said to me, "Perhaps, perhaps not; I will decide. Privileges of being the king, you see."

"Doctor's orders, even for a king," I shot back, smiling.

We were again laughing, drawing more attention from this rather somber audience. The king said to me, "You are the bright star in my evening. These political functions are usually quite boring and the people around me are not really my friends."

I said, "I know what you mean; I've been to more than my share of political functions, but at least the food is always excellent!" At that point, we both broke out in laughter again.

The king and I were apparently having too good of a time, which once again attracted the attention of Saddam Hussein, who stepped away from the reception line and came towards us. The bodyguards stood, but His Highness remained in his seat staring up at Saddam as I started to stand. The king gently put his hand on my arm, and I knew what that meant: *Stay seated.* I did.

Saddam said, "It seems you two are old friends."

The king just nodded, but said nothing.

Then Saddam stepped forward and put out his hand to me, and at that point I felt obligated to stand.

I used the standard greeting of friendship in this part of the world, taking my right hand, making a fist, and slapping it across my heart as I uttered, *"As-salaam 'alykum."*

Saddam returned my greeting in kind, and then I said, "Thank you for inviting me and my Houston, Texas TV news crew." There was a brief and almost awkward silence as Saddam regarded the king, who still resolutely remained seated. I explained, "I am a physician and surgeon to His Highness."

At that, Saddam whispered something in the interpreter's ear, after which the interpreter told me that Saddam would like me to be his physician as well. I didn't say anything, but just nodded and smiled in what I hoped was a noncommittal manner.

Saddam then turned and went back to the reception line.

The king said to me, "We don't associate with him and his people."

I said, "That is understandable. He is not to be trusted. And I will try to avoid any further contact."

I knew that King Fahd had sent a powerful message by refusing to stand when we were approached by Saddam Hussein, or during the entire time we were conversing. And I am quite certain that other Arab leaders, who were sitting all around us, took note of this as well.

His Highness then turned to me and said again, "You really have been a bright star in my evening. It couldn't have gone better." I had to agree.

As it turned out, the Saddam birthday bash did not become the major news story that Marvin and his team had hoped for. The world – and the news cycle – had moved on. and there was no longer such intense interest in Saddam Hussein. But at least we all had a good time, and, more importantly, we got home safely. It was definitely a trip to remember.

But the trip I would take to Iraq a couple of years later, post-Saddam, proved to be even more memorable.

PART 1

THE MISSION

CHAPTER 1

MOBILIZING THE TEAMS

I am always up for a challenge, and in 2004, thanks to my good friend Marvin Zindler, and a man who would become my good friend, acclaimed Canadian journalist Don North, I had a challenging new mission that would occupy me for the coming year, and beyond. The mission was to help locate seven Iraqi businessmen whose right hands had been amputated by Saddam Hussein's henchmen as punishment for various political "crimes," and then bring them back to the Texas Medical Center in Houston for restorative surgery. As you know if you read my introduction, Don had set the ball in motion when, after he heard about these men's suffering, he had followed the recommendation of a Houston oil businessman and had contacted Marvin Zindler. Marvin in turn contacted me. After that there was no turning back.

Originally there were nine "brothers" in this tight circle of Iraqi men who had become close friends in Abu Ghraib prison as a result of their common suffering. But one man had died shortly after his amputation, and another had been released from prison and had escaped to Europe, whereabouts unknown. That left seven.

Unfortunately, these seven men were hardly unique. According to estimates by Amnesty International, thousands of Iraqis had had their hands amputated for similar "crimes." Don North once called Baghdad "Amputation City," telling a reporter that within a block it was routine to run into two or three people without a leg or an arm or an ear. For now, though, our focus was on the seven men.

My objectives, apart from helping out in any way possible with the preliminary arrangements, were to fly to Iraq, meet up with Don, go to Abu Ghraib prison, and locate the men. Like so many things, these objectives sounded straightforward and almost simple in theory, but I knew they would be anything but easy. Besides, getting to Abu Ghraib and locating the men was only the first part of the mission.

Once we found them, we faced the potentially lengthy process of transferring them to Houston. Our understanding was that they possessed no real form of identification – a nearly unimaginable state of affairs to those of us who live in more developed and efficiently-run countries. And they certainly didn't have passports. We hoped we would be able to get them out of Iraq on military transport to a base in Germany, then get them seats on one of the public international air carriers that would bring them to Houston.

How do you get seven men through immigration and customs in three different countries, maybe more, without any papers, and without any passports? You generally don't, especially in a post-9/11 world. But I did have "The Letter" – an executive memo from the Oval Office that authorized the trip. It would be my ticket to getting the men, and the rest of us, through the routine tangle of military bureaucracy and multi-government red tape. (It would also prove to be valuable in giving me the clout I needed for a secondary mission, which had been suggested to me during conversations I had with certain government officials ahead of my trip: to investigate and report on abuse of prisoners in Iraq, in order to help bring an end to these deplorable practices.) I can't over-emphasize the significance of this letter; it's no exaggeration to say that I simply could not have made this trip without the document.

Lori Reingold started making telephone calls and sending emails and faxes to the German government, the German consulate, and the German ambassador. She also spent many hours contacting different airlines to see if we could acquire seven complimentary seats from Frankfurt, Germany to Houston.

I then stepped in and called a friend of mine, Gordon Bethune, who at the time was CEO at Continental Airlines (now United Airlines), and finally convinced him to fly the seven men from Frankfurt to the U.S. on available seats on Continental. I told Mr. Bethune that Marvin Zindler and the Channel 13 news crew would be at the airport to film their arrival and to give due credit and praise to Continental Airlines for their participation. I thought that was the least I could do in return.

Was I surprised when he barked at me over the phone; *"No TV, NO press coverage! Do NOT show our logo."* At first, I didn't understand, but then the light bulb went off in my head, along with the thought: *No good deed goes unpunished.* Mr. Bethune did not want to put Continental Airlines on the front lines of this war. And I can't say that I blame him.

We agreed we would have the seven brothers de-plane on the tarmac, away from the terminal and removed from the airport grounds through a maximum-security gate when they arrived. They would never go through immigration or passport check. There would be no public mention of how they arrived in Houston. Mr. Bethune felt comfortable with that, and we were one step closer to bringing the seven brothers to Houston. As time goes on and events in various parts of the Middle East threaten to boil over more each day, I more fully appreciate Mr. Bethune's abundance of caution back then, not to mention his selflessness.

Now it was time for me to begin my personal preparations in earnest. I have been to the Middle East on many medical missions with the Children's Foundation that Marvin Zindler and I founded. It was very similar to Doctors Without Borders, but our major areas of interest were children. Out of necessity, however, we had expanded to provide treatment to other family members, particularly those who had suffered injuries as a result of ongoing conflicts in the area. As a result, we had already established a reputation with the populace and even some of the warlords in the region.

In some areas, I was known as "Doctor Angel," and in other areas, I was known as the "Crazy Texan." I gladly claimed both titles but have to admit to a special fondness for the "Crazy Texan" moniker. I often wore Western boots and a ten-gallon hat, and was generally armed with a classic six-shooter or my own sniper rifle, modified with a scope and a collapsible stock that made it possible to stow away in my duffel and out of sight. (Actually, given some of the places I've been, being armed was anything *but* crazy.)

On some of my previous trips to the Middle East, however, I had dressed more to blend in with the populace than to advertise my presence, setting aside my Western hat in favor of one of the many multi-colored skullcaps that I owned. The color and design of each would identify from which tribal area and community the wearer came. By changing the skullcap I wore, as I traveled, I would better fit in with the local population. Over the years I had also learned some Urdu and Pashto language, as well as other tribal dialects, and I made it a habit to scan my notes and journals in order to improve my vocabulary. I have found in my travels that the more you fit in, the safer and more likely to be respected you are.

According to the customs of the region, respect was initiated by the visitor bringing a gift to the local tribal leader or to those in the community counsel. Throughout my years of travel, back in the days before nearly everyone on the planet had a cell phone with a camera, I found one of the best gifts was a Polaroid instant photograph.

Most of these people had never had a photograph taken of themselves or their families, and watching the magic of a Polaroid develop before their eyes as I held it in my hand was unbelievable to them. I once had an elderly gentleman up in the mountains tell me, "Only a god can make this happen." If that gentleman were still alive, it's very possible that he would have his own smart phone, with which he would be snapping photos everywhere he went. But back in the day, a Polaroid camera was an awe-inspiring device in many remote parts of the world.

I know that we in the United States hear all the time that you are forbidden to take pictures of the women and even the men in some tribal areas, but that is not usually the case. Barring photographs was one of the controlling principles of Al-Qaeda and ISIS, and not a demand of any religious or social traditions. Those with any education pay no attention to these rulings, and most despise ISIS for what they have done to family members or others in their tribal area. It's no surprise that having a photograph became a badge of honor – a form of rebellion against the oppressors.

Once my personal items were prepared and Lori Reingold was working the telephones and fax lines at Channel 13, our plan seemed to be falling into place quite nicely. I continued my due diligence by acquiring the best maps that I could of the areas into which I would be traveling.

Every rabbit builds its hole with a back door, and having good maps of the area was my back door, should it be required for a quick departure or escape. It took several days to locate and assemble the detailed maps of this part of the world. I had one foot well into the operation and the planning, but one foot was still out. How exactly would we get there?

Abu Ghraib is just north of the Euphrates river and about halfway between Baghdad, the Iraqi capital, and the city of Fallujah. I could get a commercial flight to Kuwait City on the Persian Gulf with a stopover in Frankfurt, Germany. Kuwait City was just a few minutes away from the Ali al Salem Air Base. With The Letter from the White House, I could then get an outgoing military flight to Baghdad. It would be twenty-four hours of travel, but I thought that was probably the most direct route. As it would turn out, that route would not be nearly as direct as I had assumed, but of course I had no way of knowing this as I continued merrily on with my "best-laid plans."

Meanwhile, as usual, I worked outside at my ranchette, Eden, in the heart of Bellaire, an incorporated city within the heart of Houston. Temperatures in the Houston area that summer reached 105 degrees with 100% humidity. I developed a deep bronze tan, which I felt would serve me well in my efforts to "blend in." I also made a special effort to increase my physical fitness and general endurance, because I knew that I would be working in harsh conditions. Instead of using my tractor, I carried the fifty-pound bags of oats and grain on my shoulder, and seventy-pound bales of hay. I limited my water intake and developed a tolerance to the heat. The physical labor gave me the stamina and muscle I would need for the upcoming trip.

Other preparations were equally important. I took the time to assemble any surgical kits, medications, and instruments that I felt I might need for others or even for myself, and that would not be readily available on the ground in the region.

Several weeks elapsed while the international and political ramifications of the trip were smoothed out, the appropriate ambassadors and consulates contacted, and the required identification papers and special visas obtained. At the same time, my hair grew longer, my mustache and beard filled out, and my skin tone darkened even more from my working out in the sun. My tolerance to work in triple-digit temperatures improved, and intentionally limiting my water and food intake prepared me for the physical hardships that are inevitable in the regions where we would be travelling. I was acclimating well, but this was hardly my first rodeo.

Over the course of many years, I had traveled to Egypt, Syria, Jordan, Iran, and Iraq (before the war), as well as to Pakistan and Afghanistan, and across the northern Afghan border to China. From enduring the searing heat of the desert to climbing the freezing cold but disappearing glaciers of the Himalayas in the north, I had grown very familiar with the Middle East and Central and South Asia, and the people in these regions.

With Channel 13 backing me, and with the hard work of Lori

Reingold, the day finally came when we had acquired the travel documents that I needed, as well as other paperwork necessary for bringing the seven brothers into the United States. Our preparation efforts were done privately – with no government involvement apart from The Letter, which remained in a secure place in my home but had not yet been utilized.

I can't say enough good things about the many volunteers, doctors, nurses, and rehabilitation and ancillary personnel who would be required to care for these seven men, and who had all agreed to donate their time and efforts free of charge. The Methodist Hospital of Houston and the Texas Institute for Rehabilitation and Research (TIRR) joined with us, and my good friend and colleague Dr. Fred Kestler would help with the revisions required in order to fit the prostheses. We had even made arrangements for post-op accommodations. Following their surgery, the seven men would stay in my home and the homes of several of my wonderful neighbors. I was overwhelmed by the generosity of all these Houstonians who stepped up to assist and support us in this undertaking.

I still had some personal preparations to do. Shortly before leaving, I had some articles of clothing modified with hidden pockets, one of which was to conceal and protect The Letter. I also had a special belt made, into which I stuffed as many gold coins as possible, and a fanny pack that I wore in front under my clothes. Being muscular and slight of build gave me a fullness at the waistline which looked quite natural.

Finally, all was ready.

CHAPTER 2

NOT QUITE BAGHDAD

I left from the George Bush Intercontinental Airport in Houston, with a stopover in Frankfurt, and then flew on to Kuwait City. The flights were on time and uneventful, and my duffel bag with all my equipment arrived intact. That was the only thing I had really been worried about at that point.

At the airport in Kuwait there was no problem hiring a car and driver to take me to Ali al Salem Air Base, about 39 miles away from the Iraqi border. The Ali al Salem Air Base is where American soldiers were marshaled in for their 2003 preparations for the invasion of Iraq, which, as mentioned earlier, had been based on the assumption, ultimately proven to be erroneous, that Saddam Hussein retained stores of chemical weapons and other weapons of mass destruction. Many folks, including me, had been skeptical from the very beginning about the assertion that Saddam Hussein actually possessed WMDs, and as I also mentioned earlier, to this date, nobody has proven that he ever had any. Nevertheless, I have heard from some of the American soldiers who took part in the initial invasion that even in the 110-degree heat, many soldiers slept in chemical protective suits or with gas masks at the ready.

My plan was to get to Baghdad as soon as possible after my arrival in Iraq so I could take some time to explore the city on my own, and get an idea of how the people and the economy were faring now that Saddam was out of power. I thought I might also be able to pick up some more information about the seven brothers. Then, if all went according to plan, I would meet up with Don North at a Baghdad tea shop a couple of days after my arrival.

Arrangements had been made for me to bunk at Camp Cropper, a U.S. Army operated facility near Baghdad International Airport, for as long as I needed to stay before going on to Abu Ghraib prison. Camp Cropper had been established in 2003, initially as a High Value Detainee

(HVD) holding area that was soon expanded to also be a Corps Holding Area (CHA). The original intention was for Camp Cropper to be a small temporary camp that held detainees for no longer than 72 hours, after which they would be sent on to other detention facilities in Baghdad and around Iraq. But this plan didn't work, since most prisons had been looted and vandalized after the fall of Saddam's Ba'athist regime. (Abu Ghraib prison was still up and running, of course, but they were only accepting a limited number of new prisoners.)

I was looking forward to seeing Camp Cropper, and learning all that I could about the treatment (or mistreatment) of the detainees there. I had heard rumors, some of which were as disturbing as the rumors about Abu Ghraib. I needed to find out for myself what was really going on, and then do whatever I could do to stop any abuse that might be taking place. Addressing the problem of prisoner abuse was also Don's and my secondary goal at Abu Ghraib prison, our primary one being to find the seven brothers. But first things first.

Baghdad is on the Tigris River, and the city of Fallujah is on the Euphrates River. Between the two is Abu Ghraib. American forces had advanced to Baghdad in 2003 and had immediately taken the international airport there.

Most of the major cities in Iraq were established along a river, most notably the Euphrates River or the Tigris River, but there are several other less well-known rivers in Iraq as well. From Kuwait City, if you travel along the Euphrates River you pass through Nasiriyah and onto Najaf, and about halfway between Kuwait City and Baghdad there are Karbala and the City of Musayyib. At this point lies the Karbala Baghdad Highway, which spans the Euphrates River and had been taken early in the fighting.

The area along the river is heavily farmed, with palm plantations and well-tilled fields. In the spring of 2003, a U.S. Army Special Forces convoy was moving along this highway when it drove head on into Saddam Hussein's Republican Guard. Some of the trucks of the Special Forces unit crossed the bridge, while others remained on the west side of the Euphrates River, splitting the unit.

Baghdad was still forty-five miles away, leaving the convoy isolated and on its own. A good decision was made to retrace their steps across the bridge and join the other half of their unit. Running the gauntlet, the trucks had to drive through the gunfire a second time, with small arms fire cracking all around them and rocket propelled grenades flying past at seemingly random targets. The randomness was far from reassuring to the American troops; at best, it seemed to be an illustration of the old saying that even a stopped clock is right twice a day.

The Special Forces cleared the gauntlet, passing through the town of Musayyib, west of the Euphrates, and continuing south. God was apparently with them, and no American soldiers were injured, much less killed. Since then, the cities of Musayyib, Fallujah, and Baghdad had been taken and were relatively quiet, although in that region at that time in history, "relatively quiet" didn't mean much.

As we approached the main gate to Ali al Salem Air Base in our beat-up excuse for an automobile that could barely be described as a taxi, several guards came forward, their automatic weapons pointed at us. I was waving my passport out the window while yelling, "American!" – which I think startled and confused them. I played it safe and had the driver stop a distance from the gate. Then I slowly opened the door, hands in the air, and continued to wave the passport and to yell, "American, American!" I think that when they got a closer look at me, they were even more confused by my long hair, beard, and deeply tanned complexion. I probably looked more like a Middle Eastern terrorist to them than an American.

Then I yelled, "I am undercover Special Envoy American," and I just stood there. One of the guards proceeded toward me with his automatic weapon pointed at my chest. Trying to appear non-threatening, I addressed him, saying, "I would feel a lot more comfortable if you would point that thing in another direction. Here. Take my passport and check me out." I took a few steps forward to hand him the passport, and the guard raised his hand, indicating that I was to stop, which I immediately did. But I continued to address him, saying, "Lieutenant Commander, Retired, Special Envoy – either you come get the passport or I'll bring it to you."

This really confused him. I just stood there holding up the passport, and left the decision up to him. He had the weapon, after all.

Several MPs appeared from the opposite side, the leader of the unit barking an order to both his own men and the guards who had detained us, "We have them covered. Go get the passport."

As he took the passport, I addressed him, simply saying, "Good afternoon. I am here to catch a flight to Baghdad."

Now they were all confused, and the unit leader stood there silent, with his mouth half open. While we were still being watched closely by the other MPs, he walked back to the guard shack and picked up the phone. From where I was standing, I could not hear the conversation. Moments later he returned, handed me the passport, and said, "Sir, you need to get back in your taxi and return to Kuwait City."

I told him, "I have a letter in my inside pocket that I think will change things. I am going to open my jacket slowly, and I can either hand it to you or you can take it." With that, I slowly unzipped and opened my jacket, then turned toward him so he could see the inside pocket from which I carefully withdrew the Ziploc bag that contained The Letter. Opening the bag and taking out The Letter, I said, "You need to read this and immediately return it to me, and I don't want to see a line or wrinkle or even a fold in that letter when you hand it back to me."

He glanced at the heading on the document, and his expression immediately changed. Feeling emboldened by the change, I decided it was time to further press my authority and get him to cooperate fully. With barely constrained disdain I continued, "It would nice if you would come to attention and salute before I decide to put you on report for insubordination."

He responded, "I need to make a call."

I corrected him. "You need to make a call, *'sir!'*"

He said, "Yes, *sir.*"

Then I said, "Tell those Bozos on the other side of the road to put their weapons down."

He responded with a crisp, "Yes, *sir*" and waved them away.

I walked back to the cab and assured the driver, who was understandably quite upset at having all the guns pointed at him, that everything was fine.

The other MPs gathered around the guardhouse where the lead MP was on the phone, and where I could see that The Letter was being passed around. It wasn't long before the lead guy came running back to the taxi, where he snapped to attention, saluted, and handed The Letter back to me. Then he said, "The base commander is waiting for your arrival, but the taxi will not be allowed on the base." Returning The Letter to its safe place in my inner pocket, I told him that my duffel was on the backseat of the taxi, and that I needed to pay the driver and have him return to Kuwait City.

The MP then paid the driver, collected the duffel from the back seat for me, and then we walked through the gate, where a jeep was waiting to take me to headquarters. Once there, the MP and I headed to the administration building and were directed to a conference room. A young man brought me a cool drink, and the MP set my duffel by the door while I waited. Several men and a young lady entered the room, all trying to look very important. I stood and shook hands with them, introducing myself. The first words spoken to me were, "May we see that letter?"

I replied, "You may see it, and you may read it, but you may not make a copy of it, and it must not leave this room. And when you have satisfied yourselves of its authenticity and meaning, you must return it to me."

After they had reviewed The Letter, the base commander handed it back to me. I said, "I was told I could get a flight from here to Baghdad. It is urgent but not an emergency. If you have a regular flight in the next 24-48 hours, I would appreciate being on it."

The C.O. responded, "We have regular flights to Baghdad, and I can accommodate you tomorrow."

"I appreciate that very much."

He continued, "We have a place where you can bunk tonight, and I hope you will join us in the officer's mess at 19:00 for dinner." Then there was silence. I knew what they were thinking. They wanted to know exactly why I was here, which was understandable, as The Letter raised even more questions than it answered.

Finally, the young lady gave voice to what was on all of their minds. "May we ask why you have come all this way, and can we be of some help?"

I replied, "From Baghdad I need to get to Abu Ghraib. The specifics of the mission are on a 'need to know' basis, and at this point, the President of the United States and myself are the only ones who need to know. I'm sorry, but that's all I can tell you at this time."

The young lieutenant said, "Let me show you to your room, where you can freshen up and rest, and then we'll have a Jeep to take you to the mess hall for dinner."

I walked over to pick up my duffel, but one of the other officers had already taken it for me. As we left the command center and were walking to the barracks area, the young lieutenant asked, "Where are you traveling from?"

"Texas."

With a big smile, she responded, "Of course it would be Texas."

I wasn't sure what she was implying, but I accepted it good-naturedly and answered her back in my best Texas twang, "Yes, darlin', where else would it be?"

She laughed and looked me over, saying, "You look more like the men we are fighting against than one of us."

"Good! That's the whole idea when you want to fit in."

Before long we reached my room, and after the lieutenant left, I lay down on my bunk and got a short but badly needed power nap. I awoke feeling refreshed, and prepared to join the officers for dinner.

The attractive young lieutenant and a driver came to take me to dinner. I wondered whether they had reasoned that a young woman might captivate my imagination and cause me to have a slip of the tongue, perhaps revealing the answers to some of their most burning questions, such as why I was dressed the way I was, where I was going, and even what I had been assigned to do once I got there. In other words, what was the purpose of my trip? Though I knew they were brimming with curiosity, I was determined to tell them as little as possible.

The dinner was good, and as I'd expected, the conversation centered on me. They pretty much all asked the same questions, although from many different angles, perhaps thinking they might trick me into providing answers. But I was very careful, and they all received the same vague answers. I realized that my noncommittal responses made them even more curious, so I decided to give them a break, ending the evening by saying I wanted to put their minds at rest, and that no one was in trouble. I let them know that my reasons for being here would not affect any military personnel. Then I added, "I mean, that's if I get your cooperation and can successfully carry out my assignment."

The curiosity remained, no doubt stoked even more after that last statement, but they also seemed somewhat relieved by my comments. *Typical military attitude*, I mused to myself. *They hate surprises, since most surprises involve them trying to protect their own backsides*. The least I could do was to assure them that their backsides were covered.

I got a much needed good night's sleep, and in the morning, they offered to take me to the mess tent for breakfast. I thanked them but explained that I was only eating one meal a day, in the evenings. And I needed to be ready when my flight arrived.

A few hours later, I was driven out on the tarmac, where I

offloaded and then walked up a ramp onto a C4 transport plane with several platoons of combat-ready Marines and their equipment. As we took off from the air base on what I thought (foolishly, as it would turn out) would be the last leg of my journey to Baghdad, I chatted with the young Marines, who were looking at me very curiously. My only comment to them was, "This is how we dress in Texas."

The all laughed, and one young man shouted out, "I get it! You're on some secret undercover assignment."

I shouted above the thunderous drone of the plane, "You're a smart young man; you figured it out. But please don't tell anybody." Apparently everyone either believed me or thought it best to humor an officer by laughing at his jokes.

A little while later, we landed and the Marines deplaned. The pilots came walking past and I went up and thanked them for the lift to Baghdad. They looked at me with stunned expressions, and after standing there staring at each other for a few seconds, one of them said, "We are not in Baghdad."

That took me by surprise. "Then where the hell are we?"

The pilot replied, "We're actually about 96 kilometers north of Baghdad – at Forward Operating Base MacKenzie, just north of the city of Duluiyah. Last minute orders. They told us they needed the fresh Marines in the north, and we were rerouted to FOB MacKenzie."

I said, "I know this is not your fault," but followed that by a string of expletives. Once I had finished letting off steam, I turned and apologized for my outburst.

Then the co-pilot said, "Who the hell are you?"

I removed The Letter from my inside pocket and handed it to him. After glancing at it, he handed it back to me and said, "Somebody really fucked up. We're only pilots, and we followed our orders to go to FOB MacKenzie."

"Maybe you can take me to the base C.O., and we can get transport in the morning from here to Baghdad," I said. I waited in the reception area as the pilot and copilot went in to see the C.O. Shortly afterward, the C.O. came out of his office with a big smile on his face and put his hand out front to shake mine, but then gave me the same startled look that everybody else had. I was getting used to that by now. I shook his hand and thanked him for seeing me. As was all too typical in these situations, the first thing out of his mouth was not, "How can I help you?" but, "This screw-up is not my fault."

"Let's start this off in a friendly manner," I responded calmly. "I'm not here to cast blame. I just need your help. Can you get me either air or ground transportation to Baghdad?"

"There are convoys every day that bring supplies north and then return south to Baghdad and Fallujah. I am sure we can accommodate you on a convoy either later today or in the morning."

I shook my head, saying, "I don't want to travel these roads at night."

The C.O. said, "That's smart."

I said, "Thank you for your consideration."

"We will get you onto one of the convoys first thing in the morning going south to Baghdad," he said. "I'll arrange accommodations for you here at MacKenzie. I am sure they will be adequate. You can get a good night's rest and leave with the convoy at first light tomorrow. And I hope that you'll join the officers and me at dinner tonight."

I said, "I couldn't ask for more. And look how lucky I am to again see the countryside going to the town of Duluiyah and then, I assume, on to the little city of Balad, and to LSA Anaconda and then along the Tigris to Baghdad." Okay, so I was showing off a little bit.

The C.O. chuckled and said, "You know your geography."

"I've traveled the region numerous times. I've been threatened, attacked, and shot at, but God willing, I'm still alive and here again. Before I go any place, I memorize the maps, rivers, roads, alternate routes."

"That's a good policy," he said.

I was just warming up, and I continued, "When I was traveling through Pakistan along the Afghan border up to China, I always made it a point to pick the drivers who knew every town, village, and side road. I've found that the best drivers are the ones that run contraband, guns, and illegal drugs through the mountains. I like a driver who is 45 to 55 years old and has been doing it for several decades, because he's established that he too is a survivor. In these situations, knowledge of the terrain, the people, the language, and alternative routes is what keeps you alive. I hope you can find me a driver with some experience for this trip south to Baghdad."

"Well," he said, "Most of the drivers we use are young Marines, some of whom have run the routes several times. For many it will be either their first or second caravan trip. But don't worry; I'll make certain that you will have the best and most experienced driver for your trip in the morning."

That didn't make me feel all jolly inside, and no doubt my concern showed in my face, because the C.O. was looking at me questioningly. I thought I'd better explain.

"It's just that I've found that Marines are rarely corrupt enough to have the kind of experience I need in a driver," I said. "But I'll take what I can get. I know it's a crapshoot. That's why I pray every day, and sometimes multiple times a day, especially when I'm in a situation like this."

Just as I turned to leave, the C.O. asked, "May I see that letter everybody is talking about?"

I said, "You are most certainly entitled to read it, but you can't make a copy of it. It must remain in my presence and be returned to me after you have read it. I apologize for acting less than trusting, but I know you will understand how the success of any mission – particularly a very important one – is less assured the more people know about it."

In a couple of minutes he had read it, and then he looked me in the eye-and said, "This is the real thing?"

"You better believe it," I replied. He still looked a little doubtful, so I added, "I served as a Lieutenant Commander in the USPHS, and I also served in the FBI *and* the FBP. I have been on Air Force One, I've been to the State Department and to the Oval Office, I've met with senior personnel at numerous embassies throughout the world. You don't think I would be suntanned, bearded, long-haired, and dressed like a *mujahid* for the fun of it, do you?"

We stood there silent but eye-to-eye for a moment, until finally the C.O. said, "I see your point. Got it! Dinner at 19:30?"

"It will be my pleasure to join you and your officers."

I came to attention, gave a formal salute, and did an about-face. Then I picked my duffel bag up from the floor, swung it over my shoulder, and headed out the door without looking back.

CHAPTER 3

THE AMBUSH

O nce I was shown to my quarters, which were austere but more than adequate, I plopped down on my bunk for what I intended to be a brief cat nap. But apparently I was more weary than I had realized, and the nap lasted longer than I'd intended. When I awoke I saw that it was nearly time for me to join the C.O. and his officers for dinner, so I quickly got up, refreshed myself, and headed for the mess area.

After a surprisingly pleasant and uneventful dinner I returned to my quarters, reflecting on my experiences so far, and particularly on the people whom I'd encountered. One person who had made an impression on me was a sergeant major named Justin Roberts, whom I had met at dinner. Sergeant Major Roberts was tall and muscular and carried himself with the utmost confidence – intimidating upon first impression, but amiable and very likable. He and I hit it off right away.

Roberts told me that he was only visiting FOB MacKenzie and was actually stationed at Camp Cropper. When I told him that arrangements had been made for me to bunk at Cropper for at least one night before I headed off to Abu Ghraib prison, his eyes lit up and he said, "That's great, Doc. Look me up when you get there. I'll show you around."

As I undressed and got ready for bed, I was still bone-tired and looking forward to more sleep. Instead, I tossed and turned most of the night. Though I had tried to accept the unwelcome detour with good grace, the whole thing was still not setting well with me, and I wondered if this might be an omen of some sorts, a sign that my entire trip to Iraq would be a failure. Or maybe it was some higher power's warning to me that I was in danger and that I'd better turn back while I could. I kept reminding myself that this was superstitious thinking and that sometimes, shit happens – especially when the military is involved – and you just have to accept it, but those thoughts failed to bring on the restful sleep that my body still so desperately needed.

I had set my alarm so I would be ready to go at first light, but I was up well before the alarm went off, and I prepared myself the best that I could for the trip ahead. Emerging from my quarters, I took the short walk to where the convoy was ready and waiting, as the C.O. had promised. In short order we had all boarded, and the journey to Baghdad, which I silently but fervently prayed would be uneventful, commenced.

The convoy consisted of eight trucks: six lightly armored with .50 caliber machine guns mounted on top, and two heavily armored vehicles. The truck in which I was riding contained supplies, ammunition, a few new recruits, and a couple of CIA guys. I was given a flak jacket, a gas mask, and a helmet. I was particularly uncomfortable, wedged in between two fully armed 6'2" 240-pound soldiers who were discussing running an area just southwest of Duluiyah going toward Balad. I sat there with my arms folded over my chest, and all I could hear in my head was, "Ambush Alley."

I began to dislike this drive even more as we proceeded, and I wondered what would help us more, prayers or luck. I decided we needed both. Danger would be all around us, and I knew I had to accept this. I tried to calm my thoughts, but the soldiers were discussing recent attacks on convoys such as ours – not exactly conducive to a tranquil mind.

I knew that the lightweight trucks in our convoys had little armor to protect those inside as they drove down these dangerous roads. I also knew that because only a couple of trucks had the heavy armor, and because we were all huddled together, made us more vulnerable. On the other hand, our truck only carried a few recruits, a couple of CIA men, and myself, limiting the number of us who would be injured or killed in an attack. That was beneficial in the larger scheme of things, I supposed, though it didn't do us much good. As these uneasy thoughts ran through my mind, all I could think was that I was not having a good day. Not a good day at all.

The day was about to get worse, and we would all soon get a firsthand lesson about why the road we were traveling was known as "Ambush Alley."

I was the first person in our vehicle to spot the white Toyota pickup truck that seemed to emerge out of nowhere from the distant desert. My time in Pakistan had taught me that no good ever came from white Toyota trucks driving towards military caravans. These trucks were killing machines, and their drivers suicide bombers, presumably expecting a greater reward in the next life. As it hurtled closer to us I saw that this truck had a machine gun mounted on the back and was clearly loaded with high explosives – and that was all I needed to see in order to conclude that we were about to be attacked.

But nobody else in our truck appeared to be aware of what was happening. The recruits were novices and hadn't seen much if any combat, and the CIA men, to put it politely, didn't seem to be on top of the situation either. From what I could see, nobody in any of the other vehicles in our convoy had yet responded. Had they not seen the white truck? I had no way of knowing.

One of the recruits, catching on to what was about to happen, said, "None of us is qualified or trained on a .50 caliber machine gun."

"Well, somebody's got to do something!" I shouted, both surprised and exasperated. There was no more time to argue, because the white pickup was rapidly approaching us, and there was still no sign that anyone in any of the other vehicles was responding. So I did what I've often done in my life, though admittedly most of those occasions have been less dangerous situations: I took matters into my own hands.

Without giving it another moment's thought, I jumped up into the turret and positioned myself at the machine gun. Taking no more than a few seconds to cycle the action, aim, and pray that my aim would be reasonably accurate, I let loose, hitting the truck when it was only a few hundred yards away from us. This caused the truck's driver to crash into a boulder, resulting in a spectacular explosion that, I am certain, left everyone in the convoy as shaken as the occupants of our vehicle were (particularly me). The incident was all over, almost before it had begun. We all survived, our attackers did not, and the convoy rapidly moved on, continuing to Baghdad with no further threats.

I would soon learn that the tale of my impulsive action spread like wildfire, earning me both praise and criticism, and without a doubt reinforcing that "Crazy Texan" nickname. For the moment, I was simply glad to have reached Baghdad in one piece. It was time for the next phase of my adventure.

Even though my most recent visit to Baghdad had been a couple of years ago, when the ABC-TV Channel 13 news team and I were treated to a guided tour of the sites that Saddam Hussein's PR team wanted us to see, I had visited that city in earlier years as well. When I first visited

Baghdad, it was a thriving, busy metropolis. The outdoor markets were jammed shoulder-to-shoulder with buyers and sellers, the shopkeepers busily hawking their merchandise. Shelves were packed full of goods for sale, food was plentiful, and prices were reasonable, if not cheap.

But these were memories of a Baghdad of the past, and I was shocked by what I was now seeing, when left to my own devices and not being steered by members of Saddam Hussein's propaganda ministry. Under Saddam's rule, the city of Baghdad, and Iraq in general, had been transformed by the many years of war – a transformation that was only accelerated after Saddam was ousted from power. A large portion of the city had been destroyed by bombings, mortar attacks, and other destructive forces, and I found myself surrounded by devastation. Buildings were shells of their former selves. Many buildings were now just piles of rubble. I passed a communications tower, still standing amidst this devastation. Whether or not it was functional, I had no way of knowing, but given the surroundings, I seriously doubted it.

After the first Gulf War ended in the early 1990s, which failed to oust Saddam from power in Iraq, he used his connections with other Middle East leaders, and his extreme wealth, to stay in power despite his military defeat. Oil wealth was preserved as well, and Saddam gave Iraq a national identity to which the public could relate.

It was a one-family, or more specifically a one-man, rule, and you went along with it or you were placed in one of the numerous prisons scattered throughout the country, including the one in Abu Ghraib. People who even mildly challenged those in power were often simply killed. No doubt about it: the prosperous city of Baghdad had been dramatically transformed – and not at all in a good way – by years of war and one man's ruthless rule.

The United States and European countries had placed harsh sanctions upon Iraq, which were further expanded by a United Nations resolution at the end of the Gulf War. Together, these punishments removed Iraq from any position of prominence, or even viability, in the global economy. Baghdad and Iraq as a whole were subjected to a ban on all financial transactions. There was a suspension of international flights to Baghdad and other cities in Iraq, but the most devastating action by far was the freezing of all Iraqi government funds and financial assets.

The U.S. had hoped that the sanctions and the resulting economic and physical devastation would result in a regime change in Iraq, but it didn't. And there was a significant unintended consequence: the greatest effects of these sanctions and controls were not suffered by Saddam Hussein himself, his family, or his Ba'athist Party, but by the average Iraqi citizen.

As such, living conditions for the poor and for what passed as the middle class had reached subsistence levels. People were starving, and food rationing was set in place. The bombings had destroyed much of Baghdad and other major Iraqi cities, devastating the civilian infrastructure upon which an economic recovery so greatly depended – including the ability to generate power for both industries and private homes. Without electric power, water purification plants couldn't run, irrigation systems on the farms were at a standstill, sewage systems backed up, and functioning hospitals were virtually nonexistent.

Along with Baghdad, the city of Tikrit, located about 97 miles northwest of Baghdad, was home to many members of the Ba'athist party and other Saddam Hussein loyalists, as well as inner circle regime members. Saddam doled out benefits such as food, medications, clothing, and money to these Ba'athist Party members and other loyalists, as well as to members of his military. This left the Iraqi public even more dependent on Saddam's largesse, ensuring their loyalty to him and his Ba'athist Party. The greatest toll was on those who were most vulnerable: older people, children, and women without husbands. The per capita income in 1990 had been about $3,000, but a mere seven years later, it had dropped to only $200 per household.

To make the situation even worse, inflation in Iraq skyrocketed, and the middle and upper middle classes were the most affected, as regular salaries could not keep pace with inflation. Even the salaries of people in the educated classes could not keep up. Education, therefore, was deemed useless and played almost no role in the advancement of individuals or of society as a whole. Those who had special skills, but no education, could earn more money than university professors, teachers, engineers, and other professionals.

In many households, the only choice people had was to sell their personal possessions for a paltry amount of cash in order to feed their families. It was a buyers' market – but only for buyers who had the cash.

On the streets of Baghdad, I saw a preponderance of secondhand stores and auction houses, filled with furniture and household appliances, but it appeared that nobody was buying anything, even at the very reasonable asking prices. The bookstores on Mutanabbi Street were filled to capacity. I stopped in some of the shops and spoke with the owners, who told me they were purchasing entire libraries for cash. Rare books and first editions by such well-known authors as Eliot, Milton, and others were available for unbelievably low prices, yet only for cash buyers. I continued along Mutanabbi Street into the market area, and there were medical textbooks in English, paperback novels, hardcover poetry books, and television sets with satellite antennas – some brand new and still in the original boxes. All you needed was cash!

One vendor told me what I already knew: that with many of the schools in Iraq having been destroyed, the Iraqi education program was disrupted, and illiteracy was becoming commonplace as a result. There was a severe shortage of schoolbooks and supplies, further decimating the schools themselves. Even the meager cost of transporting a student to and from school, as well as of meals and school uniforms, added to the difficulties. Most children simply left school, and the rate of older children dropping out to take jobs to help supplement the family income was on the rise.

Sadder still, childhood mortality was at an alarming high. It is estimated that between 300,000 and 350,000 children died at this time due to the lack of food and adequate medical care. The World Health Organization (WHO) estimated that more than one million children were malnourished.

Given that many years of war and strict sanctions had effectively destroyed Iraq's social and economic backbone, it was no wonder that those who had saved money and were educated fled the country for employment abroad. By some estimates, over two million of the most educated Iraqis left. Many of those who remained under desperate economic conditions turned to corrupt activities such as theft, illegal trade, bribery, prostitution, and smuggling. The members of the Ba'athist Party and Saddam's immediate family were also in the business of smuggling, increasing their wealth while the general population suffered.

Before leaving for Iraq for this mission, I'd had no clue as to the scope of destruction and deterioration of the economic system. I also did not appreciate the extent of the terror that Saddam and the Ba'athist Party had inflicted upon the general citizenry. Now I was getting a raw, unfiltered view of the country – and particularly of its capital – that I most likely never would have been allowed to see when Saddam was in power.

CHAPTER 4

BAGHDAD, UNFILTERED

As I walked through the markets in Baghdad, I met and spoke with several Kurds who deeply despised Saddam and had wanted to see him overthrown. I was now getting a more complete understanding of why the Kurds and Shia who had been forced into the military under Saddam had had no intention of dying for this man. The Kurds had welcomed the liberation with the arrival of U.S. and coalition forces. They just threw down their weapons, discarded their military uniforms, and donned civilian clothes, then ran back to their villages.

I spoke with a Kurd named Mohammed, who spoke good, if heavily accented, English. He said that under Saddam, he had lost most of his family.

"How many children did you have?" I asked him.

"I had nine children, five boys and four girls."

"Why so many children with the economic conditions as bad as they were?"

"We did not have good medical care. Several children died of disease in infancy. Several more of my children would die in the military or at the hands of Saddam Hussein. The girls would need a dowry or be sold, hopefully to a family of better means. And the one or two of my children that remained, I would need to stay and take care of me if I live to an old age."

Mohammed then asked me, "Are you staying in Baghdad? Are you visiting Tikrit or other cities?" I told him I was staying in Camp Cropper for now, but would soon be on my way to Abu Ghraib prison, and his eyes widened. He threw his arms in the air and began to breathe deeply. He seemed to be at a loss for words. As I'd seen with several other people, the very name "Abu Ghraib" was terrifying unto itself for him. But after a few moments he began to calm down, and told me that the American military did not understand the situation, and that the coalition forces did not know who their real friends were. As we chatted, Mohammed painted a bleak picture of a country still filled with fear and uncertainty, but whose citizens loved it, nonetheless. He asked me about my own country, and I responded – with deeply felt and well-practiced pride, "I am from Texas."

He laughed unabashedly, but just as I was feeling tempted to challenge what I at first thought was his disrespect of my beloved adopted home, he spoke, and the first words out of his mouth were, *"Dallas! You understand oil, then. You ride horses, you have guns, right? Everyone loves Texas!"* I smiled. Add this little exchange to the many times I'd had to remind myself to hold my tongue a bit longer than I normally would.

Mohammed said he wanted to buy me tea at the local shop, where we could talk more about my Texas and his family. I agreed to go with him, but only if he allowed me to buy the tea and some food. I could not bring myself to allow this kind gentleman to spend what was probably more than a day's wages for him. As we walked toward the shop, his demeanor grew serious and he said, "Please do not go to Abu Ghraib prison. They will kill you there."

I reassured him, informing him that the Americans had taken over the prison.

"I have heard terrible things even with the Americans there. Tortures still continue. Saddam and his sons, Uday and Qusay, could have eliminated all of us with a nod of the head or a wave of the hand if they so wished. But I have heard that things are not much better now."

I really wasn't in a position to argue with him about that point, so I simply responded, "I am sure I will be okay."

After walking a few more blocks, we arrived at a small, family-run café where just as soon as we sat down we were served tea and some small biscuits – or "cookies" to us Americans. Once the server had walked away, Mohammed asked me, "Why are you going to Abu Ghraib?"

At that point I did not want to mention the seven brothers. I can't say exactly why, but I suppose it was out of an abundance of caution. So instead I replied, "I am hoping to help make some changes…big changes that are long overdue." That was true, as far as it went.

"You say that with conviction," Mohammed said, "and your words are strong, but I fear it will take more than one man's commitment and strong words to banish the evil from our lands. I wish you luck, and hope you will achieve your goals. If you are not in too much of a hurry, I would like for you to meet my friend Quasam, who owns this shop. He speaks good English too. You may speak plainly and without concern, as Quasam has a good heart, and like me, longs for the day when our country is once again peaceful and prosperous and has been completely rid of the evil ones."

"I would be happy to meet with Quasam and continue our discussion," I replied.

Mohammed got up and walked to the rear of the shop. I sat there alone, looking at the other customers as well as the passersby on the street. A few minutes later Mohammed returned with his friend, who was bearing a fresh pot of hot tea and a plateful of the delicious biscuits. Quasam pulled up a chair and joined us, saying, "I'm honored to have you in my humble shop. I am lucky to have what little you see here because of the looting that has taken place throughout Baghdad. I understand you are going to Abu Ghraib prison."

I nodded, preparing myself for yet another warning about the dangers of my mission, and Quasam did not disappoint. He said, "I know many who have been taken there but have never returned. It was more than just a prison; it was one of Saddam Hussein's torture centers. I was told of bodies hanging from meat hooks, live prisoners hanging upside down being beaten on their feet, private parts and backs, then left to die. There was a room where they hanged prisoners on a daily basis, and a stone wall where they shot prisoners in front of the entire compound. Others were given suicide vests to wear and test. They all died. Most were in their teens and twenties, with mobile phones attached to the suicide vests that were detonated… They were blown to pieces as a warning to others."

He paused to let me absorb what he had said, and then continued, "Under Saddam, Abu Ghraib and similar prisons throughout Iraq were places where family members simply disappeared. Most did not know the fate of their family members who had been taken, but they just assumed, after weeks and months, that they were dead. Members of my family – an uncle, some cousins – were taken as political prisoners and have never returned They all disappeared without a trace. Some say they are buried in mass graves in the desert just outside the walls of Abu Ghraib."

After another pause he stood up and, with tears in his eyes, he said, "Walk with me for a minute to the back of my shop. There is something you must see."

Quasam led the way to the back, and as we parted the curtain we entered the small kitchen area, then continued through a back door to a small garden. Once we were there, he lifted his loose-fitting blouse to his neck to show me the scars on his chest and abdomen. The scars, which crisscrossed his chest and upper abdomen in a tic-tac-toe configuration, were wide, thick, and angry looking – the type that physicians typically describe as being keloid-like. Then Quasam turned around and showed me more scars of a similar nature on his back. When he turned again to look at me, I could tell by his facial expression that he wore the scars as a badge of honor. He seemed to take pride in having suffered this type of torture at the behest of, if not directly at the hands of, Saddam Hussein. Finally he lowered his blouse and tucked it into the rope-like belt he had around his waist.

I asked, "Are they still painful?"

Quasam said, "They're not painful, but some days they itch continually."

I replied, "That is consistent with the keloid-like nature of the scars. I have dealt with these for many years in my plastic surgery practice on dark-skinned individuals." Then I added, "If you could get some cortisone, preferably in the injectable or topical form, it would help."

We returned together to the front of the shop, rejoining Mohammed, and I asked Quasam what I owed him for the tea and food. At first, he didn't want to take my money, but I insisted that he take the money and a little extra for his children. We talked for a few more minutes and I told him I was going to be meeting my friend, Don North, at another tea shop in Baghdad tomorrow. When I told him where it was, Quasam said he knew that shop, that it was only a short distance from where we now sat, and he would be happy to walk me over there now so that I'd know exactly where it was. So he and Mohammed and I set out on our short journey.

As we walked, I asked Quasam and Mohammed about the war. They said they had been glad when the Americans and coalition forces invaded, but that what they'd heard about the current conditions at Abu Ghraib prison did little to encourage them that the American military forces were any better. Then Quasam looked at me and said, "I really can't believe you want to go to Abu Ghraib." Mohammed nodded emphatically.

"I must go," I said, and then decided that it was time to be completely honest about my primary purpose for going there. "I told Mohammed a little while ago that I need to do what I can to help make some changes in what has been taking place in Abu Ghraib prison. As you said, Mohammed, even with American supervision, the so-called intensive interrogation – torture – of the Abu Ghraib prisoners, is still going on.

"But I am also looking for seven men – they're called the 'seven brothers' – who had their right hands cut off by order of Saddam Hussein for political reasons. My friend that I mentioned, Don North, is going to help me. If we can locate them, we are going to make arrangements to fly them back to America, to Texas, and my team and I will give them artificial hands. We consider it to be an expression of our hope for them and their future, and for the future of Iraq."

Mohammed said, "I thought there might be another reason for your visit." He smiled.

Quasam put his arm around my shoulder and said, "You are a good man. I will pray at the mosque that Allah will watch over you and that you will achieve your goals. When you get to Abu Ghraib, I want you to look into some rumors that I believe to be true."

"What rumors are you referring to?" I asked.

"I mentioned to you just a while ago that there are rumors of mass graves there. I believe them to be more than rumors."

Mohammed spoke up and said, "I heard the same thing. I heard there are thousands buried there and at other sites in and around the Abu Ghraib facility. I believe there are thousands of corpses in graves dug by the prisoners, who themselves were then buried in the sands around the prison."

Quasam then pulled me in closer and squeezed my shoulder. "Jews suffered under Hitler, with the concentration camps and the crematoriums. We have suffered with Abu Ghraib and similar prisons. The more stories I have heard of the mass graves, the more I am convinced they are true. I have heard that there are even more graves, all over Iraq, as well. You need to get the Americans to look more closely at these accusations. To dig and open these mass graves, to give these families the chance to say goodbye to their loved ones."

Mohammed then said, "We are not trying to scare you. This is information the world should know about. You should also know that the fighting in and around Abu Ghraib continues. There is no such thing as security, even here in Baghdad. There aren't enough American military forces to keep the place safe."

I told them, "I understand this only too well. I traveled in a military convoy from FOB MacKenzie through the city of Ad Duluiyah. We passed south through an area they call 'Ambush Alley' on the way to Baghdad."

"Oh, yes, we know about Ambush Alley," said Mohammed.

"My convoy was ambushed," I continued. "It was a white Toyota pickup loaded with explosives. It was headed our way but swerved off the road. The suicide bomber struck a boulder and his truck exploded. We were not bothered further as our caravan continued south, but it was a close call." I didn't feel that it was necessary to mention that I was responsible for the truck swerving off the road.

I added that I knew the war was not at an end; the ambush had driven that point home for me. Roadside bombs and ambushes were still all too common, and U.S. and coalition forces relied on private contractors to maintain their bases and their safety. The American military was spread over such a wide area that it simply did not have the logistical capability to keep itself supplied. Add to that the continuing abuse of Iraqi detainees at Abu Ghraib prison by American interrogators, and one would have to be willfully blind or ignorant to declare that the war in Iraq was over.

Mohammed said, "I'm sure you realize you and your friend Mr. North are risking your lives for those you know nothing about. Because of the war, Iraq is full of danger everywhere, as you have already experienced. Allah be with you; may whatever God you believe in be looking out for you."

I thanked him for both his warnings and his prayers, reassuring him that Don and I were aware of the dangers and would be exceedingly careful. Both he and Quasam looked doubtful, but did not make any further attempts to dissuade me.

This exchange served as yet another reminder to me that most people in the United States – not just the general public, but also the Bush Administration and even most of the American military – had very little idea of what was really going on in Iraq. I knew I had to contain my feelings, keep my mouth shut, and not reveal my profound disappointment, which was now beginning to border on distrust and disgust. I had to ignore what had happened in the past few days, I had to put aside what I was seeing in Baghdad and what I was hearing from

Mohammed and Quasam. For the time being, I had to focus on my immediate mission.

As I thought back on the suicide bombers' attempts on my life and the lives of my military brothers who were with me in the convoy, my adrenaline level surged again, flowing into my bloodstream and rushing to my head. I was both electrified and profoundly saddened by the evidence of torture that I had just seen on Quasam's body, but it helped me refocus upon the task before me.

After we'd walked for a while longer, Mohammed stopped in front of the tea shop in which I was to meet Don North the next day. Quasam said, "I know the owner and his family very well. Let me introduce you. They will take very good care of you when you meet with your friend here tomorrow."

We entered the shop; it was simple and minimally equipped. Introductions were made, and of course tea was offered. I explained to the owner, Ishmael, that I was to meet a Canadian news reporter here at his tea shop tomorrow, and that we would be going on from there to Abu Ghraib prison. He stood there for a few seconds in utter silence, staring at me with the same shocked expression I had just seen from Mohammed and Quasam. I was going to have to get used to having a similar reaction every time I mentioned the prison.

Ishmael, like nearly everyone else I would encounter in Iraq, had a story to tell about Abu Ghraib and family members who were never heard from again. He stood there, trembling with an energy that he could obviously neither channel nor contain when discussing the prison and his family's experiences there. At that moment, I too was trying to hold my emotions in check as he described what he knew firsthand about the prison and what had happened to his loved ones who had been incarcerated there.

Finally Ishmael's emotions broke free and tears streamed down his cheeks as he recalled hearing the news of a family member who had been commandeered and dragged to the prison. He said that every time it happened, the news had left *him* imprisoned inside his own head, drained of all emotion and barely able to rise the following day to carry out his daily duties at the tea shop.

He told me that the news always overwhelmed him, leaving him in a daze and a state of physical exhaustion. For a while, he said, he was so worried about the fates of his imprisoned relatives that he became withdrawn and unable to sleep. Outwardly, he tried to keep up appearances for his immediate family and his customers on whom he depended for his livelihood. But internally, he said, he felt numb, and his mind screamed every time he thought of it.

Finally Ishmael took a sip of tea and regained his composure, saying that it was getting late and would soon be dark. He added that the local police units in Baghdad were thinly staffed, and continually shrinking due to desertions. "The remaining police in Baghdad are afraid of everyone, particularly foreigners," he warned.

Ishmael said the police stayed inside their stations most of the time, smoking and drinking tea. He suspected many of them were informants who were being paid by the insurgents, and that I would be a target for kidnapping and ransom, or they might just kill me. To make matters worse, even if the police wanted to protect the shopkeepers or myself, they did not have the equipment or the ability, and by extension the incentive, to do so.

Ishmael and Quasam had a short conference together, after which Quasam said they had a trusted friend who was a local taxi driver, and he could take me to Camp Cropper. They even volunteered to accompany me on the ride for my own safety, but I said that wouldn't be necessary.

Quasam told me that the taxi driver was once a prosperous gas station owner who had been forced to quit his business after having voiced complaints about being the victim of extortion, and about having to compete with purveyors of black-market fuel. His gas station had been located at a busy hub that was used by many truckers as a rest stop. He had also owned a profitable food kiosk located next to his gas station that had been popular with the truckers, but which he also had to leave.

Having met these three men and hearing their stories, I decided to dismiss their warnings about interacting with other civilians. I felt I was a good judge of human nature. What they and their families had been through under the regime of Saddam Hussein, and were still suffering in the aftermath, had torn at my heart. I realized that there was nothing left to say, yet so much to do.

CHAPTER 5

CONFRONTATION AT CAMP CROPPER

I said my farewells to Quasam and Mohammed, and then Ishmael walked me outside and introduced me to my driver. The car looked as if it had been through a war. I'm sure that my expression made it pretty clear to the driver that I wasn't sure whether I should even get into the vehicle, but Ishmael noticed my hesitation, and told me, "Best taxi. Good engine. Good tires. And most important, a good driver."

The taxi driver stuck his head out of the window and greeted me, and I returned his greeting. He put out a hand and we shook. He asked me where we were going, and I told him I wanted to go to Camp Cropper. The driver looked at me as if he did not know what I was talking about. I clarified, saying, "I want to go to the Baghdad International Airport – BIAO – to the southwest road."

His reply came immediately, "Yes, yes. BIAO Airport. Many American solders there."

"Yes, that's where I need to go. How much?" We haggled for a few minutes, and settled upon a price. I gave him half up front and told him that he would get the other half when we arrived at my destination. He agreed to the arrangement. I got into the backseat, which, like nearly everything else in this country, was covered by a fine layer of sand.

Settling into my seat, I found my thoughts racing again. I wondered if I should be worried about Don's safety. Mohammed, Ishmael, and Quasam all knew who Don was, and said that even though they had seen him around on almost a daily basis for a while, he hadn't made an appearance in several days. I tried to tell myself that his absence wasn't necessarily something to worry about, and that even if he didn't show up tomorrow, when I was supposed to meet up with him, that wouldn't automatically be cause for alarm. In Iraq, things happened on their own typically inefficient schedule. It was difficult getting anywhere safely, much less sticking to anything resembling a schedule. A day or two's delay for pretty much anything was quintessential Iraq, and not necessarily a crisis. I'd long since learned to quit worrying about many things until and unless there was real cause to do so.

But then, inevitably, I recalled what had already happened to *me* on this trip so far. That ambush wasn't the type of thing you can just get over. Danger was everywhere. Even so, that didn't mean that Don was in danger. All I could do for now was pray that he was okay, and that he would be at Ishmael's tea shop the next day as planned.

Camp Cropper was approximately ten miles away on a relatively good road, but my driver never exceeded 30 mph, and it took us almost a half-hour to get there. When we could see the gate about a hundred yards in front of us, the driver slowed down considerably. I urged him to keep going, but he suddenly came to a full stop and shook his head excitedly. I could see the fear in his expression in his rearview mirror, and I asked him what was wrong.

He continued shaking his head and said, "Americans, many guns. You get out here."

I said, "Just go a little further, please. It's hot and I do not want to walk that far."

He just kept shaking his head and saying, "No, no."

This was not getting us anywhere. This guy was really afraid of what he might encounter at Camp Cropper. The taxi was probably 120 degrees or more inside, so, reasoning that I probably wouldn't be that much worse off by walking the rest of the way, I got out, reached through the window, and gave the driver the other half of the money I had promised. We shook hands, and I barely had time to get out of the way before he turned the car around, floored the accelerator, and fled back towards Baghdad.

I walked with purpose, my thoughts focused on a cold drink, a shower, and dinner at the officers' quarters. As I approached the front gate, I saw that there were no more than a few strands of razor wire strung across the road and anchored to a steel post. There was an MP guarding either side, and clearly they didn't know who I was. Once again, I had forgotten that I looked more like a local or a terrorist than a member of the American military. I hoped that the arrangements that presumably had been made for my arrival were solid, and that there was at least *someone* at Camp Cropper who was expecting me.

As I drew closer the two guards pointed their weapons at me and shouted. "Halt!"

I went through my routine again. I held up my passport and waved it at them, yelling, "American, American. Undercover operation."

After their first blustery demonstration, pointing automatic weapons at me, the two guards settled down. One of them kept his weapon pointed at me while the other approached and took the passport. I chose that moment to drop the name of Sergeant Major Roberts, my new friend whom I'd met during dinner at FOB MacKenzie. Normally, of course, I would have asked to see the commanding officer first, but I had a gut feeling that Roberts had more clout here than the C.O., whoever he was.

My mention of Roberts didn't elicit an immediate verbal response, but judging from the expressions on the MPs' faces, it tilted the exchange in my favor. After both men stared at me for about half a minute, one of the MPs said, "You the guy that took out the truck with the explosives the other day?"

"Yes, I am. And you will please address me as 'sir.'"

I asked the MP where Sergeant Major Roberts was, but he said he wasn't aware of the sergeant major's location at this time. "Who is the C.O. here?" I asked. "I want to see him and let him know I'm here."

"That would be Colonel William Dunbar," the other MP replied. "He's in a meeting now, but we'll tell him you are here."

"He should be expecting me, since prior arrangements have been made for me to stay here," I said. "At least, that's my understanding." Given the glitches that had already occurred on my trip, I felt I couldn't take anything for granted.

As my escorts and I headed through the gate, I decided to continue the conversation with them. I asked them about several mounds of dirt that I had seen off in the distance. "What are they?" I asked. "Keeping grunts busy moving holes around?"

It was a casual question, and I expected an equally casual answer, so I was a little taken aback when one of the MPs replied, "There are several hundred Iraqi soldiers buried in mass graves under those piles of dirt. They died during the battle for the Baghdad airport. We don't know who they are. But someday someone will probably dig them up and try to identify them." I shook my head, because I doubted that very seriously.

As we moved through the gate, I asked if the guards could point me in the direction of the officers' barracks where I would be staying. I

71

told them I wanted to clean up before I met with the C.O. "We'll take you there," said one of the MPs. Apparently they didn't quite trust me running wild and free through Cropper yet. I took it in stride, though, thanking them.

Suddenly a soft breeze arose and as usual, it carried a helping of sand with it. But it also carried something else: a very pungent smell that reminded me of a time when I had passed a pig farm and a meat processing plant years ago. The scent I detected now was an acrid burning smell similar to that, and I thought to myself, *They are cremating bodies!*

"What is that god-awful smell?" I asked. At first, the MPs looked at me as if they had no idea what I was talking about. I suppose that was understandable, since in Camp Cropper the misery index was quite high, and the pungent odor from the burning was one more thing that the soldiers most likely took for granted and put out of their minds. Once they realized what I was talking about, one of the men hastened to explain to me that on the perimeter of the camp, beyond the gate, there was a trash dump. The maintenance people would occasionally burn trash, and that's what I was smelling now. Burning the trash in this heat just added to the indignities that the service members – and the detainees – had to endure. "It's not pleasant," the MP said, "but what else can we do with all of the trash that's generated here?"

I thought, but didn't say, that they could just dig a pit and bury it, since they had the equipment to do it with, but that was not my decision. I decided that I should just be thankful for little things, such as the fact that they were not keeping their AK-47s pointed at me.

By now the temperature had risen to more than 130 degrees, and my ride in the non-air conditioned taxi had only made it worse. My clothes were soaked with sweat, and in some areas there were white circles where the salt from my sweat had collected and dried. As my escorts and I walked through the camp towards the officers' quarters, I saw what must have been hundreds of Iraqi detainees sitting shoulder to shoulder, huddling in whatever patches of shade they could find. The Cropper military camp was originally designed to hold 250 to 300 prisoners who, as I mentioned earlier, were to be processed in two to three days, then transferred to permanent facilities. But by the time I had arrived, Camp Cropper could no longer be called a small temporary holding facility, as its population of detainees had risen to over a thousand.

The core problem was that there were never plans for a permanent prison facility to be built to hold such a large group of detainees. One result was that conditions in the "temporary" facility were atrocious, and I was told that prisoner demonstrations were a frequent occurrence.

As we continued walking past the razor wire-enclosed retention section, I noticed that there were women and children, who were separated from the men. The women were covered from head to toe, wearing all black in the oppressive heat. They looked like the refugees you see on American television news programs.

One of the MPs said that many of the detainees, men and women, had contagious diseases such as tuberculosis. I noticed others had abscesses and boils on exposed areas, infected and covered with sand flies and other pests. "There's a limited medical facility, but the detainees are afraid to go there," said the other MP. I shook my head in disbelief.

Then I spotted Sergeant Major Roberts coming in our direction, and I could tell by the look on his face that to him, my appearance was no better than that of the detainees. But he smiled as he approached me, and we greeted each other like long-lost friends. The MPs, seeing that I was in capable hands, said their farewells and walked quickly off in the other direction, no doubt relieved to be rid of me.

As Roberts and I strolled down Camp Cropper's main street together toward the officers' barracks, I asked him when I would be able to see the C.O., Colonel Dunbar. He looked at his watch and said, "I can take you to see him now. He was in some sort of meeting, but he should be getting out about now."

"Actually, if you don't mind, I'd like to get cleaned up first; that's why I'm headed towards the officers' quarters," I said. Looking at me and grinning, Roberts nodded, saying that was a very good plan. I didn't ask him to elaborate; I had a pretty good notion of how I looked – and smelled. As we continued to walk, I asked him about the camp's medical facilities. He said they were far less than adequate, and had not been designed to take care of the number of military personnel stationed here, let alone the thousand-plus detainees. Most of the prisoners had never seen a doctor or received even rudimentary medical care for their ailments. He added that in a few months, most of the detainees at Camp Cropper would be released or sent on to Abu Ghraib prison.

Of course, all of that would be determined after they were thoroughly interrogated. Roberts said the interrogations had proven most

73

of the prisoners to be just ordinary civilians and not active military. Some were involved in minor offenses of no interest to the American military. I found it outrageous that trained military personnel were being used in this manner, not to mention the expense associated with it.

Stationed out here in the middle of nowhere, these soldiers had become casualties of circumstance. Everyone here stayed busy swatting at the biting sand flies and keeping an eye on mostly civilian detainees – but that was not what these soldiers had been trained to do. The desk jockeys in Washington, and the high-ranking officers, were refusing to even admit that they were maintaining a civilian detention facility such as Camp Cropper. And they reinforced and compounded the stupidity of what was taking place at Cropper by having the interrogators go repeatedly through the same fruitless exercises – exercises that yielded no worthwhile intelligence.

This unorganized American military stupidity was taking place at significant taxpayer expense. In many places throughout the country, Ba'athist insurgents formed criminal gangs, along with the tribal gangs that were sprouting up everywhere. And these efforts were dwarfed by the somewhat more organized and better equipped Al-Qaeda terrorists and Shia and Sunni militants. These insurgent groups placed roadside bombs on roads that were heavily trafficked by American military convoys, and they usually moved about in small pickup trucks laden with explosives – as I had learned the hard way.

All of these insurgent gangs were armed with stolen AK-47s, and some even obtained rocket-propelled grenades, or RPGs. The gangs did not wear uniforms or otherwise identify their affiliation. They were nothing more than loosely organized tribal gangs that were appearing everywhere throughout Iraq, indiscriminately killing young American soldiers wherever they went.

For me, seeing so much of this close-up drove home the point that there really had been no clear plan from Washington D.C. or the military higher-ups for the occupation of Iraq. And it was difficult now for me to keep my mouth shut, knowing that the Washington "mission-essential" paper pushers were covering for each other so they wouldn't be sent to Iraq. The more I learned, the more I realized how extensive – and outrageous – the problem was.

We finally reached the officers' quarters, which Sergeant Major Roberts said were new and that I would probably find to be well-appointed, at least by the standards of officers' quarters in the middle of a godforsaken desert. He said he would wait outside for me to get cleaned up and changed, and then he would take me to meet the C.O. "I appreciate that," I said. "I'll be quick."

I couldn't wait to get out of my clothes, which were glued to me from the sweat and the salt. I headed to the showers and peeled them away. As I stood under the cool water, nothing in recent memory had ever felt so good, and I wished I could linger. But Roberts was waiting. Dressed and refreshed, I rejoined him, and he promptly took me to the office of Colonel Dunbar.

After brief introductions, Dunbar asked me to have a seat. Roberts discreetly departed, and the C.O. and I were alone. Then Dunbar said, "So, Doc, tell me why you're here. I wasn't told much when they were making arrangements for you to stay here at Cropper – just that you and some journalist friend of yours are going to be searching for a group of Iraqi citizens who may or may not be detained at Abu Ghraib. But why are you really in Iraq?"

I supposed he was right to be a little suspicious of me, and while I found his question slightly annoying, I also understood the reason he'd asked it.

"You've heard correctly, sir," I said. "The seven Iraqis – we call them the 'seven brothers' – had their right hands cut off by order of Saddam Hussein years ago. My friend, the journalist Don North, heard about their plight and wanted to help them. If – when – we find the brothers, they're going to be flown back to the United States, where I and some of my medical colleagues will perform restorative surgeries on them, and where they'll be given new prosthetic hands."

"Is that all?" Dunbar said. "On whose authority are you here?"

My annoyance level went up a notch, but I remained calm, pulling The Letter out again, in a ritual that was already becoming second nature for me. I imparted my usual instructions about the restrictive conditions under which I was allowing Dunbar to read it, stressing that he was to tell nobody else about The Letter without my express permission. He nodded and then read it with a dispassionate expression. Once he had finished, he said to me, in a calm voice that sounded as if he were struggling to remain neutral, "So this is the real thing, I assume." That was the same question the C.O. at FOB MacKenzie had asked. It was a question I was probably going to have to get used to.

"Of course it's the real thing," I replied.

"Just reading between the lines, it would appear that this letter grants you the authority to do whatever you want while you're here. So I want to ask you again, why else are you here? Don't bullshit me." He didn't sound so neutral anymore.

"As far as I am concerned," I said, "my primary mission here is, as I've explained, to locate those seven men and get them to the United States. But since you asked, and since I believe in transparency to the extent that it is possible, I will be also be looking at the conditions under which the detainees are being kept at Abu Ghraib prison and other locations. And I will be filing reports on my findings."

Dunbar looked at me for a long moment, saying nothing. Finally I said, "I'm sure you have nothing to worry about, sir. Now, if you'll excuse me…"

He opened his mouth as if to speak, then closed it again. I waited patiently, and at last he said, "Before you go, Doc, I have some more questions for you."

I cut him off, saying, "Everything else is on a need to know basis."

Seeing that he had reached a dead end the C.O. sighed, then said, "Okay, Doc. I'll see you later." I stood up and we shook hands, and I exited his office.

I was really famished by now, and dehydrated to boot. I walked the short distance to the officers' dining area, where I got an iced tea, finished it in just a few gulps, and asked for another. Suddenly realizing just how exhausted I was, I sat down at an open seat at the nearest table.

A young man in his thirties sat down across from me and looked at me in a questioning manner. I estimated that he was about my height – 5' 7" – but he looked as if he worked out with weights, displaying a solid, thick neck and powerful upper extremities. I could also see the edges of otherwise covered tattoos. He looked more like a gangbanger in a past life than military. I nodded toward him when he sat down but continued to sip on my iced tea, waiting for his response.

In a deep voice he said, "My name is Rodriguez. I'm an interrogator for the OGA." He continued to stare at me as if he felt that I didn't belong in the officers' mess.

Before embarking on this mission, I hadn't really known the true significance of the OGA here. OGA is a catch-all acronym for Other Government Agency; officially, an OGA can be any permanent or semi-permanent Federal organization, including support contractors, established by the executive or legislative branches of the U.S.

government – and in some cases, state, local, or tribal governments – to carry out a specific government function. This, of course, can cover a multitude of sins.

But here at Camp Cropper – and, as I was soon to find out, at Abu Ghraib prison as well – OGA referred to a group the military called "the real spooks" or "The Agency People." They were actually CIA. It was well known that "The Agency People" were unencumbered by limitations in the interrogation techniques they utilized. It was also well known that the interrogators enjoyed showing up in the evening, because being grilled at night was extra intimidating to the detainees.

After a brief stare down with Rodriguez, the OGA joker who had just introduced himself to me, I said, "I haven't eaten all day, and I'm hungry. I am going to get myself something to eat. Excuse me, please!"

By the time I got my food and another iced tea and went to sit back down, I noticed Rodriguez had disappeared. Before I could get the first mouthful, a crowd was gathering around my table. A rising commotion was taking place, right there in the officer's commissary. Then I felt a brawny arm leaning heavily on my shoulder. It was Rodriguez. I finished chewing, slowly swallowed, took another sip of my iced tea, looked up at him and said, "Remove your hand, or you'll spend the rest of this war behind bars."

He began to laugh, and some of his other Agency buddies joined in. I suddenly stood, shoving his arm away and saying, "Don't do something you'll regret for the rest of your life." I don't think he had expected such a response. I realized that my response might be a bit foolish, but my patience was wearing thin. My food was getting cold, and my annoyance was increasing with his taunts. The depressing surroundings, the oppressive heat, and the sand flies biting at my ankles, even here in the officers' mess, were taking their toll.

Rodriguez and I were roughly the same height standing there, eye to eye, face to face, inches apart. Clearly, he was looking for a fight. But I wasn't, and I realized that the intelligent thing for me to do was to just sit back down and return to my meal, which I did.

The door opened just then, and as I looked towards it, Camp Cropper's commanding officer, Colonel William Dunbar, entered, along with several of his aides. I silently took a deep breath. The C.O. saw the group gathered around me and said to Rodriguez, "I see you have met our very special and honored guest. From the look of things, you seem to have learned why he is widely known hereabouts as the 'Crazy Texan.'"

The group of OGA interrogators stood there without saying a word. Rodriguez was wordlessly practicing his mouth-breathing.

As I gently slid my chair back and stood up again, the group moved back a few feet. I shook hands with Colonel Dunbar, who said, "May I and my staff join you for dinner?" To which I responded that it would be my pleasure.

While his group settled in around me at the wobbling Army field table, I sat back down and said to the C.O., "Colonel, Mr. Rodriguez and I were having an interesting conversation, and his Agency buddies seemed to share that interest. I had informed Mr. Rodriguez and his crew that if they continued to harass me while I was having my evening meal that I would have them put behind bars for the rest of the war. Mr. Rodriguez and his buddies apparently thought that was funny."

With that, Dunbar stood and gave them a look that only a commanding officer seems to be able to generate. He turned to me and said, "Would you like me to call the MPs and take care of that now?"

I stood again too and said, "A salute and an apology from Rodriguez will be sufficient. I also request that they leave and not return until we finish our meal."

Dunbar turned to Rodriguez and said, "Will you accept those terms, or would you prefer that I call for the MPs?" One by one the Agency men came to attention and saluted. Then Rodriguez stepped up, gave a very formal salute, and remained standing at attention. The C.O. and I just stood there, focused on him. Finally, voice barely above a whisper, he apologized to me.

I told him, "Before you attack, you should know whether you are indeed facing an enemy or a friend. And in any case, you should measure the strength of the opposing force before taking such a foolish step."

Dunbar then went on to say to the OGA group and particularly Rodriguez, "You men came up against a man who, in the current state of affairs, outranks even me, and probably everyone else in this war." Then he began to chuckle, and I laughed with him.

The Agency men left without saying a word, clearly confused and very embarrassed. I walked with Dunbar to get a fresh plate of hot food, since my plate had gotten cold during all the foolishness. As we settled down to eat, I admitted to him that I had really enjoyed the confrontation.

On a more serious note, however, I silently wondered what tomorrow would bring.

CHAPTER 6

ACCOLADES...AND WARNINGS

I had a restless night; I did not sleep well in this heat. I woke up early the next morning, took a shower in the officers' barracks, and then returned to my bunk. I looked through the few things I had brought with me, selected what I was going to wear, and shook out the ubiquitous fine particulate sand. Once dressed, I went to the officers' mess for breakfast. I spotted an unoccupied table in the corner, got my breakfast and hot tea, and looked out over the room. On the opposite side of the room was a table with the OGA boys who had taunted me the night before. They glanced my way, but I kept my head down, determined to enjoy my breakfast.

Several officers came in a few minutes later, and Sergeant Major Roberts was with them. They came directly to my table, shook hands, patted me on the back, and gave me a big smile. A couple of them said, "Good morning, sir." Then one of them bent down and whispered in my ear, "Good job. I've wanted to do that for a long time myself." I looked at my friend Roberts, who said nothing; he just smiled and winked.

I was a little puzzled, not knowing exactly what the officer who had said, "Good job" was talking about. I thought to myself, *What is this all about? What's going on now?*

As others entered the room, they all gave me a big smile and either came over and shook my hand or patted me on the back and walked off. With the exception of Roberts, these were all people I'd either never seen before or who only looked vaguely familiar, and I had no idea why I was apparently being hailed as some kind of hero. I was thoroughly confused at this point. I then noticed that everyone took seats as far away as possible from the Agency table. It seemed that no one wanted to have anything to do with the OGA interrogators.

A few minutes later, Colonel Dunbar entered with some of his staff members. They got their breakfast and pulled up extra chairs to join me.

I was glad to see them, intending to ask them what was going on this morning with all of the accolades from people I didn't know and who I could only assume didn't know me either. After the usual good mornings, and some small talk, Paul, one of Dunbar's staff members, came right out with the answer to my unspoken question. "Congratulations are in order, Doc. You stood up to the OGA guys. That's something that a lot of us around here have been itching to do."

"Is that what all this shoulder patting and hand shaking have been about this morning?" I asked. "But at least half of those who've been coming up to me are people I've never seen before. I know for a fact that they weren't all in here last night to witness my encounters with Rodriguez and his buddies. It really wasn't that big of a deal."

"First of all," said Paul, "Nothing is secret at Camp Cropper, regardless of whether it happens in the mess hall or the officers' quarters or the latrines. And secondly, it *is* a big deal. The incident has already been told and retold throughout the camp. It seems that a lot of people have run into the Agency guys sitting over there, and would like to have done the same, but were afraid of them. You're the only one that stood up to them. Now they're cowering at their little table on the far side of the room, but they have more to worry about than just you."

"So, what else is happening?"

Dunbar spoke up then. "Last night, the OGA boys grabbed several detainees for interrogation. Two of the MPs heard moans coming from a cell located in a little-used section of the prison and found several of the detainees there, obviously worse for the wear after their 'interrogation.' Two of the detainees were taken to the hospital. They're doing better this morning, and should recover, but heads are going to roll."

"Should I go to the hospital and see them?" I asked. "Perhaps I could help."

Dunbar responded, "Our docs are really good. I was told this morning that the detainees' condition is much improved, and I don't know what additional help you could offer. But if you would like to visit them you're welcome to do so."

One of Dunbar's staff members then said, "This place is spinning out of control."

Someone else said, "If the other Iraqi prisoners find out about this, there are going to be massive riots. We don't have the manpower to control it. I don't want to be around here if that occurs. We can't just shoot all of the prisoners."

Dunbar said, "The injured men will remain in the hospital until they are well, and then we're going to return them to their villages with some supplies and money. They will not be re-entering the detainee areas."

Shaking my head, I said, "So the OGA guys just left them there after they were done with them? It must have been a hell of an interrogation. I really didn't expect to come across this type of interrogation by the OGA team here. I expected that's what I would find at Abu Ghraib prison...but not here. I thought a regular Army interrogator was supposed to accompany OGA team members during any of their interrogations."

Dunbar replied, "I tried to find out which of our regular trained Army interrogators were assigned to the evening interrogation with the OGA, and I learned no one had been assigned. And no one was requested by the OGA men."

"I assume a report was made."

"Yes, it's been well documented."

"I would appreciate a copy of that before I leave today," I said to Dunbar.

Everyone at the table except Dunbar looked a little surprised, so I said to them, "As I've previously explained to your C.O., one of the reasons I was sent to Iraq is to investigate and help put a stop to the mistreatment of detainees and prisoners, including unacceptable interrogation techniques." As they exchanged glances with each other, I stood up and walked a couple of feet away from the table, beckoning to Dunbar to join me for a moment. Once we were out of earshot of the others, I asked, "Is anyone else besides you aware of The Letter?"

"No, you asked me to keep it strictly confidential, and I'm honoring your request."

"Good," I said. "As you know, I'll be leaving today, and if you feel it appropriate *after* I leave, you can mention The Letter to the OGA guys sitting over there. Let them know that a report about what they've done is going all the way to the White House. Of course I know that it's not my decision to make, but I will strongly suggest that those jokers be shipped out of Camp Cropper as soon as possible, and that a mention of The Letter accompany your report. Now let's sit back down."

Once we were seated again, I said to the others at the table, "Colonel Dunbar and I were just discussing a course of action for dealing with those OGA goons. Of course this is ultimately his decision, but as I told you, one of the reasons I'm in Iraq is to help bring these kinds of inappropriate actions to an end, and I'm going to do everything in my power to accomplish that."

Dunbar's staff member Paul said, "That could put you on the wrong side of a bullet, Doc."

I said, "A friendly fire incident? That's going to cause a lot of paperwork for somebody." Everybody at the table broke out laughing.

Paul changed the subject. He said, "We don't know much about you. Can I ask something about your background and where you're really from?"

"I've been living in Texas for almost 50 years."

There was a whisper behind my back, "He's the '*Crazy Texan!*'"

They all laughed even harder at this. Whether they were laughing at me or with me didn't really matter; I was and am, as I've said before, damn proud of the nickname.

"Where are you from originally?" Paul asked. "You sure don't have a Texas accent. What's your story?"

"Well, if you really want to know…" I said. He and several other guys nodded. So I told them.

Life began for me in Brooklyn, New York, not too far from the old Ebbets Field Baseball Stadium in Flatbush. My dad, a dentist, and his brother, a physician, owned a beautiful white stone house on the corner of Maple and Rogers Avenue, a main thoroughfare. The first floor was a combined medical and dental office facility.

It was a happy, secure life, but it was soon to change for all of us. My dad died of a heart attack on Thanksgiving after a big meal, at the young age of 48. I was only 10 years old and had two younger brothers: brother Bob, who was nine, and Paul, who was eight. My mom was petite, beautiful, and hard-working – a real go-getter who loved to dance, especially the Charleston. She didn't feel that Brooklyn provided the atmosphere she wanted for her three growing boys. So she moved us to the New Jersey shore, to a small town called Asbury Park. We didn't have much money and we rented a downstairs flat in a three-story home on 4th Avenue. The living room became the bedroom for us three brothers. My mother had her own room, and we had the kitchen, and that was it.

Although you might not guess it now, I was big for my age back then, and told everybody I was fourteen years old, which was the required minimum age for obtaining working papers. I started out at 35 cents an hour working on the Asbury Park boardwalk running bumper cars, the Ferris wheel, and other amusement park rides. To make extra money, I went into the Jersey swamps and trapped animals for their skins. I would sell the furs at the New York fur market.

Later, I started cutting grass and found that the landscaping business could be very profitable. I hired other high school friends and we began landscaping the larger homes along Deal and Sunset Lake. I had another friend, David Allard, whose dad was an auto mechanic. David had worked in the shop with him. We purchased some old junky cars, pulled the engines and rebuilt them – and we had transportation. We worked hard for everything we got, and appreciated it all the more.

Living only a few blocks from the ocean, my brothers and I went on to fix up an old boat, then built another boat from scratch. We could water ski on Deal Lake or go out on Asbury Park's stone jetties for striped bass fishing.

I graduated from Asbury Park High School, and being good in math and the sciences, entered Rutgers University, where I studied engineering. In the back of my mind, however, something told me I should go to dental or medical school.

I was accepted at Temple Dental School in Philadelphia and graduated at the top of my class. I was more interested in oral and maxillofacial surgery but quickly found out that at that time, a dentist could not even admit a patient to a hospital for a surgical procedure without having a physician do the history and physical and sign the patient into the hospital – that is, if you were even able to get a friendly physician to do this for you. Moreover, my physician colleagues only allowed dentists on the hospital operating schedule on Saturdays. The physicians controlled the operating rooms during the week.

What was even more humiliating was that dentists could not legally write prescriptions at that time. You would have to go to one of your medical colleagues and ask him for a favor again. A medical doctor had to write the prescriptions for dental drugs to be administered to your patients. This was not right, but I had no control over it, because I was "just a dentist."

I made a decision: with my engineering background and a dental degree, I would apply to medical school and request advanced admission and also a scholarship. I was given credit for all the basic science courses and began classes in the second year of medical school. I graduated at the top of my class again and easily obtained a prestigious general surgical residency at the University of Pennsylvania in Philadelphia under Dr. Jonathan Rhoads.

The general surgery residency at the University of Pennsylvania was a six-year "pyramid program." That meant the university would take twenty-six applicants but would only graduate eight of the residents after they had spent six years in the general surgery residency program. Those who were bumped out along the way would have to choose some other field of medicine. Their surgical careers were over. Talk about competition! It was the survival of the very best, but thankfully, it's not that way anymore; those "pyramid programs" have since been eliminated.

I completed five of the six years and was looking forward to my senior year. But that was put on hold when I felt a call of duty to my country.

The armed forces and USPHS – the United States Public Health Service Commissioned Corps – were short of surgeons because of the Vietnam war. I was given the rank of Lieutenant Commander and served from 1969 to 1971, and was sent to the Los Angeles Naval base. I was also sworn into the FBI as a surgeon and made physician-in-charge of the Terminal Island Penitentiary just outside of Los Angeles in the City of Long Beach. It was an experience I will never forget. At that time, Terminal Island was the only co-ed penitentiary in the Federal prison system. As you would imagine, that presented some really interesting situations. But that's a topic for another book.

When I completed my two years of military service, I returned to Philadelphia. Many other young men and women were also returning from military service in Vietnam at that time. Although my intention was to begin my senior year of the training that had been interrupted because of my military service, there was no slot for a senior position at the University of Pennsylvania. Unfortunately, without serving as a senior surgeon, you could not take your board examination or get licensed.

My chief of surgery at that time, the aforementioned Jonathan Rhoads, made inquiries and said he thought there might be a position available only a few blocks away at the Hahnemann Hospital. It seemed the senior resident at the Hahnemann Hospital had contracted meningitis and was quite sick. He was also told he was not allowed in the operating room for at least one year after the disease had gone into remission. I now had my senior residency spot. At that time, general surgery was a six-year program, and you learned to do everything. I was a very good general surgeon, my forte being abdominal procures. I know my way around the belly blindfolded, but that took me a long way from my primary interest, maxillofacial and head and neck surgery. I still intended to put my dental degree and surgery experience together and go into Plastic and Reconstructive Surgery, in particular head and neck or maxillofacial surgery.

The application process started all over again, only this time I was accepted by every program to which I applied. My background was far more extensive than other applicants. I chose Dr. Reed Dingman's program at Ann Arbor, Michigan for three more years of study, including six months of hand surgery at the Henry Ford Hospital in Detroit. I was in the operating room almost every day; that's what I lived for.

We had two very rough winters in Michigan. At times there was so much snow that they actually sent snow blowers and plows out to my home, as well as to other physicians' homes, so they could bring us to the hospital. There was no trash collection for several weeks due to the heavy snow, and we built igloos with snow and ice in which we burned trash.

But life was not all snowbound drudgery. Everything in Ann Arbor centered around the 100,000 seats in the Michigan football stadium in which the Wolverines played, and the team was at the top of the league during those years.

Upon completion of three more years in a plastic surgery residency, my letters of recommendation couldn't have been better. I passed the surgery boards very easily and was licensed.

After going through those Michigan winters, however, I wanted to live someplace where it was warmer. I also wanted a situation where I would have residents and students to teach and a lab in which I could do research. I applied to major universities for positions in plastic and reconstructive surgery in the southern and southwestern United States. I received invitations to visit and assess many of the university programs. At each interview I was given an extensive 30-page contract, and was told that I would begin as an assistant professor.

Before signing anything, however, I received a phone call from the renowned plastic surgeon Dr. Sidney Baron Hardy and the famous heart surgeon, Dr. Michael DeBakey. I knew something about them, having read some of their articles in the surgical journals. They said they were mailing me two tickets to fly to Houston. Texas wasn't exactly at the top of my list of places to live or work, but two free tickets and a few days to look over Houston and the famous Texas Medical Center sounded good. I met with Dr. Hardy and the chief of the plastic surgery section, Dr. Melvin Spira, and I was invited to dinner with Dr. DeBakey.

I was intrigued by what they offered. It was not the money, but a combination of other factors: the facility, the promise of future new facilities, the lab, the teaching opportunity, and, not least of all, the warm weather. At the end of the third day, after I had toured all of the facility and the Baylor College of Medicine, they sat me down and asked if I was interested.

I asked to see their contract. I was upfront and showed them contracts I had from other universities offering me positions in plastic surgery. Dr. DeBakey stood up, walked around the table, and said to me, "We do things different here in Texas. Foremost, we are gentlemen, and secondly, when we make a promise, we keep it."

He added, "You will get the teaching position you want. The lab is yours. We will help fund any of your research projects. You'll have a private office. The first day you walk through the door at Baylor College of Medicine, there will be a stack of charts on your desk and you will immediately begin seeing patients and operating. Do we have a deal?"

He put out his hand, and we shook hands and agreed. And yes, this being Texas, the handshake *was* the contract.

I was absolutely fascinated by all of this. I also felt I was a little crazy doing it, but then again, that's partly how I earned the "*Crazy Texan*" nickname.

The next question to be settled was where I would live, and Dr. DeBakey was on that too. "In the morning, I'm going to have a Realtor here to take you around and see if you can find a place before you leave," he told me.

Then he added, "You've been working your butt off in hospitals and universities and the military for fourteen years. I want you to take the rest of the summer off; go someplace and enjoy yourself. Show up in August, and we will pay you as of July 1."

And I've been in Houston ever since. I was good at what I did, and later on, with the help of my good friend Marvin Zindler, I formed my Children's Foundation, which I mentioned earlier in this book. Speaking now to my small but attentive audience at Camp Cropper, I explained that the purpose of the Children's Foundation was to help kids all over the world. My surgical team and I traveled to more than seventy countries across the globe, repairing cleft lips and palates, burns, and war injuries, mostly in children but in many adults as well. I also treated those who could least afford medical care in Houston.

But patients who could well afford my fees also came to the Texas Medical Center: luminaries such as the past King of Saudi Arabia, and highly-placed military and state officials throughout the Middle East, Europe, and Central America; this included Presidents and Prime Ministers. I treated my share of Hollywood celebrities as well. These contacts allowed me to do what I loved more than anything: take my medical teams to Third World countries where we were needed the most.

I added that I knew President George H.W. Bush and Barbara Bush, as well as George W. Bush and Laura and many of their family members. I said that I had traveled on Air Force One and visited the White House, and was tentatively invited to visit the White House and President Bush again once my mission in Iraq was complete.

Then I told my audience a little bit about Marvin, and explained that it was through him and his staff that I made my connection with Don North, who had made my trip to Iraq possible. "I owe more than I can ever express to Marvin," I said. "We've traveled the world together on many medical expeditions and adventures." I explained that taking my surgical team to places with difficult medical and surgical working conditions and even worse living conditions had conditioned me to be equally at home in an Army field tent or in a palace in Saudi Arabia. "No matter where we went and how many difficulties my team has encountered, putting a smile on a child's face always made it all worthwhile," I added.

I wrapped up my narrative by saying, "So now I'm on my way to Abu Ghraib. When I accepted this assignment to Iraq, I actually believed that the trip would be less difficult than many that I've endured in the past. But I'll be honest with you: after what I've seen and heard here, I just pray each day that I get out alive. And that's no exaggeration."

The military officers' group sat there, seemingly fascinated, staring at me. No one asked me any questions. Out of the corner of my eye I could see several MPs enter the dining hall and escort the OGA men from the dining area, and I couldn't help it; a broad smile crossed my face. I noticed a similar reaction by those who were sitting with me, as well as other people who were scattered throughout the room.

I said, "Well, gentlemen, it's been fun. But I'm going to have to get going." I then turned to Colonel Dunbar and thanked him for his hospitality and help. I told him I had a last request. "I would like a driver to take me into Baghdad for my meeting with Don North, and then drive Don and me to Abu Ghraib prison in the afternoon. A Jeep would be nice, but I would feel much better in an armored Humvee going into the area around the prison."

One of the field officers sitting at the table said he knew I was leaving for Baghdad and then Abu Ghraib, and he had already checked all of his sources for word on expected conditions today and tomorrow.

"The roads have been quiet between Camp Cropper and Abu Ghraib, but the extra protection of the Humvee is a good idea," he told me.

The C.O. stood up and stuck out his hand, saying, "You've got your Humvee and a driver. Do you want additional escorts?"

"I'm happy with what your field officer here told me about the roads and the territory between Camp Cropper and Abu Ghraib," I said, "and we're probably less of a target in a single vehicle than in a convoy. Thank you again for your hospitality. I'll be ready in thirty minutes."

"Stop by the command center and see me just before you leave," Dunbar said.

"Will do," I replied, and then without further delay I exited the dining hall and headed for the officers' quarters. I had seen all I needed to see at Camp Cropper, and I couldn't wait to get out of there.

CHAPTER 7

THE JOURNEY FINALLY BEGINS

Thirty minutes later, an armored Humvee was waiting in front of the command center, per my request. As I approached the Humvee, the front driver's side door opened, and a young man in full battle gear stepped out and took my duffel from me. He said, "We have a helmet and flak jacket for you, sir."

"Thank you," I replied. "I'm going in to speak with your C.O. for a few minutes, and then we will leave."

I entered the command center, and was shown directly to Colonel Dunbar. I thanked him again for his hospitality and the use of a driver and vehicle for my trip to Baghdad and Abu Ghraib prison. He nodded, and then I said, "Did you have something else you wanted to say to me before I leave, sir?" I had assumed he had something important to convey, since he had, after all, asked that I stop by and see him before my departure.

He looked at me with a big smile, and then he began to laugh. I didn't understand what he was laughing about, and my face must have shown my puzzlement.

Dunbar then said, "The Letter, son, The Letter! Whatever you do, don't ever lose or misplace that piece of paper. I'll be honest with you. You showing me that letter made more of a difference here than you probably realize. And unless I miss my guess, it's going to get you through some rough situations throughout your stay in Iraq, however long that might be."

"So it was The Letter?" I asked, in mock disappointment. "And all the time I thought you were accommodating me solely out of the goodness of your heart… taking care of a stranger in a strange land." We were both laughing at this point.

We shook hands and he said, "Keep your head down, Doc."

"Will do. And thank you again for everything."

As I walked through the command center to exit, several people waved or shook my hand and wished me good luck.

I had the feeling I was going to need it.

I put on my flak jacket and helmet, climbed into the Humvee, and introduced myself to the young soldiers who had been sent to accompany me.

This, I thought, was the true beginning of my journey. I was full of hope that Don and I would locate the seven brothers and make arrangements to get them to the United States, as well as help end the atrocities that were taking place at Abu Ghraib prison. The first stop, of course, would be Baghdad so I could meet up with Don as planned. Then together we would begin our trip to Abu Ghraib prison.

I was already tired, after my long days of travel and the stressful situations I had experienced. I'd also lost several pounds, especially in my face. I had always been muscular but lean, and couldn't really afford to lose any weight. I knew I needed much more sleep and rest, but now was not the time for kicking back and relaxing.

I told myself I should think about the here and now and trust in God on this trip, but I couldn't help being worried. In the back of my mind there was always the concern about another ambush.

After the driver had ascertained that we were all settled into the Humvee, it began moving. The young men I was sitting with were from all across the U.S. – New York, South Carolina, Tennessee, Texas, Montana, and Washington State. While they were attending school, they had participated in the Reserve Officers Training Corps (ROTC) program, and when the Iraq war began, they were called up for active duty. They had heard about our little skirmish in Ambush Alley, but knowing how facts can get twisted in the telling, they wanted to hear my firsthand account. They had a lot of questions about what had actually happened, whether their fellow soldiers had really frozen when the attack occurred, and most significantly, how they should be expected to handle such a situation.

I told them what I have often said in similar conversations: "Read the booklet you've been given on how you're supposed to act as a trained member of the American military, but always keep in mind that that book was written by some desk jockey in Washington who has probably never even seen a battlefield. Follow your gut. If you feel threatened, then respond and let the chips fall where they may. The Rules of Engagement booklet tells you that you don't fire until you're fired upon, but if you always follow that rule, you'll be sent home in a box."

In about fifteen minutes, we were entering Baghdad proper. The soldiers who were in the Humvee with me had never been into the central area of Baghdad. We circled the area where a crowd of Iraqi men with ropes had recently toppled the statue of Saddam Hussein – yet another memorable media moment. An American flag had been draped over the base of the statue: a powerful symbol, in my mind, of the fall of Saddam Hussein's regime. But to me, it was also a reminder that even though Saddam was no longer in power and his Ba'athist Party had been officially disbanded, that didn't mean the problems were over, given the groups of armed insurgents that still operated in Baghdad and throughout the countryside.

The driver made his way to Mutanabbi Street. I gave him directions to Ishmael's tea shop, where I was supposed to meet Don, but even as I was speaking I was wondering to myself if Don would actually be there. And if he wasn't, would it be time to start worrying about his welfare? So much for those attempts at reassuring myself the day before…

Going was slow, as many people were on the streets walking through the flea markets that had once been open only on weekends, but had recently begun operating every day to provide some level of income for the many former owners of cafés, shops, and other businesses that had been closed down, casualties of the war. I noticed again, as I had the day before, that deprivation was everywhere. Many of the children and even the young men looked chronically malnourished due to the war and the current economic hardships resulting from the sanctions imposed on Iraq.

Our Humvee moved slowly down the street towards Ishmael's tea shop, and even before I recognized the shop I saw Don North sitting outside, dressed in military camouflage and flak jacket. Both relieved and excited, I yelled to the driver of the Humvee, "Stop, stop! That's the man I'm looking for."

A few seconds before the Humvee came to a full stop, the soldiers jumped out and took their defensive positions. When the vehicle stopped, I jumped out and walked over towards Don, who had gotten up from his seat and was making his way towards me. When we both stopped I looked him up and down, nodding to his choice of apparel, and saying, "Once a soldier, always a soldier," to which we both laughed. Then we hugged and I said, "Great to see you Don." Pointing in the direction of the Humvee, I added, "This is our transportation to Abu Ghraib prison."

"What makes you think they're going to let you into the prison, even in all *your* battle gear?" North asked, grinning, as we walked back to his table.

"I have a secret weapon."

"You think this small group of young and green soldiers is going to shoot their way in?" he asked.

"I have something much more powerful than even a battalion of soldiers," I replied.

"You have a suitcase bomb in there?"

"Almost as good. I have The Letter." Don knew about The Letter, having been informed about it during the time we were making preparations for the trip. But I knew he was skeptical about how effective it would actually be, regardless of the fact that it came from the highest level of the United States government.

He looked at me now with a smirk on his face, and I could see that he was thinking, *The "Crazy Texan" has just arrived.* Aloud he said, "Sit down and have some tea. The pastries are very good here too."

"Thanks, but I had a big breakfast at Camp Cropper. But I'll sit with you until you're finished eating, and then I'd like to leave for Abu Ghraib."

We sat and talked about family, and then I updated Don on the photos of enhanced interrogation appearing in the newspapers and on American TV. Though Don was a journalist, he had been somewhat isolated from some of the news from the West since he'd been in Iraq, but he didn't seem at all surprised by my updates. He told me that whenever he spoke to Iraqis about Abu Ghraib prison, their common reaction was one of fear, as it had been during the reign of Saddam. In that regard, nothing had changed since the Americans took over.

I told him that it seemed clear to me that America was once again in the business of perception management, a tried-and-true propaganda technique. "It's similar to what took place during the Persian Gulf War, but now we're perpetuating the falsehood of Saddam having a cache of weapons of mass destruction as the reason the U.S. was fighting here."

And the perception management folks were good, I noted – so good that even many news reporters embedded with the troops actually seemed to believe that the WMDs might be here, despite nobody having yet found any evidence to support the assertion. I added that most of the

American public, and even many members of the press in the United States, have no idea that perception management even exists, much less the extent to which it is used on all of us, since it is generally shrouded in government and corporate secrecy.

Don put forth the idea that perception management was making some fat defense contractors even richer, which was almost certainly a motive for at least some of the perception management efforts about the Iraq war. "Someone always gets rich off of war," he said.

I replied that where war is concerned, different factions have different motives – usually economic and/or political, and occasionally humanitarian. "But you know as well as I do that even the most 'justified' war causes destruction and suffering and death," I said. "Because of that, war can be a hard sell. And if there's no compelling justification to go to battle or keep the hostilities going, those who benefit from a given war have to invent a justification. That's where perception management comes in, the idea being to convince the public as needed, but primarily to thoroughly distract and confuse the operatives on the ground and make believers – and supporters – of them.

"In the case of this war, sure, there are fat cats... defense contractors, oil interests, all of that. But there's something more basic going on, I think, and it has to do with America flexing its muscles – again."

Don nodded. "Yep, America is very good at that," he said.

As he was finishing his coffee, I grabbed one of the pastries to go. They were indeed delicious, almost addictive. I said, "War, torture, fat cats getting fatter...all of that is enough to make a cynic of anyone. But hey, at least there's good pastry." Don grinned.

There were many onlookers at this point, and I could see that the young soldiers standing by the Humvee were getting a bit anxious, as was I, notwithstanding my attempt at levity. So without further chatter, Don and I quickly walked to the vehicle. We all piled in and took off for Abu Ghraib.

The prison was only about 30 miles away, located between Baghdad and Fallujah. There was a direct road connecting the two that had supposedly been cleared of IEDs, and we were told we should not have any problems on that stretch. Once we left Baghdad central, the trip across the desert was almost monotonous; there was nothing to see for miles and miles except more miles and miles. It was not exactly a sightseer's dream, but the advantage was that if an enemy did approach, we would have a good lead on them in order to make our escape. Abu Ghraib prison had been planned very well, intentionally located in a barren and isolated area, where you could see someone coming long before they could you.

As we drove, the soldiers began asking me questions about the press coverage at home regarding Abu Ghraib and the Iraq war in general. They expected that public perception would be dramatically different than what they were seeing day to day. I tried to answer all of their questions that I was at liberty to discuss. I said that so far, no weapons of mass destruction had been found, and I recapped some of the recent events that had made the news.

This led us to discussion about Abu Ghraib prison, and the types of torture that had taken place within the prison while Saddam was still in power. I reiterated some of the horrible things I'd learned, most of which Don also knew, but clearly it was news to some of the soldiers. "Some prisoners were beheaded, others were hanged, and some were shot in front of a wall in the inner courtyard of the prison," I told them. "Many prisoners had their ears cut off or their hands amputated. The prison was designed to hold a few thousand inmates, but more than 15,000 were housed there, jammed like sardines into stifling cells. There was little or no sanitation, and they were underfed and malnourished. It could be compared to the camps that the Japanese ran during World War II, using the prisoners as slave labor and working them until they died. The only real difference between Saddam's prison and those run by the Japanese was that Saddam had no interest in having prisoners perform work. They were there to suffer and die, period."

"I'm sure glad we got rid of that S.O.B.," one of the soldiers said, and there were murmurs of agreement throughout the Humvee.

This naturally led to talk about conditions now that the prison had been taken over by the American forces, who were using it for their own detainees and employing it as an American interrogation center. Don said, "Just the idea of being sent to Abu Ghraib prison used to strike fear in the minds of those who were to be transported there. Even now that it's under American management, the fear persists."

I added that with the downfall of Saddam, massive looting took place in the cities and towns, and when the looters were caught, they too were transferred to Abu Ghraib prison. As a result, an interesting mix developed in the prison's population.

Then I explained what I knew about tribal politics in the Arab world, where family and tribal feuds lasted for many years. It was like our own Hatfields and McCoys, carrying on their family disputes from generation to generation. As a result, many people were falsely accused, and they too ended up in Abu Ghraib prison. The American interrogators at Abu Ghraib had to have the ability to detect these instances of false accusations, as well as to quash the frequent violence that broke out between the inmates as elements of the family feuds.

Unfortunately, violence continued behind the prison walls and extended out into the general populace. Other Iraqis wanted reward money from the U.S. military, so they fingered individuals in their local neighborhoods against whom they had grudges, marking them as "high-ranked Ba'athist Party members," despite the targeted individuals having neither any relation to nor association with the Ba'athist Party. This was a way the accusers could actually get paid and let the American military settle the family dispute for them by putting their tribal enemies into Abu Ghraib. Fingering your neighbor and getting paid for it was common in the early days of the American occupation of the prison. It took a while for interrogators to learn about these types of inter-family and tribal relationships. In this way, U.S. forces were being duped.

Others in the prison told their keepers that if the Americans would get them better food and pay them, they would act as counter-intelligence agents for the U.S. interrogators, and as guards at the prison. This made finding the truth even more difficult. "Since so many of these people are the victims of family grudges, it isn't always easy to determine who's telling the truth and who's lying," I said. "False accusations because of family and tribal grudges have led to the arrest of who knows how many innocent people, and not just at Abu Ghraib. And the informants responsible for putting them there... well, they're either professional frauds or sociopathic liars, or both. To them neither truth nor justice matters."

I lapsed into silence for a few minutes, thinking sadly that despite the severe impact this mass imprisonment had on the prisoners themselves and the Iraqi population at large, few Americans knew what was taking place here, and many probably wouldn't care that much if they did know. Even many who had an inkling of what was going on would most likely forget it once things began settling down in Iraq and the war no longer made the nightly news. This was a realization that I'd come to some time ago, and I found it both disappointing and deeply troubling. But it made me even more motivated to do what I could while I was here to help make things a little better for these people who had suffered so much.

I had no doubt that working under these difficult and dangerous conditions had worn down some of the MPs and even the trained military interrogators. That left a vacuum, which the notorious OGA people were all too willing to fill, with their extreme measures allegedly designed to get actionable intelligence from their prisoners. The detainees were in American custody, yet there was nothing resembling due process, no lawyers or judges. The interrogators made the decisions, sent the reports, and then waited. It was a broken system to begin with, and the interrogators only made matters worse. I had no doubt that Abu Ghraib prison would be an even bigger mess than what I had seen at Camp Cropper, and I had little reason to believe that conditions there would improve any time soon. Still, I was determined to do what I could.

I closed my eyes, trying to bring some semblance of order into the kaleidoscope of these past few days. I thought to myself, not for the first or last time, *What the hell am I doing here?*

On one level it was preposterous that I was in this inferno of choking dust, in a place of danger and brutal beauty that was habitable only to the swarming sand flies, the snakes, and the poisonous scorpions. The desolate and untamed desert through which our lone vehicle was barreling was a stark reminder that "Mother Nature," far from being a benevolent force, seems to thrive on a never-ending cycle of death. And Don and I, and for that matter the young soldiers, were working amidst those who would have no compunction about killing any or all of us, and for what? For trying to help those who often did not want to be helped, in a place a world away from our relatively safe and comfortable lives. Viewed from that perspective, and especially considering my own privileged life at home, my presence here seemed absurd.

But as I continued my mulling, I came to the same conclusion I always did when questioning and re-examining my own motives. I was hooked on novelty: a new day, a new adventure, a strangeness I'd never felt before. It was a freedom from the everyday routines of what people in more "advanced" cultures consider to be a peaceful and conventional existence. Here there were none of the things we Westerners take for granted. No endless flow of talk. No cell phone service. No sounds of traffic filling the roads. Only piercing hot shafts of sunlight, the vicious, arid wind, and the endless grains of sand blowing at us and stinging any skin not shielded from its wrath.

I noticed that the young soldier sitting directly across from me was red-faced, looking like a baked apple bursting in its skin due to the heat. And he looked so terribly tired. Noticing that I was staring at the young man, the soldier sitting on my right said, "He's from the north. He's 'thin-blooded.'"

I said, "Well, I guess I will have to add 'thin-blooded' to my own list of possible medical ailments."

The man on my right responded proudly, almost triumphantly, "I'm from Texas. The Texas heat is so rich you can slice it with a knife and be nourished by it. Texas has hot prairies and even deserts that could give the deserts out here a run for their money. And maybe you've heard the saying that Texas is a country unto itself. We're certainly big enough and rich enough to be our own country. We call ourselves the Lone Star State; that big star is on our flag."

I said nothing, opting to just let him ramble on, reciting the typical Texas boasts that tourists parrot about the state that had been my home for decades.

Then he added, "See those pools of water on the road?" I didn't even give him the satisfaction of looking puzzled about his apparent non sequitur. Instead, playing the dumb-ass, I said loudly, "Wow, yeah! And look, there's another pool of water in the road!" Of course once the Humvee reached the spot, it vanished, and another pool suddenly appeared a few yards beyond our speeding vehicle.

Still playing dumb, I said, "The pools of water are in the middle of the road... then they suddenly aren't there. Go figure!"

By now it was clear that the other soldiers were listening closely to our conversation, and I nodded and winked at the men sitting across from me, which my sparring partner did not see. But smiles were appearing on the faces of our audience.

The young Texan said, "They're not real. They're mirages."

"Okay," I said. "So what does that have to do with Texas?"

"Texas is full of mirages," he said cryptically, with an all-knowing expression on his face.

At that, everyone else began to laugh. Finally I said, "Son, I am going to tell you a few things that you clearly don't know. First, *I* am from Texas, and secondly, you are sweating through your shirt. Look at me, cool and comfortable – not in need of water – *that's* a real Texan.

You must be from the Panhandle, where it's cold." Everyone except the butt of my harassment broke into raucous laughter in the oven that our Humvee had become. I continued, "Next, you are going to tell me Texans are open-minded, hospitable, kind folk, but I should warn you, we all carry guns in Texas. Which of course you would already know... being from Texas."

More laughter.

He responded, "Well, Texas *is* free and open."

I countered, "So is Iraq, but you better carry a gun. Better make it an automatic weapon in this open desert."

We were now having a good time bonding on what was otherwise a very hot, miserable, and potentially dangerous trip from Baghdad to Abu Ghraib. Perhaps the heat was getting to us all, more than we cared to admit. In any case our designated victim seemed unfazed by our laughter, proudly proclaiming, "Well, like I said, I'm from Texas too, and we have our own way of doing things. Which of course you would already know...being from Texas." He smirked with the satisfaction of throwing my words back at me.

I shrugged and responded, "When you think about it, though, what's geography got to do with any of what we've been talking about? In Texas, just like Iraq, the rule of thumb if you want to stay alive is shoot first and ask questions later. Oh, wait! That isn't what it says in the Rules of Engagement book that you were given, is it?" Of course I was exaggerating about Texas, but not by much.

Now everyone was losing it, laughing until tears rolled down a couple of the men's cheeks. For some reason, that made me recall a line from a book I'd read years before, the science fiction classic *Dune*, by Frank Herbert, which took place on an extreme desert planet. The line was spoken by a dweller on that planet who, upon seeing a stranger weeping over the death of a dear one, said, "He casts water for the dead."

Yes, the heat was definitely getting to even me.

One of the young soldiers across from me said, "You should know about shooting first and asking questions later, sir. Weren't you the one who fired on the truck that went off the road and exploded? I hear you saved the convoy and a lot of lives."

Suddenly, everyone's eyes were on me. I quietly replied, "Yep. I'd say that was one of those cases where experience and gut feeling can keep you alive when the Rules of Engagement can't."

In response to that, no one said anything; they just stared at me. I couldn't blame them, and I was thinking that it probably wasn't because they were gazing in admiration. More than likely it was because I was quite a sight: long, unkempt white hair covering my ears and curling at the ends; full bushy eyebrows; and sunburned, leather-like facial skin. To top it off, literally, I had my favorite smudged Stetson on my head.

I felt the conversation definitely needed to take a lighter turn, so I pulled my trouser legs up almost to my knees and said to the soldier who claimed to be from Texas, "Tex, what do you think about these?" Now all eyes were on my high-top, hand-worked, dark brown leather boots with ostrich tips and bulldogging heels. I continued, "You say you're from Texas; do you have a pair of boots to match these?"

He said, "It would take six months of military pay for me to afford a pair of boots like those."

Just then the driver said, "Now, *that's* not a mirage up ahead." In spite of the blinding sun and swirls of sand, there appeared in the shimmering distance the ghostly outline of a fortress with massive walls and watchtowers. The driver slowed down considerably, and all of us looked ahead, quiet, breathless, waiting. Was Abu Ghraib prison really this sinister? Up until now, the rumors and the stories I'd heard about the prison hadn't really hit home, and I wasn't sure what was true and what was exaggerated, but now, being here and seeing this massive complex, I was inclined to believe even the most seemingly fantastic tales.

Don and I began talking again about some of the scandals and atrocities that had been reported about the goings-on at the prison. For instance, there were rumors of an unofficial "Morale, Welfare, and Recreation" program that had been established by some business-minded soldiers. A room in a portion of the prison that was seldom used had reportedly been partitioned off and hidden behind a false wall, with the help of American contract engineers. The room was given the code name, "Boom-boom Room." In the Boom-boom Room was a brothel, and women prisoners were forced to prostitute themselves there. Cold beer was also available, albeit at an inflated price. The clandestine business operated in a hidden section of the cell blocks run by American soldiers stationed in Abu Ghraib, all to supplement their low military income.

But it was the general mistreatment of detainees that generated the most shocking reports. Male prisoners had dog leashes put around their necks and were made to crawl on all fours in the cell blocks naked, while female soldiers tugged them along. Other prisoners were sent from the interrogation rooms naked with female underwear on their heads. These were titillating yet disgusting practices in a military setting.

"Some regular Army soldiers who objected to these practices photographed what was taking place and sent it to the papers back in the United States," I said, for the benefit of some of the young soldiers in our vehicle who might not be aware of this background. "From there, the pictures went viral and the Abu Ghraib prison scandal grew. It got a prominent spot on a popular weekly news show on TV, and over the next month, a fairly steady flow of disgusting photos and stories continued to appear, minimally censored, in the American press."

The opposing political party used this scandal against the Bush Administration, as opposing parties have long done to their opponents. Conspiracy theories abounded, and the Bush administration realized that it needed to alter what was taking place. It was already paying a political price for an unsuccessful war, and a failed search for the WMDs that did not exist in Iraq. Covertly-taken photos coming out of Abu Ghraib prison and publicly circulating just made things worse for the administration. Of course as far as I was concerned, even though I supported both Presidents Bush and am a long-time Republican, the political ramifications for the Bush administration were nothing compared to the gross inhumanity of what was being done to these prisoners.

Even so, the coverage in the American press troubled me. While much of it was probably true, I felt it was important to find and tell a more comprehensive truth, even if it didn't fit neatly into anyone's narrative or agenda. As it was, the reporting that was being done about Iraq in general and Abu Ghraib in particular seemed only to be increasing the divisiveness in America. While the polarization of the populace never reached the level it would achieve in subsequent administrations, it was, at the time, historic.

I would go to hell and back for my country and the U.S. military, but I also felt very uncomfortable, caught in the middle of the politicized but, I suspected, largely accurate findings. As Don and I wrapped up our discussion, I could tell from the expressions on the faces of the soldiers sitting with us that they were taken aback. Yet none of them said anything. They were good soldiers, trained and conditioned not to question authority.

Don said, more to me than to our fellow travelers, "I think our job here will be to find out what's true and what's politically motivated BS.

Then we have to and develop and present an unbiased narrative, something that the media can get on board with."

I nodded, adding, "But we also need to do a little bit of what you and I were talking about earlier – perception management. Sure, we need to make sure the truth is told about the atrocities committed by Americans at Abu Ghraib prison, but we also need to temper that by focusing on the good things America is capable of. And I think we can both agree that the best way to do that will be to do what we can to help the seven brothers, and let them tell their own stories."

"Can't argue with that," Don responded. "But first, of course, we need to find them."

"Yes, there's that," I said, thinking but not feeling a need to say aloud, *That may be a lot easier said than done.*

The conversation ended as we drew closer to Abu Ghraib prison. It was truly an unsettling experience. My time working at Terminal Island Federal Prison in California, and my visits as a physician to various other jails, prisons, and penitentiaries over the years, had made me all too familiar with such facilities. I thought I'd seen just about everything, having worked with the FBI for several years, in addition to my international travels as a physician. But as we approached the prison at Abu Ghraib, I was taken aback by the sheer size of the structure.

As we drew closer, all I could think of was that it reminded me of European fortresses I had seen in the course of my travels. It looked like a crude rendering of a cathedral or castle, with multiple guard towers evenly spaced along its outer perimeter and one at each corner. The closer we got to the entrance gate, the more I was convinced that this was a perfect monument to the brutality of Saddam Hussein and his sons. In the eerie stillness, one could easily imagine the screams and the other sounds of the sadistic acts that were committed therein.

And in just moments, we would be right in the middle of it.

CHAPTER 8

INSIDE ABU GHRAIB PRISON

A bu Ghraib prison had been built in the middle of nowhere, surrounded as far as the eye could see by sand dunes and desert. We were told by our driver, who had been here on several occasions, that the prison compound covered an area of several hundred acres. There were a number of other walled-in areas within the main structure. The enormity and construction of the compound were impressive, to say the least. In previous travels, I had visited the concentration camps that Hitler had built in Europe, but this prison dwarfed them all.

The gusts of wind and the Humvee together stirred up heavy clouds of sand, obstructing some of my view as we slowed and approached the gate, which was centered in the front wall. I had a sinking feeling when I noticed that there were no military, not even MPs, in sight anywhere. Was no one on guard duty? I had expected to see armed guards in the towers, at the gates, and along the walls, as was standard in so many of the prisons I had previously visited.

There were a few soldiers at the main prison gate, but they just waved us on through without so much as stopping us, much less checking our identification. I had assumed that I would have to go through some level of challenge before entering the facility, similar to those that I went through at Camp Cropper and other places, but that didn't happen here. My unease grew stronger, and I could sense that Don's did too, as we drove through the main gate to the secondary compound where several thousand Iraqi inmates were cordoned off behind razor wire.

And then our Humvee entered the inner compound of this very scary place.

As we drove, I could see there was even a helicopter landing pad inside the prison. There were more walls and more gates, and compounds within compounds, in this massive facility. There were also prison wings within the inner compound, all in similar degrees of disrepair. Compared to Camp Cropper, Abu Ghraib prison was far more primitive.

Our driver stopped in this inner sanctum and we disembarked, stepping into the dust with our duffels slung over our shoulders. Still, no one came to greet us. I walked to a shady spot along the wall and sat down, then leaned forward with my forearms resting on my knees. Don joined me. I couldn't believe the casual air of those who walked past us; except for everyone being in uniform, we could have been anyplace. As I'd experienced earlier, I was getting an occasional stare – not surprising, since as I mentioned, I looked more like one of the detainees than a military man.

Finally, one of the officers came over and introduced himself as Lieutenant Casey. He said he had been at Abu Ghraib prison most of the summer and asked how he could be of help. The first words out of my mouth were, "I didn't see any MPs posted at the gate as we drove through."

Lieutenant Casey replied, "The MPs have all they can do to manage thousands of detainees. We just don't have the manpower to secure the outer or inner perimeter walls."

"That was all very apparent to us on our way into the prison, not only passing though the outer wall perimeter, but also through the inner compound as well, without being stopped," I said, realizing that these walls within walls had given me a false sense of security that I was now painfully aware did not exist.

Lieutenant Casey continued, "We use some of the Iraqi prisoners to clean up the place. They all dress the same and look the same, and we really don't know whose side they're on. It could be very dangerous in here."

Needless to say, that did nothing to reduce Don's and my feelings of unease. I said, "We need to meet your C.O. I would also like to see your hospital facility since I am a physician. Don and I would like to bunk where the doctors are staying." I felt that would be the cleanest and safest area within the compound.

I wanted to wash up and get something to eat and drink, and I really wanted to know where I would be staying. But the lieutenant apparently wasn't through with his warnings, though I couldn't really tell if he just wanted to scare us as newcomers or was serious when he told us that every other night or so, insurgents fired mortars over the outer wall.

"We never know where they're going to land," he said. He explained that the detainees were the ones at the greatest risk when the mortars landed, because their areas weren't well protected at all. He also told us to prepare for the sound of MPs in the only tower that was presently being manned, as they returned fire with their .50-caliber weapons. "We don't know if they ever hit anything," Lieutenant Casey said.

Great, I thought. *Abu Ghraib is more than just a prison; it's a walled-in compound where you're in danger of mortar fire landing on your head every couple of nights.*

The lieutenant added helpfully that there were "fallout shelters" in Abu Ghraib, and that they theoretically provided some degree of protection from the mortar fire, but they were little more than walls of sandbags stacked about three to four feet high. Don and I just looked at each other, and I knew he was thinking the same thing I was: *What a joke!*

I said aloud to Don, "I sure hope the seven brothers are still alive and are somewhere in this compound, and that we can get them – and ourselves – out as soon as possible. We're no better off in this prison than the prisoners."

I told Lieutenant Casey that I was adamant about visiting the medical facilities, and I repeated that Don and I would like to be accommodated in the same area as the doctors. He made no reply but looked at us with an expression that pretty clearly said, *Who the hell do you think you guys are?*

I said, "I have a letter that I wish to show to your C.O. It will explain why we are here. I also want to know if you can tell me anything about a group known as the seven brothers – Iraqi businessmen missing their right hands."

The lieutenant said, "Are those the men that had their right hands amputated under the Saddam regime, with the amputations themselves supposedly photographed and videotaped?"

Don and I looked at each other again when we heard this. This statement told us our trip was most likely not in vain. It appeared that the seven brothers might indeed be here at Abu Ghraib prison.

Then the lieutenant added that according to intelligence briefings, there were hundreds and possibly thousands of videos supposedly stored here somewhere: videos that showed the atrocities that had taken place –

not just the removal of the right hands of the seven brothers, but perhaps hundreds of other amputations and even executions as well.

This we hadn't known, but now that we did, Don and I realized we had yet another task at Abu Ghraib prison: to find out exactly where that stash of videos was hidden, assuming that the intelligence was valid, and report our findings. Lieutenant Casey also said that he'd heard credible rumors about the seven brothers being here, but he didn't have any specific information that could help us find them.

All of a sudden I felt revitalized. I stood up and swung my duffel over my shoulder, and Don followed suit. I said to Casey, "Thank you for the information, Lieutenant. It's been very helpful. Now, would you please take us to the hospital facility so we can wash up and find some bunks, and then take us to the C.O.?"

But Lieutenant Casey merely looked at Don and me as if we were two crazy men.

I said, "Lieutenant, you need to get us bunked in, and we need something to eat and drink, and it is imperative that we meet the C.O."

Still the lieutenant continued to just stand there.

I really didn't want to show him The Letter; I'd only wanted to bring it to the attention of the C.O. But I could see that we were getting no place in this conversation, so I reached into my inside pocket, removing the plastic Ziploc bag and extracting the document. I went through my usual song and dance about The Letter with Lieutenant Casey, saying that he could read it, but that he must not say anything about it to anyone but his C.O., especially not the details of its contents.

When I unfolded it and held it up for him to read, I got the usual response. Just seeing the heading on the document, his expression changed. He scanned it in less than a minute, after which I folded it, returned it to the Ziploc, and placed it inside my secure pocket. He just stood there. At last I said, "Lieutenant?" That seemed to snap him out of his trance.

He said, "The C.O. isn't available right now, and won't be until some time this evening."

Feeling like a broken record, I patiently said, "Fine. But we would like to go to the medical area first. We would like to be shown two bunks. We would then like a chance to wash up. Then we would like you to escort us to the dining area. While we are eating, perhaps you can have someone go to the C.O. and tell him we would like to have a meeting at 09:00 tonight. I am asking nicely, but basically this is an order."

Lieutenant Casey immediately turned, commandeered a first sergeant and a young corporal who had been walking past, and told them to take us to the hospital facility. He then said, "I will go to the administrative building and speak with the C.O. myself."

I said, "As I mentioned, you can speak to *him* about the content of the letter, but to no one else. Mr. North and I are here to find the seven brothers, and they will be transported from here back to the States. In addition, we will observe the status of the prison retention facilities and the OGA interrogation process."

The look on his face immediately changed. He was all business now.

I added, "If you could help us locate the seven brothers as quickly as possible, I'm sure you and the C.O. will be happy to see us leave."

He stood at attention, saluted, and said, "I understand perfectly well, sir."

"Thank you for your help. You are dismissed."

Don and I chuckled as the lieutenant walked away, and then we followed the sergeant and corporal to the medical area. We passed the enclosures where the detainees were huddled together, then went through several archway gates, none of which was manned by MPs or soldiers.

This pit of hell was divided into several detention areas: some for common criminals, some for detainees from the Ba'athist Party, and others for women and children. There was also an area for teens and those in their early twenties, who could be the most trouble at times.

Don and I were appalled by what we were seeing. The further we progressed, the more the misery level seemed to increase. Everywhere the population was tormented, not only by the heat and the flies and the lack of sanitation, but also, we had the strong sense, by the fear that came merely from being *in* Abu Ghraib prison. It was without a doubt a grim and terrifying place, to which one would hope never to be sent.

I'm sure many of these detainees wondered how life had managed to deliver them to this surreal crossroads in their lives. Others inside these walls knew very well why they were here, but I was willing to bet that they all felt a pang of hollowness within themselves, as well as sadness and fear and anger, and I also suspected that the longer they were confined here, the more powerful these emotions grew inside them. I felt that we were facing a battle, not only for the seven brothers, but also for the souls of all of those incarcerated here. Should that battle not be won, I knew that many if not most of these detainees would be dead within a period of months, if not weeks.

I could only think of the story of Dante's *Inferno*. This place was a living embodiment of Dante's nine-ringed hell, which seemed far less like fiction now and more like a prophecy that was uncomfortably close to being realized. These prisoners were wretched; their days were filled with torture and misery, and I suspected that their nights were haunted by the groans, the screams, and the final death gasps that marked the "merciful" end of others' suffering. Here was proof that humankind, left unchecked, could and likely would operate like a plague in hell, devouring the bodies and souls of all who dwelt there for too long.

Saddened and yet with a pounding heart, I glanced back as we passed the enclosure where the women and children were interned behind a razor wire structure. I felt as if I were indeed an observer in hell, looking upon these detainees who were terrified of what awaited them next. They sat there cramped, starving, and withering in the heat. Like many other people, there was a time when I simply couldn't have imagined anything like this happening in any place controlled by the American military. But here, I didn't have to imagine it; it was real. I have always supported our military, even when some of their actions were questionable, but what was happening in Abu Ghraib was indefensible.

Walking through the compound with the sergeant and corporal, I was thinking that what we were seeing here were examples of humanity overrun by its most primal instincts for survival. I thought to myself that when human beings succumb to this type of desperation, they are no longer really human; they become animals in cages.

A core tenet of most cultures and civilizations throughout history has been that religion and laws are two factors that make us human beings, safeguarding us from total savagery and self-destruction. Yet those same elements – religion and laws – are too often subverted to the point where they become efficient vehicles *for* savagery, driving our species closer to the self-annihilation that they should be helping us avoid.

As a physician, I couldn't help but have deep concerns for how these prisoners were being kept: their overcrowding, lack of sanitation, and limited food supply upset me. I tried to temper my concerns by thinking, *Nothing is permanent, and this will all change for the better.* But I knew that I was only trying to convince myself, and that change for the better in a place like this was far from guaranteed.

It hit me again that Saddam and his sons were psychopathic madmen; that fact couldn't be overemphasized, I thought. I was beginning to more fully comprehend the misery in which I had become involved, and I was appalled by it. In a land where compassion and cruelty seemed to be equal partners, I found myself questioning even my most deeply held beliefs.

We finally reached the old barracks that were now used as the medical facility, and the sergeant and corporal who had accompanied us told us that they had to be elsewhere, but that we should ask for the physician in charge, a Lieutenant Jacobs. I thanked them, and they saluted and then departed. When Don and I entered the barracks, all eyes were immediately on us. I asked for the physician in charge, and we were told he was in the room at the end of the corridor. As we walked in that direction, both Don and I had a fresh energy in our stride.

We knocked on the only door that I'd seen in a while, and when we entered I immediately spoke up, introducing myself and Don. In turn, the physician in charge introduced himself as Lieutenant Jacobs, but he did not make any move to shake hands with us. I requested that Don and I be put up in the medical facilities for a few days, and I gave him a brief rundown of our reasons for being here. Lieutenant Jacobs stood there, seemingly in shock, and said nothing.

I said, "Take us to where we're going to bunk for the next few days, and then we need to wash up and get something to eat."

The lieutenant continued to just stand there, dumbfounded, until I added, "This carries the weight of any order coming from a senior officer."

That apparently awakened him from his stupor, and he finally stepped out from behind his desk, shook hands with us at last, and said, "Please follow me."

My intuition had been correct: the hospital facility was the cleanest area that I had yet seen in the compound, and they had air conditioning. After showering, we felt somewhat refreshed, and we were taken to the officers' mess, where we had cool drinks and a light snack to tide us over until dinner. We were starting to feel human again.

Lieutenant Jacobs rejoined us and told us a little about himself. He said he had served at many military installations throughout the world, but that he was also wondering to himself what he'd done to get himself stationed in Abu Ghraib prison. I confessed to him that I was troubled, that finally seeing Abu Ghraib was making me feel as if I were in Dante's *Inferno*, having descended through the underworld and ultimately arriving in the lowest point of hell. "I can't help but wonder now how Don and I are going to leave this hell and return to the world above," I said, and I wasn't really exaggerating. "It's like Dante said, *'Abandon hope, all ye who enter here.'* That might as well be inscribed on the entrance gate to this prison."

The lieutenant replied, "I know what you mean. But I think that just the fact that you guys were able to get here is going to help, maybe more than you think. It's possible that 'outsiders' like you can jump-start some changes. I'll tell you the truth: my medical team and I were unaware of what was being done in any of the 'interrogations' – and the other things that were being done to the prisoners – until we actually received emails from friends back home with some of the photos."

He added that the "enhanced interrogations" – a term that, we all acknowledged, was a euphemism for torture – were going on in isolated areas of the prison with only a small group, the OGA, involved, and that these interrogations were unknown to most others in the prison facility – even, apparently, some who were in command. It might seem unbelievable that such atrocities could be going on under people's noses without their knowing about it, but I believed the lieutenant.

I was very unhappy that the torture was taking place, but somewhat relieved to hear that for the most part it was only within that small "Agency" group. This would definitely make our job easier. Lieutenant Jacobs said he had heard of the seven brothers, but none of them had presented themselves for medical care. He added that he would ask other patients where they were located within the prison. I thanked him for his effort and for putting us up for the next several days. Actually I had no idea how long we would be at Abu Ghraib, but I was assuming that it wouldn't be for more than a few days. As it turned out, that would be another one of my overly optimistic assessments.

The sharp pangs of sadness I'd experienced as we moved through the prison were now tempered somewhat by a new hope that change was indeed on the horizon. I felt I was on my way back to a state of optimism that I'd not experienced for quite a while. I was finally feeling like myself again, for the first time since we'd left Baghdad. No doubt the hot shower and the refreshments had played a role in this change of attitude. I suddenly realized I was still hungry – famished, actually – which worked out well, because it was apparently time for dinner.

At dinner, Don and I and Lieutenant Jacobs were joined by several other physicians and medical corpsmen, but none of them said a word. It was pretty obvious that the rumor mill was fully operational here in the prison, and that these men had their concerns about our arrival and about this unusual rendezvous, but they kept their thoughts to themselves. My guess was that they'd accepted that decisions had been or were about to be made, but were not theirs to make. That's the military way. Even so, some of them appeared vaguely worried as they looked at Don and me. But we were getting used to that.

All of a sudden, Lieutenant Jacobs looked up, and as we followed his glance we saw a lone figure standing motionless a few feet away. He was peering down on us with a somber expression. Jacobs immediately pushed his chair back, stood up, snapped to attention, and saluted. Returning the salute, the new arrival said, "As you were. You mind if I join you?"

At that, the other physicians and corpsmen who had joined us stood up, saluted our new companion, and then moved on to other tables. We were curious about the reason for their sudden departure, until Lieutenant Jacobs introduced Don North and me to the C.O. of Abu Ghraib prison, Colonel Robert Stevens.

After we all shook hands, Colonel Stevens asked what we thought of the prison, and I replied, "Frankly, although I've only seen a small portion of the prison facility, I'm still struggling to believe what I'm witnessing. I look forward to your arranging a tour for us, including the interrogation area."

The C.O. didn't seem fazed at all by this request, merely replying, "Yes, Lieutenant Casey informed me that one of your purposes for being here is to investigate interrogation… issues."

"That's right," I replied. "But as Lieutenant Casey also may have told you, our other main reason for being here is to locate a group of men known as the 'seven brothers,' who had their right hands amputated by Saddam Hussein for political reasons. We plan to take them back to the United States as soon as possible. Everything is still upside down at home because of what the press is reporting – especially with the photos that they've obtained that were taken in the prison. There are almost daily scandals because of the perverted forms of torture committed by interrogators. It's become a distraction from the war effort… but I'm sure you're aware of all of this."

Stevens said he was aware of some of what had been happening, but not all of it. Similar to what Lieutenant Jacobs had indicated to us, he confessed that he felt isolated from what had happened in the interrogation area. But as commanding officer he felt as much at fault for what was taking place by not knowing that it was happening on his watch.

"I want to talk to you about that," I said to him, "but before we go any further, I would like for you to read something."

"Would it be that 'Letter' I've been hearing about?" he asked.

"That's right," I replied. I discreetly pulled The Letter out of its hiding place and handed it to him. He read it, raising one eyebrow slightly, then handed it back to me. Unlike a couple of the others who had read it, he did not ask me if it was the real thing. He knew.

As I tucked The Letter safely back into the Ziploc bag and then into my pocket, I said, "Sir, regarding the interrogation issues, it's understandable that you might not know about everything that's been going on, but we have to fix it. In a way, we are now involved in perception management of a *good* kind."

I could see from the C.O.'s facial expression that he had no idea what "perception management" was all about, so I gave him my explanation. He nodded as I spoke.

Up until then, in the interests of discretion, we had been conversing at a low volume. But I was on a roll now, and I no longer cared who heard me as I mounted my virtual soapbox and continued, "Where would this country be without those serious looking, shaven-headed dudes who are always skulking around, telling people that what they actually saw happening in the interrogation rooms didn't really happen? Some people might call that 'gaslighting.' And it seems those OGA guys have made it pretty clear that they think they have the authority to do whatever they want, including torture and murder."

It was then that a big burly man who was sitting at the next table spoke up, making me realize that perhaps I had gotten a little carried away, volume-wise. "*I'm* one of 'those OGA guys,'" he said. "We do the important things." And without asking our permission, he scooted his chair over to our table, sliding into a spot right next to me.

That was my cue. I don't seek out confrontations, but this guy was just asking for it.

CHAPTER 9

GOOD DECISIONS,
BAD DECISIONS

I calmly asked the OGA man if he could provide me with a list of the men and women who were members of the group doing "important things," as well as a detailed account of exactly what "important things" they were doing. He just glared at me, so I changed my approach, and asked him how one joined this unit of the OGA.

He said, "It's not a group that you apply for. If we see something in you that we like, we will come to you. We don't make any guarantees except one: our group can promise that its members will see action – maybe more than they'd ever hoped for. And our work is critical to the security of the United States."

I just stared at him, not responding, so he continued, "The men and women in this group, I promise you, are committed to be serving the interests of the United States without having to put up with a bunch of bureaucratic mumbo-jumbo. And yes, we have what you might call a... *robust*... style to our interrogations that's absolutely second to none. But we're doing our jobs and we are making a difference."

"Really?" I said, not bothering to disguise the contempt in my voice. I was looking over his shoulder as I spoke, gazing out of the open door at the barbed wire-enclosed pens in the distance, and imagining the suffering detainees in the pens, almost all of whom had done nothing wrong and had no information to provide.

He continued, almost as if he were talking to a potential recruit, "Those who join us are provided with in-house promotions on a regular basis, and that means an increase in pay scale greater than all but the highest commissioned military officers can expect."

I said nothing, but thought to myself that despite the promises of regular promotions and pay increases, someone would have to be an unacceptable sociopath to be one of these OGA people.

But he seemed quite proud of his participation in the group. "Say what you will about us, we're not here twiddling our thumbs like so many others," he declared. *"We* are actually having an impact."

Looks like this guy is stupider than I thought, I mused to myself. *I just caught myself a big stupid fish.*

Through more questioning, I found that he had started off as a teacher, was later promoted to an analyst, and then turned into an interrogator, drawn by the allure of direct involvement in the CIA. He said that working with the OGA interrogators got his adrenaline pumping and infused him with a single-minded sense of purpose. He truly believed that he was performing life-and death-actions, and getting results.

I didn't respond, content for now to just let him talk, so he continued, "I was originally warned to stay away from the OGA interrogation groups before something horrible happened. Well, I knew that was a decision I had to make for myself, so I ignored the warnings. Glad I did."

How stupid is that? I thought to myself, but still said nothing.

I thought again of the terrible things that had happened here: the detainees who were interrogated and later found dead, the others who had been tortured and humiliated in all sorts of creative ways – and the fact that many of their stories and photos had been published by the press all over the world.

Still maintaining my silence, I got up and walked slowly around the room. My feet felt heavy and my back pain was gradually increasing from sitting in the very uncomfortable folding metal chair. I could not sit and listen to this man any longer. I returned to the table and just stood there, with the uneasy awareness that everyone in the room was looking at me.

I felt a sudden and nearly irresistible urge to just pack it up and go back home, but the feeling passed quickly. My mother had always taught me that quitting was not acceptable. She always said that you must set a goal for yourself, work harder than everyone else, stick to the basics, execute your plan as perfectly and confidently as possible – and most importantly, you need to be brave and never quit, always trusting in God, because He is never far away.

After having already been kicked around a few times since I'd been here, I realized again just how important my mother's words were and are. Even as I stood there facing down the OGA interrogator, I could almost hear Mom's voice urging me to pick myself up, do better, and never quit. I miss that voice, but I have never forgotten the lesson.

Glaring at the interrogator, I finally said, "Well, despite your delusions about the sanctity of your duties, Don and I are here to help put a stop to OGA activities in Abu Ghraib prison. We are here to help make a change. We're also here to find the seven brothers and show the world that some good can come from all of this."

The room grew deadly quiet, and then this broad-chested, thick-armed bull of a man, who was obviously used to getting his own way, slammed his fist down on the table. He looked at me as if he had me in the interrogation room as he said, "Who the hell are you to talk to me in that manner?"

I opened my jacket and reached inside. It was a simple gesture, but this big brave man pushed back in his chair; then the legs of the chair caught on the uneven floor and he tilted over backwards, landing on the floor with a loud thud. Everyone had a smile on their face, and some laughed out loud. Clearly he had thought I was reaching for a pistol and was going to shoot him. As much as I might have liked to shoot him, though, that's not my style. He got up, dusted himself off, moved his chair back, and sat down again with as much dignity as he could muster under the circumstances.

Not inclined to do anything to help restore his dignity, I then asked him, "Can you read?"

"Of course I can read."

"I am going to hold this letter. Read it very carefully, maybe even a second time through, if you don't understand it the first time. You are not allowed to discuss this with anyone else. You understand these requirements?"

"Yeah, yeah," he said, visibly aggravated by my condescension.

I unfolded The Letter and held it in front of him. He reached out with his right hand, and I chopped him across the wrist. He was startled.

I said, "I'm giving you an order. You may read this, but you may not touch it."

I followed his eyes as he was reading. Then his eyes shifted back to the heading. At that point I folded the document and put it back in the Ziploc bag, returning it to my inside jacket pocket.

I said, "You get to live your life, son. You make some good decisions and you make some bad decisions. Some folks will hate you; some folks will love you; some folks haven't made up their mind about you yet, but I have. Matter of fact, I think everyone else in this room has made up their minds about you and the OGA."

The room was very quiet for what seemed like an impossibly long time. Finally the OGA guy said, "Is that… that letter… for real?"

Colonel Stevens was sitting next to me on my other side, and with the authority befitting his stature as C.O., he said, "You can bet your life on it, and you and the other 'interrogators' involved in the torture and killing need to rethink your goals." That chilled the conversation for a while.

Then the OGA man started to stand up, but the commanding officer fixed his eyes on him and said, "Sit."

Settling back into his chair, he shrugged and shook his head, and there was another gap in the conversation. We watched him struggle with what had just happened. There was no talk for a long time, but all eyes were affixed on him.

He finally said, "I had no choice."

The C.O. said, "We all have choices in this life. The difficulty is in making the right ones."

I added, "Besides, you just said a while ago that you made the choice to join up with the OGA interrogation group, even though you'd been warned by others to stay away." He looked like he was about to sputter a response, but no words came. He said nothing for a few long moments, but there was murmuring all around us in the room.

I waited until all was quiet once again. This evening there would be no rush. I was not watching the clock. Finally the OGA guy folded his arms across his chest and leaned forward, his demeanor making it clear that he wanted to get in my face again.

After a while he said, "I just figured out who you are. You're the crazy guy that everyone is talking about who took out that truck with explosives and saved your convoy."

I put up my hand and stopped him, saying, "I am *not* 'the crazy guy.' I am the '*Crazy Texan.*'"

He responded, "Yeah, okay. You're the *Crazy Texan* who doesn't believe in the Rules of Engagement manual. Well, neither do I, so we have that in common."

I immediately responded, "Don't you dare compare what I did to what you do. I was saving American lives. You, on the other hand, are defaming the U.S. military and taking lives unnecessarily."

He drew himself up and said in a huffy voice, "Those who are timid and frightened have no place among the victorious."

"What the hell is that supposed to mean?" I asked. "Do you consider *your* actions to be courageous, and the torture and murders you've committed to be victorious in some way? Or are you insinuating that *I'm* 'timid and frightened?' I've made my peace with my God, and am not afraid of very much. I'm certainly not afraid of dying. What I am sometimes afraid of is that I might fail to make the world a little better in my life. And stopping the evil done by people like you falls pretty clearly within making the world a little better. So I'd say that I'm still on track."

I paused, glaring at him. His face was turning all shades of red, but he said nothing, so I continued, "You are torturing these detainees and they're suffering horribly, and you are accomplishing *nothing*, because you don't understand that they believe death is just the beginning. Even as you're inflicting intolerable pain on them, they know that the pain will pass. A lot of the people you torture and kill are looking forward to going to Paradise and enjoying all kinds of rewards. Even if that promise is false, in their minds it's as true and real as any suffering you might inflict upon them.

"So all you and your other OGA goons are accomplishing is inflicting pain upon people whom you have no way of knowing. Your supposedly noble cause is doomed, its only accomplishment being the torture of your fellow humans. This war, to them, has strong religious overtones. You clearly don't understand this, any more than the bureaucrats in Washington understand it. Unfortunately, your ignorance and that of the bureaucrats can only produce more ignorance and spread more hate. If spreading ignorance and hate is your life's goal, I pity you."

He remained silent. I leaned forward, placed the palms of my hands flat on the table, and got right in his face as I continued, "Unlike you, I'm a lucky man who's lived a wonderful life with few regrets. I've never had to look back in regret, because there's still too much to be done by moving forward.

"Don and I need to do what we can to help clean up this mess and find the seven brothers so we can get home to the people we love. But I'll tell you one thing: We're not leaving Iraq until we accomplish what we came here for. What will *you* have accomplished when you eventually leave?" I knew I was rubbing it in, but once I get started, I sometimes can't stop myself.

The sweat had soaked through my shirt by now, and was pouring off my forehead, but as I looked at this big OGA interrogator, it was not sweat that was pouring off his face, but tears in his eyes – tears that were now dripping down his cheeks.

I said to him, "If you're crying, please… just stop."

Everyone sitting around the table seemed to be holding their breath. I moved behind the OGA guy, put my hands on his shoulder, and gently – well, maybe not so gently – pressed down. Then I looked at the commanding officer and said, "Send for the MPs. We are done here." Colonel Stevens nodded, but apparently the OGA guy didn't notice it.

"You're not the C.O. here," he said to me. "You have no authority."

Then Stevens spoke up. "Well, first of all, he does have authority here, and second of all, *I* am the commanding officer, and I concur. You and your buddies are on the fast track out of here." Stevens signaled to two MPs who were standing nearby, and they rushed over and grabbed the OGA man, whisking him away towards the door.

The C.O. looked at me and said, "That was just the beginning. We're going to be cleaning house here." I nodded, still glaring at the rapidly departing OGA goon.

Despite my bravado, part of me still desperately wanted out of this place, but I knew that was not an option for Don and me. Our job was just beginning. We had perhaps taken small steps towards shining a light on and bringing an end to the activities of the exclusive little OGA club at this prison. Even though there was no way of knowing what the results of this evening's confrontation would be, I felt that something had been accomplished and that it was now time to move to the next step.

But first, I needed a good night's sleep.

CHAPTER 10

MORTAR ATTACK

Unfortunately, the longed-for and much-needed good night's sleep continued to elude me. That night more than a dozen mortar shells struck inside the walls of the prison, proving that Lieutenant Casey hadn't just been trying to scare us with his warning. Some of the shells even landed in the detainee area, where hundreds of Iraqis being held within the wire pens were caught unprotected. I was certain that a number of them had been hit by the shrapnel that hammered even the occupants of supposedly "safe" areas of the prison.

In the midst of this shock, my thoughts were racing in several directions. I was picturing in my mind the slender minarets rising elegantly above the domed mosques that I had seen throughout the Middle East. The remarkable architecture of these beautiful structures seemed incongruous with the brutal and destructive actions of the insurgent fighters who were attacking us here in the prison – yet both the elegant architecture and the vicious attacks were presumably inspired by faith. In my view, however, the violence was and is a perversion of Islam, making a bitter mockery of the dignity and beauty of that religion.

The sad truth was that Iraqis were routinely being killed and wounded by the mortar fire the attackers unleashed upon their own people. The insurgents didn't care how many of their fellow countrymen and women they killed or wounded if in the process they could injure or kill even just one American soldier.

The initial shock of the mortar attack passed quickly, as Don and I threaded our way through the narrow passages, seeking shelter as more mortar rounds struck. In truth, although we moved decisively through the prison, we didn't really know whether we were heading away from this inferno or going directly into it. Solders, private contractors, and prisoners were taking cover wherever they could. I found myself studying the faces around me, some reflecting fear, and others numbed by shock. I was trying to quell the morbid rage I was feeling; I wanted these insurgents dead. I wondered, *Why not drop the big bombs as President Truman did during World War II, and just walk away from all of this?*

I thought about the MPs, who had apparently grown accustomed long ago to their role as the puppet masters – the ultimate force that pulled the strings in the prison. And yet, under the mortar fire raining down on them, all of their power had been suddenly snatched from them as they too ran for shelter.

As Don and I took cover in a windowless holding cell, I began to wonder if my luck had run out. Did I make a mistake in coming here? Could this current situation be a kind of karmic retribution for a lifetime of taking risks that I had deemed necessary at the time, but which had actually been foolish? What the hell was I really doing here… and for that matter, what was the U.S. doing here?

But I already knew the answer to the latter question, and it all came back, again, to perception management. Whether trying to prop up the administrations of national leaders or to justify a war, the world's power brokers have long relied upon schemes of massive disinformation. The disinformation campaigns are always designed to shape public perception and to help powerful people such as the American president, and other national leaders, expand and retain their power. The current situation in Iraq, of course, was no exception to this longstanding pattern. At some level I had known that from the beginning, but it wasn't until shortly after I took this assignment and accepted The Letter that I fully understood what was really going on.

At the moment, I was beginning to doubt myself and my own motives again, which sometimes happens when I'm in an extremely stressful situation. I began wondering if perhaps I had been *too* altruistic this time; maybe my grandiose wishes to help save the world were profoundly misguided. As the mortar shells fell around us, I was struck by the realization that it was very possible that this time, I would die.

I was thinking that every epic in my life could be traced back to a single chance moment, leading to a decision that had seemed, at least at the time, to be good and guided by some Divine Power. Now, however, listening to the deafening crash of the mortar shells exploding and the screams of grown men, some of whose bodies were almost certainly being ravaged by the attack, my decision to come here seemed like a bad one, to say the least.

Don and I curled into a fetal position, shoulders slumped, backs pressed hard against the concrete wall of the empty cell, trying to hide ourselves from any shrapnel that might come our way. At first we didn't notice him, but one of the prison MPs had taken shelter across from us, and he looked as alarmed as we felt. He drew a deep breath as if he were going to say something, but there was no sound; he apparently thought better of it. Turning away and stretching out flat across the cell floor, the MP listened to the loud report of the mortar shells for a few moments before turning back toward us, shaking his head in disbelief. Then in almost a whisper, he said, "How is this possible?" Apparently he was new here. He lifted his head from the dust and rubble on the floor and listened intently for a few moments until it apparently registered in his mind that the attack was over, at least for tonight.

With this realization, the MP let out a big sigh. I studied him lying there for a long moment, and then he looked at Don and me again. His eyes drifted toward the door, and in a conspiratorial voice he whispered, "I won't tell anyone you guys were here."

"Good," I said. "And we won't tell anyone you were here. Deal?"

"Deal," the MP said. He lay in the sand and dust on the floor and studied us a while longer.

Finally Don looked up towards the ceiling and said, "Thank you, God!" The MP and I both knew he was expressing gratitude that we were all still here, uninjured.

I found myself musing again about the contradictions that often exist within organized religion. It was interesting, I thought, that in the Islamic tradition, it is held that only God can create life, but man has the right to take life. Of course these contradictions exist in other religions as well, certainly in Christianity. But since Islam is the prevailing religious influence in this region, that was the focus of my reflections now.

I thought that if the horrors that had plagued inhabitants of the Middle East were proof of anything, it would be proof of the great lengths to which people are sometimes willing to go in the name of faith. I knew that the conflicts in Iraq and elsewhere constituted a religious war to many – a *jihad* – which, of course, was one of the points I'd tried to drive home to the OGA guy earlier. Beyond the religious factors, however, war and conflict seemed to be embedded in the culture, and while I couldn't speak for other outsiders who had been stationed here, this culture of war served as a shock treatment to me. Experiencing such circumstances firsthand and up close can be devastating. Your sense of your own importance shrinks to a mere speck.

Don and I stood up at last, taking stock, looking out towards the tangled web of wire cages where the prisoners were kept. The shock waves of terror that just a few minutes ago had run through our bodies had now been replaced with an adrenaline rush, fueled by a desire to help those who had been injured. The crashing of the mortars falling all around us had ended and the screams had finally subsided, and all at once the world seemed strangely peaceful. We felt almost hypnotized by the sudden silence as it passed over us.

My own sense of peace was brief, and before long, my thoughts were racing again. I have endured some terrible things as a physician traveling in war zones – things that I sometimes had trouble moving past, but ultimately did. Perhaps that's why in times of crisis, the only forces that keep me going are my Hippocratic Oath and the belief, however irrational it may seem at times, that humans are capable of being better than we often demonstrate in our actions. I remain hopeful that we can, and at some point will, take action to avoid a catastrophic future defined by our most ignoble actions.

And yet, although in general I reject the theory that our species is on the brink of collapse, we seem alarmingly close at times to a calamitous future. Sometimes it feels as if we are racing toward our own doom, knowing that we're doing so but unwilling or unable even to slow down. Such a fear is not wholly groundless when you realize that a number of "civilizations" that are constantly at war with each other have developed and produced weapons capable of causing our extinction hundreds of times over, faster than anyone cares to admit. What truly saddens me is the awareness that my own country is itself one of those constantly warring nations.

Even though no weapons of mass destruction had been found in Iraq, the mere desire to develop them was and is disturbing in its own right. A core problem is that science is progressing so much faster than humans are evolving, and it seems that no one, particularly those in power, recognizes where the lines of acceptable behavior are drawn anymore. In times like this, there is no greater sin than inaction, but nobody can seem to agree on the right actions to take, further compounding the problem.

A Show of Hands • Joseph Agris, M.D.

As idealistic as it may sound, I had hoped that by rescuing the seven brothers, and helping even in some small way to end the atrocities that had been taking place at Abu Ghraib prison, my team and I would be part of a larger pattern of transformation – or at least we would be part of a good step in the right direction. When I accepted this assignment, I was looking not only to the near future but to a more distant one as well, believing in my heart that with the powers of technology and a span of several generations, humans really can evolve into a species that is socially, emotionally, and mentally more advanced than we are now. I sometimes envision a time when humanity will be more compassionate, smarter, stronger, and generally healthier.

I still cling to these hopes and beliefs, two decades after my visit to Abu Ghraib prison, even in the face of global and national upheavals that threaten to destroy everything we claim to hold dear. Most days, I'm still inclined to believe that we are in fact headed in the right direction. But my idealism is tempered by the question that won't go away: Will we as a species live long enough to realize our most lofty goals? Or will the monster lurking within us, and feeding our fears and greed, set the stage for one madman to push the wrong button, releasing a monster we cannot contain, and annihilating the human race as we know it?

I also sometimes find myself wondering if a "doomsday" scenario would result not in total annihilation of our species but rather in a dramatic but brief reduction in our numbers, causing a dip in human population on this earth, and possibly fixing what I feel are the fatal flaws of human evolution. Could even the horrors of launching weapons of mass destruction have an upside, ultimately resulting in a new birth of sorts, a second renaissance? If so, would such a blood-fueled renaissance provide humankind with the opportunity – and incentive – to redefine our species? Or are the darker aspects of our nature so hard-wired that even dire circumstance would fail to effect any substantial change?

What *will* fix the fatal flaws in our evolution – most notably, the flaws of simply being too bellicose and too prolific? We think of ourselves as intelligent beings, but cannot seem to control our instinct for war or our own terminally profuse expansion, which together will ultimately lead to our turning this planet's lands and waters into barren wastelands incapable of supporting many of its life forms, including us humans. Clearly we need to redefine our priorities before we go extinct like the dinosaurs and so many other life forms on this planet. If that makes me an alarmist, I'll gladly claim that title, because as far as I'm concerned there is genuine cause for alarm.

Unfortunately, my travels around the world have conditioned me to expect the worst from the people who hold the power, or at best not to expect anything that will truly produce change. I have never encountered anyone in power who dared engage in meaningful conversations about atomic weapons or a human population out of control.

Looking around me now, I mused that places like Abu Ghraib prison are the constructs of people with too much power taking their personal priorities and agendas into their own hands. But in the idyllic future that I envision on my better days, prisons such as this one, and the terrible things that take place within them, will be reduced to little more than a series of ugly footnotes in our history. Most of the time, though, such a future seems to me to be a long way off, and in the wake of the mortar attack at Abu Ghraib, it seemed like a pipe dream. I found myself wondering, as I've wondered a few times in other extremely stressful situations, if perhaps humankind is on the brink after all, and if our warlike attitudes and catastrophic overpopulation will ultimately require an uncomfortable solution: sacrificing limbs to save the body.

All of a sudden, the sound of generators being activated beckoned me to set aside my reverie and deal with matters more immediately at hand. Overhead lights began coming on throughout the central garrison area. People were emerging slowly from where they had taken shelter, and others, who had been injured in the attack, were calling out for help.

Don and I grabbed the medical kits we had brought, and we ran into the compound without really considering our own safety. The fact that we were in amongst the prisoners without any MPs around did not really occur to us. People were suffering, and some were likely dying. In situations where lives were in danger, racing towards trouble instead of away from it had become second nature for Don as an investigative journalist and me as a physician: the path of least resistance and greatest familiarity.

The inner compound, where the prisoners were being held, was deplorable, and that's putting it mildly. As Don and I walked through the area, I was shocked all over again by the extreme carnage the insurgents inflicted on prisoners, and was still trying to wrap my mind around the fact that these insurgents were waging war against their own fellow Iraqis.

Tonight, fortunately, there had been no deaths, only a few prisoners with minor injuries. I'd expected to find serous wounds, but upon checking some of our soldiers and the Iraqi prisoners as we moved through the compound, I found none that were serious. I also couldn't help but observe that unlike the prisoners, the soldiers had on their Kevlar and flak vests. In a sense, I was as exposed as were the prisoners, for even though I typically carried a concealed weapon in the uniform, sweats, or *shalwar kameez* that I sometimes wore to blend in with the populace, tonight I had perhaps unknowingly opted to trust in God and not wear a vest.

Previously I'd thought that our military had a system for tracking the insurgents' mortar installations and eliminating threats such as that we had just experienced. Now it seemed clear that regardless of what was going on elsewhere, no such system was being employed at Abu Ghraib prison.

As Don and I continued to move throughout the compound, we warmly greeted every one of the soldiers we encountered, inquiring about injuries as well as their general health. It was also an opportunity for us to ask about the seven brothers.

We spotted an older man sitting in the corner against the wall, his head down against his knees and his arms limp at his side. He had a small forehead wound, and blood was dripping into his eyes. I cleaned his wound and then applied a head bandage. He thanked me, and I asked him why he was being held.

In heavily accented but understandable English, he said that a false accusation against him had led to his arrest, and that American solders took him into custody for no apparent reason, but he trusted the American solders to treat him justly. He was missing many of his teeth, and I asked him what had happened. He replied that a couple of years previously, Ba'athist guards had arrested him and wanted him to sign a confession. "It was a false confession," he said. "When I refused to sign it, the secret police began to pull my teeth with a pair of pliers. When I couldn't stand the pain any longer, I signed the confession."

He added, "But I was one of the lucky ones. My torture was minimal compared to what they did to other prisoners, and many of those other prisoners lost their lives."

I asked if he had ever heard of the seven brothers. A big smile came across his face.

He said, "Yes. Yes. They are an example of the torture that Saddam Hussein had his men perpetrate in this prison. They all had their right hands cut off under Saddam's orders. None of them did anything except speak out against Saddam's ruthless political and social management of the country." He gave us detailed information regarding what he had heard about how they got by in the prison by helping each other with everyday tasks, but he stressed that all of this was just hearsay. He had never actually *seen* the seven brothers in the prison; he had only heard the stories. Still, we took his information as a hopeful sign.

Now that the mortar attacks were presumably over for tonight, teams of Iraqis supervised by the American contractors began to clean up. I noticed that one wall in the middle of the prison facility looked freshly painted, and I asked about it.

One of the Iraqi workers spoke up. "Since the Americans arrived, it has not been used anymore."

"Used for what?"

"Prisoners were placed against the wall and shot." He added, "That's why they filled the holes and painted over the evidence." He gave Don and me a moment to let that sink in, then continued, "There was also an execution room where there are some gallows. Many of those who were executed were political prisoners. They were tortured first and then taken to the gallows where they were hanged."

He paused again, then added that other prisoners weren't as lucky; they were used for biological and chemical experiments as well, and some were the victims of ritualized tortures. He hesitated once again, then looking carefully at Don and me, he said, "That happened under Saddam. But unfortunately, some of the American guards have seemed to have the same attitude toward their Iraqi prisoners and mistreated them, though not to the extremes that took place under the Saddam administration or the insurgents who managed the prison."

I smiled, telling him, "Looking into this mistreatment is actually one of the reasons why my friend Don and I are here, but first and foremost, we must find the seven brothers."

But before any of that happened, Don and I were going to have to finally get some very long overdue sleep. We had certainly earned it.

CHAPTER 11

THE SEARCH BEGINS

A fter finally getting our wish for a relatively restful, though brief, night's sleep, Don and I got up early the next day, and my first stop was the communication tent, where I finally was able to put a call through to my fiancée Terry in Houston. (Later that year, after having dated her for more than 10 years, I would propose to Terry in a very public venue. Fortunately she accepted my proposal, and I can't say it enough: marrying Terry was the best decision I have ever made in my life.)

The first thing I heard from her was, "I miss you. I worry about you. I still don't understand why you felt you had to go." Then after a moment's hesitation, she added, "I know you feel like you're doing the right thing... but I can't help worrying."

By the tone of her voice, I thought she was being remarkably reasonable about this dangerous trip.

I told her I missed her more than I could express and was glad she understood.

"It's just that I worry about your safety there," she said again. "You can't fix everyone's problems."

"No, but I feel that with Don's help, I'll be able to fix some of the problems here."

"I just hope you can count on some people over there for help if you need it," she said. When I didn't respond, she added, "You do have people who have your back, right? Like the military police? Anyone?"

I had always been open and honest with Terry, with whom I intended to spend the rest of my life. This was not the time for me to tell her there was nothing to worry about. I knew she wouldn't believe that anyway. Still, I tried to lighten the conversation by saying, "Look, I'm mostly just doing some sightseeing. As far as most of the people here are concerned, I'm just a tourist."

Terry responded, "A tourist that might inadvertently tangle with Al Qaeda or ISIS. A tourist that might inadvertently get shot."

"Terry, There are hundreds of soldiers here, including Special Ops guys."

"And that might be a problem. Remember there's a camera on that device you're using, and I can see you. You look like a terrorist. I'm more worried that one of those Special Ops guys might take a shot at you!"

At that, I knew I needed to change the subject. "I miss you, but I'll be home soon. Everything is going reasonably well; we've gotten some good leads. I love you." As we said goodbye, however, I was remembering that she had seen photos of some of these places from my previous trips, and I realized that she probably didn't believe any of my reassuring words.

I then went to the officers' mess, where I met Don and we had something to eat. As we were leaving the mess hall, our military interpreter arrived, along with two MPs, and we began our trek through the barbed wire fence and into the innermost part of the prison. We started there because the seven brothers had been incarcerated for a long time, and it was highly unlikely that they would be in the outermost ring where new detainees were being held. We also knew we could eliminate the women's and children's sections and the teenagers' section.

It was another beautiful sunny day, but that was nothing new because it was always a sunny day in Iraq. It probably was about 110 degrees at this time, and I could taste the sand with every breath. Even when I had been home in Houston for months after previous trips, there were times when I could smell and even taste the sand in my dreams. Awakening from those dreams, I routinely felt anxious, as if I were back in the hottest areas of the Middle East – and by "hot," I don't just mean the temperature.

While we walked in the heat, I started to think about my phone conversation with Terry about what it was that had beckoned me to Iraq. My two reasons for being here – locating the seven brothers, and doing what I could to disrupt the cycle of extreme interrogations – were not separate and independent. Each was as important as the other. After my confrontations with some of these interrogators at both Camp Cropper and here at Abu Ghraib, I felt we had made good progress so far on that part of our mission, but time would tell. In any case, I did not want to be known as the "cop within the prison," who is trusted by neither the prisoners nor the prison staff. The prisoners had long ago learned that outsiders were rarely there for the inmates' benefit. And while many of the prison staff had grown accustomed to having complete power over their prisoners, they also feared the potential consequences for committing or ignoring the prisoners' mistreatment, torture, and even their murder. If I did anything to foster the mistrust of prisoners or prison staff, it would render Don's and my mission even more difficult, if not impossible.

As C.O. at Abu Ghraib prison, Colonel Stevens understood the many obstacles that Don and I had gone through so far, just to get there. This task had become a part of us now. That didn't mean the C.O. was going to keep quiet about his ongoing concerns. While I had been relieved and grateful that he had seemingly backed me in my confrontation with the OGA bully at dinner on the previous evening, and had verbally committed to "cleaning house," it was clear that he still had some reservations about Don's and my presence here. It was possible that he might even throw some obstacles in our way. So as we saw him striding purposefully towards us that morning, and saw that he wasn't smiling, Don and I were prepared for the worst. To brace myself for any resistance we might get, I just tapped my chest a few times – a reminder that I still carried The Letter in my pocket.

The first thing that Stevens said to us was, "Look, guys, don't take this the wrong way, but I'm more worried about you two inside this prison than outside of it. You've already made some enemies, and people get killed every day in Iraq. Just be careful, and watch your backs."

With that said, he smiled at us for the first time, then turned and left us. Don and I just looked at each other in surprise. We hadn't gotten a dressing-down, but on the other hand we clearly hadn't received a full endorsement. Despite the C.O.'s lack of encouragement, however, I believed he really understood that we had a job to do, and that we were intent upon doing it right.

Our interpreter was no more encouraging than Stevens had been. After the C.O. left, the interpreter stood there and stared us down very intensely, apparently trying his best to intimidate us. But I was resolute, and played his little game to establish who was in command. I'd already seen the horrors behind these walls, and I wasn't about to let anyone get in our way. I also noticed that the two MPs were looking at Don and me as if to say, "You guys must be crazy." But that was nothing compared to the stare-down we were still getting from the Iraqi interpreter.

Finally the interpreter looked straight at me and said, "Okay, Mr. Hotshot, I'll get you your *seven brothers*." His voice carried with it a tone of dismissiveness and disdain, which was not only unnecessary, but inappropriate.

I stood silent for a second, as the interpreter mumbled something snide under his breath. I turned toward him and told him that if he had something to say to me he should just come out and say it.

He replied, "You must have heard a distant radio from one of the tents, or the wind is playing tricks on you."

I said, "Nobody can tell me I didn't hear what I just heard."

Suddenly, I felt an uncomfortable and compelling urge to strike the man. I knew that Don and our two MP escorts could see it in my facial expression and my body language, and I could see the interpreter's hand tremble ever so slightly. My seething passed rather quickly, though, and I didn't give in to my urge to hit him. I tried to look at the situation from his perspective. There was no doubt in my mind that he was under a lot of pressure from multiple sources, and he obviously had no idea what consequences he might face as a result of his having worked with us. Nor did he really have an idea what he could expect from Don and me.

Still, I didn't want to just let his rudeness slide, so I took a deep breath and said, "Just do your damn job."

He stood up a little straighter, nodded, and said, "Okay. Then, let's make this happen, and get it over with. You might like being called the Crazy Texan, but I don't want any part of it. People who do crazy shit frequently die over here, and I don't want to die because you do something foolish."

It turned out that after all of that bluster, however, the interpreter knew little more than we did about the whereabouts of the seven brothers. We spent a frustratingly futile day of searching, conversing with numerous detainees with the help of the interpreter. But by the end of the day were no closer to finding them.

After that first long day of searching, it had become clear to Don and me that finding the seven brothers most likely wasn't going to be as easy as we had hoped. It was equally clear that my original assumption that our quest to find them would only take a few days had been too optimistic. The C.O., recognizing the possibility that we would be at Abu Ghraib prison for the long haul, graciously offered us private accommodations in the officers' quarters, which were much more comfortable than our bunks in the physicians' barracks. While we were thankful for the more cushy quarters, we were also unhappy about the prospect of an extended stay.

Of course, we had no intention of giving up. We were still highly motivated, and I became even more motivated a couple of days after the confrontation with the arrogant interpreter, when I met some unlikely new friends who would turn out to be an invaluable help to us in many ways.

It happened on a very hot afternoon, when I was sitting by myself in the commissary. Don was off on his own; he had said he was going to be in his quarters for a while, consolidating some of his notes and reviewing video footage he'd taken. After a while I felt closed in at the commissary and felt that I needed to get outdoors. There was a sitting area outside, with some wobbly plastic tables and chairs, so I took my sandwich and iced tea out there and sat down. Because of the heat, it wasn't the ideal setup for al fresco dining, but at least the area was shaded by an overhanging tattered tarp. And it was considerably less claustrophobic than the indoor dining area.

I had come out here hoping to be alone, but no sooner had I sat down than two young men approached. They were carrying sandwiches and were obviously looking for some place in the shaded area to sit and eat. I immediately noticed that their facial features and dress were different from most of the others I had seen at the prison.

The taller of the two gave a low grunt and checked his surroundings, moving his head from side to side as if it were on a swivel. The shorter, younger man stuffed his cell phone into his pocket and gave me a hard look.

I gave them a thumbs up to let them know I was friendly, but they only continued to stare at me. I pointed to the plastic chairs across from me and to my right, indicating that they were welcome to join me. After a few moments, the thinner and taller man sat down in the chair across from me, but still seemed hesitant. The shorter one then pulled out the chair to my right and sat down as well.

I said, "My Arabic is poor. My Urdu is satisfactory. But my English is very good."

They both began to laugh. In excellent English, the younger man said his name was Aziz, then he pointed to his companion, whom he introduced as Hussein.

I nodded at each of them and said, "My friends call me 'The Crazy Texan,' but those who have met my knife call me Doc." This comment earned me an immediate smile from Aziz, who appeared to be at least five years younger than Hussein. I studied him, noting that his black hair was slicked back with grease, from his forehead to the curls around his neck. I speculated that he had done that to make himself look older and also perhaps more menacing. Superficial appearances aside, Aziz was bursting with youthful exuberance, and it was apparent that he could hold his weight in conversation.

Hussein, on the other hand, was considerably more reserved. He had long and quite unkempt hair, almost to his shoulders, and the stubble of a new-growth goatee. I suspected that he too was trying to appear older and more formidable.

I thought they both deserved a B-minus for their efforts, but of course I said nothing about that, instead merely giving them a big smile and a gentle nod as I took a bite of my sandwich. I felt it best to just let them lead the conversation, and if it ended up being nothing but pleasant small talk, so be it; at least I would have made a couple of new acquaintances.

Aziz explained that he and Hussein were not really close friends, but that they had met on their job as interpreters for the Americans stationed at Abu Ghraib prison. Then he told me that they were both Yazidis, and I sensed that the conversation was about to go beyond small talk.

I knew, of course, about the Yazidis, a group of people closely associated with the Kurds in northern Iraq. As I've mentioned elsewhere, for years Saddam Hussein had tried to exterminate them – a clear case of mass genocide that most of the world knew almost nothing about. Whole villages of Yazidis and Kurds had been killed in poison gas attacks perpetrated by Saddam and his military.

But there was so much more that I wanted to know about the Yazidis. I wanted to learn more about their tribal life, their religion, and their families, but I knew I had to approach the subject with tact; after all, it was an extremely sensitive area to embark upon with two young men I'd just met. So I decided just to open with a casual and neutral statement, and see where it went. "That's very interesting," I said. "I really would like to learn more about the Yazidis."

I expected Aziz to be the first to respond, since he had been so outgoing and talkative at first. But now he was silent, moving mechanically as he ate, and looking warily back and forth between Hussein and me. After a tense and somewhat awkward pause, Hussein put his right hand flat on the table and made eye contact with me. *Okay, that's a start,* I told myself, and waited; I could see that Hussein was trying to decide whether or not to speak.

Then a moment later, in accented but otherwise perfect English, Hussein said, "Okay, Doc. What do you want to know?" He had a look of exaggerated seriousness on his face, and I couldn't help myself. I began to laugh, and after a moment they laughed with me. The tension had been broken.

"I'm guessing that there is a lot you can tell me," I said.

Hussein chuckled. "Quite a bit." He took a bite of his sandwich and looked across the table at Aziz for support. But then he paused again.

Sensing that he needed a nudge, I said, "I assure you that I'm one of the good guys. That is the most important thing you need to know."

Aziz looked down at his hand, which was still on the plastic table, and said, "This is a lot to take in at one time." When he said this he locked eyes with me.

I said, "You two have been interpreters with the American Army, doing whatever you do since they arrived in Iraq – is that correct?"

Hussein lifted his head, took a sip of his drink, then nodded and said, "This kind of work has a way of finding the right persons for the job. The Americans also pay quite well."

I gave him a big smile and a wink and said, "When you guys came down and sat with me I thought you were pretty cool. I have a feeling we are going to become good friends." They both smiled, and I added, "You are probably wondering what 'The Crazy Texan' is doing in Abu Ghraib."

Both men nodded but said nothing, waiting for me to continue.

"First of all," I explained, "I'm not regular Army. I am not CIA or OGA. I am independent and I'm looking for a group of men known as the seven brothers, who are supposedly imprisoned in Abu Ghraib. By order of Saddam Hussein, their right hands were amputated and their foreheads tattooed. They are all businessmen. They are not political. Their only mistake was to speak out in their villages and towns against Saddam and his regime."

Aziz's face lit up as he said, "That is the most kick-ass thing I've ever heard of." I was a little surprised by his use of American slang, but it made me smile.

Clearly the more pragmatic and wary of the two, Hussein asked, "What do you want with these men?"

"I made a promise to the President of the United States that I would locate them, take them back to Houston, Texas, surgically repair their amputation sites, and provide each of them with a functioning, state-of-the-art, electric-mechanical new hand."

They both looked at me as if they thought I was indeed a little crazy, but I was fully accustomed to such reactions to me on first meetings with the people I met on my travels. It didn't faze me.

I decided to remain silent and wait for Hussein or Aziz to speak next. If there's one lesson that I'd learned on my many trips around the world, it is that there is often tremendous weight and power in the things that I leave unsaid, sometimes even more so than in what I say. Sometimes it is to my advantage to simply remain silent, either as a diplomatic strategy or to keep others guessing and slightly off balance. I knew that this was not one of those times, however. I felt that these two young men could be of help to me, but only if I were as honest as possible with them. As usual, though, I would have to wing it, for there really is no guidebook for these situations, no single correct course of action.

That's understandable, since as I learned long ago, there is no such thing as a strictly routine mission. Years of education and training, a passion for one's work, and even intrinsic factors such as aptitude and a high IQ can only take a person so far. At the risk of sounding immodest, all of those factors have worked in my favor, but in my experience my gut feeling, more often than not, was the force that saw me through complex or even dangerous situations and brought me home safely.

I took another bite of my sandwich, while Aziz and Hussein looked at me quizzically, waiting for me to continue. Overall, I had a good feeling about these two young men. And I knew that in the end I was going to have to trust somebody; after all, if I could not trust at least some of the people around me, all could be lost. Even so, I felt I needed further reassurance that I could trust my new friends, and it was pretty clear that they didn't entirely trust me yet either.

Then I had an idea about something that might go a long way towards reassuring all of us. Abandoning my plan to remain silent until one of my companions spoke, I looked up from my sandwich and said, "Can I trust you, Aziz? And you, Hussein?"

In the brief silence that followed, it hit me once again how terribly hot it was. I used my sleeve to wipe the perspiration from my brow, then adjusted my glasses and waited patiently for a verbal response from the two men. I could see that both Aziz and Hussein were suddenly quite intrigued, their minds no doubt brimming with curiosity, but they still did not say anything. In a subtle, or perhaps not so subtle, effort to elicit an answer, I said, "I cannot protect you if you disclose to anyone the information that I am going to present to you now."

Aziz, petulant youngster that he was, finally broke their silence, saying, "I am with you, boss!"

They say that those who are slower to respond are more reliable. I don't know if that's always the case, but at any rate, I was reassured when Hussein, after another moment, gave me a quiet "Yes."

I picked up my glass of iced tea and took a long drink – I've never denied having a flair for the dramatic – and then I finally unzipped my flak jacket, reached inside, and brought out The Letter. Returning my attention to the two men, I said, "Your spoken English is good, can you read English as well?" They both nodded their heads.

Slowly I unfolded The Letter and handed it to Hussein. He and Aziz immediately moved closer together, both reading at the same time. As I had done with everybody to whom I'd handed the document, I watched their expressions closely. I still got a thrill each time I did this. It never got old.

After a minute, when it was clear that they had finished reading, I reached across the table and they handed The Letter back to me. I carefully folded it, placed it back into its Ziploc bag, and returned it to the same pocket inside my vest.

They looked stunned, and we sat there in silence for another minute or so. I was the first one to break the silence, saying, "So, can we trust each other with this secret?"

They looked at each other and then once again nodded their heads vigorously up and down.

"Can I depend upon you?"

"Yes," they both said simultaneously.

"Will you help me find the seven brothers?"

They nodded again.

My gut feeling kicked in again; I felt comfortable with these two men at last. This seemed like the beginning of a solid friendship, and I knew that Don and I were going to need all the friends we could find if we were going to be successful in our quest.

CHAPTER 12

THE TRAGEDY OF THE YAZIDIS, AND ANOTHER CONFRONTATION

I t was time to change the subject and get Aziz and Hussein to open up, because I was very interested in learning more about the Yazidis. So I broached the topic again.

Aziz didn't seem to be paying attention to my cue at first; he took a few deep breaths and sighed. It appeared to me that he was still trying to process the information in The Letter.

It was Hussein who spoke first. "I do not know what all you know about us, Doc, so I will start with the basics. The Yazidis are one of the oldest religious minorities of Iraq, Turkey, and Syria. Some Yazidis live in Armenia as well. We have some things in common with Hindu culture, because long ago we were nomadic and migrated to India. But we are not Hindu. Our religion has elements of several other religions as well, but we are unique."

"That's interesting," I said. "Tell me more about the Yazidis in Iraq."

Hussein continued, "Iraq is really two ethnicities, Arab and Kurdish. Kurds and Yazidis function well together and occupy the north of the country. The reminder of the country is ethnically Arab, and they are mostly Muslim." He paused and then asked me, "Do you know very much about the Muslims in Iraq?"

I said, "Well, I know that Islam consists of two sects, the Shia and the Sunni Muslims. I know that despite their being in the minority in Iraq, the Sunni controlled the Ba'athist party under Saddam Hussein, as well as the political and military power. My understanding is that the Sunni used their power, privilege, and wealth, lording it over the Shia majority, as well as the Kurds, Yazidis, and other smaller groups of people."

Both men nodded as I was speaking. Then Aziz said, "It is also important to know that the Kurds and Yazidis are separate ethnic groups. The Kurds dominate in Northern Iraq. Kurdistan actually would like to be independent from Iraq."

"But it is complicated," Hussein added. "Aziz and I and many others consider Yazidis to be a distinct group, but there is actually disagreement among scholars, and even among some Yazidis, about this matter. Some say that we are simply a religious sub-group of Kurds."

Aziz continued, "To Saddam, the distinctions did not matter. He hated all of us, and ordered the army to eliminate the Yazidis and Kurdish people in their villages and towns with chemical weapons. He bulldozed our villages and forced us into collective housing, then confiscated our land, which he then gave over to Arab Sunni Muslims. Because of that, the Kurds and of course we Yazidis have been grateful for American presence in our country."

An air of sadness had suddenly fallen over the young men, and there was another long silence. I sensed that Aziz and Hussein might have more to say about the atrocities committed by Saddam against their people, but I didn't want to force the issue. No doubt they would come back to that subject if and when they felt up to it. I could wait.

Meanwhile, I had many other questions. Plunging right in and hoping that I would not offend them, I told them that I'd heard the term "Yazidis" used in relation to devil worshiping.

Aziz and Hussein both sighed; clearly they were all too familiar with this misconception. With a patience I had not seen in him before, Aziz explained, "Our religion has great regard for the Peacock Angel, one of seven angels who according to our beliefs run the universe. We call the Peacock Angel Melek Taûs. Unfortunately the Abrahamic state equates our deity to the 'fallen angel' that many consider to be the devil and the ultimate embodiment of evil.

"The confusion is understandable because we do believe that Melek is a fallen angel, and once he was a force of evil. But we believe that he was reformed, and has been forgiven by our creator deity, Khude, so now he is a force for good like the other six angels. We don't worship our creator deity, and we don't worship Melek, but we do believe that he needs constant attention to prevent him from going bad again and bringing more evil to the world."

Hussein nodded. "But all of that seems to be lost on the outside world. We Yazidis are considered by the religious majorities to be purveyors of evil, and we have been looked upon with fear and suspicion for centuries. For hundreds of years the Yazidis have been persecuted not only by Muslims, but also by Christians and even by some Kurds."

"And yet," Aziz interjected, "Yazidism has thrived for centuries, long before the births of Christianity and Islam. Yazidis considered themselves to be God's original creation."

"In that sense," I said, "they're not much different than hundreds of other ethnic or religious groups all over the world. That belief seems to be part of human nature." Both men smiled at this.

"Whether we are the original creation or not," Hussein said, "our faith is older than Judaism, Christianity, and Islam, perhaps one of the oldest religions in the world. And we consider it to be an all inclusive religion."

"But there is one very important point," Aziz said. "There is a lot about the Yazidi religion that we do not discuss with non-believers. Tenets of our faith are private. And we have strict rules and rituals for marriage and actually for every aspect of life."

He then explained that in Iraq, the Yazidi people had secluded themselves in the remote mountainous region around their capital city in the Sinjar region, and they dominated that region. "But life in the region changed with the Muslim invasion," he said, and that air of sadness was back for a moment.

Hussein now took up the narrative. "In the North, the Yazidis functioned and traded and did business side by side with the Kurds," he said. "That is one big reason that we have not slaughtered each other like Saddam Hussein has done in more recent decades, and the Muslim invaders historically were doing to our villages and towns."

Then, changing direction slightly, he added, "As we told you, Aziz and I are translators for the American military. There are two similar dialects spoken by the Kurds and Yazidis – referred to as Kurmanji, or Northern Kurdish; and Sorani, or Central Kurdish. Then there is a whole separate group of non-Kurdish languages spoken by ethnic Kurds."

"Like you said, Hussein, it's complicated," I responded, eliciting laughter all around.

Aziz said, "That is why the interviewers need us. We work with them side-by-side, and we translate written material as needed. We also talk to strangers who enter this region."

"I would say that you two have become invaluable to the American forces here," I said, smiling, and both looked pleased.

After a few minutes of companionable silence, Hussein said, "Since we are talking about complexity, Yazidi culture is very complex. We have a rigid caste system of three main castes, and within each caste there are many tribes. To make things even more confusing, there is also a co-existing class system within some of the castes. And there are strict and elaborate rules about who can associate with whom across these groups and even within them. It would probably take many days to explain it all." We all laughed again.

Hussein continued, "There is a lot that remains hidden about Yazidi culture, much that is not obvious to outsiders. But what *is* obvious are the attitudes that outsiders in this region have towards us. Most of us have had the experience of being treated with suspicion and anxiety by many Muslims when they are in the presence of a Yazidi. This is most likely because they think we are agents of the devil. Even those who don't necessarily fear us have apparently always felt that there was little to be gained by association with us. As a result, we are routinely avoided by local merchants, cab drivers, civil servants, and others throughout the region."

"But in a way this has been good," said Aziz, "because it also allowed us to preserve our religion and rituals by protecting them internally. And as we have said before, our relationship with the Kurds has been cemented because we have all been targets of Saddam Hussein's Ba'athist Party killing squads."

Hussein explained that the Yazidis living in northern Kurdistan are rural people, consisting mostly of farmers and shepherds. They do not participate in national politics, and they limit their activities to their own people and the region in which they live.

"Over the years," Aziz said, "There have been several attempted revolts by Yazidis seeking independence from Iraq. But all of those revolts collapsed under pressure and time."

"And Saddam and his vengeful Ba'athists took down the Kurds as well as the Yazidis," Hussein said grimly. "As we said before, the Yazidis lost their land. Our villages and towns were bulldozed under the order of Saddam Hussein and by the Iraq central government."

"Hussein and I have been witness to decades of war," Aziz said. "All of our relatives and friends bear the scars of trauma from the war. We have all lost family members to the violence and hatred. This is true of every Yazidi in Iraq."

Hussein nodded and said, "Yazidi village life was almost completely destroyed. Many of the Yazidis escaped across the Tigris river to Syria and then applied for refugee status to the United States. Thousands of Yazidis and Kurds came as refugees and were resettled in the United States."

What none of us knew at that time was that in the years to come, many more Yazidis would emigrate to America. This time it would not be to escape from Saddam but rather from ISIL/ISIS, the terrorist organizations that represented some of the most prevalent unintended consequences of the destabilization resulting from Saddam's removal. In August 2014, in what became known as the Sinjar massacre, the terrorists crossed the border from Syria and abducted and murdered thousands of Yazidi men, women, and children. Nearly half a million Yazidis were forced to flee and take refuge in other countries, including the United States, and the repercussions of that awful event are still being felt even today.

In the wake of the atrocities committed by Saddam and his Ba'athist party thugs, Aziz had been one of those who were fortunate enough to escape to America. Life improved for him but was far from easy. Aziz said, "I felt so isolated, not only from other Yazidis, but from the people all around me. This was true of other Yazidis I met. We were all outsiders. But Yazidi parents sent their children to the local American schools. We all learned English. We were provided with the opportunity to find better jobs. And now here I am back in Iraq in Abu Ghraib prison, with the American Army, as an interpreter."

Then he paused, and when he spoke again he seemed hesitant, and what I could only interpret as a sheepish expression came over his face. "I don't want to insult you, Doc, but, living in America has taught me that many Americans are very narrow minded."

I laughed. "I am not insulted, Aziz," I said, and he was visibly relieved. "In fact I happen to agree with you."

Encouraged, Aziz continued, "Americans are educated, but that education is limited in scope. In other words, Americans are not worldly. Most of those whom I encountered did not know what a Yazidi is, or a Kurd, or even a Muslim, for that matter. Most of them could not locate Iraq on a map if you asked them."

"I won't argue with you about that!" I said, chuckling.

Aziz was on a roll now. "It seems to me that Americans are more interested in football, baseball, basketball, and other sports activities than about what is going on in the outside world, or in some cases even what is going on in their own communities. They have no idea how we and many other groups throughout the world have suffered."

Hussein jumped in. "Aziz is correct. Even most of the young military men we work with and interpret for here at Abu Ghraib prison do not really seem to understand why they are here or what is taking place in Iraq." I nodded, waiting for him to go on.

"When American troops arrived in this country," Hussein continued, "many barely knew who Saddam Hussein was, and they knew nothing about his crazy sons, Uday and Qusay. They surely did not know what the Ba'athist party was and what it was doing in this country to minority groups such as ours. They knew nothing about the genocide that was occurring. Or if they knew, they didn't seem to care. And again, it is not my wish to insult you, or America, or the American military. I think it must be something in American culture or maybe in your education system that causes this limited outlook."

"You are exactly right, Hussein," I said.

Aziz looked at me then, and said, almost shyly, "You are the first American person we have met who seems to have insight and understanding about what is going on, and who actually seems to care about our history and about what is currently taking place in Iraq and Kurdistan."

This comment both pleased and upset me. I was pleased because my new friends acknowledged and appreciated my interest in them and in the events in and around Iraq and the entire region. But I found it slightly upsetting, assuming their observations were honest and accurate (and I had no reason to believe otherwise), that virtually none of the other Americans they had encountered seemed to know or care much about these matters.

Hussein then said, "Be assured that we will make inquiries, and we will help you find the seven brothers you speak about."

At that moment the conversation ended abruptly, as Aziz and Hussein looked up from the table, clearly uneasy. I immediately saw why, as three men who were obviously OGA spooks had emerged from the commissary and were just standing there, looking around the outdoor dining area as if they were searching for something, or someone. I hadn't seen these men before and I was both surprised and disappointed. Then it hit me that despite the commanding officer's responses to the OGA bully during my recent dinnertime confrontation, and notwithstanding his promise to me that he would be "cleaning house," it was unrealistic of me to expect instant results. Getting rid of the OGA was one of those tasks that was easier said than done. The appearance of the OGAs here and now was a harsh reminder to me that even though Abu Ghraib was a vast and constantly changing place, some troubling aspects might not be so quick to change. And it was also possible that I had overestimated my own influence – not the first time that had happened.

I wondered if a new group of detainees had just arrived, meaning that interviews – or, more accurately, interrogations – had been scheduled, and perhaps the powers-that-be had turned to what had long been their default response of calling in the OGA team. As much as I hated to think about this, it was possible that the place was in fact still crawling with OGA, despite my best efforts and the commanding officer's promise.

As the newcomers settled at a table a few yards from ours, I tried to suppress a groan. Well, at least I had The Letter, which had served me well so far. Noticing that Aziz and Hussein were glancing with an apparent mixture of puzzlement and anxiety from me to the OGA group and then back to me, I explained to them in a quiet voice, "I have already pissed off the OGA interrogators here at the prison. I wanted them all gone, and I thought that they were, but apparently I was overly optimistic."

Hussein rocked silently in his chair across from me, obviously trying to remain calm. Aziz was also clearly uncomfortable, but he too was trying to maintain at least an outward appearance of calm. No words passed among the three of us for what seemed like a long time, but was probably just a few minutes. It was clear to me that Hussein and Aziz held the OGA men in the same disdainful regard as did I.

Feeling that it was time for me to leave, I began pushing back in my chair slightly, not wishing to draw any more attention to myself than necessary. Speaking softly again, I said to my new friends, "I have just one favor to ask of you now, and that is for you guys to accompany me to the C.O.'s office. I need to speak to him again, and I don't feel comfortable walking there alone with these OGA men – and who knows how many others – still at Abu Ghraib."

Aziz rubbed his hand across his face and frowned, wrinkling his nose as if he smelled something rotten. He said, "We have much to be concerned with now that we are going to be helping you look for the seven brothers. We need to make this quick."

Hussein gave a cursory nod but did not speak for a minute or two. He began tapping his fingers on the table, and then, struggling to keep his voice calm and dispassionate, he said to me, "Those OGA men all have their eyes only on you."

I nodded. "Yes, I'm aware of that. Now we just need to figure out how we are going to get out of here, hopefully without being followed or attacked."

But even as I was saying this, it occurred to me that simply trying to avoid the newcomers wouldn't improve the situation, and might make it worse. Besides, it wasn't like me to actively avoid confrontation, at least not in situations where my best option was most likely the direct approach. No longer trying to prevent drawing attention to myself, I pushed my metal chair back across the floor, perhaps with a little more emphasis than was necessary. It made quite a racket, which apparently caught the attention of some of the officers inside the commissary, a few of whom had gathered at the door to see what was going on.

I got up and walked over to the table where the OGA men were sitting. They were staring at me now, their faces expressionless as I asked them in a calm but ever so slightly threatening voice, "Is there a problem?" Then I just stood there, rubbing my forehead with thumb and forefinger and trying to tamp down my anger, as they continued to stare.

I didn't realize until that moment that I still had my teaspoon in my hand. I made a show of pushing the spoon across their table, and at that moment, Aziz and Hussein rolled their chairs around, directly facing them.

One of the OGA men leaned back in his chair and glared at me. He nervously patted the table with his hands but said nothing, and neither did his companions.

"Do I need to put in a call to the MPs?" I asked.

Hussein and Aziz now joined me at the men's table, each giving me a subtle nod that plainly said, *We are with you.* One of the OGA men began to flex his hands and arms, an obvious sign of his stress in this situation.

At that point I noticed that the officers who had been observing from within the commissary had come outside to see what was going on, and they slowly circled around me, as if to say that they too had my back.

I had a strong sense of *déjà vu*. As with my previous public confrontations with OGA guys, I was doing what the service members had very likely been wanting to do for some time. There was clearly a lot of bottled-up hostility towards the OGA in this place.

Finally one of the OGA men – apparently the leader of the small group – leaned back against his seat and closed his eyes for a moment. He then pushed his chair back and slowly stood, as if trying to make it seem that he had intended to do so anyway, and that my somewhat aggressive behavior had nothing to do with it. He tapped the shoulder of the man who was sitting to his right, then did the same to the one on his left, and in a few seconds they were all standing. Their leader gave me a curt nod and a broad but clearly menacing smile, then the three of them headed back into the mess hall, obviously trying their best to preserve their dignity. I wanted to laugh out loud.

Instead, I simply looked at the group of men standing around me and said, "Sometimes the blade cuts. Sometimes it just gets waved around. Either way, it needs to be sharp and pointed." They all nodded, and then some began laughing, and I joined in.

Then I looked at Aziz and Hussein, who seemed frozen in their spot. I asked, "You men good?"

They both nodded at me, solemn at first, but a moment later their faces broke out in broad smiles. Then Aziz began to laugh out loud, and he said, "Outstanding." Hussein bowed his head towards the ground, and I could see the relief washing over him. The rest of the men who had been observing filed back into the commissary, and I said to Aziz and Hussein, "Before we go speak to the commanding officer, why don't we get some more refreshments? I think we could all use something after that encounter."

"Yes, I need a fresh coffee," Aziz said, and Hussein indicated that this sounded like a good idea to him too. I told them that I could use a hot tea to help me relax, hoping that my voice and manner didn't betray just how rattled I had actually been by the confrontation with the three OGA men.

The three of us walked into the commissary, heading straight towards the food line. As we were getting our coffees and tea, two officers entered the dining area and looked at us quizzically. No one said a word, but the new arrivals made no attempt to hide their curiosity as they gave us the once-over. Trying our best to ignore their stares, we took our drinks and sat down, this time electing to stay inside rather than return to the outdoor area.

As we settled in I said, "Now let's get back to what we were talking about. I'm very interested in hearing more about the Yazidis."

Aziz opened his mouth to speak, but he hadn't gotten a word out before the commissary door opened with a loud bang. A young corporal entered, out of breath and panting. He shouted out, "Is the doctor in here?" I assumed he was referring to me, and naturally the worst possibilities immediately went through my mind: had someone been severely injured, or was somebody gravely ill?

The room had grown deadly quiet, and as I stood up to identify myself, the young corporal said, "Doctor, you are wanted in the C.O.'s office for an urgent phone call." Well, that was convenient, since I had been planning to drop by Colonel Stevens' office anyway, but now I had something else to be concerned about besides the OGA issue. An urgent phone call? What if something had happened to Terry or to someone else I loved?

Unexpected phone calls do have a way of putting matters in perspective.

CHAPTER 13

A CHAT WITH THE PRESIDENT, AND ANOTHER DIRE WARNING

I slid my chair back, making that god-awful annoying squeaky sound as the metal scratched across the concrete floor. Standing up, I faced the corporal and asked, "Who is calling?" It was more of a demand than a question, but I didn't have time for niceties at the moment.

"I don't know, sir. I was only told by the C.O. to bring you to his office on the double."

Naturally, all kinds of thoughts were going through my mind by now. I noticed that Aziz and Hussein were looking at me with strange expressions on their faces.

A young lieutenant in the far corner of the room shouted, "Hey, Doc, it's probably the President of the United States calling you!"

Then someone else said, "Nah, most likely just the Secretary of State."

Everyone in the room was laughing as I got up and double-timed across the mess hall to the corporal, who had the door opened and was waving me out. *Good to know I'm a source of entertainment for them,* I thought to myself, a little annoyed. A minute later I was in Colonel Stevens' office and being handed the telephone by Stevens himself, who then excused himself and left, even though the corporal remained.

Not knowing what to expect, I said, "Hello?" in an apprehensive voice.

The response on the other line was, "Hold for the President of the United States."

A few minutes that seemed more like a few hours passed, and then finally I heard some static. It was quickly followed by a pleasant and unmistakable voice that said, "Good day to you, Doctor."

I responded, "Good morning… or is it good evening there, Mr. President?" With so much on my mind these past few days, I had lost track of time zones. Then, without waiting for the President to respond, I continued, "I take it that you have been kept informed through channels as to what's going on here at Abu Ghraib prison?"

"You could say that, yes. Which is good, since you and Mr. North have been remarkably uncommunicative."

"Would your source of information be Colonel Robert Stevens, the C.O. here at the prison?" I asked, knowing that I might be crossing a line, which come to think of it might be a mistake, perhaps a foolish one. This was the President, after all, and he was under no obligation to reveal his sources of information. Then again, sometimes you have to cross lines and test the bounds of protocol in order to obtain necessary information.

"I have multiple sources of information keeping me apprised of your progress there," replied the President, with a somewhat terse edge to his voice, or perhaps I was just imagining that. "But I would like to know what you and Mr. North have found out about those seven men – the 'seven brothers' – that you're looking for."

"What we've learned is that they are apparently here in Abu Ghraib, sir." Then, throwing caution to the wind, I asked, "Sir, is that really the main reason you called me?" I wondered what else he had been hearing about my activities here, and it seemed to me that the only way to find out was to ask him directly. I wasn't being disrespectful, just looking for information.

There was now an unmistakable edge to the President's voice when he replied, "I didn't see any other way to get direct answers than to call you." He paused for a moment before he continued, "Maybe you and I have different ideas about your purpose for being there, and about what you're really doing in Abu Ghraib. From what I've been hearing, you've been doing a lot more than just looking for those seven men. I understand Abu Ghraib is a big place, but I would think that you'd have found them by now, and that you all would be on your way back to the States."

That statement was a little puzzling to me, since I had assumed that the President would have been made aware of the conversations I'd had with other government officials prior to my departure, in effect giving Don and me the green light for our "secondary mission" of investigating and reporting on abuses within Abu Ghraib prison. But, not wanting to risk getting anyone in hot water with the President, I wasn't going to name names now. I had no intention of revealing any information unless asked directly.

So I simply said, "I just need a little more time. I admit that we've gotten sidetracked by what the OGA has been doing here with their intensive interrogations...resulting in injuries to detainees, and sometimes even in their deaths. Not to mention seeing firsthand some of the horrifying aspects of Saddam's 'legacy.' If it hadn't been for all of that, I assure you that Don and I could have made more rapid progress."

"So what you're saying is that while you were tracking down these seven men, you've actually been working as an undercover agent in Abu Ghraib."

Without stopping to think that this conversation was not likely being held on a secure line, and speaking a bit more boldly than I was feeling, I replied, "That is exactly what I'm saying, sir."

There was another pause on the other end of the line – a pause that was just long enough to give me time to start worrying if maybe this time I really had gone too far. Maybe I should have simply said, "No" to his question, or at least tried to qualify my affirmative response in a way that wouldn't get anyone else in trouble.

A wave of relief washed over me when he finally spoke, this time in a much lighter tone. "Well, Doctor, I happen to agree with what you're doing. In fact, from what I've heard, I think you and Mr. North are doing great work there. I encourage you to do whatever is in your power to help clean up that mess. God knows the press have been going on about it for a while now anyway, after those pictures were leaked, and it seems that what you and North are doing, at the very least, is helping confirm that the reports about what's been going on there weren't exaggerated. It may not be what some people want to hear. Sometimes the truth is ugly. But it needs to come out. Still, I'll be frank with you – the CIA/OGA and even some of the military personnel stationed there are not happy about your presence there."

"Yes, they've made that abundantly clear," I said, laughing. I was enormously pleased by the turn the conversation had taken, by knowing that the President was indeed aware and supportive of Don's and my secondary mission. Most of all, I was pleased by his compliment. I would be sure to convey the compliment to Don too.

The President continued, "One of the reasons you're resented there – besides the fact that you're a thorn in their side – is that they think you're getting some kind of special treatment. And in fact you are.

But they know that they can't do anything about it because it's coming from the top."

"I appreciate that, sir, more than you know," I said. "But I just need a little more time… hopefully not more a few more days." (There I was, being overly optimistic once again.)

Now there was another pause, this one even longer than the previous one, and I was afraid that the President had hung up or that the connection had been lost. Finally he spoke again. "So you've really witnessed firsthand evidence that some of these intensive interrogations have resulted in death?"

"Yes," I said quietly.

"Okay, a few more days. Actually, take as long as you need. And let me know if you need any backup, any help getting those men out of Abu Ghraib."

"Will do. And thank you, Mr. President."

"And by the way, I thought you'd like to know that the C.O. and top brass at Abu Ghraib have…let's just say…been duly informed about what you're doing."

"Well, I *have* shown a few people The Letter," I said. "It's actually been very helpful to me on this trip."

The President chuckled. "I'm glad, but what I'm talking about goes beyond that letter," he replied. "Let me just say that they know in no uncertain terms that even if they don't necessarily believe what you say, and disagree with what you're doing, and don't want you there, they will follow your orders… again, because it's coming from the top."

I was not expecting that, and was momentarily at a loss for a response. All I could manage was another "Thank you," which seemed a little lame, given the import of what he'd just said.

"And in case you don't know it, the press has shown an interest in what you're doing," the President continued. "So you have to finish this and bring those seven men home with you. Make us all look good. You got that?"

"I got it," I said. "And thank you again for your support, sir." I wanted to say more, but the President had already clicked off, clearly not one for long goodbyes.

The conversation left me with a renewed sense of determination, as well as a fresh sense of urgency. I knew without a doubt that Don and I had to bring our secondary mission to a close as quickly as possible – even if it meant accepting that the most we could accomplish would be to stir the hornet's nest enough to prompt real action regarding the atrocities at Abu Ghraib. We'd certainly done plenty of nest-stirring since we'd been here.

At the same time, we had to complete our primary mission, also quickly, meaning that we needed to double down on our efforts to find the seven brothers and prepare them for the long flight to Houston so their healing could truly begin. It was this imperative that was foremost in my mind as I slowly put the phone down.

After I hung up, it took me a moment to realize that the young corporal who had come to fetch me at the commissary was still standing there. I turned to him and said, "Is there a problem, young man?"

"No, *sir*. Absolutely no, *sir*."

I turned and walked out of the C.O.'s office, knowing that the corporal wouldn't be able to keep this conversation to himself. Even though he had most likely only heard my side of the exchange, it was clear that, mess hall joking aside, I had indeed been talking to the President of the United States. It would be all over Abu Ghraib prison within the next few hours, and since there was nothing I could do about that, I intended to make the most of it.

I walked slowly back to the commissary, where I got myself a fresh hot tea. I was pleased to see that Aziz and Hussein were still there, waiting for me, so I sat down with them, ignoring the stares of the other men in the room.

The same brazen lieutenant who had ribbed me before I left to take the phone call shouted out, "Did you have a nice chat with the President?" His voice was dripping with sarcasm, and he had a smirk on his face that made me want to get up, go over to him, and slap him. Of course I resisted the urge.

"Actually, we did have a very good talk," I said, after taking a long sip of tea. "And Mr. Bush gave me some very good advice on how to handle wise-ass lieutenants." Everyone in the room began laughing, except for the wise-ass lieutenant, who didn't seem to see the humor. The smirk was gone from his face, which had turned a bright shade of red.

This time when I slid my chair back, I did it more quietly than I had before. I stood up and faced in the lieutenant's direction, saying, "Lieutenant, please join me at my table for a minute. I need to show you something." I had decided that in spite of the seriousness of my mission – or missions, to be more precise – and the need to wrap them up as quickly as possible, there was no reason I couldn't continue to have a little fun along the way.

The young man stood up slowly, then brought his chair quietly over to our table. Aziz and Hussein looked up at him with big smiles on their faces, anticipating what was about to happen.

I said to the lieutenant, "Sit."

But he just stood there defiantly, saying nothing. I said nothing either as I slowly lowered my hand and reached into one of my boots. Today I was wearing a pair that I particularly liked; it had the American flag etched on one boot and the Texas flag on the other. Continuing to move slowly, as if I had all the time in the world, I pulled the flap that was inside the boot with the Texas flag, and I removed a small Beretta pistol, placing it quietly on the table in front of me. Then I casually took a sip of tea, looked up again at the lieutenant, and said, "Sit your ass down NOW."

Instead of sitting, he continued to stand there. He looked at the weapon I'd placed on the table, then looked back at me, then at the weapon again, and finally he focused on me, all the while remaining silent and expressionless. I refused to let his behavior ruffle me, instead nodding towards the chair that he'd pulled over, and then suddenly looking directly at him with a big smile across my face.

He didn't smile back, but continued to look at me. I'm not sure how long the two of us remained frozen there, staring at each other, but eventually I won the staring contest, as evidenced by the fact that he began to blink rapidly, his defiance all at once replaced by what was clearly anxiety. Finally he sat, and then I did too.

After I gave him a moment to compose himself I said, frowning slightly, "The thing is, Lieutenant, you have unfortunately walked into the middle of a very serious undertaking. And I need your support." He looked at me, shaking his head in bewilderment. His attitude now was quite a contrast from the arrogance he had displayed only a short while ago.

I removed the little Beretta from the table and slipped it back into my boot pocket, then laughed. This was fun, and I decided to do my best to further confuse the lieutenant. With a well-practiced air of drama, I slowly took the Ziploc bag bearing The Letter from the inside pocket of my vest and took out the document, looking at him with a grave expression on my face. "You should read this," I said. "You must read it here and return it to me immediately when you're finished. Once you've read and understood what this letter represents, you are not to speak of it to *anyone.*" Then I handed The Letter to him.

Like everyone else who had read it, he first scanned the top and then looked at me. Our eyes met and I nodded slightly toward the single sheet of paper in his hand, and he continued reading. I noted that once he finished reading it, he went back to the beginning to read it again. When it was clear that he had completed the second reading I reached across the table and he returned The Letter to me. I carefully tucked it back into the Ziploc bag and returned it to my vest pocket.

"I only showed this to you because I need to make this point as clear as possible," I said to him. "It's true that I just got off the phone with your Commander in Chief, the President of the United States. You all have been joking about this, but it's a very serious matter. So what I want you to do now is go back to your buddies and sit down. Get your head straight. You do not want this to become your problem. You will absolutely not discuss what you have just read with anyone, or I will personally see that you suffer the consequences."

He gulped and said, "Yes, sir. Thank you, sir. And I apologize for my behavior." He stood up, grabbed his chair without looking at me again, and went back to the table where he'd been sitting. As he sat down, I could hear him say to his table mates that I had just been talking to the President of the United States a few minutes ago. "That's all I can tell you, so don't ask me anything more," he said, and I had to suppress a laugh.

A hush passed over the room then, and I turned back to Aziz and Hussein with a big smile on my face. "Now, what were we talking about?" I said. I'd decided that I had had enough excitement for the day. My conversation with the C.O. could wait until tomorrow.

We talked for a while longer, and it was very enjoyable and informative for me. When it seemed that we had finally exhausted the subject of the Yazidis, or at least had carried the conversation as far as my new friends desired, I looked at my watch and said, "Hey, guys, I usually take a walk around the prison at this time. I talk to the guards and visit with the detainees to determine their state of health and nutrition, and to find out if they underwent any 'procedures' at the hands of the OGA men. Would you two like to join me? Your service as interpreters would be very welcomed." I was thinking that their company would be much more enjoyable than that of the arrogant military interpreter who had treated Don and me with such disrespect.

Aziz and Hussein both nodded, with big smiles on their faces. I pushed my chair back, as did they, and we left for our tour of the prison. I was struck again by what a monstrous building it was: about a thousand feet in width but many acres in depth – certainly larger than any American prison I had ever visited.

Beside the main facility there were hundreds of feet of corridors, sleeping accommodations for staff, eating areas, and of course the cells where the prisoners were kept. At the far end of one of these unused cell blocks, unfortunately, were the remains of yet more detainees who had obviously undergone severe "interrogation." And then there were the rumors Don and I had heard about the brothel – the infamous "Boom-Boom room" –where young female inmates were used as prostitutes, and chests of ice, beer, and hard alcohol were available. We intended to investigate those rumors, and soon.

As we approached each area, the MPs who served as guards saluted and hustled us through each checkpoint without a word. Then we came across one of the few MPs whom I had befriended. He saluted, smiled, and said, "I'm not on duty, Doctor, I have come here with news. More than that, I bring a warning."

I stopped and looked at him, waiting for him to continue as Aziz and Hussein stepped away a few feet, as if assuming that the MP might want our conversation to be private.

As soon as they had retreated, the MP said, "There are those who work in this prison who... how can I put this... don't agree with your intentions to change how things are done here." It was obvious that he was choosing his words carefully as he continued, "They've chosen to see only the limits that they think you are putting upon them. They know you have significant influence at the White House, but it seems they don't care. From what I can determine, they are members of the OGA who remain here and who feel that you are not only treading on their territory but have also begun taking action against them."

"This is your *warning*?" I asked him. "I appreciate it, but you're not really telling me anything that I don't already know."

The MP replied, "But maybe you don't know how serious it is. There are some of us who care and are open to change, but there are still quite a few who take your judgments personally, and will likely do whatever they can to see your efforts fail." Then he lowered his voice, clearly not wanting Aziz and Hussein to hear what he said next. "They

wouldn't hesitate attacking — even killing — you if they got the chance. *That* is the warning."

Then he led me to an open doorway and said, "Perhaps we should talk more privately." I nodded, looking back at Aziz and Hussein and signaling for them to stay put for a few minutes.

As the MP and I passed through the archway to the more private area, he said, "I can't stress enough that any misstep could bring an end not only to your good work here, but possibly to your life. Unfortunately, what the OGA men did here has attracted unwanted attention in the international press."

I said, "I already knew that too. So what exactly are you trying to tell me?"

"There are problems with the prisoners. Not just about food, sanitation, and overall poor conditions, but also the intensive interrogation techniques used by the OGA. Now, the men inside who have been responsible for running the everyday functions in the prison feel a lot of pressure and are beginning to complain loudly.

"With your presence here, Doctor, they now feel free to speak out and have become really angry, but they're also puzzled. The things they're saying now are no longer veiled accusations of unpleasant actions by the prison's security forces. They're making clear and provable accusations of the worst kind of criminality. And the perpetrators know that if you aren't stopped, they might find themselves facing the same kind of treatments that they're being accused of. They've become like frightened animals, and they're ready to respond accordingly."

At this point I took a very deep breath. My MP friend put a strong arm around my shoulder and started to walk me back. "I assure you it won't take much for you to find more than you can even imagine," he said. "Be careful! This is a war zone. You already know that we take mortar fire here every couple of nights. Control within the prison is far from being absolute. You understand what I'm saying, Doc?"

I stopped, and he did too. Facing him I said, "I appreciate your concern, but I plan to always have several people with me when traveling through the prison facility. I have a job to do; I need to locate the seven brothers, and now I find myself deeply involved in a genuinely more disturbing situation. But again, I thank you for your concern and for the information. I appreciate that you're watching out for me."

We shook hands, and as I stood there watching while he made his way toward the main corridor and away from me, I noticed that sweat had begun trickling through my hair and down my neck again. This time it was not from the heat.

I waved to Aziz and Hussein to rejoin me, and we completed our walking tour of the prison, as planned. But something had shifted within me. On the surface I remained calm, but I was feeling more unsettled than ever.

PART 2

MISSION EXTENDED

CHAPTER 14

THE TAKEDOWN: THE BOOM-BOOM ROOM

A part from our task to find the seven brothers, and our concerns about the enhanced interrogation, torture, and even murder of inmates at Abu Ghraib, the credible rumors of the hidden brothel known as the "Boom-boom Room" had been weighing on my mind, and Don's as well. It wasn't a mere distraction. As it was yet another example of abuse of detainees, we reasoned that it was well within the purview of our secondary mission. We'd heard enough buzz around Abu Ghraib to be fairly certain that the brothel was still in operation. The information we had gathered so far had provided us with a general idea of where it was, and what exactly went on there. Hearing stories about the sexual exploitation of female prisoners, some of whom were mere girls, made both of us furious, and we were determined to do what we could to stop it.

At dinner on the evening of the day that I had met Aziz and Hussein and had my conversation with President Bush, Don and I talked about the Boom-boom Room. We knew we needed to speak with the C.O. about the matter, and the sooner the better. As far as I was concerned, this issue was even more urgent than the conversation I had intended to have with Colonel Stevens about the continuing threat of the OGA men. Accordingly we scheduled a breakfast meeting with Stevens the next morning.

Don and I arrived early for the meeting and selected a table at the far end of the dining room, where we were not likely to be overheard. Fortunately there were few other people in the room at the time. I strongly suspected that Stevens and most of the other command officers stationed at the prison knew – at the very least, unofficially – about the

Boom-boom Room. But I still felt that discretion was called for in this matter.

As Don and I sat down I had an edgy feeling, though I was doing my best to control my anxiety. I hoped it didn't show. Soon we were joined by the C.O. and two other men, whom Stevens introduced to us as Lieutenant Allard and Lieutenant Heineg, adding that they were his top aides. We had seen them around the facilities, sometimes accompanying the C.O., but up until then we hadn't known who they were. "You can say anything to Lieutenants Allard and Heineg that you would say to me," Stevens assured us.

For some reason this made me feel even more anxious, but I had no intention of backing down now. I knew Don was as determined as I was to see this through. After the introductions had been completed, Stevens and his lieutenants excused themselves and went to get their breakfasts. Once they were seated again, Stevens took a couple of bites of his breakfast and said, "So just what is this meeting about, Doc?" He didn't seem overly concerned about what my reply might be, or indeed about anything except the heaping plate of bacon, eggs, and toast in front of him.

I had done my best to prepare myself for a range of reactions from Stevens – from anger to defensiveness to denial – so it was now or never. Tentatively I said, "We want to talk about something we've been hearing about hidden in the prison...something called 'the Boom-boom Room.' Does that ring a bell?"

I was somewhat taken aback when the C.O. didn't even look up from his plate, and neither did Lieutenants Heineg and Allard. Then I looked at Don, and saw that he was grinning so hard his face must have hurt. But the C.O. and the other two remained silent, their faces impassive as they continued eating.

I started to wonder if Don and I were the only ones at this table who knew what I was talking about. I could tell that my face was flushed; the heat was rising and the sun was baking this building, but I was pretty sure that wasn't the cause of my facial color change. I sat there a few more moments in silence, wondering what in hell to say next.

Then I snapped out of it, realizing that I had to press the matter, regardless of what the consequences might be. I had been sitting at the edge of my chair, but I suddenly pushed it back from the table and stood up, facing the C.O. He and the two lieutenants remained quiet, but they had at least stopped eating, and they were now looking at me as if they thought I was a bit unhinged.

I knew I was smiling hard, and my brow was furrowed as I said, "I don't know exactly how to say this." I began pacing around our little table, with those who remained seated following me with their eyes. Don was still grinning, and while Stevens and the other two still hadn't said a word, the C.O. was closely observing my facial expressions and mannerisms, as if steeling himself for whatever the Crazy Texan might say next.

Then, Lieutenant Allard put down his fork and knife and said, "Doctor, what is this all about?"

Apparently I hadn't been direct enough in my initial statement, so I just came right out and declared, as forcefully as possible while still trying to keep my voice down, "You're running a brothel inside Abu Ghraib prison!" Stevens looked up at me with an unchanged, mask-like expression, and it occurred to me that he was probably a great poker player. "Look, sir," I said to him, my anxiety rapidly being replaced by annoyance. "I asked for this meeting to get your thoughts about suspicious activity in an on-base brothel known as the Boom-boom Room – a whorehouse within the prison. You can't tell me you didn't know about it."

Then suddenly Stevens burst out laughing, and Allard and Heineg chuckled as they picked up their utensils and began eating again. That was not the reaction I had expected. Now I was really beginning to get annoyed. I said, "Sir, in the few days that we've been here I have found you to be a fair man. I couldn't ask for more, but this is not a joke."

Lieutenant Heineg said, "So, Doc, is there something that's happening here that we need to know about?" I found myself wondering whether he was being sarcastic or was just a little slow. Trying to control my exasperation, I said, "Do I need to send you an incident report? Or maybe a semaphore signal? Get me some flags and I'll get started."

Heineg shrugged, and he and Allard continued to regard me with what appeared to be slightly mocking expressions. The C.O. was grinning nearly as widely as Don had been a few moments earlier.

Something in me snapped. No longer caring about discretion, I said in a voice well above my previous whispers, "You guys are running The Best Little Whorehouse in Iraq – right out of Abu Ghraib prison! And some of the victims reportedly have been children." I glanced around and saw that the few other soldiers who were within earshot were looking a little shocked. I didn't care.

At least Stevens had ceased grinning. He said, "Doc, really, is this some kind of a joke?"

"I already told you, sir, that this is no joke," I said, lowering my voice to a more conversational level. I began giving him some more details about what Don and I had found out. Or at least I tried, though without much success, because now Stevens was talking over me, and not very quietly. He kept saying things like, "For Christ's sake, this can't be! I don't believe it! Not on my watch." His grin had been replaced by an expression of outrage; either he was a damn good actor, or he really had been unaware of the brothel inside the prison. Judging by the expressions that were now on the faces of the two lieutenants, this was news to them as well. Part of me was still skeptical about how that was possible, but then I reminded myself that Abu Ghraib was a sprawling facility, and like all prisons, it had its share of unsavory "benefits" for the detainees and even some of the staff.

I began circling the table again, though I changed course and was now pacing in the other direction. When I finally stopped I stood directly in front of Stevens, looking down at him, and in an obviously worried voice he said, "Perhaps we need a one-on-one conversation."

I said, "That was Don's and my original intention, sir, but the secret is out, and I'm sure we can trust the lieutenants. Now that it looks like we're all on the same page, all Don and I want to do is give you our input. I'm inclined to believe that you and the other officers at this table were unaware of what's been going on in one of the hidden spaces in this prison. But I'm also willing to bet that almost everyone else stationed or confined here knows about the Boom-boom Room." Stevens and the lieutenants were quiet now, waiting for me to say more.

I continued, "Sir, my understanding is that not only do they have under-age female inmates for sale, there are chests of ice with beer, and they're serving hard booze too. This is a big ongoing operation, right here in your prison."

"Where is it?" Lieutenant Heineg asked.

"From what we've been hearing, it's at the end of a wall in an unused hallway at a far end of the prison," I replied. "No detainees are housed in that area. We've heard that the hallway comes to a dead end."

Don took up the narrative. "Apparently it's a very clever wall, built with a secret sliding door. If you're taking a casual walk down the hallway, it looks like any other section of the prison. The secret door opens to the Boom-boom Room, and adjacent facilities where the...um... young ladies are plying their trade."

I added, "I don't know if some skillful soldiers with previous construction experience put up this wall and the secret door, or guys from the engineering division helped put it together, but it sounds like this has been going on for a while. I'd say that it's time to break up the party." Looking directly into the C.O.'s face, I said, "So what else do you want to know?"

No answer.

I wasn't really certain what was going on in his mind now, nor was I sure exactly what Don and I had set in motion, but my instincts were on high alert. The dynamics had changed at the table in some way, but I couldn't quite put my finger on it. I could see, however, that Stevens was studying my facial expression again – no longer because he suspected that I might be a little crazy, but perhaps because he was pretty sure I wasn't. I felt certain that at any rate, he was uneasy because he didn't know what I planned to do next about the discovery of the brothel.

I wanted an answer, in the form of some promise from Stevens that he would take immediate action to end the exploitation in the Boom-boom Room. Thinking that he might need a small nudge, or perhaps a shock, I said, "Do you want Don and me to get some pictures and then tell this story to the press, or perhaps just put it online? Don't we already have enough problems at Abu Ghraib?"

As I spoke, I noticed that Lieutenant Heineg was sweating, and his lower jaw was jutting forward, which made him look like a pit bull dog. But he said nothing.

Stevens asked, with a tinge of anxiety in his voice, "You're dead serious? You'd do that?"

"Yes sir," I said. "We would, if we had to." Even as I spoke, it occurred to me that rattling cages at even the most professionally-run prisons in the U.S. could have serious repercussions not only for the prison staff, but also – and especially – for the whistleblowers.

Stevens said to his lieutenants, "We need to move on this immediately."

Heineg responded, "Sir, the mayhem this could set off could bring a congressional investigation down on us."

"Maybe," I said. "But you can't just let this keep going on, now that you know about it."

The lieutenants and Stevens looked at each other. Stevens appeared somewhat agitated now, but I knew that wasn't going to do any of us any good.

As for me, I probably just looked a little empty; that's certainly how I was feeling at the moment. Don appeared subdued as well. I didn't know exactly what he was thinking, but the thought that was going through my head was that the two of us had risked a lot by coming here. We had put a great deal of thought into presenting what we knew about the Boom-boom Room to the C.O. The ball was now in his and his lieutenants' court. They needed to act immediately.

I finally sat back down, waiting for a response.

But the only response was a soft, "Oh, my God" from Lieutenant Allard.

Finally Stevens said, "I assure you that I would never ignore something like this if I had known about it."

"I believe you, sir," I replied. "This is not your doing. But you can stop it."

Lieutenant Heineg spoke up again. "We have enough problems in here, but yeah, I hear you. We'll deal with this immediately."

I could tell that Stevens was upset and angry about what we had told him. I wasn't unsympathetic to his position and to the emotions he was experiencing, but mostly I was glad that he finally believed us and seemed motivated to quickly deal with the problem. As I studied the expression on his face, it was clear that he was mentally preparing himself for what he had to do.

After a couple of minutes, Stevens snapped out of his ruminations and was suddenly all business. He said, "Lieutenant Heineg, you will accompany North and the doctor to the area where the Boom-boom Room is located. They will conduct a reconnaissance mission investigating hallways, adjacent passageways, rooms, and so forth. Then, Lieutenant Heineg, you will report back to me in an hour.

"Lieutenant Allard, you will put together a strike force with at least twenty men in full CQC (Close Quarters Combat) gear. Your primary weapons will be nonlethal, loaded with only bean bags or rubber bullets. Take along enough flash-bangs. Sidearms will be loaded with, and team members will carry, only standard-issue ammunition, to be used only in the event of a life threatening situation.

"So, Lieutenant Allard, get your men together, give them their orders, and if anyone objects, add them to a list of suspected collaborators and replace them. And send the list to me, sealed and marked Eyes Only. Understood?" The lieutenants nodded, as did Don and I. Looking directly at his two lieutenants, the C.O. said, "We don't want anyone to get hurt. Be sure the men you select are levelheaded, and tell them not to do anything stupid."

Two hours later, the entire group was assembled, including Colonel Stevens, the two lieutenants, their team of twenty trustworthy soldiers, and selected MPs. Stevens said, "Those weapons have rubber bullets?"

To a man, they shouted, "Sir, yes sir."

Stevens turned to Lieutenant Allard and said, "You have flash-bangs with you?"

Lieutenant Allard answered, "Yes, sir."

Don and I led the team to an area where we had been informed that the Boom-boom Room was most likely located. The men took their places along both sides of the hallway facing a dead-end wall that, frankly, didn't look any different from many others within the prison.

Lieutenant Heineg directed Don North and me into a side passageway and told us, "Keep down." He then handed a bullhorn to the C.O., who took a deep breath and shouted, "Give yourselves up! Give it up! Give it up!"

After that it was completely quiet in that passageway for a few moments. Stevens said, "We've warned them. Now we are going in." I was thinking to myself that I hoped the information Don and I had been given about the location of the brothel was valid. Distant memories of former TV talk-show host Geraldo Rivera and mobster Al Capone's vault came to my mind.

From our relatively safe space in the side passageway, Don and I watched the men move forward. The MPs were forming a barrier on either side of the hallway, and Lieutenant Allard, who now had the bullhorn, began shouting, "Hold your fire, men, hold your fire!"

I thought to myself that even if we had accurately determined the location of the brothel, even a seemingly minor tactical error now could launch a firefight that would costs dozens of lives in this narrow space. It could – and probably would – continue until every last one of us was gravely injured or dead.

Two men then stepped forward and using a battering ram, aimed it at the center of the wall where they thought a secret door might be. To our surprise, almost the entire wall came crumbling down. Stevens had the bullhorn again and began shouting to the occupants, "Do not do anything stupid! Step out with your hands above your heads!"

As I've mentioned elsewhere, I have been in plenty of war zones, and I've had the experience of coming under fire, but it is something to which you never really get accustomed. The close quarters of this hallway, combined with the bullhorn commands echoing in my ears, and the fear that someone might actually use a flash-bang and set off a firefight, left me shaking. I just wanted it all to be over.

I lifted my head and looked around the corner to the main hallway to scope out the scene. My first thought was that Don and I had been correct about the location of the brothel. That was both good news and bad news. All at once, a group of young girls began to frantically dash through the now-demolished entrance way, some in various stages of undress. Clearly, they were terrified; most were sobbing uncontrollably as they struggled to get away. Sadly, freedom wasn't presently in the cards for these young girls, who were, after all, still detainees. They ran down the main hall towards the perimeter, even though there were no other doors or windows through which they could escape. More MPs, who had been standing at the end of the hallway and waiting patiently, grabbed them gently and cuffed them.

Stevens now stood to the side of the remaining fragment of what had been the door. He kicked it down and then kicked it out of the way. All at once, a young man in military fatigues came running out of what was left of the Boom-boom Room, arms up, yelling, "I give up. I give up."

One of the commandos from the tactical team grabbed the man by the arm, and in one smooth movement threw him to the ground, putting his knee on his back as another commando cuffed him.

With the broken segments of the Boom-Boom Room's walls and secret door scattered as a pile of rubble, other young soldiers surged forward out of the former brothel, holding their hands above their heads. Commandos quickly ran through the Boom-boom Room facility, calling out, "All clear, all clear!"

Stevens, unwilling to relinquish his bullhorn, shouted to his team, "You should all be proud! No casualties, problem solved!"

Mission accomplished? It sure looked like it, but I knew that probably wasn't the end of the story.

CHAPTER 15

AFTERMATH

The next morning when we went to get breakfast we saw Colonel Stevens and Lieutenants Heineg and Allard at the same table where we'd all been sitting yesterday. Stevens was in a good mood and shouted out to us, "Doc, North, come over here and sit with us!"

I was so emotionally exhausted from all that had gone on yesterday that I hadn't put much care into the day's outfit; I was wearing a camo pullover, jeans, and my Western boots. Don, looking equally worn out, was dressed in fatigues. As we shook hands all around the table, I thought to myself, *To hell with anyone who takes issue with my fashion sense!*

But our apparel didn't seem to be an issue. Stevens said to me, "We've already had our breakfast. You and North sit down, enjoy your breakfast. I want to see both of you in my office at 1300 hours today."

We both nodded and said, "Yes, sir."

As the C.O. and the lieutenants gulped down the rest of their coffee and got up to leave, I thought to myself, *That went well...I guess.* But I wondered what the meeting that afternoon was going to be about.

That morning, Don and I made our usual rounds through the corridors and cells of the prison, unaccompanied by either MPs or the unpleasant military interpreter. I was hoping to meet up with Aziz and Hussein soon, introduce them to Don, and formally establish them as our interpreters going forward. For now, however, we felt secure walking on our own through the prison. Things seemed quieter. That was good, but we really didn't make any progress regarding the seven brothers. We did, however, hear some scuttlebutt about the previous day's bust. It was apparently a popular topic of conversation throughout the prison.

At 1300 hours sharp, as requested, Don and I showed up in the base command offices. As we entered the C.O.'s office, I got the impression that Stevens was still in a decent mood, based on his sunny greeting, "Hello again, you two! Please come on in."

We all shook hands. Stevens looked cool and calm as he sat behind his old metal desk, with its usual neat stacks of papers and folders arranged at one end, and the rest of the desktop perfectly clear. When he indicated that we were to sit down, Don and I were already so exhausted from the heat that we dropped like lead balloons into the two chairs that were positioned in front of the desk.

Stevens began to explain the situation. He stated that the Boom-boom Room was now officially closed. "I don't have to tell you that a whorehouse in a military facility is not a good thing," he said. "If the press gets hold of this story, those of us who are stationed here are in for a hell of a lot of trouble."

Don and I nodded, and then I said, "I assume that the men we caught in the Boom-boom Room will be shipped out, court-martialed, and dishonorably discharged. But realistically, it probably won't end there. As commanding officer, you are ultimately responsible for everything that takes place here, and other heads could roll."

Don added, "And it's very possible that this is not the end of the whorehouse operation. More than likely you just got the low-hanging fruit."

"That's right," I said. "I wouldn't be at all surprised if there were other ambitious young men stationed here who are likely to take up where the business left off. This problem isn't over. There needs to be an ongoing investigation and a clear set of regs that all personnel will be required to follow."

"What do you suggest I do?" Stevens asked.

"Judging by what we saw yesterday, and have heard today, the young men involved in the Boom-boom Room seem to be of average intelligence," I replied. "They don't seem particularly greedy, and they're not sociopaths. They saw an opportunity to have fun and at the same time make some money. I understand they were also smart enough to stop talking when they were arrested."

"So what are you saying?" Stevens responded. "I'm listening."

"I'm hoping you will drop some of the charges and just have the men transferred from Abu Ghraib prison duty," I said. Don nodded in agreement. I continued, "Honestly, these young men are not criminals. If they receive dishonorable discharges, they'll be marked for life. In some ways, just being out here and assigned to Abu Ghraib may have been punishment enough. As I said before, this needs to be an ongoing and fully transparent operation. And as Don said, the ones we caught are just the low-hanging fruit. If you proceed with the court martials, the press will get wind of it, and that won't look good for you or for the White House."

"If I may add a suggestion," Don said, "I recommend that you handle this as an in-house problem."

Before Stevens could respond there was a knock at the door, and he said to us, "I took the liberty of having one of the men we arrested from the Boom-boom Room brought to the office this afternoon. He said he needed to talk to me about what was going on. I assume that's him now." In a louder voice, the C.O. commanded, "Enter!"

A young man came through the entrance, accompanied by two MPs. His hands were cuffed behind his back, and he held his head down, not looking at any of us. He had a crewcut and a clean appearance, and wore a standard camo outfit, perfectly starched and pressed. His belt buckle was polished like a mirror, and his shoes were freshly shined.

I asked that the cuffs be removed, and Stevens nodded to the MPs, who promptly removed them. Then Stevens asked the MPs to leave the room but to remain just outside the door. After they left, the young man spoke for the first time. Turning towards the C.O., but still refusing to raise his head to make eye contact with him, he said, "My name is Corporal Charles Thomas. Thank you for seeing me, sir."

"Find a chair and have a seat," Stevens responded.

Corporal Thomas looked around the room, and finally found an empty chair against the far wall. He brought the chair forward, close enough to our group to speak with us without infringing upon our space.

Looking at Stevens, I said, "May I?" He nodded, and I stood up and positioned myself in front of Thomas. I imagined myself looking like Perry Mason as he delivered his surprise final interrogation in every episode of the classic television show. First, I introduced myself and Don to the young corporal, who nodded in my direction and then Don's, though he didn't look at us directly, and he said nothing.

Then I began, "Corporal Thomas, why are you willing to come forward now to discuss what took place in the Boom-boom Room?"

Instead of answering my question directly, he said, "Sir, it was fun while it lasted. It wasn't meant to hurt anyone." None of us responded. We just looked at the young corporal and waited for him to go on. Finally he did.

"I'm a prisoner now," he said, "and really, I'm not much different than the detainees held here. The problem is, I don't feel safe."

"Explain that to us," I demanded.

"After we got caught, we knew we'd be interrogated. And we were all actually afraid we were going to be tortured, maybe killed. We've heard about some of the things that have been done to the prisoners here by the OGA men."

Don started to say something, but I stopped him, thinking it would be better for now just to let Thomas talk.

"The thing is," the young corporal said, "I realize my mistakes, and so do the others involved in the whorehouse. We know we deserve punishment, that more than likely we'll be court-martialed, maybe imprisoned, dishonorably discharged. Our lives are ruined."

His body language spoke clearly of both his submission and his contrition: his head was down, and tears welled up in his eyes, only to drop and land on his uniform. His tears were silent, and his shoulders shook convulsively. Nobody else said a word. I was patient. I stood there and waited for him to pull himself together.

After a few minutes he raised his head and almost looked at me, then lowered his head again. I said, "Can you tell us, Corporal Thomas, how you came to be involved in the whorehouse?"

He nodded. "I'm just a corporal, sir. It was the Master Sergeant, and a couple of others, who got me involved. They...well, they gave me money to get things for them."

"What do you mean by 'things?'"

"Beer from the PX, chests of ice from the commissary, and... things. It all started about a year ago. And you have to understand, I'm in the Army, sir, and anything my Master Sergeant said was to be taken as a direct order."

The frightened young corporal sighed deeply and continued, "I knew that what I was doing was wrong, but the Master Sergeant and the others who were involved said they would be watching out for me." His tone shifted at that point, and I could literally feel the corporal's sense of betrayal by his superior. Head still down, he clasped his hands in his lap and sat there. I waited for him to say more, but when nothing more was forthcoming, I said, "Go on, Corporal Thomas."

"The more I did for the guys who ran the Boom-boom Room, the more they had me do, and the more deeply I became involved. But the Master Sergeant and I guess most if not all of the other organizers who started and ran the whorehouse are gone now. Now I get arrested with a few others, and we get blamed for everything."

Stevens, who up until now had been closely watching and listening but had said nothing, spoke up now. "So, Corporal Thomas, clearly you knew some things, but not everything," he said. "Here is what *we* need to know now. We need to know more about how they got the beer, booze, and other things that were provided in the brothel."

"Sir, all I know is I was sent to the PX and the commissary, where I would be given most of the items on my list, with no questions asked. I don't know their source." Corporal Thomas paused, and said, "Look, *everyone* in Abu Ghraib knew about the entertainment room." The C.O. glared in his direction and started to say something, but Thomas quickly corrected himself. He still hadn't looked directly at Stevens, but sometimes a glare is louder than words. In a faltering voice he continued, "Sorry, sir, what I mean is that I just figured everyone knew, though I never saw any evidence that you or any of the lieutenants were involved. I just jumped to a conclusion, and I apologize."

He hesitated, then continued, "Anyway, it was a pretty popular spot. The visitors changed daily and there were too many to keep track of. I mean, it's not as if we really could; no one signed in or out. Nobody kept track of who the visitors were as long as they paid."

"Do you know the names of all of the organizers?" Stevens asked.

"I…um… I just know about the Master Sergeant, but he's been transferred out. There were others, but I really don't know who they were or what or how they participated in the facility."

"Corporal Thomas, are you saying you really do not know the names of all of the people responsible for this criminal enterprise?" It may have seemed that I was hounding him, and maybe I was, but I wanted to leave no stone unturned. I suspected that he was still concealing information, most likely from fear of retribution.

There was a long silence. Thomas again had tears in his eyes, and he still refused to look at any of us. His face had assumed an expression of defeat, and it was as if his mind had gone blank. But I was pretty sure that his mind was anything but blank; no doubt he was focused on the fact that if the C.O. decided to go through with a court martial, it would be a sure conviction, resulting in a dishonorable discharge.

I was now in my Doctor Angel mood, though it wasn't immediately apparent to Thomas. I stood in the center of the room facing him with my hands at my sides as I said to him, "Corporal Thomas, I have a feeling that you're not telling us everything you know. Do so, or I will be happy to call for the MPs and have them take you to one of the cells."

The young man lifted his head, looking past me toward the doorway as if planning to make a run for it. But that was impossible with the two big MPs standing on the other side of the door. Besides, there was no place for him to go in the vast desert surrounding Abu Ghraib prison.

"If that is all you have to say, Corporal, we won't take any more of your time."

For the first time, Corporal Thomas raised his head and looked directly at me; it was also the first time he made actual eye contact. Seeming to realize that he had now reached the point of no return, the corporal spoke softly, almost in a whisper, "Do you want me to try to make a list from memory?" When I didn't answer he went on, "I really don't know what else you would want. If I give you a list, how are you going to stop one of the guys who were involved from coming back and killing me? Or telling someone who's running it now that I ratted them out?"

"From what you're telling us now, it seems we really need to get you out of Abu Ghraib prison and into a protection program," said Stevens. At that, Corporal Thomas' demeanor immediately changed; he appeared to be almost overcome with relief. He asked for a pen and something to write on, which Stevens supplied. Pulling his chair up to the desk at the C.O.'s invitation, Thomas began writing – slowly and shakily at first, and then more rapidly until he was almost scribbling. After a few minutes he was finished, and without a word he handed paper and pen to Stevens.

"That is all, Corporal," the C.O. said, after glancing at the list. "Thank you." Turning to Don, Stevens asked him to get the two MPs back into the room, and Don got up and opened the door. I stood and walked Charles Thomas to the open door where the MPs were waiting, and said to him, "Thank you, Corporal. This will help us make a just decision for you and the others."

That night, Don and I had dinner with Colonel Stevens at his request. The C.O. informed us that he and his men had had a busy day. Several others who had participated in the organizing of the pleasure facilities, but who clearly were not the leaders of the enterprise, had now been arrested. The decision had been made that there would be no trial for these men, no military discharge. Don and I smiled, because this was what we had really wanted. Upon hearing Stevens' announcement, it was as if a major weight had been lifted from us. We felt that we could now relax and enjoy eating and talking about what we'd really come to Abu Ghraib to do: find the seven brothers.

But Stevens didn't seem to be as relaxed and comfortable as we were. We could see that there was still something on his mind, and we didn't have long to wait to find out what it was. Looking at us and slowly running his fingers through his hair, he said, "I'm hoping we have been able to contain this…ah… problem, and that it won't be all over the media."

Immediately I replied, "I understand your concerns, sir, and I want to clarify that this is one of those cases where what takes place in Abu Ghraib prison stays in Abu Ghraib prison. Too much has leaked to the press already. President Bush sent us here to help turn the situation around. Don and I feel that with your help this is going to happen, and when we locate the seven brothers and bring them back to the states, we will have completed what we set out to do. *That's* what we intend to spread all over the media. And we're going to keep working, seven days a week, until we find those seven men."

The C.O. looked somewhat relieved, then said, "Well, the weekend is coming up, and most people take weekends off."

"Sir, as a physician I don't know many who do," I said.

Stevens responded, "What worries me is how you two look right now. You guys look exhausted."

"I must admit I'm beat," I said. "I feel like I've been run over with a steamroller." Glancing at Don, I said to him, "And you look like you don't feel much better than I do."

Don had finished his meal, and he moved his plate to the side to make space for him to place his elbows on the table.

Looking more closely at him, I said, "Are you okay, Don?"

He replied, "Stop looking at me like that. I was just trying to block out all thoughts of this place."

I responded, "I get it, but let's face it, what we've seen here will be with us for the rest of our lives." I knew that would be the case, and there was a lot that I wished I could block out and forget, too. Even so, I was even more convinced than I'd been before that our story had to be told:

the good, the bad, and the nightmarish – but especially the good. It was up to us to ensure that there would be something good to tell.

Working together in this hellhole had deepened my friendship with Don, and I was grateful to have such a wonderful friend by my side. We enjoyed the type of closeness that only occurs among comrades in arms in a war zone or other life-and-death situations, and I wouldn't have traded that bond for anything. But there was another bond that was even deeper, and looking down at the table now, my mind was suddenly flooded with thoughts of home and especially of Terry. I missed her terribly.

I turned my attention back to my dinner companions, and saw that Don was staring at me, unspoken questions filling the space between us. Collecting my scattered thoughts, I raised my glass of iced tea and toasted our little group.

At this, Don emitted a long sigh, leaned back in his chair, and said, "We're all going to make it through this." I wasn't sure exactly what had prompted his apparent burst of optimism, but it was contagious, and I felt a surge of confidence myself. Yes, our situation here was less than ideal, but we still had a job to do, and I felt more certain than ever that we could do it with a little help from our friends, such as Aziz and Hussein, whom I hoped that Don would meet soon. We might be on a plane back home before we knew it. I began to relax, enjoying the break from my anxiety.

Relaxation gave way to drowsiness; indeed, I was so tired that I nearly fell asleep right there in my chair. But I came fully awake when the C.O. pushed his chair back, stood up, and said, "Gentlemen, see you tomorrow." He left without waiting for a response from us.

"I guess it's time for us to turn in, too," I said to Don. "We have another long day tomorrow." He nodded, and I said good night and pushed my chair back. Walking back to my quarters, I had an almost overwhelming desire to scratch my ankles where the sand flies were attacking me. But I resisted the temptation, as I knew it would only make it worse. I walked the fifty yards, kicking up the sand and gravel in a failed attempt to alleviate the itching and the frustration. Not surprisingly, it didn't work.

Once in bed, however, I fell asleep fast and slept deeply. It was one of the few nights when my mind and body seemed detached from the nightmare of Abu Ghraib prison. It wasn't much of a respite, but I would gladly take whatever I could get.

CHAPTER 16

MOVING ON

A lmost before I knew it, the sun was coming through the small window over my bunk. It seemed I had only been asleep for a few minutes, but it had actually been most of the night. My mind had become empty and dull by the time I'd gone to bed the night before, but with the bright sunlight and a good night's rest, it crackled with thoughts of what this day would hold for me. My stress level was almost nil and I was ready to take on whatever the day might bring.

I was fully awake within minutes, focused and feeling competent. Even though I personally felt hollow and cold at what was taking place in Abu Ghraib prison, I wasn't ready to accept it. I thought to myself, *I am here now, I have a job to do and I'm going to make the most of it.*

When I pressed my lips together, they were dry and cracked. But that didn't matter; I was in full "Crazy Texan" mode, and I knew that I needed to get out of this bunk and get to work. So I got up, slid on my cowboy boots, and placed an eight-inch stiletto in the left boot and my .45 caliber pistol in my right boot. I put my Glock 43 in my inside-the-pants holster as well. *That's what that space is for in the small of your back,* I thought to myself. Indeed, my Glock fit perfectly there and was quite comfortable. I was all gunned up for action should it happen.

As I exited the building, the intensity of the sun shining down and reflecting off of everything almost blinded me. I could also tell that the ambient temperature was already well over 100 degrees – another typical day in Iraq.

I walked to the officers' mess hall, where I met Don North. Soon after that, my new friends, Aziz and Hussein, showed up, and I happily introduced them to Don. "These two are going to be our new interpreters," I told him.

"I'm glad to hear it," Don said. "I was getting tired of putting up with that joker that the military sent us."

The four of us shared an early breakfast together on a plank table, and then it was time to begin our rounds. Maybe today would be the day that we would find the seven brothers. We began by walking into the holding area and surveying a new part of the minimum security area. As usual, the C.O. had assigned two MPs to be with us. Even though Aziz and Hussein and I had made a round the other day without the benefit of the MPs, I was grateful for their presence now. Don and I had been hearing rumors of escalating threats from the few remaining OGA men. and now that the Boom-boom Room had been busted and closed down, God only knew what other types of dangers we might face.

As we entered the first cell block, we encountered three members of the OGA team; it was as if they had been waiting for us. I immediately saw that it was the same three with whom I'd had the confrontation in the dining area outside the commissary. My understanding had been that they'd been ordered to pack their things and go back to Baghdad, but either the order hadn't been issued, or they were defying it. Upon seeing them still here, my uncharacteristic anxiety and paranoia set in. So much for a stress-free day.

The two MPs who were following at our six were proactive and wasted no time. They immediately stepped forward and took positions on the right and left side of the OGA men. But all I could think was that I didn't want to be today's story on the Internet or TV. I wasn't the only person who was uneasy; Aziz exhaled rather loudly and ran his hands through his hair, a clear expression of his anxiety.

Now, all three of the arrogant OGA men were standing directly in front of me. There was the hulk who was obviously the leader, and then there were the other two, whom I immediately decided to christen "Dumb and Dumber." Granted, I couldn't quite decide which one was Dumb and which was Dumber, but it didn't really matter; let's just say that neither appeared to be MENSA material. As the leader stepped forward, I had a sudden visceral reaction to his movement. This guy looked to be six feet and 200 pounds to my five-seven and 160 pounds. He had a large cheeky grin on his fleshy face, and was missing a couple of teeth. On the upside, he had a huge gut, and it didn't appear that he worked out too hard – not exactly a perfect specimen of physical fitness.

He folded his arms across his chest, and his body language was saying, "I own you." I did not see a weapon on him, but that didn't mean there wasn't one. After all, *I* was packing multiple weapons, and he could just as well be armed too.

He said, "You disrespected the uniform. You're not part of the military, and we don't have to take orders from you."

With this he unfolded his arms and dropped them to his side. In response to his textbook offensive posture, I had taken a half step to his right. I firmly set my left foot and shifted my weight to my left leg. If he took one more step forward, he was going to get a lesson on the intricacies of Article 128 of the UCMJ, the Uniform Code of Military Justice.

He did take that step forward, and I could smell his sweat and see his five o'clock shadow. I was now in the perfect position. Due to a previous trauma, my right hip and femur had been replaced with titanium. With my weight on the left leg I drove my right foot upward with all the force I could muster, and my bionic titanium leg struck him where no man wishes to be struck.

His reaction was to bend over and reach down with both hands in a protective yet painful stance. In that bent-over position he was very vulnerable, and my right knee came up and struck him solidly on the jaw. He toppled over, and you could hear the sound of his skull hitting the sandstone. I immediately pressed my boot on his neck, with my heel compressing his windpipe, then I gradually eased up so he could take a breath. Dumb and Dumber were obviously in shock at seeing that their leader was down for the count, and the MPs quickly and easily subdued them.

I then applied more pressure to my essentially supine adversary, knowing that I could rupture his trachea and he'd be dead. That, of course, was not my intent, but he didn't know that. I just wanted to send him a message. I pulled my pistol from my boot and pointed it at his head, then slowly decreased the pressure on his trachea and finally lifted my boot from his neck. He began coughing and sucking in air, then started to move again. While he was still down, I told Aziz to frisk him quickly and remove any weapons, and then to back away and let him stand.

I said to him, "Don't you dare lie to me again. You are going to be on the next flight out of Abu Ghraib to Baghdad and then back to the United States for trial. I may not be in uniform, but you just assaulted a superior. Originally, I didn't want to have you arrested, but now you *are* under arrest. It seems you don't have the brains to understand when you've been given a chance, and you can't seem to get a grip on yourself."

My anger was beginning to cool, and I holstered my weapon and told the MPs to cuff all three of the men. I added that they were then to be placed in a confined area to await the next flight to Baghdad, and were to be escorted in chains onto that flight.

One of the OGA men who'd had better sense than to challenge me – I think it was Dumber, but it might have been Dumb – said, "If you don't mind me asking, in what capacity are you here?"

Now that they were under arrest, I felt obligated to let them know the mistake they'd made and with whom they were dealing. I opened my vest, removed The Letter from the inner pocket, and, glaring directly at the leader, I said, "I assume you can read." He glared back and said nothing. I took a step closer, held the document up so that all three could read it, and waited for their response.

Their expressions quickly changed, with Dumb and Dumber nodding their heads almost simultaneously. Their leader was a bit more subtle – no head nodding, but his eyes widened just a little and his face turned red, assuring The Letter conferred, had had the desired effect, not only establishing my legitimacy and most importantly, my loyalty to my country, but also the authority under which I was here.

The faces of all three men were now taut with fear. Finally the leader spoke to me, and all of his arrogance and bluster were gone. I could see how resigned he was now feeling. Then the uneasiness in his face disappeared and he let out a long breath, as if to relieve his tension. The man was plainly exhausted, but I didn't feel much compassion for him.

I couldn't help thinking of this small win in terms of the popular notion of ancient Roman audiences in the Colosseum deciding the fate of gladiators with a simple thumbs-up or thumbs-down gesture. (Historians say that this belief is inaccurate, but it has been firmly entrenched in popular culture, so it was good enough for me now as I was dealing with these three jokers.) Flush with my firmly re-established power and authority, I raised my right hand in the thumbs-up position and grinned. I could see a look of relief and even the faint beginnings of smiles on the faces of all three of the OGA men, including the man on whose neck my boot had been resting such a short while ago. I'm pretty sure that they were thankful to finally be freed from a twisted endeavor in which they no longer believed. But if this threesome had imagined that I might now be willing to accept them as allies, or that I would at least recommend leniency for them, they were quickly disabused of that idea when, after a few seconds, I rotated my wrist and turned thumbs-down.

I turned toward the MPs and said, "Take them away." The MPs nodded their heads, and the OGA men grew deathly quiet.

Now my thoughts were bouncing like a tennis ball rattling around in my skull. Anything could happen in Abu Ghraib prison, and I had to be on guard and prepared. And I still had many questions, but the most important ones right now were this: were the seven brothers still alive, and if so, where exactly were they?

I took a deep breath, realizing that the worry I had been carrying about the OGA team ever since our arrival was gone. All of my attention was now focused on Don's and my primary mission. As the MPs escorted the three OGA men away, I took one last dig and wished them a good flight. Then I put one foot in front of the other, and at a rather jolly fast pace moved down the corridor between the cells, with Don, Aziz, and Hussein hurrying to keep up with me. I had things to do. True, we no longer had our MP escorts, as they were now busy with their OGA detainees, but for some reason I no longer felt any anxiety about that.

As we walked briskly along the corridor, I wondered to myself why those interrogators seemed to be so obsessed with killing, even to the point of feeling eagerness for their next victim. Were they psychotic? I didn't know. Narcissistic sociopaths? Most definitely. But the result I'd achieved today – actually witnessing some of these tormenters being taken into custody by the military police – made me feel good. I felt sure that regardless of what they faced before a stateside court martial, they wouldn't be back.

I suddenly realized that nobody had spoken for a while, so I slowed down, looking around at my companions. There was an expression of shock on Aziz and Hussein's faces. My easygoing partner, Don, who had been so quiet and observant throughout this entire exchange that we had almost forgotten he was there, was the first to break our silence. He said, "Maybe now we'll stop seeing military guys and contractors around here who are addicted to torture and killing."

"I hope so," I replied, "but at this point I'm not taking anything for granted."

"It was almost inevitable, when you think of it," Don continued. "For people who were already predisposed to that kind of behavior, this was the perfect setup. They had the means. They had the permission.

And for some of them, torture and killing became their drug of choice. That's even how they talked about it in the mess hall. These guys are totally lacking in anything resembling a conscience."

"You nailed it," I said. "And it seems pretty obvious that they already considered the detainees in Abu Ghraib prison to be enemies, bad people. From that point it was easy to dehumanize the detainees and justify whatever they did to the prisoners. That's how it always works."

"Right," Don said, and then after a moment he added, "And I know we've talked about this before, but it really bothers me that most of the prisoners aren't even members of the Ba'athist party. They're completely apolitical… just a bunch of poor locals who were at the wrong place at the wrong time, getting caught in the crossfire of tribal politics."

Aziz and Hussein, who were well acquainted with this issue, joined in the conversation. They spoke again about the fact that many of the detainees had been thrown in prison simply because a local tribal leader or clan member had falsely accused them of some crime or misdeed, either as retaliation for some imagined wrong, or as a means to continue a longstanding tribal feud. Then there was the fact that the Americans paid a substantial fee to those who supplied information about potential threats. And the accusers were perfectly happy to let the American Coalition forces do their dirty work for them while they sat back collecting their bounties from U.S. forces, and basking in the satisfaction of having dispatched their "enemies" so effortlessly.

"Yet as you were saying when we were talking about this before, Doc, most of the American military and the interrogators have been clueless about the role tribal feuds play in this region," Don said. "That point has really been driven home for me since we've been here. I think some of the military members stationed here do care about things like cultural and historical context, though it's been a pretty steep learning curve for them. But apparently there are a lot of others here who just can't be bothered."

"That is the truth!" Aziz said, and Hussein nodded his agreement.

Fortunately for my nerves, the rest of the day was relatively uneventful. Unfortunately, we still didn't make any real progress on finding the seven brothers, but at least I had another deeply restful night's sleep, and given the circumstances, I took that as another small win.

I had scheduled another morning meeting with the C.O. I wanted to check in with him and let him know about our progress, or lack thereof, as well as to find out about any fallout from the Boom-boom Room bust and my confrontations with the OGA trio. The C.O. said he wouldn't be able to join me for breakfast, but he asked me to stop by his office afterward. I'd told him that I wanted to bring Don North along, as well as two Yazidi interpreters I had met, Aziz and Hussein, and he said that was fine. So after we ate, Don, Aziz, Hussein, and I walked over to Colonel Stevens' office, where we found the commander sitting at his desk. He was sweeping his hands across the top of the desk as if looking for something. Hesitating for a few seconds, he patted his chest and finally reached into his side pocket.

The four of us stood there watching this, waiting for him to acknowledge our presence. Finally, Stevens touched his face, apparently realizing that his glasses were sitting on the bridge of his nose. He looked up at us and said, "These glasses are so light you can't even feel them when you're wearing them." We laughed.

I then said to him, "Colonel Stevens, do you know Aziz and Hussein?" I motioned my two new friends to step forward.

The C.O. replied, "Ah, yes. I've seen you guys around here, but we haven't been formally introduced." As he stood up and shook hands with them, he added, "I understand that you two are working as interpreters here in the prison."

Aziz and Hussein nodded, and I said, "Yes, and Don and I plan to have them accompany us on our rounds from now on, so you can tell that other guy who's been interpreting for us that he is officially relieved of duty, as far as we're concerned."

Stevens chuckled and said, "I will do that." He then motioned for all of us to sit down, and as we did he said, "I haven't had much of a chance to talk to you about this matter, but I assume you've still had no luck in finding those 'seven brothers?'"

"Not yet," I replied.

"So, if you don't mind me asking, why are you visiting with me today?"

I said, "We just wanted to touch bases with you about our progress, or more accurately our lack of progress so far. And I'll be honest: I wanted to see if there have been any repercussions from the Boom-boom Room bust, and from my latest encounter with the Three Stooges from the OGA."

Don spoke up. "We also want to thank you for what you have already done, and to ask you where we should meet our MP escorts for today?"

"First things first," Stevens said, picking up his desk telephone and giving some orders. He then turned to us and said, "The MPs will be here in a few minutes."

We nodded, and then the C.O. said, "Regarding your questions about repercussions, Doc, there hasn't been anything significant from the brothel op, not yet anyway, but you need to watch your back re the OGA. I have a feeling you probably knew that already."

"I've been hearing some whispers about escalated threats," I said. "That's why I'm glad we are going to have the MPs with us." I didn't mention that Aziz and Hussein and I had taken a short tour of the facilities the previous day without protection, and fortunately my new friends didn't mention it either. In retrospect, walking the halls of the prison without police protection seemed foolhardy.

The C.O. said, "I want to make sure you have all of the protection you need for the duration of your stay. Now, on to another subject. You probably know that we were shelled again late last night. Fortunately it was only for a few minutes, and the mortar rounds fell short of any important targets."

That was news to me. "I was so tired I must have slept through it," I said.

"I didn't hear anything, either," Don admitted.

"You guys slept through a mortar attack? You've got to be kidding me!"

"We wouldn't kid about something like that, sir," I said. "I really did sleep through it, and apparently Don did too. We must be adapting to this place. I don't know if that's a good thing or not."

"Believe me, it's not," Stevens said. "You *don't* want to adapt to this place. You want to get out of here alive."

"Hopefully with the seven brothers," Don said.

"Of course," said Stevens.

"Did you lose anyone in last night's attack?" I asked, in full physician mode now. "Any of the detainees injured?"

"No, as I indicated, most of the mortar shells fell short of the wall," he replied. I relaxed a little.

"What are your plans for today?" Stevens asked next.

"We're going to the main courtyard where the majority of the paddocks are," I replied. "Then we'll continue on to the inner secondary courtyard, where I understand more prisoners are being held, who are more independent and living on their own."

The C.O. said, "That's true. There is even a well in that area. You haven't ventured that far into the facility yet?"

"No sir," I replied. "This place is endless."

"Well, not quite, though I can see how it seems that way," Stevens replied. "It's huge, all right, and the countless rooms, cells, passageways and so forth have made it very difficult for us to maintain control. As you probably know, that's what made it possible for the OGA to get away with everything they've been doing, hidden from the regular Army and administration. Not to mention the Boom-boom Room…"

"That's behind us, sir. At least this is what I have been led to believe, and I sure hope so. The OGA guys are presumably on their way out for good, and I think we can be reasonably certain that the Boom-boom Room has been closed down, for now, anyway. But as we've discussed, there needs to be an ongoing internal investigation, which I assume is being done."

As I said this, I thought about Marvin Zindler and his involvement in the real-life story that had become a popular stage play and later a movie, *The Best Little Whorehouse in Texas*. Back in the early 1970s, Marvin had been responsible for shutting down a couple of houses of ill repute in some small Texas towns near Houston. The most famous of these houses was known as the Chicken Ranch, located in LaGrange, but its sister institution, operating out of the former Wagon Wheel Motel in Sealy, was also shut down. Marvin's dogged reporting about these beloved institutions (well, they were beloved by several generations of red-blooded Texas boys, anyway) drew an enormous amount of attention, and one thing led to another, and before long a couple of the worst-kept secrets in Texas had become a full-blown scandal. The authorities had no choice but to shut the whorehouses down because, after all, prostitution is illegal in Texas. Thus ended more than 100 years of tradition, at least in the case of the Chicken Ranch, and there are people who, half a century after the shutdown, have still not forgiven Marvin Zindler for this.

Feeling that the C.O. needed to lighten up a little, I broached the subject of the Texas whorehouse saga, wondering if he was at all familiar with the story, either the real one or the fictionalized version. My words had the effect I'd hoped for; he began laughing and said, "Oh, yes. I saw the stage play many years ago, and later I saw the movie with Dolly Parton and Dom DeLuise. I was laughing so hard I missed parts of it and had to go see it again."

Never one to miss an opportunity to promote one of my books, I told him about my book, *White Knight in Blue Shades*, the authorized biography of Marvin Zindler. "There's a whole section in there about the 'Whorehouse' story," I said. "The book has sold thousands of copies over the years, and I'm told it's currently out of print, but there are still a few copies available. It would be my pleasure to send you one."

"I'd like that," Stevens said, and he and Don and I continued to chuckle about the Texas whorehouse saga. Then we noticed that the MPs had arrived. Along with Aziz and Hussein, they were standing there, straight-faced, not having a clue as to what we were talking about. Aziz and Hussein looked particularly puzzled.

I turned to my two Yazidi friends and said, "While we're doing our rounds through the prison, I'll explain more about what the C.O. and I were just discussing." They nodded, still looking a bit uncertain, and to tell the truth I wondered if these two men would appreciate that whole story the way we Westerners did. Perhaps they might find it more offensive than humorous. But since they were curious, and they were my friends, I would tell them anyway, choosing my words carefully and gauging their reactions.

Then Don spoke up. Addressing the MPs, he said, "Today we're going to want to go through the main courtyard and into the secondary courtyard in the inner depths of the prison." They looked at me as if for confirmation, and I nodded. I was anxious to get started.

As we began our rounds along one of the impossibly long corridors, I carefully told Aziz and Hussein the story about the "best little whorehouse in Texas." They didn't seem offended, and I was relieved about that, but they didn't seem to find it all that amusing either. Cultural differences, I guess.

Our conversation was cut short when we saw one of the inmate trustees excitedly approaching us. He stopped and stood silent before us for a moment, then suddenly broke into a machine-gun flow of unintelligible words that he seemed to believe would be of great worth to us. He definitely had something to tell us, but he was clearly having trouble getting his thoughts together. Where he was eager, I found myself growing impatient, which, in my defense, was understandable after days of too many false leads and not enough good information. I couldn't help but wonder where this was going. But then as Aziz finally stepped up to the prisoner, and none too soon, my frustration faded, replaced by a twinge of compassion and something approaching optimism.

Aziz greeted the man, who stood there wiping his bald head with his forearm. He had the shoulders of a man who had endured heavy toil for decades, and the gut of one who had been rewarded for his effort. He arched his back, making himself look a few inches taller than he had appeared at first. His voice was husky, sounding as if it had been ground down by decades in the unforgiving desert and then filtered through to my ears. I was glad to have my interpreters there to tell me what the man was saying.

He started off by saying that being placed in Abu Ghraib prison was God's punishment, but now he was able to do something good. Then he put his hands over his eyes as if he were going to cry.

Don and I looked at him, and I removed my dark black-rimmed glasses. With a big smile, I told Aziz, "Tell him that he is a man with a good heart, and Allah will bless him for it."

I suddenly felt an almost irrational surge of the optimism I had barely tasted a few moments earlier. Don, as if reading my mind, looked at me and said, "This could be the break we've been looking for."

"Maybe," I said. "We'll see." I didn't want to get too carried away with hope, but this really might be our big breakthrough. That thought gave me an extra burst of energy and enthusiasm, even though some part of me was acutely aware that I was getting ahead of myself. After all, we still needed to locate the seven brothers, or everything that Don and I had been through would have been for nothing. (Well, nothing if you don't count breaking up a criminal operation and saving some sex trafficking victims from a life of exploitation, not to mention helping to rid the prison of the brutal OGA interrogators.)

While all of these thoughts were racing through my head, Aziz had continued to quietly chat with the man who had approached us. He said his name was Habib. Aziz told me that he had been trying to establish a rapport with Habib, finding out a little bit about him and offering him what he hoped was helpful advice, but not trying to push for information at this point. Habib had one big concern, according to Aziz: "When will I get out? When will I be released from Abu Ghraib prison and returned to my family?"

Of course, none of us could answer that. But I told Aziz to tell him we would get that information for him and that if Habib helped us, we would try very hard to secure his release date. Aziz conveyed the message, and the man nodded, and then began talking again, this time more rapidly. I could only understand a few words, but Aziz soon filled in the blanks for me.

"He says he is getting too little food, too little sleep. And he is made to work eighteen hours a day."

"Tell him that we can help him with those things now," I said. "Let him know that we will do what we can about the food and work and sleep situation, and that he does not have to worry about being tortured or killed." As Aziz repeated that message, a look of relief came over Habib's face, and he smiled slightly, though his eyes were still filled with fear and uncertainty.

It was a good beginning, I thought. We needed to get Habib's confidence and hear what he was so anxious to tell us.

CHAPTER 17

LIBRARY OF HORRORS

Aziz continued to interpret for me as I asked Habib more questions about his life in Abu Ghraib prison. I told Habib that the more details we had, the better the chances that we would be able to help him. It was clear that Habib could see that I was genuinely interested in his well-being, which was almost certainly a new experience for him here. He told us that according to what he had been told at the time of his sentencing, he should have been released months ago, yet he was still here. This made me even more determined to help him.

After a few more questions about conditions within Abu Ghraib prison, I began asking Habib about his family and his life outside the prison – a life to which he would soon be returning if we had anything to do with it. I could see Habib growing a little more at ease as we spoke.

This was progress, I felt, but as for getting information regarding the whereabouts of the seven brothers, we were getting nowhere. It was time to move things up a notch, so I told Aziz to ask Habib if there was anything else he wanted to tell us. I didn't want to be too pushy and risk intimidating this prisoner who had already suffered so much and was justifiably wary of other people's motives, but I was getting impatient again. After all, Habib had sought us out, and had initially seemed very eager to tell us... *something*. What was it?

Adding to my impatience was my physical discomfort. We hadn't been here in the bowels of the prison complex for very long, but already I was feeling the effects of the extreme heat, the infernal sand flies, and near-dehydration, despite taking frequent drinks from my water bottle. I wanted to help Habib, of course, but I also wanted to get some usable information so we could either follow any leads that he might provide, or alternatively, we could proceed with other avenues of inquiry. Either way, we would try to facilitate his release, but we also had a greater agenda and couldn't afford to waste time.

After Aziz conveyed my question about whether there was anything else he wanted to tell us, Habib considered it for a few moments. Then he said slowly, as if choosing his words carefully, that his passions were videography and photography. This statement didn't seem terribly earth-shattering on the surface, but I immediately thought of what we had heard about Saddam supposedly having had video recordings made of countless cruelties to Abu Ghraib prisoners, and I thought about the rumored secret stash of videos. I looked over at Don and could see that he had grasped the connection as well. Don and I were all ears now, and our interest heightened when Habib added that he had a secret he wanted to tell us, but he needed another reassurance that we would go to the prison administration and see about his release.

Once again, through Aziz, both Don and I reassured him that we would do everything possible to help him. Though Habib nodded, there was still some reticence. I was convinced, however, that his mention of his love for videography and photography was somehow related to that "secret" he was harboring – and almost certainly to the buzz about Saddam's obsession with videotaping the brutalities he had ordered – so I decided that it was best to let Habib take his time getting to the point.

I asked him what he photographed, and he replied that before he came to Abu Ghraib prison, he had taken the usual family photos, weddings, events to commemorate the birth of a new child, school events, and so forth. "He says that that the photos and videos he shot were nothing of great importance until he came to Abu Ghraib," said Aziz. "Since he knew about photography and videography, he was told that if he did this type of work within the prison he would get 'special treatment.'"

I asked if that had happened, and Habib said "Yes" – at least regarding the first part. He explained that he had agreed to do what was asked of him, but soon found that the "special treatment" he had been promised wasn't all that special. "He says that he finally figured out that his captors' ideas of 'special treatment' were that they would let him live, with all of his bodily parts intact," Aziz told us.

I asked, "What did they want you to do here? How did they want you to put your skills to use?"

Habib replied that he was told his job would be to record certain things.

Now it seemed that we were getting somewhere. I asked him the next logical question: "What did they want you to record?"

Again the hesitation. And then Habib looked directly at me and, with Aziz continuing to translate, he said, "Doctor, I do trust you. I hear good things about what you did here, and I believe that what you told me is true. I trust that if I tell you my secret you will go to the administration and try to secure my release."

He paused, and after I had reassured him once again he continued, "First you must know that I am not a soldier. I am just a civilian. And I did not participate in any of the things Saddam Hussein and his two sons did, or told others to do. I only did the recordings so I could receive the special treatment they promised me."

It was obvious that this was difficult for him, and I tried not to let my mind race ahead to the horrors that I imagined he was preparing to describe. I put out my hand to him, and then realized that it was probably not the right thing to do, so I placed my hand across my heart in the classic Middle Eastern gesture of loyalty and trust. Habib relaxed again, and even smiled at me. "I do trust you, Doctor," he said again. I nodded and smiled back, waiting.

I didn't have long to wait. In a rush of words flowing so rapidly that it was a challenge for Aziz to keep up with the interpretation, Habib continued, "My job at Abu Ghraib prison was to take videos of all of the atrocities that have taken place here under the orders of Saddam." His smile disappeared, and tears welled up in his eyes.

"And what were some of those atrocities?" I asked gently. "Take as much time as you need to tell us. We know this is difficult for you, and we appreciate any information that you can give us."

Habib took a deep breath and said, "I am sure you heard rumors that men were hanged nearly every day. Those rumors were true, and I had to make videos of those hangings. I am also sure that you have seen the wall that was stained with blood, and you probably heard that prisoners were made to stand up against the wall so they could be used as target practice. Those stories are also true, and I was required to make videos of those shootings. And perhaps you have seen the room where you were told they did medical experiments. Also true, and I was made to shoot video and record audio of the horrible experiments. Then there were other rooms where body parts were removed, hands were amputated, and some prisoners even had their eyes burned out with a hot iron. Some had their tongues cut out for speaking against Saddam."

The tears were falling in earnest now as he added, "I had to record all of it."

I could see fear as well as sadness in his eyes, and my heart ached for him as he said again, "Remember, I did not support any of these terrible things. My job was to do audio and visual whenever I was told to do so. The things that I saw will haunt me for the rest of my life."

Eschewing formalities and cultural differences, I put my arm around his shoulders and said, "We know, and everyone to whom you tell your story will know, that you are not responsible for Saddam Hussein's cruelty."

He nodded and said, "I know that is true, but some part of me feels that maybe I should have tried to stop it anyway. I know it is not rational, and that if I had tried to stop these things from happening, or had even spoken out against them, I most likely would have been tortured or killed myself. But I still wonder if I could have or should have done *something.*"

"You're doing something now," I said to him. "By telling us, you will help ensure that Saddam's victims did not suffer in vain."

Habib looked at me with an expression that clearly conveyed that he not only wanted, but desperately *needed*, to believe me. Then he lowered his head as more tears came.

Slowly I continued, "Now I have a question for you, Habib, and if you can answer it you will be helping us even more. Do you know if the videotapes and audio recordings still exist? And if so, do you know where they are?"

Habib, now drying his eyes, lifted up his head. His eyes came into contact with mine again as he said, "There is a hidden room in this prison in which all the records are kept – including the videotapes and the audio recordings."

"And do you know for certain that the videotapes and recordings are still in that room?" I asked.

Habib nodded.

"Where is the room?" I asked. "Can you take us there?"

Habib nodded and said yes, but then suddenly looked as if he might be reconsidering his reply. I forced myself to maintain my air of patience as I turned my attention away from Habib and looked around at the others in our small group.

The two MPs were steadfast and silent as usual, betraying no emotion. But I could see that Aziz and Hussein were appalled by these latest revelations, which was understandable because even though they too had been aware of the talk about the existence of videos, they hadn't put much stock in it. On the other hand, and despite the horror of the events that Habib had described to us, I was feeling a combination of relief and excitement, and I could tell that Don was too. Here was the promise of a solid lead at last. Finally we were on the verge of something more than rumors, in the form of an entire audio-visual library of evidence that was located, conveniently enough, right there in the prison. This was assuming that what Habib told us was true, of course, and at this point we had little reason to doubt him.

I turned my attention back to Habib, and was on the verge of asking him again if he would take us to the hidden video library when he said, "Doctor, I am telling you this not just because I want you to help me leave this prison, but because this information will be needed when Saddam Hussein and his sons are captured and brought to trial."

I told him, "Saddam Hussein was captured last December by U.S. soldiers, after spending months in hiding like the coward he is. The soldiers finally found him huddled like an animal in a six-foot-deep 'spider hole' a few miles outside of Tikrit. He was dirty and unkempt, with matted hair and a bushy beard. They dragged him out, but he did not resist arrest."

As Aziz interpreted my words, Habib's eyes widened, and he began to smile. I continued, "Saddam will eventually be brought to trial, though I can't tell you when that will happen. Regardless of whether or not the information you have is used at his trial, it will likely be very helpful in telling the full story of his crimes against humanity."

As it turned out, Saddam was eventually brought to trial for human rights violations, and in fact he underwent two trials. One was for violations he had committed back in 1982 following a failed attempt on his life, and the other was for genocide that took place during a military campaign against the Kurds in 1988. Neither one was for the brutalities committed on prisoners at Abu Ghraib, but we had no way of knowing that at the time. It was reasonable for us to speculate that the amputation and torture tapes might be the focus of a future trial. In any case, we knew we needed to follow every lead we were given, and it seemed obvious that Habib was providing a valuable lead for us.

"What about his sons, Qusay and Uday?" Habib wanted to know. "In many ways, they were even worse than their father." He shuddered, no doubt at the thought of some of the atrocious acts that had been ordered by one or the other of the sons, and that Habib had been compelled to record.

"There will be no trial for the sons," I said, "because they were killed by American forces in July of last year."

Habib's eyes widened even more, and he broke out into a big grin as he said, "You can see that we prisoners do not always get news about what is happening. I think we are kept in the dark about these things so we will stay afraid."

"I think you are right about that," I said. "But you don't need to be afraid of Saddam or of his sons anymore. Now, can you take us to the room where all of those tapes are being kept?"

Habib said, "Yes, I can take you there, but…" He hesitated, then looked around the group, and then looked back at me before he continued, "But Doctor, only you and Mr. North and Aziz and Hussein can come with me. No one else."

It was clear that Habib did not trust the MPs. I shot a quick glance at them, but their faces remained expressionless as Aziz translated Habib's words to us. When he was finished, however, one of the MPs said to me, "We're under orders to remain with you at all times, Doctor."

"I appreciate that," I said. "But I think it's important to honor Habib's wishes on this. He poses no threat, and the information he says he has will be very helpful to all of us. It's best that you two remain here, and we'll be as quick as possible. More than likely the C.O. will never find out, but needless to say, if word of this gets to him, I'll cover for you. This is all on me, not you guys. I take full responsibility." With some reluctance, the two MPs consented.

Turning back to Habib, I lifted my right hand and placed it over my heart, then made a slight bow and said to him, "Agreed. The five of us will go, and no one else."

Habib relaxed, and then said, "Good. Let us go now."

We began walking, and Habib took us through musty-smelling corridors that seemed to wind on endlessly, until we came to an area in the prison that I'd not yet visited. Habib led us to a cell block that contained two rows of empty cells, and at the end of that very long cell block there was an entrance to a large area that appeared to be an administrative office suite of some sort. "We are almost there now," Habib said, and we followed him into the suite. The place was nearly bare of furniture, except for a few ancient desks and chairs, and there were no pieces of office equipment or supplies that I could see. But there were electrical outlets, and a few lights were on.

As we followed Habib further through that stark suite, I was beginning to feel a little uneasy. We were very deep into the prison now, and nobody, not even the MPs who had been tasked with guarding Don and me, knew where we were. *But we have to trust Habib,* I thought.

We walked some more until finally, approaching a wobbly old desk that was flush against a wall in a corner of one of the rooms, Habib gave us the sign to halt. He dragged the desk a couple of feet from the wall, creating a loud and extraordinarily unpleasant racket that made me wince. "I hope nobody heard that," I said. "I mean, since this is all supposed to be so secret."

Aziz told Habib what I had said, and Habib smiled grimly, saying, "Do not worry. There is nobody back in this area to hear us." I found his reply both comforting and disturbing.

Habib reached down to a pair of metal rings that had been concealed beneath the desk. Pulling on the rings, he opened a trap door that revealed a stairway leading into murky depths – which, of course, did nothing to abate my unease. But we had come this far, so I nodded to Don, Aziz, and Hussein, who were also looking less than enthusiastic. Using the flashlights in Don's and my cell phones to guide us, we followed Habib down into the depths. Once we reached the bottom of the stairs, Habib, with the help from the lights in our phones, located the string attached to a single light bulb in the ceiling.

He pulled the string.

The light came on.

And there it was.

Though the light was barely adequate, and the bulb was flickering as if on the verge of going out, it was enough to illuminate a large room with shelves and metal file cabinets, as well as some old but presumably still usable audio-visual equipment. What caught our attention were the shelves, for they were lined with what appeared to be thousands of audio-visual tapes, all in cases that were labeled as to their contents.

Habib said, "It is all here, Doctor. I have told no one but you and your companions about this place, and you are the first outsiders to see it."

As our group slowly made its way along the first row of shelves, with Habib in the lead, we could see that the tapes were numbered and dated. I could read the numbers on the labels, but not the other information, which was rendered in Arabic script. Habib told us that it appeared the tapes were filed alphabetically by name, which I wouldn't have been able to tell one way or the other, since I had yet to master the art of reading Arabic. I was glad that we had Habib, Aziz, and Hussein to guide us. I was also glad that both Don and I had a list containing the names of the seven brothers, in both the Latin and Arabic alphabets, the latter courtesy of our two Yazidi friends. Our lists also included the approximate dates of the men's amputations.

I quickly took out my wallet and pulled out my list. Even with the assistance of our Arabic-literate companions, finding the tapes I was looking for would have been an arduous task indeed had it not been for the fact that the library was apparently so well organized. Thank goodness for small favors. Showing the list to Aziz, I told him to ask Habib to look for any video material related to the brothers. Aziz showed the list to Habib, pointed to the names, and explained what we wanted. Habib nodded and said, "I will certainly try."

The light bulb was still flickering madly, and it suddenly dimmed, a clear warning that the room would soon be plunged into darkness. Thankful for the light provided by our phones, Don and I, along with and Aziz and Hussein, followed Habib as he began the search. After a few minutes Habib suddenly stopped and pulled out a tape. He studied it for a moment, then handed it to me. I strained my eyes to look at the label, which, of course, did not make the Arabic script any easier for me to decipher. But Habib, through Aziz, explained that the tape I was holding was a videotape, including audio, that showed the amputation of the right hand of one of the men on our list.

I was now shaking, and I'm pretty sure Don was too.

We continued our slow and methodical search, and thanks to Habib, recovered several more tapes with names and dates that matched our list. After another hour or so, the moribund light bulb finally gave up the ghost, and the room was pitch-dark except for the lights in our phones. I worried that our batteries would run down, and we had no way to charge them down here.

I said to the group, "I think we'd better head back up before we lose what light we have. I'm pretty sure that the tapes we did find are sufficient to prove that the seven brothers were here in the prison, and unless I miss my guess, they're still here. And more than that, these tapes, and the thousands of others in this room, are further proof of Saddam's crimes. I imagine they'll be very useful. Meanwhile, the tapes we have will help Don with his documentary."

I got no argument from the others about leaving this dark and stuffy chamber. I put the tapes in my backpack, and we headed back up and out of the darkness, carefully closing the hatch and replacing the desk over it.

Then I turned to Aziz and Hussein and said, "Needless to say, you are not to speak of this to anyone. The information will have to be released at the proper time. But I'm keeping these tapes related to the seven brothers, and Don will be using them for his documentary to help tell their story to the world. And please convey this to Habib too."

Aziz interpreted my words to Habib, who nodded and responded, "Of course. I have been keeping it a secret for a long time. I will rely on you to decide when to release it to the proper authorities. And Doctor, you will see about getting me out of Abu Ghraib prison, yes?"

"I promised you that I'd do that, and I intend to keep my promise," I replied. Habib beamed as Aziz translated my words.

After that, with Habib leading the way, we made the trek back through the suite of desolate rooms, then traversed the long cell block, and retraced our steps until at long last we reached the area where we had left the two MPs. They were still waiting there, and I detected a look of relief on both of their faces when we emerged.

Then it was time to say farewell to Habib, thank him once again, and offer a final reassurance that his case would be a top priority for me. Through Aziz, I had obtained Habib's full name and the details of his sentencing – everything I would presumably need in order to facilitate his release. There were tears in his eyes as we left him, and while I felt sad on his behalf, I was happy that I was going to be able to help him, and downright jubilant about the evidence we now had, thanks to him. I confess that on the last leg of our journey back to the point where we'd begun our tour that morning, I came as close to skipping as a sixty-something physician could come while still maintaining a modicum of dignity.

Finally, parting ways with Don, Aziz, Hussein, and the MPs, I returned to my quarters to rest a while before I went to see the C.O. Once I was alone in my bunk, I put the audio-visual materials in a separate bag with other personal items and locked it.

I lay back on my bed to rest and possibly even take a brief nap, but after about twenty minutes I sat up. I was too pumped to rest, much less sleep. I needed to see the C.O., and soon.

As I walked towards Colonel Stevens' office, the smoke from the prison's burn pits was particularly strong. The smell from the pits at Camp Cropper was bad enough, but this was even worse. The smoke filled my lungs, choking me with its nauseating odor. *How could anyone live under these conditions?* I thought. And yet thousands had, day after day, week after week, month after month, year after year. I couldn't wait to get far away from this hellhole as quickly as possible.

As I approached the administrative offices, the first person I saw was the C.O.'s secretary, who told me to take a seat and wait for him, and he would be with me shortly. I said, "I'm sorry, but this will not wait." Perhaps that was a little arrogant, but I rationalized to myself that I had earned the right. Walking straight up to the C.O.'s closed office door, I knocked. Seconds later he opened the door, looked at me, and then gave his secretary a look. The secretary shrugged and said, "Sir, I told him he needed to wait, but he insisted..."

"Well, never mind," Stevens said, with a sigh. "Come on in, Doc." He shook my hand, walked around his desk to sit down, and indicated that I should pull up a chair and have a seat as well. Once I was seated, the C.O. said, "So what can I do for you? How did your search go today?"

"Sir, I have bad news and good news about that," I said.

"Well, let's get the bad news over with first," Stevens said.

"The bad news is that we didn't find the seven brothers."

"That may be bad news, but it's not really much of a shocker," he said. "I'm assuming there is some good news too? Let's have it."

"The good news," I answered, "is that we may be closer to finding them. We ran across some concrete evidence that they have been prisoners here, and I'm pretty sure they still *are* here."

"Okay, that's good. Tell me more."

"First of all," I said, "I need your help in securing the release of a prisoner who was actually supposed to be released months ago. His name is Habib al Abdullah, and he's the one who led us to the evidence concerning the seven brothers, not to mention a whole room full of damning evidence about crimes committed under order of Saddam and sons. We would still be virtually nowhere in our search if it weren't for Habib. Don and I met him when he approached us in an open courtyard in a section for nonviolent prisoners. He needs to be released as soon as possible."

"Can you give a reason? Is there a medical problem?"

"No, not that I know of," I replied. "But as I said, he was supposed to be released months ago, and yet he's still here, living under abominable conditions."

"As are most of the prisoners at Abu Ghraib," said the C.O. "We're trying to improve conditions for them, as you know, and you and Don have been very helpful in that regard, but all of this takes time, as you also know. Why should we single out this one prisoner for special treatment? It seems you're taking his word for it that he's overdue for release, but how do you know he's telling you the truth?"

"Let's just say that I've developed a sixth sense about these things," I said. "I've gotten pretty good at detecting BS when I hear it, and this man was not BS-ing me. But I don't expect you to take *my* word for it, of course." I took out the piece of paper on which I had written the information about Habib, and I handed it to Stevens.

"Here is the information Habib gave me," I said. "Surely there are records that are kept here, that you can check against this info. And there are officials with whom you can verify the information. I think you'll find that Habib was telling the truth. The sooner he's released, the better."

Sighing, the C.O. looked at the paper I'd handed him, and said, "I'll look into it."

"Please do it as quickly as possible, and keep me apprised of the progress," I said, a little more forcefully than I'd intended. I did not want this to be another one of those matters that might possibly be "looked into" eventually, if and when it suited the C.O. I knew he was a busy man, and I considered him to be a basically honorable one, but for Habib's sake I needed a more definitive commitment than, "I'll look into it."

I saw by his expression that my forceful response had annoyed the C.O. He was equally forceful when he asked, "Doctor, on what authority are you making this decision and giving me this order?"

It was not my wish to escalate the situation, but sometimes I can't help myself. So I responded, "Sir, do you want to re-read The Letter, or do I have to take this further up the chain of command?" I placed a slight emphasis on the words, "The Letter," which caused him to raise his eyebrows.

He said, "I prefer that you didn't."

"That suits me fine," I said. "I would greatly prefer to keep this between us, and in-house. I believe that you and I have developed a relationship of trust, and there's no need for this to go any further. I urge you to investigate Habib, interrogate him if you need to, but I would like to see that he is out of this prison within the next 48 hours."

"I'll take your request under advisement." Seeing my raised eyebrow, he hastily added, "I believe it can be handled quickly and quietly."

"I will of course be following up on this matter," I told him.

"I would expect nothing less of you, Doctor," the C.O. said, obviously resigned to the fact that he had no choice but to follow up on Habib's case as quickly as possible. "Now tell me more about this evidence you found, with Habib's help."

"For now, let me just say that I can verify the truth of those rumors we've all been hearing about Saddam's library of videotapes. There is indeed a whole library of those tapes in this very prison, in a section that apparently hasn't been used in a while. It isn't easy to get to because it's in a dark underground chamber that we could never have found if not for Habib, who was forced to take and produce many of those videos."

The C.O. looked at me in surprise, and then leaned forward, clearly very interested now. "Do you have any of those tapes with you?" he asked.

"Only a few," I said, "specifically about the amputations on several of the seven brothers. We lost our light before we were able to retrieve all of the videos related to this case, but I have no doubt the others are there as well. And there are thousands more in that library, all numbered, dated, and alphabetized."

Stevens asked, "Were you planning on giving the ones you retrieved to me?"

"No, sir, I'm sorry," I replied. "Don and I need to keep the tapes on the seven brothers. But as I said, there are thousands more, and I'm sure they'll be quite useful in the case against Saddam. I am disclosing this information only to you. You can make the decision about when to notify whomever you feel needs to be notified. I believe it will be a real feather in your cap when you do."

The C.O. started to say something in response, and I quickly added, "When you meet Habib, which I hope will be very soon, he can lead you to the chamber where the tapes are stored. Don and I couldn't find our way back there if we tried." I figured this would give him extra incentive to follow up on Habib's case, while heading off any ideas he might have about me taking him on a personal tour of the hinterlands of Abu Ghraib prison.

Stevens paused to consider what I'd said, then asked, "Who else knows about this, besides you, Don, and Habib? Weren't your interpreters, Aziz and Hussein, with you too?"

"Yes, they were, but they have been sworn to secrecy. They're very loyal, and we can trust them."

"What about the MPs who were with you today?"

"Their lips are sealed too," I replied, deliberately dancing around the fact that the MPs hadn't actually accompanied us on the long journey to the video library. There was no sense stirring up trouble. If Stevens specifically asked me, of course I would have told him the truth and would have taken complete responsibility, as I'd promised the MPs, but I wasn't going to volunteer any information. To discourage any thoughts that the C.O. might have of digging deeper, I added, "As you know, the tapes in that library will have enormous importance, not just in Iraq, but internationally as well. They'll implicate Saddam and, no doubt, numerous high-ranking Ba'athist Party members."

"Saddam is already toast, as far as I'm concerned," grunted the C.O. "Over the past several decades he's committed so many atrocities and human-rights violations that it's going to be a real challenge just to narrow down specific charges for his trial. But yes, I'm sure those tapes will be useful. And I *will* put Habib's release on my priority list. I'll do my best to see that he's treated fairly, and I will definitely keep you in the loop."

"That's all I can ask, sir," I said. "Now, if there's nothing else you want to discuss, I think I'm overdue for a rest."

"Of course," he replied. "Will I see you tonight at dinner?"

"If I don't sleep through dinner, yes, you will," I said, smiling as I got up to leave. "I'm pretty beat."

As it happened, I did sleep through dinner, and beyond, waking up early the next morning feeling refreshed and ready for a new day. In regard to finding the seven brothers, it turned out to be yet another unproductive day for Don and me, but that did nothing to diminish our sense of hope and our enthusiasm. We would simply keep on searching until we either found the men in the prison, or found credible evidence that they were no longer there.

Towards the end of the day, I received the very welcome news, from the C.O.'s faithful sidekick Lieutenant Allard, that Colonel Stevens had indeed followed up on Habib al Adullah's case, had verified that the man was telling the truth, and had signed the papers authorizing his immediate release. "Did he say anything else about Habib?" I asked Allard, choosing my words carefully so as not to reveal anything about the video library, just in case the C.O. was still keeping that information to himself.

"No, Doc," Allard replied. "That's all of the information I have. Colonel Stevens just wanted to make sure that you were informed that this prisoner is going to be released as you had requested."

"Thank you, Lieutenant," I said. For now, I would just have to assume that the C.O. had asked Habib to take him, or one of his trusted men, to the chamber of horrors that we had visited a couple of days before. And presumably, Stevens would use the information in the way he felt was best. I intended to follow up on this matter within a couple of days, but in the meantime, I had more than enough to keep me occupied, beyond the task of finding the seven men for whom we were searching. At Abu Ghraib prison, it seemed there was always something else to divert me – always another "surprise" lurking just around the corner.

CHAPTER 18

MYSTERIOUS MOUNDS

I developed the habit of climbing the stairs to the outer wall of the prison and then into one of the guard towers each morning and each evening. I enjoyed watching both the sunrise and the sunset from this panoramic perch. At times, I found myself so enchanted by the beauty around me that I awakened early or stayed past sunset, just to linger in the darkness. The night sky was utterly gorgeous, filled with stars beyond count. It was unlike anything I had seen anywhere save the times when I was high in the Himalayas on the Chinese border in Pakistan, on peaks that were almost three miles high. You never see anything remotely like this if you live in a big city. Even if you live in a small town, there is generally so much light reflecting from buildings and street lamps that it blocks out all but the brightest of stars in the sky.

A couple of days after our trip to the library of horrors, I was exceptionally spellbound watching the sunset as I looked out into the distance, where the mountains began turning red and then brown as the setting sun painted them in glorious bands of color. The sky above me was a mixture of yellow, orange, and red, and there were patches of dry grasses swaying in the breeze like a carpet beneath this colorful canopy. Standing atop the prison wall, I could scarcely hear the murmurs of the thousands of humans inside the compound below. I felt at once connected to and isolated from them, and indeed, isolated from the rest of the world. A rare feeling of tranquility settled over me, and I didn't want to leave this post, or this moment.

Just after darkness fell, I saw several meteors – "shooting stars" – streaking across the heavens. The sight prompted me to ponder, as countless other humans have done when looking at the night sky, how small we really are in the vastness of the universe. For some reason this led me to reflect, as I frequently do, on how profoundly stupid humankind is to be destroying the only planet we have to live on. I envisioned all of humanity as a lone person adrift on a simple raft in the middle of a great ocean and, upon feeling a chill, sets fire to his raft. We have managed to pollute 80 percent of our fresh water, and we are destroying the natural habitat for ourselves and all other life forms – animal and plant alike – that occupy this planet. Sadly, we are losing hundreds of species each year, while comforting ourselves with the illusion that we are immune to such a fate.

As I thought about this, I naturally thought again about the fact that humans have over-populated the earth. We cannot feed everyone, we cannot clothe everyone, and we are unable to fully educate everyone, but still we keep reproducing, endlessly. Convincing ourselves that it is the natural order of things, or perhaps even a divine mandate, we have established dominion over every other animal species on earth. But instead of exercising stewardship, which many believe is the highest form of dominion and is the true meaning of the famous passage in Genesis (1:26) in the Old Testament, we have long exercised the lowest form: exploitation. For millennia we have ruthlessly subjugated our fellow creatures, in many cases nearly annihilating vast wild animal herds, and carelessly bringing numerous species to extinction.

And yet we have failed to manage the human species. The destruction our species has caused is far-reaching, but it is always a matter of controversy. Consider climate change, which is a real phenomenon, the focus these days being on the extent to which humans are to blame. But few people mention that there is a cyclic pattern on Planet Earth, unbroken for billions of years, of 25,000 to 30,000-year periods of increasingly warmer weather, followed by an intermediate period, then another 20,000 to 30,000 year period, this time of increasingly colder weather. Those of us who are alive now have been privileged to live on this planet during one of those intermediate periods. In all but the most extreme areas, it is neither too hot nor too cold, but overall it *is* changing, and it would appear that we are beginning to experience the shift to the next phase of a process that has been going on throughout Earth's existence.

This is not an attempt to refute the significant role that humans have played in climate change – specifically, global warming – in the modern industrial era, through the production and burning of fossil fuels and the depletion of earth's protective ozone layer. Most scientists today agree that climate change is accelerating beyond the rates experienced during previous cycles, and that human activity is to blame.

However, there are those who refuse to believe it, or who acknowledge it but insist that there's nothing we can do about it now. But the result is the same regardless of one's beliefs: we and all of our fellow species are suffering because of this accelerated phase.

But – and I hope you'll excuse me for climbing back up on my soapbox about this topic –almost nobody seems willing to say that if there were fewer people on the earth, there would be fewer pollutants. There would be less demand for oil and oil products, or for coal. The pursuit of clean and renewable energy alternatives is not only worthy but necessary, and I'm not discounting the value of electric vehicles, solar cells, wave and wind turbines, and the like. Unfortunately, these do not solve the essential problem of there being too many human beings on the planet. Standing in the guard tower at Abu Ghraib prison in Iraq and looking out over the desert, I wondered to myself, *When will we as a species truly realize that we are not the most important thing on this planet, and that we need to control our own population?*

Forcing myself to push my serious thoughts to the back of my mind, I looked up at the heavens again, taking in both the vastness and the silence, as the feeling of tranquility that I had enjoyed earlier slowly began to return.

The quiet and my serenity were suddenly shattered by the sound of a diesel truck engine straining to pull a heavy load. I raised my head up over the edge of the guard tower walls to see what was going on, and I noticed something I hadn't noticed in my previous excursions to the tower: there were multiple mounds of sand that extended a few hundred yards out from the perimeter wall, but which matched neither the naturally occurring nor human engineered surroundings. That asymmetry seemed odd, but I couldn't quite put my finger on what was wrong. It was hard to discern much in the darkness, but I could see enough to convince me that something just wasn't right, and that I needed to take a closer look.

My first instinct was to try to reassure myself that there was really nothing amiss. I thought, *Well, maybe there was a road there originally, used for the construction of the prison and extending around the perimeter, and now it is covered by blowing sand.* That made sense, I supposed. After all, the wind was always blowing here, constantly shifting the sand.

All at once a tower guard appeared next to me, a man I'd seen there before but with whom I had never spoken. He was a trim Iraqi man, short in stature but fit, and with a stern and almost harsh appearance. He said nothing at first, just stood there, staring out over the desert and frequently glancing at his watch.

I was just about to say something to him when he nodded to me, pointed to his watch, and said, "Four hours and twenty three minutes to go."

I assumed that he was referring to the end of his duty shift in the tower. As I unzipped my Mylar vest and sat in the guard tower window, I said to him, "Sounds like you can't wait to get out of here. In fact, I'm willing to bet that you can't wait to go back home for good and be through with this place altogether."

A smile appeared on his face – something I rarely saw with these guards. I couldn't blame any of them for not being cheery. I could only imagine the harshness of their experiences at Abu Ghraib prison. The man appeared relieved that I was someone who was actually pleasant to him instead of someone to be feared. He asked me, "I see you come up here every morning and every evening. Why do you do this?"

I replied, "Because the desert is beautiful in its silence. I think most people don't appreciate it, but like the waves in the ocean, the desert is always moving. I can't imagine this planet without deserts. They fascinate me."

He smiled warmly and said, "You like to keep your expectations low." I suppose that was his way of suggesting that perhaps I am too easily amused.

His response was understandable, coming from someone who had probably seen little except deserts for his entire life, so instead of trying to wax poetic about the beauty and wonder and importance of the deserts of this earth, I shrugged and said, "You might be right. But I've found that with lower expectations, your disappointments are fewer." That brought a big smile to his face.

Then the guard turned away from me and began scanning the desert that lay all around us. His attention was drawn to a sliver of light off in the distance. He said, "Mortar installation being prepared. We can expect to be shelled in the next hour."

"You have a good eye. I need to up my game."

"If you want to stay alive here, you need to be aware of any little thing that seems out of place."

"I'm learning that," I answered. Then I said, "You notice anything else different?"

"What do you mean?" he asked.

"Well, a difference in the look of the desert. I was noticing it a little while ago. Most likely it's been there all along, and I just now noticed it. Several hundred yards around us on the outer perimeter wall, there are mounds. They don't match the flow of the desert around them."

The guard took a minute, looking up and down the corridor and around the wall, and then he turned to me.

"You have a good eye too. There *is* a difference. I don't know what it means. But it's possible that it is just left over from when the prison was constructed."

"I had thought that too, at first," I said, "but I want to think about it some more. Maybe we'll discuss this further when I see you tomorrow evening."

He nodded, and I said good night to him. I then turned and descended the stairs from the guard tower down the inside of the wall. As I slowly walked to my sleeping quarters, I couldn't erase from my mind the picture of the desert and the subtle but very different aspects around the prison wall compared to what I'd viewed through the binoculars further out. The more I thought about it, the more it bothered me.

Late that night, a couple of hours after I'd gone to bed, we did indeed have another mortar attack, as the guard had predicted. The attack didn't last long, and it barely roused me from my slumber. Maybe I really was getting too accustomed to this place.

The next morning I got up early and walked to the far side of the prison. I climbed the stairs to the guard tower again and looked out, taking a moment to appreciate where I was in this desert. Naturally, I was still obsessed with those mounds I'd seen at the perimeter, and I studied them again. Was my initial theory, which was also the opinion of the guard, correct? Were the mounds of sand merely covering construction debris that nobody had bothered to clean up? I wanted to believe this, but in my mind and heart I couldn't.

Standing there watching the sun rise, I could not forget what this place was truly used for under Saddam Hussein's control. Finally I climbed down from the wall and went to the mess area for breakfast, still thinking about those mounds. I remembered the conversation I'd had with the two Iraqi men, Quasam and Mohammed, in Baghdad shortly after my arrival in Iraq. Quasam and Mohammed had been quite serious about the rumors of mass graves, and it was increasingly looking as if these were not merely rumors.

I got my breakfast and joined Don, Aziz, and Hussein. As we ate, I told them about noticing the mounds in the desert, explaining that the more I thought about it, the more I believed that the matter needed further investigation. Don looked mildly interested, but he seemed more absorbed in his breakfast than in anything else. Aziz and Hussein both said they'd never noticed the mounds, but that they would climb the stairs to one of the guard towers and see what they thought those mounds might be. I told them I would appreciate that, as well as any ideas they had.

I mentioned that the guard I'd been speaking with last night thought the irregularity was due to the construction of the prison itself but I didn't feel this was right. "I'm afraid it could be something that nobody wants us to see," I said.

Hussein and Aziz looked a little baffled by my comment. "What do you think is out there?" Aziz asked.

"I'm not sure, but…" I let my voice trail off. I didn't want to open another can of worms and get us further distracted from our mission of finding the seven brothers, but I also knew that I couldn't just let the matter of the desert mounds go.

In an attempt to lighten the mood, Don said, "I think the ungodly hot days and long dark nights are finally getting to you."

Smiling, I said, "Maybe so. But humor me. I want to find out more about this. Could be nothing, but could be something. In any case, I think it's time to leave here and get started on our rounds." My companions nodded, and we all got up from the table and headed for the door. Just as I was pushing the door open, it was blown out of my reach by a sudden breeze. As I swung back and turned the other way, tiny pellets of sand hit all of us. I covered my chin and face in the collar of my jacket to keep the sand out my mouth and eyes. I saw that Aziz, Hussein, and Don were doing the same thing.

I had heard about these "dust devils" – sand funnels – but had never been caught in one. This one dropped down a few yards away from us and then disappeared as if it had never occurred.

Aziz put his hands together and muttered through cracked lips, "It is a sign." But his eyes were twinkling, and we all laughed.

I said, "Well, maybe it's just a sign that we need to go into the prison courtyard again and continue our examinations of the detainees and our observations, and hopefully find someone who can lead us to the seven brothers."

"Now you're talking sense," Don said.

And so we began another day of our search, but I couldn't stop thinking about those mounds in the desert. They weren't natural phenomena, of that I was now certain. I'd trekked across deserts in other parts of the world, and had never seen an artifact like I had seen in the desert around Abu Ghraib prison. I'd seen mounds before, of course, but they had been architectural, the remains of long-lost cities.

Right now, however, I had to concentrate on the job at hand, so I decided I would speak to the C.O. at dinner tonight and get his opinion. Maybe he knew something we didn't.

It was another long, hot day. Much to our disappointment, our efforts still yielded no news about the seven brothers. In the late afternoon we decided to call it a day, and I returned to my quarters and took a shower.

After my shower, I lay down on my bunk and got in a power nap. Feeling slightly refreshed, I walked to the officers' mess, where Colonel Stevens was already seated with several of his lieutenants. Don was there too. I asked the C.O. if I could bring up a chair and join them, and he said, "Of course. You don't even have to ask." He seemed pleased that I was joining the group. In fact, he appeared to be in an unusually good mood. Seeing this, I felt that I could not only trust him with my observations about the mounds in the desert, but that he would give serious consideration to a plan I was cooking up in my mind to investigate the situation.

So I sat down and told him everything I'd told Don, Aziz, and Hussein earlier. I shared my observations about the topography around the prison versus the topography of the desert itself. "I think it's something that needs a much closer look," I told him. "I'd very much appreciate it if some of your men could take me out to the area so we can inspect it more closely." I braced myself for a refusal or at least for a barrage of questions, but Stevens surprised me.

"Now, that's what I like to hear," he said. "New thoughts, new ideas. Just tell me this inspection mission doesn't involve a psychic or a divining rod, because we don't have either." Then he laughed out loud, and everyone at the table did too.

"I'm glad to see you still have your sense of humor, sir," I said, wondering if he was taking me seriously or just thought it all a big joke. "I request an armored Humvee and four men in full battle gear to go out with me, preferably at 08:00 tomorrow. And thank you for your help."

"I didn't say yes or no yet," he said, with a suddenly serious expression on his face, although his eyes were smiling.

"May I remind you that I still have The Letter?" I responded, echoing his mock seriousness.

"So you think the President of the United States would authorize you going out into the desert and playing in the sand?" he asked.

"I do, sir, if he knew it was for a good reason, and I think this qualifies."

He paused a few moments as if giving it serious consideration, and finally he said, "Okay, you've got your Humvee and your men. Be ready at 08:00 tomorrow." As I thanked him, he and his lieutenants stood up to leave. Don and I pushed back our chairs and stood too as the officers left the dining hall.

The next morning the armored Humvee was at the front gate promptly at 08:00. Don had opted not to go with me on this expedition, saying he wanted to get some rest and catch up on organizing the voluminous notes he had been taking since we'd been at Abu Ghraib. I spent a few minutes introducing myself and talking with the men in the Humvee. I then instructed the driver to take us to the engineering compound to pick up some additional equipment. He nodded, and then without prompting from me, he informed me that he had made sure we had adequate water and food for our expedition. I thanked him, telling him I appreciated that he'd had the initiative to see to our needs.

The drive to the engineering facility was only a few minutes, and when we got there I walked in and was greeted by a sergeant whose name I did not catch. When he asked me how he could help me, I requested some shovels and pickaxes. Although the sergeant said they could supply these items, he did give me that look to which I was now well accustomed – the look that told me he thought I was a little bit crazy. That was my cue to introduce myself as the Crazy Texan, and when I did he shook my hand and said, "Oh, right, you're that crazy doc who's been making waves around here."

"Guilty as charged," I said.

"Guilty, my ass!" he responded. "From what we've been hearing, there are going to be some big improvements in this place because you and your journalist buddy have been raising hell." Then he paused and said, "We've also been hearing some rumors about some mysterious *letter* that has apparently granted you clearance to do some things that would get any of the rest of us disciplined or even court-martialed." I noticed the strong emphasis he put on the word *"letter,"* but I couldn't tell if he was gently mocking me or was genuinely in awe that such a document might exist.

I smiled and, applying the same emphasis to the operative word, replied, "I don't know anything about a *letter.*"

"Sure you don't," he said, laughing and patting me on the back. "Anyway, whatever you need we'll get it and put in the Humvee for you."

I thanked him, and we went over the list of tools I felt we would require. Then I returned outside to kill time, idly chatting with the driver and the other four soldiers assigned to me for this desert expedition. In short order the supplies I'd requested were brought out and loaded into the Humvee under my direction, and finally we were leaving the main gate, heading out into the desert for what I hoped would be a fruitful search for... what? Bodies? WMDs? It was anyone's guess at this point. It wasn't that I was eager to uncover something gruesome or dangerous, but I didn't want this trip to be a waste of resources.

The first thing I did was to instruct the driver to go about 200 yards out toward the mounds of sand that had become my new obsession. As we made our way there I said to him, as casually as I could muster, "What do you think about those mounds?"

Without even pausing he answered, "It's gotta be just a bunch of stuff left over from the construction of the prison. Probably concrete and stone that's been buried by the shifting sands. I really don't see anything unusual." His dismissive tone put me off a little, and I was tempted to attribute his apparent unconcern about the matter to his youth and inexperience – but then again, my initial impression, and that of the prison guard, had also been that the mounds hid nothing more than construction debris.

"I guess we'll find out soon," I responded. "It might turn out to be a lot more interesting than that."

He shrugged, and I had the clear impression that he viewed our expedition as a complete waste of time, and that he wasn't too enthusiastic about it. But it didn't matter, because we were already at the first mound, where I told him to stop.

Telling the others to stay put, I got out, taking a shovel with me, and I moved some of the sand around with the shovel. After a few minutes I was satisfied that there was nothing to see, so I got back into the Humvee, feeling both relieved and, I admit, a little disappointed. Maybe this would all turn out to be nothing after all. Then again, this was only one relatively small mound, and I wasn't going to turn back now. As I settled into my seat I looked around, and could see from the expressions on their faces that the men were thinking that I was possibly risking my life – and theirs – and for what?

I requested that the driver continue along the outer prison wall, and then take us further out into the desert, closer to the undisturbed sand dunes, where there was quite a large mound. He turned his head and scratched the spot below his ear where the sand flies were pestering him, then said, "You're the boss." His voice was neutral, but he looked doubtful and even a little resentful.

I said, "This vehicle is in good shape and it's fully gassed up, right? So we should have no problems with it?"

He replied, "It came straight out of the motor pool."

I patted him on the shoulder and said, "I should be satisfied with *that* answer?"

That broke the tension, and soon everyone in the Humvee was laughing, including the driver. As I laughed with the group I thought to myself, *Just let it go.* Whatever we found, or didn't find, I was thankful for these good men who had volunteered to join me on this project.

We bantered back and forth for a while, with everyone seemingly in a pretty good mood. Then one of the young men said, "Okay, Doc, I don't know what we're doing out here, but we're clearly not here to admire the scenery."

Another man asked, "Do you think Saddam Hussein buried his gold and silver in some of these mounds – or maybe his WMDs?"

I answered, "If he did, we are either going to be very rich tonight, or, if we're not careful, very dead." I figured I might as well try to make light of a potentially dangerous situation.

At my command, the driver stopped the Humvee when we reached the large mound. I said, "We're going to have to take this mound down. It's going to be less than fun in this heat."

I told the driver to stay with the vehicle and keep it running. I asked that two men, whose names were Edwards and Rogers, take positions to the front and rear of the Humvee and keep their eyes focused on the open desert. The other two, Mason and Brandon, would be joining me on the mound. I told them to grab shovels and pickaxes and leave their weapons inside the Humvee.

You can imagine the look I got from Mason as he said, "It's more than 120 degrees out there, and we're in full battle gear."

"Well, dig slowly and you won't tire out as fast – or dig fast and we can get the hell out of here a lot sooner," I said, smiling. I wasn't unsympathetic with their situation, but we had a job to do.

Brandon said, "Either way, we gotta dig."

"That's the idea," I said, and without further discussion, the two men gathered their tools and exited the vehicle.

I grabbed a shovel and pickaxe too, and just as I jumped out of the Humvee to join them, the vehicle lurched as the driver downshifted gears. I very nearly lost my balance, but regained my footing as I sank into the deep sand. I had a feeling that this was not accidental, that it was payback on the part of the driver.

But I said nothing as the diesel engine again rumbled to life, and black smoke came pouring out from behind the cab as the Humvee moved a little further up along the mound. I assumed that the idea was for the vehicle to act as a shield between us and the open desert.

As I joined Brandon and Mason, they were hard at work already, but looking none too happy about it. Hoping to instill a little bit of enthusiasm, I said, "Guys, it's probably nothing, but then again, Saddam Hussein had to bury his gold bars some place." At least that got a smile out of them. Smiling back, I began digging into the mound too.

The sand that covered the mound lifted quickly and easily, but then we came down to some rocks, and this required using the pickaxes and really putting our muscles into the job. Suddenly Brandon yelled excitedly, "I hit something. I hit something. We found it!" I didn't know what he thought "it" might be – my guess was that he was fixated on the thought of discovering buried treasure – but I had a feeling that he was about to be disappointed.

I told both men to stop and put down their shovels and pickaxes, saying that we would move the sand and dirt carefully with our hands. We gently began scooping sand, and it wasn't long before a white object appeared. Mason and Brandon jumped back as I lifted the object out, and we saw that it was the cranium of a human skull – with a bullet hole in the back. We immediately saw that there were other human skeletal remains where that had come from.

Like archaeologists, we began separating the bones and the sand slowly and intensely, still on our knees and digging with our hands, though I paused occasionally to snap pictures of the work in progress and of our grim finds, then continued working with Brandon and Mason. Our excavation yielded a rib cage, long bones, and another skull. We didn't remove those, and we carefully replaced the skull I had lifted out earlier. After that I told everyone to stop, and we just looked at each other for a few moments, saying nothing.

Then I said, "I think we can assume that what we've found here is just a small fraction of untold numbers of people who are buried here. No doubt a lot of them are 'political prisoners' who were incarcerated in the prison and killed. I'm willing to bet that there are also thousands of men and women buried here who were victims of Saddam Hussein's and the Ba'athist Party's genocide of the Kurds, Yazidis, and maybe even some of the Marsh Arabs." Mason looked at me questioningly, and I said, "We'll talk about that later. Let's get back to work."

At my direction, we carefully covered over our dig site so as not to disturb anything further. I told Brandon and Mason to get some bottles of water and to put the tools away, and I signaled to Edwards and Rogers, who had been standing guard at the front and rear of the Humvee the entire time, that we would be leaving this site momentarily and would be driving further out into the desert to other mounds.

When Mason and Brandon returned with the water, the three of us sat with our heads down, slowly sipping from our bottles and still trying to wrap our minds about what we had discovered. It was plain to see that the men were no longer skeptical about this mission, and I felt vindicated, but given what we had found, that was small comfort.

I said to them, "Guys, you've been at Abu Ghraib prison for several months. And you've probably heard the rumors that there are thousands, if not tens of thousands, buried outside the walls. Well, as of today, it's not a rumor anymore. Our little dig proved that, and unfortunately it has substantiated what I've been hearing throughout the towns and villages during my travels in Iraq – that if you're sent to Abu Ghraib prison you'll most likely never return. That sure has been true for who knows how many thousands of people." Both men nodded solemnly, saying nothing.

I continued, "Drink your water, rest up, and then we're going to drive a little further into the desert. We need to examine a few more of these mounds to confirm that they *are* all actual burial sites, or at least that most of them are – and that no WMDs are hidden out here." At the mention of WMDs, everyone laughed. It had become a running joke for us.

A few minutes later, after we had all gotten back into the Humvee, Mason told the driver and Edwards and Rogers about what we had found in the mound. Then I told the driver that we needed to explore a couple more mounds. "And you guys will be rotating duties," I said to the others. "For the next mound, Mason and Brandon will do guard duty, and Edwards and Rogers will take up shovels and pickaxes."

As we began driving, Mason turned to me and said, "So Doc, tell me about the genocide of those people you mentioned a while ago." Brandon nodded, and Rogers and Edwards looked interested, though the driver remained impassive.

I gave them an encapsulated version of what I'd learned about the Yazidis, the Kurds, and the Marsh Arabs, telling them a little bit about these people and their respective cultures. "Saddam had different reasons for killing off different groups," I said. "In the north, he killed Yazidis and Kurds simply because he wanted the oil that was under the ground they were sitting on.

"In the south, the Marsh Arab genocide was for the most part more indirect. There were political dissidents hiding in the south, and Saddam and the Ba'athist Party used that as an excuse for damning and draining or burning the marshes – the idea being to flush out rebels that were hiding in the marsh reeds. But the land was also rich for farming. Saddam was building drainage canals and using the marshes for farm land. The result was the total destruction of the Marsh Arabs' habitat, economy, culture – their entire way of life that they had maintained for 5,000 years. So again… different motives and methods, like I said, but for all practical purposes it was all genocide."

Edwards, Rogers, Brandon, and Mason listened somberly, and even the driver seemed interested. It appeared to me that they hadn't been aware of any of these practices of the Ba'athist party under the orders of Saddam Hussein.

A few minutes later I had selected another mound further out in the desert. It was at the edge where the topography was not leveled and no other mounds could be seen. There were only the undulating waves of sand, with the dunes undisturbed as far as we could see. The driver stopped the Humvee, positioning it between us and the mound once again for protection.

We lowered the drop gate and, as I'd instructed, this time Brandon and Mason were on guard duty while Edwards and Rogers and I started digging. We now knew what we were looking for, and it only took a few minutes to discover that we had come upon another mass grave. As I'd done at the first mound, I snapped numerous pictures of the site as more bones were uncovered.

Mason called out, "Don't keep us in suspense!"

I cleared my parched throat and yelled, "Same result – another mass burial mound!" Then I turned to Rogers and Edwards and said, "Fill in the dig, we're finished here." I was satisfied that there was nothing else to see by digging up even one more of the myriad of burial mounds around the periphery of the prison walls. I was now estimating that twenty to thirty thousand have been buried here – maybe more. After we closed the dig, we all stood back, at my urging, and quietly said a prayer.

As Edwards and Rogers and I headed back to the Humvee, the winds suddenly picked up and sand drifted in the air like a mist. Mason, still at his guard post, looked out across the burial mounds and said, "This sure is a depressing-looking place."

The others nodded their heads in agreement, and even though I was silently appreciating the stark beauty of this arid landscape, notwithstanding the gruesome discoveries we had made, I wasn't about to give them a lecture on the magnificence of deserts and their vital role on the planet. Instead I turned to them and thanked them for coming out into the desert with me. "For whatever it's worth, I guess you've gotten your answer about why we're here." There were rueful smiles all around.

"Now let's get back," I said, grateful that we hadn't run into any incidents so far. I was hopeful that our luck would hold out and we would have a peaceful drive back to the base, where we would all be able to kick back and unwind, and I could report to the C.O. so he could decide what to do next.

But it was not to be a peaceful ride home. Just as the men were closing the rear tailgate, we heard automatic weapon fire, and as we were all getting settled in our seats, bullets began bouncing off the side of the Humvee.

CHAPTER 19

FIREFIGHT IN THE DESERT

The driver quickly put the Humvee in gear and went to swing right to clear the burial mounds as bullets continued ricocheting off the vehicle. He then slammed on the brakes, sliding with the power change and kicking up a voluminous cloud of sand as he spun the wheel, put the pedal to the metal, and once again turned away from the onslaught of automatic weapon fire. Driving in the blinding sandstorm that he had just created was difficult, but it made us almost invisible as a target. He leaned forward over the wheel and squinted through the sand-covered windshield, trying to avoid hitting anything.

Then he suddenly swerved to avoid a burial mound, plowing through the deep sand in the process. He made another loop, trying to confuse those who were firing at us, and as he did so we could see that they were setting up a mortar. The driver made another half circle, and was now taking us back towards the prison's outer wall. This churned up a new cloud of sand which, we could only hope, would serve to further confound our attackers. The evasive action we'd taken seemed to be working for now, as we didn't hear or feel any bullets hitting our vehicle. But we still had challenges ahead of us, not only because of the dust cloud in which we were now traveling, but also because of the uneven terrain we were about to navigate.

The unspoken worry was that whoever was shooting at us might have a rocket-propelled grenade – an RPG – or a rocket launcher; it would only take one lucky shot, and we all knew this. But we had to keep on going, and the driver made another loop that brought us behind one of the sand dunes. He was going full out, keeping his foot off the brake so the tail lights would not give us away as he carefully avoided the low-lying burial mounds and headed behind another sand dune.

The Humvee picked up considerable speed as the driver exited the turn into a more direct path back to the prison, bouncing us across the dry terrain. The vehicle traversed a compact, rocky area and continued its surge toward the prison's outer wall. For a few moments it seemed that we would crash, and we prepared ourselves for an impact that would be both sudden and jarring, but to our surprise, the wheels gained traction and the driver turned away from the large mound.

Fortunately the top-heavy Humvee was holding its own so far, but nevertheless we all braced ourselves, fearing we were going to go over onto our side, especially as the wheels seemed to lose traction again. But then just as suddenly, they regained their traction, and we righted coming out of the turn. The horsepower under the hood of the Humvee propelled us forward through the sand at an unbelievable pace.

Then the driver slowed behind another large sand dune and shouted to us, "Do we fight? Do we run?"

Mason, Brandon, Edwards, and Rogers simultaneously shouted, "We fight!"

I said, "Tell me I didn't hear what you gentlemen just said."

Brandon repeated, "We fight! That's what we've been trained to do!"

Pretending to grumble, I responded, "You know I didn't sign up for this." But they could see I was kidding, and they all laughed while they were checking their weapons.

Mason said, "We have a .50 caliber machine gun in the turret. Let's open it and uncover the gun." Then he added, almost sheepishly, "But I'm not qualified on the .50 caliber."

Edwards added, "None of us except Brandon has ever used a .50 caliber!"

Brandon hastily said, "Actually, I've only been shown how to use it; I haven't really put it to use in battle. So none of us has ever really used a .50 caliber."

"Well… that's not quite true," I said.

The driver shouted, "Doc, is it true that you were in a convoy that was under attack, and you climbed into the turret and took out a jeep that was loaded with explosives? I heard that you actually saved the entire convoy."

I was quiet for what seemed like a long time, and finally said, "Yes, I heard that too."

In listening to that response, the driver seemed quite pleased with himself and said, "Okay, then, I have a plan."

"I'm open to suggestion," I said. After all, this was their bailiwick, not mine.

The driver continued, "Mason, take one of the other men to the left. Brandon, take another man to the right and flank their position. Stay low and move through the dunes. There is a good chance they won't see what is happening. We're not taking much fire now, and we'll sit here in the Humvee and keep their attention. How long will you need?"

"Give us ten minutes," said Mason. "Set your watches on my mark." As he and the other three exited the Humvee, Mason nodded, and the driver and I both set our watches.

Once they'd gone, the driver said to me, "And you, Doc, you'll be getting up in the turret when the time comes. Load that .50 caliber and be ready."

I didn't argue with him; the plan was already being executed. I sat for a few moments, leaning back with my arms folded across my chest and saying a silent prayer before going into battle. Realistically we had them out-gunned, and if the flanking procedure worked, we would have them outmaneuvered as well. They wouldn't be able to set up or adjust their mortar in time to make a difference.

I thought to myself, *If we take out this mortar, maybe we won't have any mortars fired on us tonight, maybe even for a few nights – and maybe even into the distant future. This could save a lot of lives.*

The driver shouted to me, "Are you ready?" But he already knew the answer.

I hammered my fist against the side of the Humvee and glanced at my watch. Five minutes to go. I thought to myself, *It sounds pretty simple and straightforward.*

Looking at my watch again a few minutes later, I saw that there was only a minute to go, and I didn't take my eyes off of it until, right on time, I heard the automatic fire. Then the driver put the Humvee in gear and flew over the sand dune. As we leveled out, I climbed into the turret and cranked the .50 caliber for a few seconds. I put my goggles on, anxiously waiting and trying to visualize my targets.

This action all seemed a little over-the-top, even for me, but now I was right in the middle of it. The driver swerved around a burial mound, climbed the sand dunes, and headed directly towards the enemy site. I was now in full adrenaline mode.

Soon I could see the enemy live and close up. I pulled the trigger on the .50 caliber and gently moved it left to right across the field of targets. As the Humvee launched itself over the last sand dune, I could study the enemies' body language, and could read the expressions on their faces as they were taking fire from the right and left flank, as well as the front.

I told myself I was calm and relaxed, but I wasn't very convincing. I was clinching my jaw and was coiled like a steel spring as I let loose a barrage of bullets from the turret of the Humvee.

As we crested the last of the sand dunes, I could see our men up and charging the enemy soldiers, who were unsuccessfully trying to prepare the mortar, while falling under the barrage of gunfire from three different points.

The Humvee now came to a stop at the top of one sand dune as I moved the machine gun up and back over the enemy encampment. But nothing was moving, and I stopped firing.

Our guys came charging in now from two different directions, and the first thing I thought was that I didn't want there to be any friendly fire casualties. The driver grabbed his weapon, but after a while he dropped the tailgate and exited the Humvee while I continued to stand cover from above. I could feel the sweat running down my neck and my back, and my hands tingled from the vibrations of the .50 caliber. Some of my fingers actually felt numb. I thought to myself, a la Danny Glover and later Mel Gibson in the *Lethal Weapon* movies, *I'm getting too old for this shit.*

I stayed in position for a while longer but did not hear any more small arms fire, so I climbed down from the turret, and took a much-needed drink of water. I folded my hands across my chest and then indulged in my customary self-questioning about what I'd gotten myself into this time.

Then Mason appeared at the rear of the Humvee with the mortar tube over his shoulder and the mortar stand in his hand. I unfolded my arms and helped him drag it into the vehicle. Right behind him the others were carrying weapons that they had seized, as well as what looked like a map and some paperwork that was in a language I couldn't read.

"So," I said, "it looks like you guys got a bit more of an adventure than you were expecting when you started out today. But good job, all of you."

Brandon, clearly pleased with the praise but trying to maintain a semblance of humility, shrugged and said, "Hey, we're trained to fight and take out the enemy, wherever we find them." The others followed his lead, assuring me that they were just doing their jobs.

"Personally," I said, "I think you guys are crazy, but I also realized that you were probably bored out of your minds just doing guard duty at the prison, and you needed some action." This made them laugh.

"But seriously," I continued, "I thank every one of you for standing with me and giving me a chance to examine those mounds – and for risking your lives. I've taken plenty of photos of what we found; we couldn't pay for that sort of validation. If there was any doubt left that Saddam Hussein, his two sons, and the Ba'athist party were genocidal psychopaths, what we found today should remove all doubt."

I could feel the enthusiasm of the group sitting around me inside the Humvee, including the driver, who actually cracked a smile.

I sat there quietly as we drove back to the main gate at Abu Ghraib prison, fortunately without further incident. We stopped just outside the gate, where we were greeted by two men in full body armor, whom I recognized as Lieutenants Allard and Heineg, the C.O.'s close aides and trusted friends.

Lieutenant Allard stepped up to the Humvee slowly, putting on his wire rim glasses, and after waiting a few seconds, he adjusted them and looked down at our group. "So what happened out there, guys?" he asked. Suddenly all of us were talking at once, but nobody could really understand anything over the din. Finally Lieutenant Heineg stepped up behind Allard and raised his hands for quiet.

"You talk, Doc," he said, "since it was your idea to go out there in the first place."

"Well, we discovered mass graves under those mounds out there, and on the way back we ran into a firefight, but we took out the mortar and the enemy." My five companions nodded as I spoke.

Allard said, "Clearly, you need to report this to the C.O. ASAP."

"That's exactly what we intend to do," I replied.

As we cleared the gate, a group of men on the inside clustered around the slowly moving Humvee, and soon there was more hubbub, with people yelling questions at us that were impossible to understand. After Heineg had shouted for silence again, one brave soul violated the order and said, "We heard a lot of gunfire out there, but how do we know you took out the mortar?"

As we retreated from the crowd I yelled back, "The mortar and the weapons are in the back of the Humvee." A raucous cheer broke out in the group, and this time neither Heineg nor Allard attempted to silence them.

My intention had been to report to the C.O. immediately upon returning from our desert expedition. It was essential that he be informed not only about our encounter with the enemy combatants, but also about our grisly discoveries in the desert mounds, so he could coordinate further investigations and decide upon a course of action. And although it might seem crazy, I was also formulating a plan to go back out to the mounds one more time and look around a little more. Just to be sure.

But I was told that Colonel Stevens was tied up with other matters for the evening and would speak with me tomorrow at breakfast. I was both surprised and a little disappointed, as I had really been counting on talking with him when everything was fresh in my mind, before he heard second- and third-hand versions that would very likely be heavy on speculation and light on facts.

I did meet up with Don, Hussein, and Aziz, and as we sat together at dinner that evening I caught them up on the day's events, keeping my voice low so as to thwart any eavesdroppers. As it was, there was some staring in our direction, which I tried my best to ignore, and I couldn't help overhearing some gossipy remarks at some of the nearby tables. This was understandable, but I had no intention of sharing details with the room at large before I'd had a chance to speak with the C.O., and I was grateful that nobody at the other tables tried to engage me in conversation.

My three friends listened to my account with a mixture of concern and fascination, and Don said, "I almost wish I'd gone with you. But I'm mostly glad I didn't." Aziz and Hussein just looked a little stunned.

I had a restless night. I knew there was buzz all over the prison about what had gone down in the desert, and I knew beyond a doubt that the C.O. would get wind of it. The situation was frustrating, but there was nothing to be done about it tonight.

I was up very early the next morning, deciding against making my trek to the guard tower to enjoy the sunrise; I was not exactly in a contemplative mood this morning. I was all business. I showered and then spent some time organizing my notes until it was nearly time for breakfast. Hoping to be a little early and catch Colonel Stevens alone, I quickly walked over to the mess area, only to find that the C.O. was already finishing his breakfast. And he wasn't alone; Lieutenants Allard and Heineg were sitting with him, as they so often did. Stevens looked up at me and smiled, which was a good sign, but then his smile was followed by a nervous chuckle, which didn't seem quite as promising. The lieutenants nodded at me with vague, noncommittal smiles, but said nothing.

I stood over the table for a couple of minutes, with nobody saying anything. No one invited me to sit down, and despite the C.O.'s previous amicable manner with me, and the fact that we had seemed to have a good working relationship, I didn't want to presume anything. The air of tension I sensed around the table that morning called for a little caution on my part instead of my usual assertiveness, so I continued to stand there as Stevens sipped his coffee and the lieutenants scraped up the last of their eggs and bacon. Caution notwithstanding, I was beginning to get annoyed by their seemingly dismissive attitude, but I was not going to leave.

Finally Stevens slid his chair back, took a final sip of his coffee, and said to me, "Let's take a walk." At that, he stood up and walked briskly towards the door, while the lieutenants stayed seated, finishing their meals. I followed him, grabbing a bottle of water on the way out and taking a big swallow from it. As we exited, the heat and the blowing sand hit us; it seemed even more oppressive than usual as we made our way to his office. Once we were seated, the C.O. said, "So give me an update about yesterday's action, Doc."

I went over what happened, describing how the team had taken out the enemy combatants and had confiscated the mortar and their weapons. Much of it was presumptive, but I described events to the best of my ability, knowing that a detailed account was necessary for Stevens' report to headquarters.

As important as his report was, I wanted to get past this topic and on to something that, for me, was even more important: the discovery of human skeletal remains in the mounds around the prison. To me they offered clear proof of genocide by Saddam Hussein.

I was nearly ready to burst by the time Stevens finally said, "Now tell me about those mounds you went out to explore." I drew a deep breath and began my narrative, again providing as much detail as possible, and he listened patiently. When I was finished, he sat back, looked at me, and said, "Allard and Heineg filled me in on some of this, but I needed to hear the details. I'll be speaking with the others who were with you too, of course." Then he paused for a moment and lit up a cigarette, something he normally didn't do in my presence. I really didn't like it, but I decided to let it slide for now. My multiple objectives and The Letter aside, this was most certainly his house, and he deserved respectful treatment and a degree of patience from his "guests."

After taking a couple of puffs he said, "Look, I don't like you talking to those interpreters, Aziz and Hussein, about what happened and what you found. I know you consider them to be your friends, but they talk too much, and the last thing I need is a lot of unnecessary gossip about what happened out there. There's no telling what might get out to the media, and as you know, we have enough problems here as it is."

I thought to myself, *So he's more worried about potential PR problems than about the fact that who knows how many thousands of human beings were slaughtered and buried in mass graves around this hellhole?* Not to mention the fact that he was questioning my judgment regarding Hussein and Aziz, whom I had come to trust implicitly. His insinuation that they were nothing more than a couple of common gossips ruffled my feathers. I had to bite my tongue before I responded, knowing it was imperative to choose my words carefully.

"Sir," I said, "everyone at Abu Ghraib, including the prisoners, knows at least a little bit about what happened out there on the desert. They are going to continue to run with it whether you want it or not. I had hoped to have an opportunity to give you my detailed report last night, before the rumors started flying, but that didn't happen. The minute they heard about the way it went down, the rumors took on a life of their own. With something this big, you really can't keep it a secret here. Aziz and Hussein have proven themselves to be trustworthy; they should be the least of your worries."

That seemed to rub him the wrong way, and he stomped his cigarette out forcefully, glaring at me. I looked him in the eye and calmly said, "Thank you for putting that out, sir. This is a small room, it's hot as hell in here, and the last thing either of us needs is for our discussion of important matters to be flavored with cigarette smoke." I was still choosing my words carefully, but perhaps not quite as carefully as before.

The C.O. looked away, then turned back and looked me over, finally making direct eye contact but saying nothing. If he was challenging me to a staredown, I was certainly up for that challenge. I picked up my bottle of water and took a long, slow drink as we eyed each other. I had the strong sense that something about me was really bothering him, and my intuition told me that it had to do with my possession of The Letter. I was reasonably certain that this was always in the back of his mind. After all, he knew this document meant that I was in a position of authority, and that potentially volatile events were likely to cause me to exercise that authority. Even so, and notwithstanding my dramatic flourishes when presenting The Letter during my encounters with several other people since my arrival, in my interactions with Stevens I had mostly been trying to be low-key and work with him, not against him.

Our staredown continued, with neither of us yielding any ground, until finally the C.O. said to me, "Now – about those OGA men..."

"What about them?" I asked, surprised. "After our last conversation about them I thought they'd been sent away, and that at least *that* problem was finally being taken care of."

"Not quite," he said. "They are no longer on the premises at the moment, but no final decisions have been made." Then he proceeded to ask me if I thought they should be relieved of duty, sent home, and suitably disciplined, perhaps even prosecuted or otherwise held accountable.

"Yes, I agree with all of that," I said. "It's really not my call, though."

I was beginning to get impatient again, for my mind was not only on the mass burial grounds around the prison, but also on the ever-looming reality that Don and I still hadn't located the seven brothers. I feared that time was running out. It seemed that my earlier concerns about opening another can of worms, and getting sidetracked from our primary mission, were well founded.

But Stevens apparently wasn't through with his train of thought. "Have any of the other officers talked to you about all of this?"

"Me? Why would they talk to me?"

This seemed to annoy him, and he took a big gulp from his coffee cup, then slowly took out a cigarette from his pack and lit it. Extinguishing the match, he stuffed it into an ashtray full of butts and spent matches, and took a deep puff off of his cigarette.

I looked him in the eye again, shook my head, and said, "Sir, I have allergies and I have occasional bouts of asthma. Please put that out."

After taking his own sweet time with another couple of puffs, he finally tamped the cigarette out and gave me a hard stare. Then he said,

"Doc, you're getting into some things around here that you really have no business being involved in."

"I thought we'd already had that conversation," I said, trying to contain my frustration, "with people who had something to hide, like those OGA goons. You and I are supposed to be on the same side, and I've come to you about everything Don and I have discovered here, always deferring to you as the commanding officer. Also, as an American, a commissioned military officer, and a physician, I *do* feel that what goes on here under American command is very much my business. As are the things that went on around here before the American military took over. We all have a responsibility to bring these things to light and do what we can to make sure they don't happen again."

My frustration was mounting, because I'd honestly thought that Stevens and I had already come to an understanding about what my roles were to be at Abu Ghraib prison. He had seemed to accept my assertions that I wasn't here just to find the seven brothers, but also to help bring the misdeeds and atrocities that were taking place in and around the prison to an end. We had been over that before. But now it felt as if we were starting again from square one.

The C.O. said, "The truth is, Doc, you don't know everything. Maybe you haven't been here long enough to know when you're being played, but some of the OGA and MPs have been feeding you and your buddy Don North a line of bullshit."

"Actually, I'm a fast learner," I said. "And I think Don and I have been doing a pretty good job of weeding out the bullshit from the truth. It hasn't been that difficult, actually. Besides, we've seen enough firsthand evidence to know that we're on the right track with pretty much everything."

He didn't answer that point directly, but simply said again, "You may think you have a lot of authority here, and I've been indulging you, but you need to know there are some matters that simply are none of your business."

"I think it's safe to say that The Letter gives me considerable flexibility to decide what is and isn't my business." I stared directly at him as I said this.

He stared right back, and then said, "I don't like your attitude, Doc. As a general rule, people don't talk to me in that manner."

"Well, as a general rule, there is no one else here who has The Letter."

Stevens' face turned slightly red, but he said nothing. For some reason this emboldened me to push forward with something that had been troubling me ever since the Boom-boom Room bust. I had bent over backwards to be sympathetic and understanding when Stevens had told me that he honestly didn't know there was a brothel in Abu Ghraib prison, as well as when he'd insisted that there was no way he and his men could have known everything the OGA was doing here.

No longer as intent on diplomacy as I had been a little earlier, I said, "As you are aware, there are some serious violations that have taken place here, which apparently nobody was doing anything about. If that hadn't been the case, then Don and I could have concentrated completely on finding the seven brothers, and who knows, we might even be on our way back to the States by now, and out of your hair. I don't need to remind you that these violations I'm talking about have taken place under *your* watch. You acknowledged as much the first time you and I met, and in subsequent conversations we've had."

"But as I also told you the first time we met, I wasn't aware of most of this," he responded. "For the most part, the interrogations and torture were a secret tightly held by the OGA people."

"And you are sticking to that?"

"Of course!" he said, his face turning an even deeper shade of red.

"Do you know what the lieutenants and the enlisted men think about all of this?" I asked.

The C.O. looked at me eye-to-eye again, then pushed back in his chair and took another sip of his coffee before he responded, "I do know – generally, that is."

"Well, *specifically*, I strongly suspect that their accounts would not be consistent with your story," I said. "And when an investigating committee comes here to question them, they are going to say what they really think and what really happened – and that brings us back to you, their commanding officer."

Stevens was now actually shaking, and his forehead was dripping with perspiration as he reached for his glasses. He removed them, wiped them clean, replaced them, and finally said, "I assume you're not just playing me for a fool, and that you are actually digging for answers."

"Your defense as commander of this institution is that you didn't know what was taking place regarding the interrogations. It was all on the OGA men from the CIA, or so you say. And as you recall, I have accepted that explanation for the most part. But I've been thinking about it some more. Beyond the OGA factor, do you have an actual defense for what's been happening here – just in case further investigation yields new information, or the higher-ups don't accept your explanation, and you are ultimately held responsible? With all due respect, sir, that's something you need to think about."

Stevens' eyes narrowed as he picked up his cup; he took a big gulp of coffee, obviously more hastily than he should have, and coughed a few times. He wiped some sweat off of his face, then focused on me again.

I focused on him with equal intensity, awaiting his answer. Finally he said, "I actually agree with you regarding the OGA men and the… ah… incidents."

"That doesn't really answer my question," I said.

He said nothing, but just looked down at his nearly empty cup of coffee, seemingly deep in thought. Clearly I wasn't going to get a direct answer to my question regarding any fuller explanation he might have for the goings-on at Abu Ghraib prison. I had backed him into a corner, but I felt that continuing my hard-ass line of questioning would get me nowhere, and beyond a certain point it would just be bullying. So I changed direction slightly.

"Look," I said. "You and I have gotten along well for the most part since I've been here. I don't pretend we're best friends, and I don't think we're going to be on each other's Christmas card lists. But I don't bear you any ill will. I intend to be as impartial as possible. And if it turns out that all that has been going on here does *not* really fall completely on your shoulders, my report will indicate as much. Of course I have no control over what the honchos ultimately decide, but I promise you that I will be fair."

The C.O. waved his arms as if he were a magician and could make me – and all of his other problems – simply vanish. But when he spoke, his tone was more conciliatory than it had been. "I'm still relatively young, and I hoped to have a long career in front of me," he said. "And I had thought I was pretty well-connected."

"You may be," I said. "But The Letter says that in Abu Ghraib, and throughout the military actions surrounding the prison, the president has dealt me a royal flush. There's no way I'm going to relinquish that hand, because doing so would put a quick end to the humanitarian goals I intend to accomplish." What I clearly hoped was that my subtle threat of blackmail might inspire Stevens to finally come clean with me.

"You've made your point about The Letter, repeatedly," he said, "But what is it you really want to know?"

I said, "Let's just start with a basic question, which I'm asking for what I hope is the last time, and then it ends here: Are all OGA men gone – at least for now?"

"They are."

"Can anybody else vouch for that?"

"Yes, but isn't my word enough?"

"You better hope it is, but my faith in your honesty and motivation should really be the least of your worries."

He looked a bit morose, and I softened my approach. "Sir, despite everything, I am actually on your side," I said. "Those photos of prisoners being humiliated and tortured by interrogators had already gone viral before I even got here, so that secret was out, but Don and I want to help repair the situation, not make it worse."

"I'm glad to hear that," he said, but he didn't sound or look very convinced.

"Are you really?" I said. "Realize it or not, I am here to protect you as well as the men who are working under you. It's not my job to put you in prison. Besides, I've seen what you've had to deal with here, day after day, and saying that it hasn't been easy would be a colossal understatement."

There are times when a little empathy goes a long way, and this was one of those times. The C.O.'s mood lightened visibly, and he even cracked a smile.

After taking the last sip of coffee from his cup, he said, "I appreciate that, Doc. And now I suppose congratulations are in order for yesterday – for taking on the mortar installation and confronting the insurgents. You all deserve a medal for the lives you saved here."

"Thank you," I said. "But I was just along for the ride. The guys who were with me are the ones who deserve the thanks. Write it up and give *them* the medal."

He nodded, and then I added, "Now I need to make another request, sir."

"I'm all ears." But he let out another nervous chuckle, similar to the one he'd greeted me with that morning at breakfast. In light of the heated exchange we'd just had, I suppose his nervousness was understandable. Not that I was going to let that stop me from making my request.

CHAPTER 20

RETURN TO THE MOUNDS

I said, "It's about what we found out on the mounds yesterday. You know, the reason we went out there in the first place." Now Colonel Stevens was looking a little more nervous, but he said nothing.

"It's not my area of expertise," I continued, "and I'm not an archaeologist, nor am I a forensic doctor. But as a physician, I know human bones when I see them. I also know what a gunshot entry wound looks like in the back of a man's skull."

Hearing these words sent a shudder through Stevens. He popped out of his chair and began pacing, and his frown had returned, but he still said nothing.

"Apparently you still don't trust me," I said.

"Look, this is my command. I've made mistakes; we've established that, but I will take responsibility and I will correct them."

"I thought we were finished with that part of the discussion," I said. "This isn't about you, sir. My theory is that the remains in the desert are the results of Saddam Hussein's years-long campaigns of genocide. Besides, you haven't heard my request yet. Don't you want to hear it?"

"Yes," he said, his voice barely above a whisper. Clearly he still thought he was in trouble, so I knew I'd better put him at ease before he had a heart attack.

I said, "I just want an armored Humvee again – two, actually –– and the driver I had yesterday. I also want the four other men who were with me, in full body armor. I may need additional men as well; I haven't decided that yet. And I also want my interpreters, Aziz and Hussein."

He opened his mouth as if to dispute me, but I quickly said, "Sir, as I indicated before, I trust Aziz and Hussein, and you can too. They're smart and ambitious and loyal, like most of the locals who've joined us here."

Stevens sighed as if in resignation, and I continued, "And I would like an experienced gunner, not me in the turret with a machine gun."

"What are you planning to do now, Doctor?"

"I want to completely encircle Abu Ghraib prison and count the number of mounds – or at least get a much better estimate than I was able to get yesterday – and list them as small, medium, or large gravesites. I want to move further out into the desert and see if there are any others that have been covered over by the blowing sand. I plan to excavate several of the mounds on the other side of the prison and more closely examine the remains of those who are buried there, though I can already predict that many have been shot or hung. And as some stories say, some may have been pushed off the wall from the guard towers by Saddam's psychotic sons and allowed to splatter on the stones below."

Without hesitation Stevens replied, "Put together your little group. Select your men. We will provide two armored Humvees. I'm sure it was crowded with all of you in just one vehicle yesterday, and with additional men you're definitely going to need two Humvees. We'll also help you put your water, food, and other supplies in the vehicles."

Relieved that there would be no further argument from him, I said, "Sir, this will reflect well on you. I think our discovery will prove the genocide beyond a doubt and will lend support to American military presence here. President Bush and the cabinet members will appreciate this as well. Maybe we can even get you a promotion out of this."

Now smiling, he slowly pushed his chair back and put out his hand, saying, "We have a deal, then."

To make him feel more at ease, I said, "We have always had a deal. Remember, I'm on your side. But now that we've shaken on this, let me put my team together, and when we return I'll give you a complete report. And sir, I hope you'll be able to meet with me immediately upon our return. It was my intention to report directly to you when we got back yesterday, but I was told you were busy."

He smiled a little sheepishly but didn't say anything for a moment. I sat and waited patiently, until he said, "I'll be here. Just get done what you need to do. And stay safe."

I said, "Thank you. I'll see you later, sir." He nodded, and I pushed back my chair, picked up my nearly empty bottle of water, and stepped outside.

It was another scorcher of a day, probably 120 degrees already. I longed for dusk, when it would cool off a little bit. But I had a long day ahead of me; I had to meet with my team members and coordinate our plans for tomorrow, plus possibly recruit some new members, and talk to Aziz and Hussein about joining us.

Following that, I planned to get with Don so we could make our rounds and continue the inquiries that we hoped would lead us to the seven brothers. And then, perhaps, if I had time and wasn't too tired, I would take my hike up to the guard tower to look at the stars. I felt that I was overdue for a little bit of contemplative solitude.

After leaving the C.O.'s office I returned to my room, which was marginally more comfortable, temperature-wise, than being outside. I made my list of what I needed for the proposed return trip to the desert around the prison. I listed extra water, some food, and some protein bars, if they had them. I also listed extra ammunition, just in case – I was taking no chances after what had happened yesterday – and I made a note to requisition shovels and pickaxes too so we could continue exploring the mounds.

Once the list was finished, I folded it and put it in my pocket, then went to the mess hall, where at this time of day I was sure I would find the four soldiers who were with me yesterday. I was pretty sure Aziz and Hussein would be there as well.

Entering the mess, I was pleased to see Mason, Brandon, Edwards, and Rogers sitting at a table together. When they spotted me, they pushed their chairs back, stood at attention, and saluted.

"At ease, men," I said, a little embarrassed by the military display. I'm not at all shy about pulling rank when need be, but that's generally when I am dealing with blowhards who need to be taken down a notch or two. The men at this table had more than earned my respect yesterday; if anything, I should be saluting *them*.

I pulled up a chair and sat down, then presented them with my list. I asked them to add anything else that they thought we might need for tomorrow's trip into the desert. As they were going over the list, Aziz and Hussein came into the mess hall, and I waved at them and invited them to pull up chairs and join us. I introduced them to my four team members, who recognized them from having seen them with me around the premises, but had never actually met them. They were cordial to Aziz and Hussein, but they looked somewhat puzzled, and a couple of the men gave me a pointedly questioning look. Their puzzlement turned to visible doubt as I quickly caught my Yazidi friends up on our plans, and then said, looking directly at Hussein and Aziz, "And guys, I'd really like for you two to come along on this trip with us into the desert tomorrow."

Both men hesitated, looking as doubtful as Mason, Brandon, Edwards, and Rogers. Their reaction didn't really surprise me, given the stunned expressions they'd had on their faces the previous evening when listening to my detailed account of yesterday's battle. But I also suspected that their willingness to help me, not to mention their sense of adventure, would prevail. I was right about that. After a few moments, they nodded, and Hussein said, "Of course, Doc. We will help out any way we can."

Turning to the other four, I said, "I know you've only just met them, but I would trust Hussein and Aziz with my life. They're going to be good additions to our team." I can't say that they looked entirely convinced, but they seemed to relax a little, and Mason said, "Welcome to the team, guys."

The C.O. entered the mess building at that moment, along with his two sidekicks, Lieutenants Allard and Heineg, as well as a couple of his private security men. I nodded at them, and Stevens and the lieutenants nodded back, then sat down at a table across the room from us. I could see from their expressions that they were very interested in what was going on at our table, and they weren't attempting to hide it.

But my guys continued sipping water and iced tea, concentrating on the list I had given them. A few had taken out pencils to add items to the list.

"Here's something else," I said after a while to the table at large. "I'm thinking of adding a couple more men to our team. Obviously they have to be ones we can trust. I'm open to suggestions."

This led to an intense discussion, with everyone talking at once, and I couldn't make heads or tails of what was being said. But a few minutes later they quieted down and began scribbling down names. Brandon leaned over to me and said in a low voice, "A couple of guys I trust are sitting a few tables away from us. Let's you and I go over and talk to them." He motioned towards a table where two of the biggest, burliest men I'd seen since I'd arrived here were sitting.

"Okay," I said. "But let's not cause a commotion; just you and I will go." We slid our chairs back quietly, and walked over to the table to talk to them.

As we approached, both men suddenly stood and came to attention. I couldn't help but notice that they were considerably bigger than any of the others in the room. They were tall and broad-shouldered, as solid and sturdy as tree trunks, with square jaws and a bearing that clearly said, *Don't mess with me!* These were guys who would definitely have my back, and that was exactly what I was looking for. I stepped forward to get up close and personal, wearing my best poker face so they couldn't read me or tell what I was about the ask of them.

As tough as they were, they also looked slightly anxious. I caught the biggest guy staring at me, with furrowed brows. His left eye was swollen nearly shut; the left side of his face was puffy, and there was a stain across his cheek. This man had recently been in a fight, and I thought to myself, *He stands up for himself. I want both of these men on tomorrow's trip. If they agree.*

The bigger one was the first to speak. Looking down at me he said, "We know who you are."

"Well, good, then I don't have to introduce myself. I have a simple question for you two, but the answer may not be so simple."

He replied, "No problem, Doc. We hear you're one of the good guys, so tell us about it. I'm Corporal Peters, and this is Corporal Tyler."

"Pleased to meet you both. I'll tell you what I need, but let's sit down first," I said, and the two sat down, as did Brandon and I.

"We are planning a mission for tomorrow in the desert around the outside of the prison," I began. "We want to count and uncover some of those mounds that we found. You've heard about them, I'm sure."

Peters said with a laugh, "You didn't find any of Saddam Hussein's gold out there, but the rumor is those are gravesites!"

"Yes. Rumors move quickly through the prison."

My fingers involuntarily adjusted my eyeglasses, and I realized that I was a little bit nervous about sitting with these two hulks. All I could think of was that I wanted them on my side.

Peters' buddy, Tyler, finally spoke up, saying, "We've seen some action."

"I figured that," I replied, smiling. "I can't promise we'll see some tomorrow, but as you no doubt know we sure saw some yesterday. Any time we go outside the walls of the prison we're a target. That's why I need two more men like you and Corporal Peters."

Almost simultaneously they said they were with me, and asked where and what time I wanted them.

"Front gate, 08:00, in full body armor ready to go," I replied.

They saluted, and then I returned to our table with Brandon, who was clearly pleased that I had chosen the two men he had recommended. The others at the table had heard part of my exchange with Peters and Tyler, but I could see that they were eager to hear the details. While Aziz and Hussein seemed accepting of these new additions to our team, Mason and Rogers looked uncertain, and Edwards actually appeared displeased. I thought it might be my imagination, but Brandon also noticed their attitude. He quickly reassured his buddies that despite the menacing outward appearance of the two new recruits, Tyler and Peters were men he knew and trusted. "If you trust me, you can trust them too," he said, and as they'd done when I had vouched for Aziz and Hussein, they seemed to relax a little.

We all sat in silence for a while, sipping our various drinks, with me imagining every possible disaster that could befall us tomorrow, and trying to come up with contingency plans to resolve each of those disasters. Even if we didn't run into any insurgents, we had more than a full day's hard physical work ahead of us. We would be going through the mounds carefully, picking through the remains in order to determine the sex and approximate age of the victims, and hopefully we would gain a clearer understanding of what had happened here.

Out of all the rationales offered by our leaders for going to war in Iraq, or anywhere, the most important, as far as I was concerned, was to end the killing of innocent men, women, and children. Of the many reasons given for U.S. military action in the Middle East – spurious tales about weapons of mass destruction, battles over oil, or even the seemingly endless fight against terrorism – in my mind they all paled next to humanitarian reasons, such as ending genocide and freeing innocent people from being incarcerated in brutal prisons like Abu Ghraib.

This of course was why I placed such high importance on taking the investigation of the mounds to the next step. Confirming the genocide in Iraq by examining more of the myriad graves surrounding Abu Ghraib and other killing fields was crucial to establishing what had really happened. Further exposure of Saddam Hussein's brutality would not only serve to validate the U.S.-led coalition's presence in Iraq, at least on humanitarian grounds, but it would also help ensure an accurate narrative in the history books. And with any luck, it would be a history lesson that people would actually take to heart, so that for once, history would not have to repeat itself. I wasn't terribly optimistic about the latter possibility, but nevertheless pursuit of the truth, and the accurate recording of that truth, were paramount.

As I shook myself free from my reverie, I noticed that there was still a slight air of tension around the table. Frankly, though, I was too preoccupied to deal with it at the moment. I was due to meet Don, so we could get back to the project that I had been forced to neglect for the past couple of days. I decided that I would handle any potential team conflicts in the morning, when I was fresh and focused.

Saying goodbye to my companions and telling them I would see them the next morning at 08:00 sharp if I didn't see them at dinner that evening, I stood up and headed towards the exit. Aziz and Hussein came with me. Just outside the mess hall we ran into Don, who said, "Hey, Doc, thought I'd find you here. Let's go round up a couple of MPs and get going."

It felt good to be back on our primary quest of locating the seven brothers, even though my mind was still preoccupied with the next day's expedition. We made our rounds through the prison, but unfortunately we had yet another unproductive day. Around dusk we decided to quit, and at that point I was so tired I told Don, Aziz, and Hussein that I was going to skip dinner. I also decided that I would have to put off my stargazing ritual at the guard tower for another night. Right now, I wanted nothing more than to fall into bed.

The next morning at 08:00 we all met at the front gate. All of the men were there, in full armor as I had requested, including the new team members I had recruited the previous day, Peters and Tyler. The latter two resembled nothing so much as a couple of versions of The Incredible Hulk, minus the green hue. There was yet another new member as well: I had requested a gunner and was glad to be introduced to Sergeant Davis, who told me that the C.O. had personally recruited him for this mission. It occurred to me, however, that I should have requested two gunners, since we would have two vehicles on this trip instead of only one, but it was probably too late now. We would have to make do with the men we had.

I was pleased, though not altogether surprised, to see Don, who jokingly chided me for not recruiting him to be part of today's team. Despite the fact that he had told me the other night that he was glad he had not been along for the first expedition, and notwithstanding the fact that he hadn't said anything to me yesterday while we were doing our rounds, apparently he had decided that the lure of adventure was more powerful in him than any concern about risks. Ever the intrepid journalist, he was fully prepared with his notebook, his camera, and his flak jacket.

The two armored Humvees were parked and ready, though I was beginning to wonder if perhaps I should have requested a third one, since our team had grown a little larger than I'd anticipated. But I decided that we would be okay as we were. It would be a little crowded, but we would get by. The extra supplies I had requisitioned had already been loaded into the vehicles. All that was left to do was to stop by the engineering section and pick up the shovels, pickaxes, and other digging implements.

But before that, I felt a pep talk was in order, since there still seemed to be some tension among some of the men. I said, "Listen up, guys. Before we get started I need to make sure we all agree that we're on the same team. There are some new members of the group, and some of you don't know each other very well yet, because you've just met. For that matter, I met Sergeant Davis for the first time just now, but he was chosen by your C.O. at my request, and I trust your C.O.'s judgment." I nodded in Sergeant Davis' direction, and he nodded back.

Then I continued, "The important point is that everyone who's here is qualified to be here, and deserves to be here. We have a long, hot day ahead of us working those mounds, and at the same time, we have to be prepared for another insurgent attack. I need to know that we've all got each other's six, all right?"

There was a general murmur of assent in the group. I didn't feel it necessary to assert my authority and demand that they all respond, "Yes, sir!" These weren't OGA goons, after all; they were just a group of young men who, notwithstanding any minor personality conflicts among them, were clearly willing to put themselves at risk for this mission.

As far as I was concerned, we were all going out to the desert as equals, and I was more than willing to defer to their expertise in battle, as I had done on the first expedition. I certainly had no intention of using my not-so-secret weapon, The Letter, because it didn't seem necessary or appropriate with them. Consequently, I was surprised and not very pleased when my newest member, Sergeant Davis, broached the subject. He said, "Hey, Doc, some of us have been hearing rumors about some letter you're carrying around with you that gives you permission to do just about anything, and to order us to do anything you want." Davis had a slight smirk as he said this.

Aziz and Hussein knew what he was talking about, of course, and they remained impassive, but the others were definitely interested. Clearly they had heard those "rumors" as well.

"First of all," I said, "the letter I have is *not* a free pass for me to just do anything I want to do. But it does give me a considerable amount of... authority." I performed my familiar routine of unzipping my protective vest, reaching in, and retrieving the Ziploc bag, from which I removed the document and held it up so that anyone who wanted to read it could do so. There were a couple of minutes of absolute silence, and Sergeant Davis' smirk was gone.

Brandon looked at me and said, "Why didn't you want all of us to know about this at the outset? It's like you were keeping it some sort of secret."

I turned to him and said, "I wasn't hiding anything from you. I personally am an open book. But I didn't feel it was necessary to wave The Letter in your faces. As far as I'm concerned, it doesn't mean anything among us."

Mason spoke up. "I want to know what you mean by that," he demanded, a little bit harshly, and the others gave him a look, as if he'd somehow overstepped his bounds.

I smiled to let all of them know that neither his tone nor his words bothered me, and I said, "First I want to say that I know I've been causing some upset around this place in the short time that I've been here, and that some people don't like that at all." Some of the men laughed, and I continued, "And I strongly suspect that some of you guys would have rather been tarred and feathered than to be partnered up with me." More laughter. "But I hope I've proven that my intentions are good, and that while I'm here with my friend Don North searching for the 'seven brothers' whom you may have heard about, I'm also doing my best to help improve conditions at Abu Ghraib prison. One of the things I'm trying to do is help reverse some of the damage that's been done to you men who are unfortunate enough to be stationed here – the damage caused by the leaks, and by the bad press coverage of what's been going on at the prison." I looked around at the group, and could see I had their full attention now.

I continued, "But this isn't a one-man or two-man show. Don and I couldn't have done anything we've done so far at Abu Ghraib prison without the support and cooperation of men like you who are willing to risk everything. And as for what happened on the desert the other day – I owe my life to some of you. Having something like The Letter in your pocket doesn't mean much when you're facing down an enemy that's bent on killing you. When it comes right down to it, I know my shirt stinks of sweat just like yours. I served as a Lieutenant Commander, and even though I served in a medical capacity, that doesn't make us any less brothers. I've got your back on this mission, and I'm grateful you have mine too. I mean that."

That seemed to convince them, at least enough to dissipate most of the remaining tension that had been hovering over us. Even Mason, Brandon, and my new gunner Davis appeared placated, though I sensed Davis might still have some unresolved issues.

"So, are we all on the same page?" I asked, and they all nodded.

"Good!" I said. "Now let's get loaded into these vehicles, get to engineering to gather our equipment, and then head out to the desert." We quickly piled into our respective Humvees, with Davis, Aziz, Hussein, and I, along with the two hulks, Tyler and Peters, crowding into the lead vehicle. Behind the wheel was my same driver from the other day, and we nodded to each other. Meanwhile, Don, Mason, Brandon, Edwards, and Rogers boarded the second Humvee. Once we were at the engineering compound, the equipment loading proceeded smoothly and quickly, and in short order we were headed out towards the mounds.

Despite having donned my best pair of sunglasses, I found myself squinting through the already oppressive sunlight. I told the driver that we wanted to keep the sun at our backs, and to move from east to west in case we ran into any hostiles. Pointing to a large mound out in the distance, I said, "I'd like you to take us to that big mound and put us behind it, between the desert and the walls of the prison, please."

"Sure thing," he said. I was amped-up now, running on adrenaline, and although my brain was telling me to slow down, my body wasn't listening very well.

As we were headed out to the mounds, Tyler asked me, "Doc, what do you think about Abu Ghraib prison? I mean, how does it compare to what you've seen in other places you've been?"

He might be a rough, scary looking dude, but it was a thoughtful question, and I appreciated it. I said, "I've been in war zones in many different countries, and I've seen some pretty bad stuff. But this place is among the worst, particularly in light of those mounds we're heading for, because of the genocide that's taken place here. That's what has bothered me more than anything.

"Don't get me wrong. War is hell, no matter where it happens and why. But genocide – the long-term, deliberate, systematic killing of a group of people – that's just about the worst crime against humanity there is, as far as I'm concerned. When you combine the genocide of groups like the Yazidis and the Marsh Arabs with the atrocious ways Saddam Hussein and the Ba'athist regime treated *everyone* in Iraq, or everyone except Saddam's favorites – there's no close competition with the other places I've been. And Abu Ghraib prison represents the worst of the worst in Iraq. Does that answer your question?"

Tyler nodded, and he looked glum, almost disheartened. Feeling a compulsion to cheer him up, I said, "But it's not all bad here. On the bright side, almost getting killed the other day made me feel more alive than having good sex."

Everyone laughed, including Tyler. Then Davis, the gunner, looked at me and said, "You and the others with you killed all of those insurgents the other day." He then fell into an awkward silence. I wasn't quite sure how to respond, because the inflection in his voice hadn't made it completely clear whether he was making a statement or asking a question. And his face bore a trace of that smirk I had seen earlier.

Finally I asked him, "Was that a question or a statement of fact?"

He picked up his water bottle and took a drink, and then stared back at me. I said, "Anything you want to tell me, young man?"

"Should there be something?"

"I don't know, that's why I'm asking you," I said. "I don't have much patience for conversations that run in circles."

He paused, took another drink of water, and finally said, "I joined the Army because it was something I had wanted to do all my life. But..." He suddenly looked a little nervous, making me wonder momentarily if he was the experienced gunner I needed, had requested, and had assumed he was. It was really too late for me to be vetting him now.

Then I was struck by another thought, and drawing upon the intuition that has yet to fail me, I made a decision to give him the benefit of the doubt. He wasn't trying to provoke me; instead, as I studied his face and mannerisms I could see that he was struggling to come to terms with the fears and uncertainties he had about going out into the desert to fight a very unpredictable and formidable enemy. These were understandable emotions, natural for even the most experienced fighter.

I said to the nervous looking young man, "You are a well-trained and an experienced gunner, am I right?" He nodded. "As such, you believe that you're supposed to be confident and in control all the time. And I'm willing to bet that you often are, certainly when confidence and control are most needed. But I also understand that sometimes this attitude is just bravado and that inside you're scared. And what you're scared of, if you'll pardon my bluntness, is death."

Davis hesitated, then nodded again.

"In that case," I said, "you're no different from anyone on this team, including me. Even including those two." I pointed at Tyler and Peters, who grunted in agreement and nodded. Aziz and Hussein nodded too; they weren't trained fighters, of course, but nevertheless they were willing to risk coming out here with the rest of us in order to be of service. I knew them well enough to know that despite their outer calm, they were wrestling with their own fears and doubts as well.

"In fact," I continued, "I wouldn't want to be going out on a mission like this with any of you guys if you weren't at least a little bit scared. So that's settled."

"Doc's right," said Tyler. "We also gotta remember that we're well trained to do our jobs. We'll be ready for whatever we run into."

Davis seemed marginally more at ease, which relieved me, because there were already so many ways this project could go askew, and managing my own qualms gave me enough to handle without having to also be concerned with my teammates' fears and doubts. Besides, we were coming up on the large dune, and soon it would be time to stop worrying and get to work.

CHAPTER 21

BACK INTO BATTLE

T he driver slowed down, and the second Humvee, which was close behind us, did so as well. As we stopped next to the large dune, I looked around and was satisfied that the vehicles were well hidden from the desert out to the west. First we secured the perimeter, with Davis stationed at the turret on the Humvee in which he and I had ridden, and Brandon, who at least knew the basics of using a .50 caliber, manning the turret on the other one. After the insurgent attack the other day, I wasn't taking any chances; I wanted my guys to be ready to fire. I instructed the others to get shovels and pickaxes and head towards the nearest mound, which was tall and very long. It was going to take all of us working on it to get an idea of the number of people whose remains lay beneath.

Edwards, Rogers, and Mason, having been with me on the previous expedition, had a good idea of what we would find once we began digging, and I was certain that Don, being a seasoned journalist and having seen more than his share of horrors in the world, was also prepared. But I wasn't entirely sure about the new guys, Tyler and Peters, not to mention Aziz and Hussein. So before we set to work I briefed them, explaining that, depending upon how much digging we did, we were likely to find the remains of hundreds if not thousands of people of both sexes, including children.

"Obviously it's not going to be pleasant," I said. "But we have to do this. And I want everyone to give me a heads-up the moment you find anything." They all nodded in agreement. The mood was understandably somber as we dispersed to our respective work sites along the length of the mound.

We had only been digging a few minutes when Mason called me over to his spot. He had a deeply troubled expression on his face, though it was clear that he was trying to contain his emotions as he said, "Doc...

there are bones, skulls, there must be hundreds of them – a lot more than we saw the other day."

I would be lying if I told you that I wasn't feeling a little emotional myself, even though I had known what to expect; my hands were even shaking a little because of the adrenaline that had kicked in. But I calmly knelt down to help Mason, and together we brushed some of the sand away with our hands. We carefully lifted several skulls, each of which showed a single bullet wound to the back of the head, as had been the case with the finds from the other day.

As we worked our way further into the mound, we came across cervical vertebrae that showed the heads had been crudely chopped off. Quite a few of the remains showed chest wounds, and some had fractured ribs that were indicative of having been shot in the upper torso at close range. There were yet other remains that did not display these sorts of trauma, and I knew there was a good chance that many of them had simply been buried alive.

Beside me, Mason was taking deep, gasping breaths. At one point he stood up, looking into the site and shaking his head. I empathized; it was a lot to take in. We were looking at the remains of men and women, and even young boys and girls, all of whose lives had been cut short by Saddam Hussein and his vile Ba'athist thugs.

I patted Mason on the shoulder, told him he was doing a good job, and then moved along the mound, for other team members were calling to me about their own disturbing finds. I stopped and spoke to each man, offering what encouragement and emotional support I could, and then I moved on.

Just from what I had observed so far in this one large mound, I was even more confident about the accuracy of my original estimate regarding the number of human beings buried out here. The mound we were now digging held what I guessed to be the remains of about a thousand people, and judging by the overall number of large and smaller mounds in the area, there had to be at least twenty-five to thirty thousand bodies in all, and perhaps more. I had intended for us to go around and count the mounds before the day was out, but now, seeing these hundreds of bodies in just this one gravesite, I felt as if we were in the House of Horrors. The thought that kept pounding through my mind was, *genocide.*

I was now standing beside Peters, who had taken a brief break from digging to stand up, stretch his legs, and wipe some of the sweat from his face. He wore a grimace that appeared to be a combination of anger and bitterness, with perhaps a bit of defiance thrown in as well. I didn't fault him for the defiance; after all, his area of expertise was fighting, not digging for skeletons in the desert. Nor could I blame him for being angry or bitter about what we were uncovering, because I was feeling much the same emotions.

As I had done with the other team members, I offered what I could in the way of solace. "We're on to something very big," I said. "Maybe even bigger than I thought at first. The world needs to know about this, and what you're doing will help ensure that happens." He didn't look entirely convinced, but he nodded, then knelt back down and resumed digging.

My eyes were heavy and my neck was aching as I continued to move up and down the line. I finally settled down next to Aziz, who worked steadily but looked even more grim than Peters had. Without saying a word, I set to work digging with my hands and clearing the sand from around a skeleton.

Aziz was doing the same, and I could see that he was trying to control his emotions, but there was a tremble in his hands. He continued to work for a few minutes without looking at me, and then he said, "Doc, do we really have to keep doing this?"

I said nothing for a few moments, instead concentrating on gently lifting several skulls and examining them. Each one showed a close-up gunshot wound with entrance and exit wounds. Carefully replacing the skulls, I turned to Aziz, who was looking at me now, and I replied, "I know that some of these are your people, Aziz, and I can only imagine how difficult this is for you." As I said this, I could see the tears welling up in his eyes.

I continued, "But yes, we have to do this, at least for a little while longer, because otherwise the world might never know the whole story about how your people, and others, were treated under Saddam Hussein's regime. It's important that we keep digging in order to get a better idea of how many victims are out here, and how they were killed, and maybe even who they were. And in case it isn't obvious, I'm very grateful that you and Hussein came along on this trip."

I felt that my words were a little lame, considering the devastating impact this experience was having on my young friend. But it appeared that what I'd said had flipped a switch in his mind, and to my surprise, he suddenly seemed more in control of his emotions. He said nothing but simply nodded and then got back to work, as did I.

Don, meanwhile, had been laboring nonstop, taking pictures of his finds and occasionally stopping to scribble in his notebook. "This is definitely a crime scene – and that crime is genocide, like Doc's been saying," he said at one point. "No question about it."

I uncovered a few more skulls, and then I stood up again, holding one of the skulls aloft as if poised to perform the "Alas, poor Yorick!" speech from *Hamlet*. Everyone had stopped working and was now looking at me as I began to speak in the words of a detached clinician rather than of a tragic Shakespearean character, though my words were dramatic in their own way. I explained, "This skull, like so many of the others uncovered in this mound, shows a close-up gunshot wound with entrance and exit wounds. Clearly these people were murdered at close range. The skull I'm holding shows a single gunshot wound over the right eye – clean through and though from the frontal lobe to the back of the skull." I pointed to the entrance and exit wounds as I spoke.

Edwards walked up alongside of me. He was sweating profusely, his shirt adhering to his body. Rubbing his eyes, he said, "The bastards did this in secret. And they thought it would stay a secret forever. Just bury 'em out here in the desert, and nobody will ever find out."

"That's exactly right," I said. "Saddam Hussein thought he could do just about anything and keep it a secret. And he apparently believed he could just keep on getting away with his crimes, and that nobody would ever stop him even if they found out what he was doing. But he was wrong. He couldn't hide from the American forces, could he?" I paused and looked around at the team, pleased to see that my words had had the desired effect: there were smiles all around, and a few of the men called out, "Hooah!"

I smiled too and continued, "All of Saddam's dirty little secrets will eventually be exposed. We're helping to make that happen, and I can guarantee that what we've been uncovering won't go unnoticed. We're going to honor the dead – every one of the men, women, and children buried here – by taking this story worldwide."

I could see that Aziz was struggling with his emotions again, and so was Hussein. Some of the other men looked as if they were trying to hide their feelings as well, and I felt the tears welling up in my own eyes. I was grateful now for my sunglasses; they might not provide much protection against the harsh desert sunlight, but they did shield my eyes from outside observers. I knew it was time to get back down to business before we all started blubbering, so I carefully lowered the skull I'd been holding back down into the mound, then stood up straight and said, "Okay, let's get back to work. And we'll continue to do things by the book. No mistakes. Be at your best, honor these dead. And of course, continue to document all of it."

I got nods all around, and the men knelt down and began working again. But Aziz looked as if he were going to faint. He was clearly overheated and seemed to be struggling to breathe, so I had Hussein take him back to our Humvee to get him a cold drink and let him rest a while before returning to work.

I began walking slowly up and down the line again, observing and occasionally stopping to snap a photo as the team members continued to uncover more skeletal remains. I thought to myself that it wouldn't be an exaggeration to compare what we were seeing here to the infamous killing fields of Pol Pot's Khmer Rouge in Cambodia, or even to Hitler's extermination camps. For me, this experience was strengthening my conviction that exposing and putting a stop to genocide was far and away the most important reason for America's involvement in Iraq. I was increasingly coming to the conclusion that it might eventually prove to be the only valid reason to be in Iraq, and I think history has proven me correct.

I stopped next to Tyler and said, "How are we doing?" He responded with a loud and clear, "Ready, willing and able!" I nodded and stood watching as he continued to dig, finally uncovering the intact skeleton of a young child.

Rogers, working next to Tyler, had peeled off some of his heavy battle gear. He paused, mopped his brow, and said, "I've been stuck in Abu Ghraib for several months now. Who would have known these mass graves were sitting in the desert just outside the walls of the prison? But this sure ain't why we all came to Iraq. This is *not* what we signed up for." Clearly he was still trying to process the situation, and I understood this, but he did sound a little whiny.

I was about to say something to Rogers when Tyler turned to him and said, "You got somewhere better to be?"

Rogers just shrugged and said, "It's freaking hot out here!"

"Yeah, well… it's the desert," Tyler retorted. "Deal with it." I grinned and walked on.

After a while I stopped next to Tyler again and got back to work digging. We all worked diligently for a while, with very little conversation, and then I decided to walk the mound again. As I did so, I concluded that we had seen enough of the contents of this mound to get a reasonable estimate of the number of people buried here. It was time to move on.

I said, "Everyone please take a deep breath. I think we're finally finished on this mound. Obviously we have neither the time nor the resources to excavate each and every mound. My initial plan was for us to excavate a couple of the smaller ones after we finished here; my thinking was that this would be sufficient to confirm my previous estimate and enable me to compile an accurate report." There was a collective groan, and I held my hands up in a gesture motioning for silence.

"Don't worry," I said. "It's getting late, and I think that we can probably estimate the number of dead in the smaller mounds just from what we've seen in this large one. But I do want us to walk the area together and get an accurate count of the mounds. If a particular mound stands out for any reason, we can stop and explore it more closely."

Peters said, "So how many do you think are buried in this mound, Doc?"

I said, "I'm estimating about one thousand."

We gathered up our tools and equipment and slowly and methodically made our way around the outer wall of the prison, counting the mounds. I photographed each one of them and made notations in my notebook about its size, along with my estimate of the number of dead it contained. I still saw nothing to contradict my original estimated total of twenty-five thousand to thirty-thousand bodies at the minimum, and I now recorded those numbers in my notebook, though I added a comment that the actual number was at this point still indeterminate. In this context, as far as I was concerned, "indeterminate" was an ugly word, for it meant that we couldn't be sure of the number of murdered human beings who had been discarded here like so much trash. A much more detailed investigation would be needed, but it would only happen if decreed by the powers that be. Despite my lofty ambitions, I realized that the most that Don and I and our team could do was to execute a rudimentary investigation and issue a report about our findings; how that report was ultimately used was not up to any of us.

After we had completed our inventory, I had us circle back and stop at another one of the larger mounds, because I had noticed some irregularities that made it stand out from the others. I said, "Let's just do a little digging at a few spots on this mound, to see if it warrants closer inspection. Then we'll go back to the prison; I promise." The men dutifully got into their places, but before we could even begin to get to work we heard shouts from Davis and Brandon, who were still stationed in their respective turrets on the Humvees. Looking out over the desert, Davis called out, "I think we have action out here!"

That was it. I couldn't take any more chances, so I commanded the team to halt work and prepare to get back to the vehicles as quickly as possible. No sooner were the words out of my mouth than I spotted Aziz and Hussein rapidly approaching from the direction of the Humvees, making no attempt to conceal themselves from whatever unseen enemy might be out beyond the mounds. While Aziz looked marginally more rested and refreshed, he still had an intense look on his face. Hussein looked troubled as well, but that was understandable, given the circumstances.

After I had ushered Aziz and Hussein behind the large mound, chastising them for walking back so openly with no apparent concern for a potential sniper, I quietly said to them, "I can see that you guys are really keyed up. Beyond the fact that Brandon and Davis just sounded the alarm that there might be trouble out on the desert, I know this day has been particularly hard for both of you."

Hussein said, "These are our people, and this has become personal for Aziz and me."

"I absolutely understand that," I said. "And as I told Aziz earlier, I'm very grateful to both of you for coming along today and helping out. You're showing a lot more strength and courage than many people would in your situation."

"Thank you," Hussein said. "We are going to see this through, Doc. But we are glad you can see how difficult it is for us." I smiled at him and then quickly explained that we were cutting our work short due to the possible threat of another insurgent attack, and were gathering our equipment and getting ready to go back to the Humvees. They nodded and immediately began helping.

Fortunately the preparation to leave the site went smoothly. Taking care to stay as hidden as possible behind the mounds, we then were able to get back to the vehicles without incident. We swiftly loaded up our gear as Davis and Brandon briefed us on what they had seen out on the desert.

Davis spoke first. "We thought we saw movement about 300 yards out, possible snipers," he said. "We'll be on the lookout on the way back to the prison, but..."

Then Brandon cut in. "But we also saw more mortars that have obviously been put in place since we were out here the other day. We can't just leave them out there."

Davis nodded vigorously in agreement, as did Tyler and Peters. Everyone else stood by, alert and ready to do whatever needed to be done. Even Aziz and Hussein were all business now, every trace of emotion and conflict gone.

I sighed; I was bone-tired, and more than ready to call it a day and get back as quickly as possible to the relative safety of the prison. To put it bluntly, I felt that we had already done more than enough with what we had accomplished on the mounds today and on the first expedition – not to mention the confrontation with insurgents, and the mortar retrieval, on that initial outing. I didn't think anyone would dispute my opinion that I had gone well above and beyond anything that could reasonably be expected of me, as had Don and all of the team members.

But then, looking around at this small but determined group of soldiers and civilians, I knew I couldn't just turn away. If I'd had any lingering doubts about the wisdom of going on another mortar-retrieval mission, they were vanquished when Tyler said, "Doc, I know we've all put in a long day, but it's our duty to neutralize any threats we encounter. We have to at least try to stay one step ahead of the enemy who are trying to wipe us all out. And when we go out there, we're going to have to be prepared to deal with insurgents. Davis and Brandon told us they saw movement, and more than likely whoever they saw is still out there, and who knows how many more."

Peters interjected, "I wanna kill them – all of them, because if we don't they're for sure gonna kill us." I could see and hear the rage building within him, and I knew that for him, as well as for several others in our group, this went beyond the mandate to neutralize threats and protect innocent lives: it was also about revenge for the thousands of nameless souls, lying dead in the mounds around the prison.

I glanced around at the group again and said, "Okay, but obviously, we need a plan."

Peters said, "We need to surround them."

Don spoke up. "But we really don't know how many there are." I nodded.

Tyler said gruffly, "That doesn't make any difference. We're trained, and one of us is equal to twenty of them."

The soldiers were now all looking at me, their faces nearly expressionless but their eyes burning with determination, and their demeanor signaling that they were ready to kill at a moment's notice. I had witnessed such behavior many times, most recently out here just a couple of days ago.

At this point I knew that there was no turning back. For better or for worse, we were likely going into battle again.

I knew we had no time to waste. I said, "Okay, if we're going to do this, one of the Humvees has to act as a decoy. We need to keep the sun in their eyes as we approach from the target's east. The other Humvee will flank them with the sun at the target's ten o'clock, relatively out of sight to the north. The men in the other Humvee will maneuver to the south, with the target at their two o'clock. At our signal, we will open fire, with our target caught off-guard in a crossfire. Does that sound good to you guys?"

The plan seemed agreeable to all, so I said, "Next question: how much time will you need to maneuver into position while staying out of the target's line of sight?"

"We should be able to be in position in twenty minutes," said Davis, with Brandon and the other soldiers nodding their agreement.

"Are you sure that's all the time you need?" I asked. It wasn't that I was questioning their skills or their expertise; after all, Brandon and the others who had been with me on the previous expedition had taken us successfully through battle. But I had an uneasy feeling about this, and I wanted additional assurance. There was no room for error here.

It was Davis who answered me. He said, "Doc, this isn't our first rodeo. We're trained to do this, and we can and will do it." There was hearty concurrence among the team members.

"Fair enough," I said. I wasn't entirely reassured, but we had to move forward. "We'll need a signal to begin the attack. The insurgents will be focused on the decoy Humvee. We need to move from north to south, staying behind as many dunes as possible. They'll announce that they've seen us by opening fire on the decoy. That will be the signal for us to hit them hard, from three different directions. From their defensive position, there will be less chance for them to reposition and catch *us* in a crossfire."

I paused, then continued, "When that happens, our decoy Humvee will be moving away from the action and will circle around behind the insurgents, joining up with the other Humvee. Meanwhile four men on foot will move in from the north and south and keep the insurgents pinned down in a crossfire."

I hoped that the guys couldn't see that my hands were shaking a little, even though my voice and demeanor were forcibly calm. It didn't help that I was feeling parched; my throat was as dry as the sand around us, and it was closing up, making it more difficult to speak or even to breathe. But again, we had no choice but to go forward, so I grabbed a bottle of lukewarm water from one of the Humvees and took a couple of gulps as we quickly briefed the two drivers on our plan.

As we took our seats in the vehicles, with Davis and Brandon resuming their positions in their respective turrets, I glanced at Aziz, whose eyes were closed. At first I thought he had been overcome by anxiety again, but then I realized he was praying, which didn't seem to be a bad idea at all, given the circumstances.

Running my hand over my head and wiping away the sweat that was dripping into my eyes, I waited until Aziz appeared to have finished his silent prayer. He opened his eyes and I said to him, "It's going to be okay. These men are well trained and very smart, and I trust them."

Aziz said, "I know, and I trust them too, but it is still very disturbing. I tell you the truth when I say that I do not know who those men are who are manning the mortars. I only know that they are our enemies, and that they want to kill us."

"That's right," I said. "And if we don't stop them now, those mortars will go off, and many innocent detainees and military personnel could be injured or killed. It's a constant risk, I know; there have been mortar attacks on the prison on a regular basis, and more than likely they're going to continue. But now, we have a chance to stop an attack and maybe put some more of those enemies out of commission. So we need to successfully complete this mission, because there's no help coming from the outside. We're not getting helicopter gun ships or any of the reinforcement that some of the military personnel here say they've been requesting for months. We're on our own."

The other guys listening to our exchange all nodded. But Aziz still looked worried. I sensed there was something else he wanted to say, but something was preventing him from saying it. For someone who was so expressive, he was nonetheless hard to read at times, and this was one of those times.

I was beginning to get a little impatient, but then I reminded myself again of the courage he had displayed by coming along on this trip, knowing what he might be getting into, and given that he was hardly a battle-hardened warrior. Trying to put him at ease, I said, "Whatever you want to say, Aziz, it's all off the record for now. So please speak freely. What's on your mind?"

He replied, "I know we are doing the right thing, but I fear repercussions. Even though I don't know who they are, these are Iraqis we will be fighting. Hussein and I live here, and we will probably be here long after you have gone back to Texas." Hussein, who had been listening intently to our exchange, nodded, his eyes narrowing slightly. But he said nothing.

So that was it. Aziz was worried not about the fighting per se, but about potential blowback from his participation. And it appeared that Hussein shared the same concern. "I understand," I said. "If that's your worry, I will see that you and Hussein are kept out of it when I make my report. I'll do everything I can to protect you two, and so will the others, right, guys?" I was met with a chorus of, "Right!" and "You got it!" from the others in the Humvee.

"Thank you," Aziz said. He was clearly still worried, but at least he knew we were all going to do whatever we could to protect him and Hussein. Hussein nodded, still saying nothing.

It was time to move, so I met the driver's gaze and nodded for him to proceed. He moved forward slowly, and stopped on my command. I said to Tyler and Peters, "Okay, guys, it's time for you to get out and move forward to take your positions. Be sure to stay hidden behind the dunes. Now, look at your watches, and remember you have twenty minutes to reach your objective."

Aziz, Hussein, and I remained with the driver in our Humvee while Tyler and Peters assumed their positions. Meanwhile, the second Humvee was making a wide circle, preparing to let Mason, Edwards, and Rogers off on the south side, behind the enemy. We knew that the mortars that were there would be pointing towards us and the prison.

After fifteen minutes had passed, I told the driver to start moving forward slowly at a right angle to the dunes to see if we would attract any fire. He nodded, but his brow was furrowed. In spite of the time we had spent together in the desert, I still didn't know him very well, and I had no idea how I should read his expression. But it seemed pretty clear that he had serious doubts about the wisdom of this move. Nevertheless he was willing to comply with my orders. I had to give him points for showing the same courage as that of my Yazidi friends. My respect for all of the members of our team, soldiers and civilians alike, was growing by the minute.

I stuck my head out of my window to check on Davis up in the turret. He was obviously primed for battle, unfazed by the intense heat and the blowing sand as he wiped his forehead with his sleeve. He grinned and gave me a thumbs-up, and I returned the gesture, then ducked back inside, wishing I could completely share his enthusiasm and confidence.

Yet as our vehicle bounced in and out of the dunes, coming ever closer to the target, I found my own excitement growing. I was even beginning to feel optimistic about our chances, particularly because we still had not been fired on. Either we hadn't yet been seen by the enemy, or they were just holding out and ranging the mortars. I knew that this interlude of relative peace was soon to end.

And I was right; small arms fire suddenly began to ricochet off of our Humvee. The enemy combatants were concentrating their fire on us, as we had intended, while the other Humvee, and the men on the ground, circled behind them and prepared to move in. The insurgents were in for a surprise, and I felt no small amount of satisfaction at the prospect.

Now there was a barrage of automatic fire, which told me that our men on the ground were taking action. Then the air was filled with the rat-a-tat-tat sound of a .50 caliber machine gun as Brandon began firing from the turret gun in the second Humvee. I thought of a line by Gregory Peck's character in the classic movie, *The Guns of Navorone*, "You're in it now, up to your neck!" Indeed we were.

I was at least comforted by the knowledge that the .50 caliber rounds were all headed toward the insurgents rather than towards our Humvee, whose armor would be no match for the incredibly powerful rounds.

We had now effectively surrounded the enemy, and we took full advantage of the element of surprise. From the turret in my vehicle, Davis began firing bursts into the area, and I shouted a reminder to him not to catch our own men in a crossfire. "Stay on target!" I added. I don't know if he heard me over the commotion, but I realized as soon as I had uttered the warning that it probably wasn't necessary; after all, Davis was a well-trained gunner. But I was pumped up on adrenaline and felt a need to do something besides just sit there.

Our Humvee kept going until we were behind another large dune, taking us out of the action momentarily. I leaned forward and told the driver to stop and just sit here for a few minutes, letting the other Humvee and our men on the ground do their job. After we had sat for about five minutes, I said, "Okay, time to move out from behind this dune and circle around to meet up with the other Humvee. Maintain the engagement discipline we discussed so we don't risk injuring our guys." The driver nodded, then began to circle to the north.

No mortars had yet been fired, and with any luck, I thought, none would be. Our driver was now moving across the desert at full throttle, and it only took us a few minutes to catch up to the other Humvee and join them in the fight.

In only minutes, the insurgents were taken by surprise, outflanked and outgunned, and were totally vanquished. Now it was time to take stock of the carnage, then to clean up and get out of there.

We disembarked cautiously from our vehicles, joining our men on the ground. We saw that there were half a dozen mortars, only two of which had been set up. There were four more mortars lying around but not yet assembled. It gave me no pleasure to see that there were about twenty insurgents lying dead in the sand. Granted, they had been trying to kill us, and it was either them or us, but now that the immediate crisis was past, the physician in me recoiled at being a party to ending life rather than preserving it.

The soldiers moved about taking weapons off of the dead insurgents, with Don helping them. I climbed up to the turret and told Davis to remain alert and keep an eye to our rear. He nodded and said, "Already on it, Doc." Then he gave me another thumbs-up, and I smiled and climbed back down, only to come face to face with Hussein, who seemed a little rattled. Aziz was approaching us, walking somewhat unsteadily and shaking. He stopped when he reached us, and did not look me in the eye as he said, "Well. I am glad to put this behind us."

"You and me both," I said. Hussein nodded and mumbled, "That makes three of us."

As I looked around at the dead, and took in the sight of multiple crimson pools seeping into the sand, my head was swimming. The combination of heat and the release of adrenaline had left me feeling profoundly exhausted, and it didn't exactly energize me to realize that my day was far from over. There would probably be tons of paperwork to do tonight; at the very least I had to report to the C.O., and there was no telling how involved that conversation might be. I also had a feeling that, given our second and even greater triumph in the desert, there would be festivities later on that most likely would last far into the night. Right now, though, we had a job to complete, so Hussein, Aziz, and I joined in the effort to remove the weapons from the bodies of the insurgents and store them in the back of the Humvees.

Meanwhile, Don and a couple of the soldiers were going through the pockets of the dead, looking for any identification and paperwork that could be of future help. Two men were dissembling the mortars and placing them wherever they could find room in the back of the Humvees.

The aftershock was hitting me full force now as I considered what we had just experienced. It had all happened so fast, and there were so many things that could have gone wrong. By now I was feeling almost as shaky as Aziz, but I continued to help with the cleanup, and within a half hour our job was done. I looked around at the group and said in a loud voice, "Now let's get the hell out of here!" There was no argument.

CHAPTER 22

A NIGHT FOR CELEBRATION

J ust before we boarded the Humvees, I said to the team, "Those of you who were with me on the mission the other day know what we can most likely expect when we get back to the prison. We're probably going to be surrounded by folks wanting to know exactly what went on out here. Obviously they'll have heard the gunfire. But it's best if we don't say anything until I can get at least a preliminary report to the C.O. Understood?"

There was a chorus of, "Deal!" and "You got it" and even a couple of "Yes, sirs." That was good enough for me, so we got into our vehicles. I was well aware that the desert heat was getting to everyone, even those who were more acclimated to it, and unfortunately the Humvees weren't much cooler. But at least they would get us back to the prison.

As we made our way across the desert, I looked out the front window at the cloudless sky, thinking that we wouldn't have much of a sunset without the presence of clouds. Then another thought came, unbidden, from the physician side of me: *Those insurgents will never see another sunset or sunrise.* I couldn't help but feel pity for them; some were barely past adolescence and probably hadn't even known exactly why they were supposed to hate us enough to kill us.

But that's always the case with war, isn't it? Wars cannot be effectively fought without vilifying and dehumanizing one's opponent, and while such an attitude may at times be justified, often it isn't, and this has most likely been true ever since humans first engaged in war. *So much for the idea of human progress,* I thought. *Viewed through the lens of warfare, the only "progress" we've made over the millennia is to come up with ever more efficient ways to kill each other, while our need to dehumanize whomever we have decreed to be our enemy has remained essentially unchanged.*

But again, in this situation, it was either us or them. I couldn't let myself dwell too long on the humanity of the men who had been so determined to annihilate us.

We were now driving directly across the sand dunes towards the outer perimeter walls of the prison, which appeared to be a mere haze in the distance. *It could be just a mirage,* I thought to myself. *Maybe none of this is real.* Then I realized that I was more than a little punchy from dehydration and low blood sugar, so I grabbed another bottle of water and a couple of power bars – thank goodness we were well stocked with these items in both vehicles – and I set about replenishing what my system so desperately needed. The men I was with were doing the same, as were those in the other Humvee, no doubt.

After a few minutes, I began to feel considerably better, both physically and mentally, my morose thoughts dissipating as I took in the mood of celebration that was beginning to fill the vehicle. Before long we were all smiling and patting each other on the shoulders and back, nearly giddy not only from the satisfaction of having done a good job, but from the fundamental reality of being alive and having survived another dangerous venture into enemy territory. In retrospect, I find it very strange that the twinges of compassion I had felt as we had plundered the dead insurgents for weapons and other items was gone, displaced by the celebratory mood we all seemed to share.

Actually this was the second time in two days that I had experienced these feelings, but this time around they were even more powerful. As I bowed my head to say a silent little prayer of thanks, I looked over at Aziz and saw that he too appeared to be praying again. The focus of my own prayer of gratitude was Terry, the love of my life. I was more determined than ever to double down on my primary mission of finding the seven brothers so I could get back home to her.

The conversations in the Humvee abated when we reached the front gates of Abu Ghraib prison. As the MPs waved us through, with no questions asked, there was utter silence in the vehicle. But there was a small crowd awaiting us, as I'd expected, and when we began to exit, men were shouting, "What happened this time? Is everyone okay? We heard a lot more gunfire than we did the other day."

As agreed upon, none of us said a word, but just began walking away from the Humvee while others pushed and shoved their way to the vehicle so they could peer inside. I was weary and badly in need of a shower and, with any luck, a long nap, but I was determined to at least attempt to see the C.O. and give him a brief rundown of the day's events. After all, I had chided him for not being available when I returned from the previous mission in the desert, and I didn't want to be the one responsible for yet another missed briefing.

As I walked towards Colonel Stevens' office, I was met by Lieutenants Allard and Heineg. "Welcome back," said Allard, who didn't look terribly pleased to see me. His attitude didn't particularly surprise me; I knew that even more than Heineg, Allard was worried about getting his next stripe. I also knew that Stevens wasn't the only person who was concerned that the results of my investigation might reflect poorly on the command structure at Abu Ghraib. Allard was most likely worried that any additional information uncovered in today's expedition would negatively impact his career.

Surprisingly, however, neither he nor Heineg attempted to extract any information from me. Heineg simply said, "Colonel Stevens is waiting for you in his office." I nodded and continued on my way as the two lieutenants headed in the opposite direction.

When I entered the C.O.'s office, he smiled at me and said, "Come on in, Doc! I know you're beat and probably need to get some rest, so just give me the basics, and you can fill me in on the details later when you do your report." I plopped down at the chair in front of his desk, and then, as concisely and coherently as possible, I provided a recap of the day's events. He nodded as I spoke, and scribbled a few notes on a notepad.

When I was finished, he sat back and we shot the breeze for a few minutes, with me keeping up with the small talk as well as I could, until he finally took mercy on me and said, "Good job, Doc. I look forward to reading your more detailed report, and of course I'll be talking to the other team members too." I nodded and said, "Of course."

Then Stevens said, "Well, I've kept you long enough from that nap – and hopefully that shower – that you've earned." There was a grin on his face as he said the word "shower," but then, I knew I was pretty ripe, and I didn't take offense. I smiled lamely back as Stevens said, "Dismissed!"

I had never been so grateful to hear that one word. "Thank you, sir," I said, and I beat a hasty retreat, praying I wouldn't run into anyone who would slow my progress as I headed for my room. Once I got there and had shut the door behind me, I breathed a deep sigh of relief, then stripped down and headed for the shower. My body was indeed reeking from the slimy perspiration that covered me, and despite my attempts at rehydration my mouth was dry and thick with sand particles.

But the shower began to revive me, and as I stood under the pulsing water my heart rate continued to gradually decelerate, and my breathing evened out. I put my face directly under the water, determined to let it wash everything away. Unfortunately, it couldn't wash away my thoughts about the tens of thousands of dead in those unmarked mounds. I knew I had to get past it, and I knew that I *would* get past it to the extent that I could continue to function, but I also knew without a doubt that what I had seen would never really leave me, and would be with me until the end of my days.

I was deeply saddened by the burden that would be carried by the soldiers on all sides of the fields of combat for the rest of their lives: memories of the profound carnage they would observe, inflict and suffer, too often for the sake of priorities they rarely shared, much less understood. I knew that even with the small part I was to play in this morbid theater, I too would feel that same shadow.

As I emerged from the shower and dried off, I finally realized how completely exhausted I was. Yet the adrenaline was still pumping, and I had developed a terrific headache. And even though I was pleased with the overall outcome of today's mission, I felt like crap. I knew I had to get some rest, and with any luck, at least a cat nap. As I lay in bed, however, sleep eluded me. I was still haunted by everything I had seen and done over the past few days. We had uncovered the remains of a lot of people on that desert, and all I could think about was their families back home – their spouses, their children, their parents, their friends. I said another quiet prayer for them, and that gave me some comfort. And while I was at it, I also thanked God that for the fact that nobody on our team had been injured or killed. A feeling approaching peace finally settled over me, and with it the hope that maybe I could catch a few winks.

But that was not to be. There was a knock at the door, and before I could say, "Enter," the door squeaked on its hinges and was abruptly opened, letting a steaming blast of hot desert air into the room.

It was Lieutenant Allard, who was all formality now as he entered the room and saluted.

I sat up in bed and said, "As you were."

He handed me a folded piece of paper and then said, "The commanding officer invites you to dinner at 1900 hours, casual dress, in the mess hall. Your associate Don North is also invited." I nodded and before I could respond further, he went on to say, "I wasn't asked to tell you this, but the men who went with you on the desert today, and several other officers here at Abu Ghraib, will also be at the dinner."

"It sounds like it's going to be quite an event," I responded. "Right now, I'm awfully tired, and I really need to rest some more." In fact, I was starting to feel pretty bad, and at that point was unwilling to commit to attending the dinner, no matter who might be in attendance.

The lieutenant looked at me and said, "You look like crap, Doc."

"Maybe I look like crap on the outside, but on the inside I feel worse than that."

"I'll bring you some aspirin, or something stronger if I can find it. And you need to get into the shower and get yourself presentable for tonight."

"Thank you, Lieutenant. You sound like my mother. But I have some aspirin, and actually, I've already showered. I'll be a lot more presentable if I can get even a half hour of shuteye."

Lieutenant Allard said nothing more, but simply did a formal about-face and was out the door.

I took a couple of aspirin from my small first aid kit, swallowing them without water. Then, giving up on the idea of a nap, I went back to the shower and stood under the water for a long time. My headache dissipated and I was actually beginning to feel revived, so I decided I would attend the dinner, though I was a little wary about it.

Emerging from the shower again, I changed into what was left of my clean clothes: black lightweight cotton trousers and a blue button-down collar shirt, with no tie. I also put on my favorite brown alligator Western boots with the embroidered medical caduceus on the front end and the American flag and the Texas flag on the back. And even though I knew I was in a secured space, out of habit I checked my snub nose .38 and put it into my right boot. My left boot already had the eight-inch double sided stiletto, which was as sharp as a scalpel. Then, of course, I topped my outfit off with my white Stetson hat.

The ensemble complete, I looked at myself in the mirror and thought, *Not bad, for a guy who looked and smelled like hammered shit just a little while ago, and still kind of feels like hammered shit.* But the aspirin and the shower had done wonders for me, and I now felt that I could actually make it through the night. Even so, as I sat on the end of my bunk, I continued to mull over the dinner, wondering what it was all going to be about.

Just then, there was another knock on the door, and again it was abruptly opened. There stood Lieutenant Allard again, this time in full dress. He had an intense look on his face, and I said, "Come on in, Lieutenant," at which his expression softened considerably.

"Ah, you're ready," he said, greeting me with his hand out. As we shook hands he said, "I didn't know if you were going to accept the dinner invitation – you weren't very clear about that – but if you didn't show up, I was the one who was going to catch hell from the C.O."

"Well, we couldn't have that," I said. "I'm sorry if I was a bit noncommittal during your earlier visit. I was a little cloudy, but I'm feeling better now."

"And certainly looking a lot better," he said, giving my outfit a quick once-over, and seeming pleased with my appearance. "Are you ready to go?"

"Ready as I'll ever be," I said.

As we walked out into the heat, which, true to form, had abated very little despite the fact that dusk was approaching, Lieutenant Allard said, "I've heard about what happened out on the desert today."

Deciding to play it coy, I replied, "Abu Ghraib prison is a rumor mill, and perhaps you heard too much."

"Well, I heard it from the C.O., and he presumably heard it from you, so draw your own conclusions."

I laughed, but then I looked at Allard and saw that his expression had become serious again. Clearly he was weighing the political and personal consequences, both short-term and long-term, that might result from the can of worms that the team and I had opened. It could either be the best thing that ever happened to his career, or the worst. Or it might have no effect at all. Who knew at this point?

Taking mercy on him, I said, "Lighten up, Lieutenant. We're all in this together. What we found out there in the desert isn't a negative reflection on you or the C.O. or anyone here. Those burial mounds are a negative reflection on Saddam Hussein and his psycho sons, and it's good that they're finally being brought to light. It's proof that even though no one has been able to find any WMDs, ousting Hussein was a good thing.

"And as for the insurgent activity, we've disrupted a few attacks, but they'll more than likely continue to be a danger until and unless you can get some more outside support. That's something that the C.O. and ranking officials at Abu Ghraib are going to have to deal with."

Looking marginally more relaxed, Allard said, "You're probably right, Doc. But it's a lot to take in, anyway."

"No argument there," I said.

"Still, I get the idea that you kind of like the challenges you've faced since you got here," Allard said.

"Well, Lieutenant, to tell the truth, I could do without being shot at, or huddling in corridors during mortar attacks, or cleaning up the carnage after killing people who were trying to kill me, but yeah, in general, I like a good challenge." Allard chuckled.

I continued, "In all honesty, though, I prefer to be with my fiancée Terry at our little ranchette in Texas, with our horses, llamas, alpacas, donkeys, deer, and swans and geese on the lake – preferably sitting on our back porch with a cold iced tea in one hand and a book in the other. But I have to find the seven brothers first."

"Well, considering all you've been through, and all your efforts, I would like to be on that flight out of here with you and those seven brothers when you find them."

We made eye contact, and I felt for the first time that we understood each other, which given time might even lead to our liking each other. As we continued walking towards the mess area, nothing more was said, but it was a pleasant interlude.

The walk gave me an opportunity to stretch, which resulted in an improvement in my aches and pains. Granted, it was a real effort, and a poignant reminder of the fact that I'm not a young man any more. But it is an effort that I was and still am willing to expend whenever needed, because while I may be getting on in years, I still have a lot to do.

When we reached the entrance to the mess hall, the lieutenant stepped forward and opened the door, then stood there as I entered the room. I was astounded by what I saw. The tables had been pushed together into one long table in the center of the mess hall, and that long table was fully and formally set. At the head of the table was Colonel Stevens; to his left was Don North and to his right was Lieutenant Heineg, next to whom was an empty seat which I assumed was for Lieutenant Allard.

Further to the right of Stevens were several of the men who had volunteered to go out on the desert with me, and next to them were Aziz and Hussein. I was shocked and stood there in disbelief. Lieutenant

Allard stepped forth, and said, "Follow me." He then escorted me to the empty seat which I had assumed had been reserved for him. As I sat down, everyone at the table stood and clapped. While I felt honored, I was also embarrassed.

The C.O. turned toward me and said, "On behalf of all of us here at Abu Ghraib, we thank you for what you and the men sitting at this table accomplished today. For more than three months I've been trying to get help, going through channels and command, and still the mortars were hitting this prison almost every night, endangering and sometimes injuring or killing the prison inmates, as well as the military members who are housed here."

I stood and thanked everyone briefly, stressing that I could not have accomplished anything without my good friend Don North and the team members who were also seated at this table. I added that even though we had been able to neutralize some mortars and stop a few attacks on the prison, it was very likely that insurgent activity was still an ongoing threat, but one that I was confident would ultimately be handled by the capable leadership here at the prison. Looking directly at Stevens, I added, "Don and I will do whatever we can to help you get the reinforcements you need. For now, though, maybe the actions taken today and the other day will make other insurgents think twice before mounting another attack on us." I took my seat, determined to enjoy this evening and not make it all about me.

But then I was asked by one of the attendees to give a summary of our discoveries, and I looked again to the C.O. for a cue. He nodded and mouthed to me, "Just the basics."

So, choosing my words carefully, I proceeded with a capsule summary of our discoveries – a version of the report I'd given to Stevens after our first expedition to the mounds. "The way I see it, these are burial mounds," I said. "By the number and size of the mounds that we counted, there are probably at least twenty-five thousand bodies, but most likely far more, buried outside the walls of Abu Ghraib prison." I crossed my arms over my chest and paused.

Aziz now spoke up. "Keep going."

"I'm not an archaeologist. But, I know what human bones look like. I have worked in labs and have seen many autopsies, and I know what gunshot wounds to the back of the skull look like. I do not wish to dishonor the dead buried in these mounds, so we selected several to investigate and went no further. This was all the proof we needed. I couldn't ask for more than that, short of absolute validation."

Hussein looked directly me and said, "Then why are you worried?"

"I am not worried. This is a new light on this war. It's proof of what Saddam Hussein, his sons, and the Ba'athist party in general did. This is genocide that involved the Yazidis, the Kurds in the North, and the Marsh Arabs to the South. In addition, there are men, women, and even children buried out there who were killed by political death squads. It can only be compared to what Hitler did with the concentration camps, and with other examples of mass exterminations in history."

I hesitated again, staring down at the table, and continuing to choose my words carefully. "There are no words to describe the inhumanities that took place under Saddam Hussein. And there are no words to describe some of the atrocities that have taken place within the walls of Abu Ghraib prison by certain parties, even after Saddam was ousted." I did not think it prudent to go any further on that topic, so I paused again and looked up, my gaze traveling around the long table.

Finally I said, "As most of you may know by now, I originally came here to look for the seven men who had their right hands removed by order of Saddam Hussein. I discovered more than I wanted. Change is inevitable, and Don North and I just happened to be in the right place at the right time, or the wrong place at the wrong time, depending on your point of view. If it hadn't been Don and me, then ultimately it would have been others. After all, the media were already aware of Abu Ghraib and some of what was taking place inside.

"For now, though, what Don and I need more than anything is your help to find those seven men who had their hands amputated. We need their story. We need their perspective about what happened to them, and what was happening to their country under Saddam Hussein. It's *their* stories that are important now – not mine. We can't change the past, but we can present their stories to the world. And that will be a very good thing."

As I concluded my statement, I hoped that I had helped to clear the air, perhaps reassuring those who were worried that Don and I were planning at a later date to use our findings against the military stationed in Abu Ghraib prison. I knew that some dishonorable discharges might yet result from our activities, but as I had explained to the C.O. in previous private conversations, that was not our reason for being here. I was still determined for our work here to convey a positive message to the world.

And for the first time in several days, I felt hopeful that the net outcome would indeed be positive. I thought about the fact that I still had The Letter, which placed Don and me in a unique position of power. My mind was suddenly cleared as a small rush of adrenaline surged through my body.

Then Lieutenant Allard stood up, smiling as he said, "We all know that you and Don North were sent here to locate the seven brothers. And I think I speak for all of us when I say that we'll do whatever we can to help you. We'll get started on that project again tomorrow.

"But tonight, this is a celebration. So… cheers!" He raised his glass in a toast, and everyone at the table did likewise, echoing, "Cheers!" My own voice was among the most enthusiastic in the chorus.

Whatever tomorrow might bring, tonight was indeed a night for celebration.

PART 3

MISSION
ACCOMPLISHED

CHAPTER 23

THE CORRIDORS OF HELL

As the chorus of cheers in the wake of Lieutenant Allard's toast subsided and the feasting commenced, I found that I was truly beginning to enjoy myself, despite having been so exhausted just a couple of hours ago. My mood had brightened considerably, and I sat back, savoring my dinner and enjoying the buzz of numerous conversations around me. I felt no compulsion to join in any of the chat, so I simply sat in silence taking it all in – a rarity for me, I admit.

I was drifting off into my own world, my eyes wandering around the room but focusing on nothing in particular, when a voice a few chairs down from me said, "Don't worry, Doc. We will find your seven brothers. We will get them – and you – out of here safely. That is a promise!" I turned in the direction of the voice and saw that it was one of the team members on our recent desert expeditions, Brandon. He had apparently mistaken my silence and generally unfocused demeanor as the marks of a troubled man. I smiled to reassure him, and said, "Thank you; I appreciate that. I feel confident that with the help of good guys like you, I'll be able to find them." Brandon smiled and gave me a thumbs-up.

The rest of the evening flew by, and almost before I knew it we were finishing our desserts and having our final drinks for the night. Then there was a round of handshakes and hugs as the festivities came to an end at last, and the attendees began dispersing to their respective quarters.

As I was leaving, I took one last look around the room at the departing crowd, and was struck again by the shockingly chaotic events of the past few days. I really had needed the camaraderie of this surprise dinner and was glad to see everyone celebrating together.

By the time I reached my quarters, I was so tired I could barely stand. I quickly undressed and then staggered to my bunk, looking forward to a long and restful night. I was asleep almost immediately.

But that long and restful night was not to be. I awoke in pitch darkness in the clutches of a nightmare. The details of the dream were quickly fading, but the feeling of horror lingered. Breathing heavily and heart pounding, I was covered in sweat, and my sheets were soaked.

I pushed the button on the side of my glow-in-the-dark wristwatch and I saw that it was 3:30 in the morning. There was still time to get a few hours of sleep if I could manage it, but instead of sleep I found myself staring up at the blackness of the ceiling, trying to shake the effects of a nightmare whose specifics I couldn't even begin to recall.

For a while I just lay there in the dark, controlling my breathing and calming myself. I wanted to go up and get a cold drink, but where would I go at this time of the morning in the desert of Abu Ghraib?

I started thinking again – or perhaps "obsessing" would be a better word – about what I had originally been sent here to do. All accomplishments of the past few days would mean nothing if Don and I failed in our efforts to find the seven brothers. What if we were on a fool's errand? What if the men for whom we were searching were, despite the swirl of rumors about them, nowhere in the area, or worse, were dead? My surge of optimism at last night's dinner had faded, to be replaced by nagging worry.

A couple more hours passed, and I finally gave up, knowing that there would be no more sleep tonight. I swung my legs over the side of the cot, and then headed to my shower. To my consternation there was only a trickle of water, not nearly enough for a decent shower, so I pulled on a pair of shorts and exited my quarters, heading for the communal showers. There was no guarantee that the water situation would be any better there, but I'd never know unless I checked it out.

Even though it was still quite early, the air was already very warm, as usual; in this desert, at this time of year, dawn was anything but cool and refreshing. As I took the short walk to the showers, conflicting thoughts of the men we'd killed in our two expeditions to the desert washed over me again: essentially the same back-and-forth I'd had with myself so many times previously. Clearly these men were the enemy and had wanted to kill us. Yet they surely had families as well, people who had loved them and would suffer from their loss. But my sympathy only went so far. On one level, their deaths caused me heartbreak, but again... *rather them than us,* I thought. I reminded myself that in this environment, sympathy was an emotion that, more often than not, I could not allow myself to feel.

It was still very early, and no one else had yet come to the showers. Walking into one of the shower stalls and closing the door, I turned on the water and was grateful that it was running fine, and there seemed to be plenty of hot water. I relished the feeling of washing away the salt from the dry sweat while relieving my aching muscles. If I couldn't completely relieve my mind, at least I could tend to my body, and the shower was starting to help.

Even so, my mind was still reeling over what had taken place over the last several days. I couldn't stop reviewing the horrors – not just the loss of life but the sights and sounds of battle. The noise of machine guns and small arms fire still reverberated through my entire being; clearly I was not finished processing these experiences. I knew that it would take time for me to heal, and I tried to think down the road to one year, two years, ten years from now. I had to have faith that with time and effort, I would be able to put all of this behind me.

For now, however, I was exhausted. Though none of my other experiences here compared to those battles on the desert, every day that I'd been at Abu Ghraib prison had been, in its own way, both nerve-racking and tedious, and it was all taking its toll on me. With only a few notable exceptions, my sleep had been in short little spurts, interrupted by long stretches of wakefulness as I worried about all of the things that could go wrong.

I forced myself to focus on the present reality that the shower felt incredibly good and that my muscles were finally relaxing. I was able to enter a semi-meditative state, which was actually rather pleasant. I'm not sure how long I stood there under the water, but at some point I realized that time was wasting and that I needed to get started with my day. I reluctantly turned off the water, toweled off, and pulled my shorts on, still in a bit of a haze.

I was startled out of my reverie when the door opened, and I saw the smiling face of Lieutenant Allard.

"Rough night?" he asked. "I didn't see you drinking very much at dinner; it couldn't be a hangover. But still… you look like hell."

"I'm okay. Just a bad dream."

"So I take it you didn't sleep very well?"

"No, which is probably why I look like hell."

"How do you feel other than that?"

"Better than yesterday. I think I'm getting closer to my goal, anyway, and I feel encouraged after last night that I'm going to have more support." As I wrapped my towel around me I said, "The shower is all yours, Lieutenant. I left you some hot water."

"You're all heart, Doc," he said, and I laughed, then exited the shower area and walked back to my bunk. My armpits were already soaked with sweat, but I needed to get dressed for the day. I pulled on my T-shirt, which was already stuck to my skin before I'd even reached for my pants.

Once dressed, I walked over to the mess area for breakfast, still embroiled in my moral dilemma of healer versus killer. Maybe a solitary breakfast and strong coffee would help clear my mind, at least enough for me to focus on finding the seven brothers and getting the hell out of here. Aziz and Hussein were sitting at a corner table, motioning me to join them. I waved them off, but they would not accept no for an answer, so I walked over and sat down with them.

Looking very concerned, they asked me what was wrong, and instead of evading the question and pretending that everything was all right, as was my initial impulse, I decided to come clean with them. I said, "Lieutenant Allard has already informed me that I look like hell. I'm not going to lie to you guys; I didn't sleep very well. I had a nightmare – I can't remember the details, but I couldn't get back to sleep. But what's really on my mind is that I'm stuck with what is best described as a moral dilemma. It's something I've been wrestling with for a while."

"What do you mean?" Hussein asked.

"As a person and a physician, I treasure life. And as a physician, I'm bound by an oath to preserve and protect life to the extent that it's possible. I'm sure that in general we can all agree that it's wrong to kill. Most major religions, not to mention secular law in most places, are pretty clear about that." Aziz and Hussein nodded, though they looked puzzled.

I continued, "Yet we allow ourselves, under the guise of war and with the sanctions of our respective countries, to kill human beings. The question is, *why*?"

My two friends stared at me as if not knowing just how to reply.

I took a sip of my tea and said, "This is not just an abstract question, in case you're wondering. It's about my own experiences as well. As I said, I've been wrestling with this quandary for a while. In my previous travels I've found myself in other situations where I had to take a human life. And of course it bothered me. But my experiences on this trip to Iraq have been even more disturbing, and in a way they've deepened my dilemma. After all, I took a Hippocratic oath!"

There was another long moment of silence as the two men studied me. Finally Aziz spoke up. "It's only natural to question our beliefs," he said. "I think I understand your dilemma. At least I understand what you're saying regarding the conflicting teachings about taking a human life. On the one hand we are told that it's wrong and against the law to kill. On the other hand, in a war situation we are commanded to kill. I have heard the same arguments at home growing up, at school amongst my friends, and of course in the mosques."

"As have I," Hussein said. "And I can see how the fact that you are a doctor makes the arguments even more significant." Then he looked at me intently and said, "Iraq is a country where everybody believes in 'an eye-for-an-eye.' Yet when we go to the mosque, they preach, tolerance, acceptance, equality, and of course love for everyone. Isn't that the Christian way, too?"

"I hate to burst your bubble, but I'm not a Christian," I replied. "I look on myself as an agnostic Jew."

They both looked puzzled again, but I wasn't about to explain. I did not want to turn this into a protracted ideological or religious discussion. So I changed directions slightly. "Whenever I have these arguments with myself," I told them, "It always comes down, eventually, to me concluding that sometimes it's all very simple. No matter what our holy books, our law books, our belief systems, or our training tell us, if we're faced with a situation where there are people on two sides, and it is a matter of killing or being killed, we have no choice but to kill. And on both times when I went out into the desert to explore the mounds, I had consciously placed myself in such a situation."

Aziz and Hussein nodded vigorously, and Hussein said. "So there really is no conflict, when it is just a matter of personal survival."

"That is what I keep telling myself," I said. "But for me, the moral dilemma always has a way of coming back to haunt me."

Aziz said. "That just means you have a conscience, Doc. Don't you think that it's better to have that ongoing conflict than to harden yourself to the point where you just do not care anymore, or where you actually enjoy killing?"

I smiled at him and said, "That's a very good way of looking at it. But it doesn't make things any easier late at night when I awaken from a nightmare and all those doubts come flooding back in again."

Our conversation was cut short when the door to the mess hall burst open and Lieutenant Allard and his sidekick, Lieutenant Heineg, entered. They came to the table, greeting us warmly with handshakes all around. I invited them to sit down, pointing to the remaining empty chairs.

When seated, Allard said to me, "Doc, I must say you're looking better than you did earlier this morning."

"My two friends here cheered me up," I said, indicating Aziz and Hussein.

Allard continued, "Well, we have a busy morning. The C.O. says that Lieutenant Heineg and I are to focus today on helping you find those seven brothers you've been looking for. We're also supposed to have a couple of MP escorts. So let's eat breakfast and get right to it. I have a feeling we *are* gong to find those men for you within the next couple of days, if not today."

I certainly hoped he was right, but I felt that it was best to manage my expectations at this point. As weary as I was after my restless night, I didn't want to deal with another emotional roller coaster of hope and disappointment.

I was, however, slightly encouraged by the fact that the C.O. had asked his two favorite lieutenants to aid me today. Maybe that portended a turning point in our quest. Perhaps today really would be the day we finally found the seven brothers, which would be, to say the least, a profound relief for both Don and me. This thought led me to wonder just where the hell Don was. Was he sleeping in? I decided I'd go look for him after breakfast if he didn't show up before we were finished with our meal.

Breakfast turned out to be quite pleasant, filled with small talk, which for me (and, it appeared for Aziz and Hussein as well) was a welcome break from the weighty discussion about my moral quandaries. I was actually grateful that our conversation had been cut short by the appearance of the lieutenants. I had little doubt that I would continue to struggle in various ways with my inner conflicts, but now I needed to focus on the seven brothers.

As we finished our meals, I was the first to stand up, mostly to indulge in some gentle stretching exercises to relieve the stiffness and pain that were bothering me again. *The old machine is wearing down*, I thought. I had brought some of this on myself when I was younger; as a weight lifter, I lifted more than double my own weight. I had participated in gymnastics as well, and for a while I had also taken part in an acrobatic circus team called the Atlas Jets. In short, I had lovingly tortured my bones and joints for years, not realizing the consequences that would come with age. The best I could do now was to take care of my body and try not to overtax myself.

The stretching helped a little, but I was obviously still in a state of discomfort. Lieutenant Allard jumped up, scurried out of the room, and was back within a few minutes with a bottle of aspirin. Having forgotten to bring any aspirin with me to breakfast, I thanked him, then gratefully sat down and took several of the tablets with a glass of water. After a couple of minutes I stood and stretched again, then sat back down.

Aziz said, "I don't suppose you would want to go back to your bunk and lie down for a while?"

"No, absolutely not. Let's get the day started. We need to get this done. Let's split up into teams so we can cover more area. And speaking of teams, here's another team member now. Finally!" I was looking at Don North, who had just walked into the room and was heading towards our table.

"You're late," I teased him. "Breakfast is over."

"You're the one who's running late," he said, chuckling. "I grabbed a bite earlier, went back to my bunk to organize some notes, and now I'm ready to get to work. What's the plan for today?"

"We were just getting ready to solidify that plan," I said. "Pull up a chair and sit down."

Don grabbed a chair from a nearby table, and as he was getting seated, I was unexpectedly hit by one of those waves of doubt and borderline pessimism that had plagued me on this trip. No doubt it was just the sleep deprivation, but I was troubled again by the fact that Don and I had been here as long as we had without finding the seven brothers, or even procuring any viable leads. I wasn't at the point of giving up hope, but on the other hand, I wasn't exactly in the frame of mind to provide motivation, much less a concrete plan, to the small team that was gathered around me. But I knew I had to say something.

Instead, however, I simply sat there at the table for a couple of minutes, looking around at the team members, and then out over the room. My arms were crossed over my chest, which I vaguely registered as being a defensive position, but I didn't really care. I'm sure that my frustration and doubt were evident in my face as well as my body language, which probably explained why the expressions of the team members changed rapidly from anticipation to puzzlement to, in a couple of cases, the hint of a frown.

Finally I said to the group, "First, before we get started, I want to thank all of you for your friendship. And I thank you for something far more important. You have accepted me. You have taken me in as a brother in arms, giving me this incredible opportunity. You have allowed me to perform as an equal, and I hope and believe I have done so. I apologize for not seeming to be at the top of my game today; I had a bad night's sleep. But I'll catch up on my sleep eventually; right now, we've got work to do. And with your acceptance, help and encouragement – particularly with the addition of Lieutenants Allard and Heineg to our search team – I really do believe we will find the seven brothers. It may not be today, but it'll be very soon."

There was relief on the face of every one of the men around me. Encouraged, I continued, "You have no idea what your help means to me and to the United States, and, Lieutenant Allard and Lieutenant Heineg, to your Commander in Chief in Washington. I'm grateful to all of you guys, so let's get started – and let's not get killed trying to figure this shit out." I smiled, and so did everyone else.

We decided to split into two teams. I would team up with Lieutenant Allard, and Aziz would be our interpreter. Don would be with Lieutenant Heineg, with Hussein accompanying them as their interpreter.

It was still fairly early in the morning as we left the commissary. We each picked up several bottles of water, knowing that the heat would only get worse as the day progressed. After some light chatter and discussion, I suggested that we go into the depths of the prison, to one of its furthest points, where it split into two corridors. Lieutenant Allard, Aziz, and I would take the north corridor, and Lieutenant Heineg, Don, and Hussein would take the one on the south. We had been in these corridors previously, but had not yet ventured to the end. That was going to change today.

As we walked towards the area where the prison split, we were joined by two gruff-looking MPs whom I'd never seen before. We explained to them that we planned to split up into two search groups, one group taking the north corridor and the other the south corridor. They nodded, looking none too pleased about their day's assignment.

The eight of us continued in silence towards our respective destinations, and the lack of chatter gave me more time to think – and worry. Memories of some of the close calls that my medical teams and I had experienced on previous mission trips over the past couple of decades flitted through my mind again, adding another layer to my constant recall of what had happened so recently at the desert mounds around Abu Ghraib prison. I couldn't help thinking that at some point, my luck was bound to run out. Or, to look at it another way, the "angel on my shoulder" that my dear friend Marvin Zindler had so often teased me about might finally grow weary of protecting a fool who, to evoke the famous quotation from Alexander Pope, was constantly rushing in. I knew this was not exactly the ideal frame of mind for the present task, and I struggled to refocus.

Peril aside, I was proud of the fact that my medical teams and I went to places where others wouldn't go and were able to accomplish things that others could not. As a non-profit, and in essence what one would call an NGO, my Children's Foundation depended solely on donations for our budget. There was virtually no governmental oversight by the countries that we entered, and our structure was completely outside of the United States government. This gave us a lot of latitude, but it also put us at risk.

I may be an adrenaline junkie, but I have never been one to intentionally seek out danger. Our medical teams, however, always seemed to find ourselves in the midst of some type of peril, whether it be from war-zone situations or natural disasters. And although the present trip to Iraq was not a medical mission per se, I'd already experienced more than my share of personal danger in the time that I'd been here.

I was determined not to let it get the best of me. I was equally determined not to let those accompanying me see that I was churning inside as we reached the area where the prison divided. Just before we split into our respective groups, we wished each other good luck, and agreed to meet back here at the main corridor.

"If the other team isn't here, we'll assume that they're still searching, and we'll wait for them right here," I said. "We will wait for a period of one hour; that should be long enough for the other team to catch up. After that hour is up, or if for some reason we need to leave the area before the time is up, we'll depart, but we'll leave a message for the other team with the guard on duty. Agreed?" With everyone in agreement, we were good to go.

I regretted that there was not a more efficient way for the teams to communicate with each other while separated, but there was zero cell phone service in this remote part of the prison, so texting was out of the question (not that I was then, or am now, proficient in the fine art of texting), and we didn't have walkie-talkies or any other means of remote communication. Our mutual agreement would just have to suffice.

As Lieutenant Allard, Aziz, one of the MPs, and I began our trek along the north passageway, there was no conversation for the first few minutes. Then, seemingly out of the blue, Lieutenant Allard said, "Doc, everyone in Abu Ghraib is talking about what you guys did on the desert, taking out those mortar installations."

I replied, "We just did what we had to do." I wondered why he was bringing this up now, when I was already very aware, especially after last night's celebratory feast, that our actions on the mounds had been a source of conversation for the past several days. I waited for him to say more about the subject, but he was silent, as if trying to decide exactly what to say next.

Then Allard surprised me when he said, "We recently received information that operatives from Iranian special forces had implemented a series of ratlines to funnel thousands of foreign fighters into Iraq from all over the globe. Their objective has been to try to reverse the gains that Americans and the Coalition forces have been making in Iraq. And Abu Ghraib is reportedly one of their retake targets. We have evidence that Iran has played a major role in arming the insurgents."

Now, that *was* interesting. I was all ears, as were Aziz and, it appeared, the MP as well. Allard went on to say that he had information that American and Iranian operatives had actually been in firefights with each other. He added, "More and more of our military in Iraq are feeling that we went to war with the wrong Middle East country."

Well, I could have told them that, as could numerous other ordinary citizens, journalists, and politicians who had been paying attention from the beginning. Of course, many people had advised against the invasion of Iraq, but the powers-that-be weren't listening. But don't get me started on that again...

Allard questioned whether the war would have been different, whether things would have been better, had we gone into Iran first. Then he shook his head and said, "Well, no use speculating now. Maybe we'll have learned our lesson this time."

"Maybe," I said. "But I wouldn't count on it."

As we continued our walk through the narrow, damp, and musty corridor, Lieutenant Allard continued with his train of thought. He said, "Iran was actually losing the war in Iraq, but it had expanded its activities across the globe. Its influence had been spreading for years, not only to other Middle Eastern countries, but as far away as Latin America. It was Iran that directed the bombing of the Israeli Embassy and the Jewish Community Center in Buenos Aires in the 1990s. And they've operated an intelligence network in Latin America since at least the early 1980s."

"No doubt about it," I agreed, "Iran's terror reach is now worldwide."

"So then… why are we in Iraq?" Allard said.

"I assume that's a rhetorical question, Lieutenant," I replied. "But just in case it wasn't… Please understand that I'm not speaking ill of your Commander in Chief. But in my opinion, and I'm not alone in this opinion, the Iraq invasion was a personal decision for President Bush, with a lot of support and encouragement – and that's a gross understatement – from Vice President Cheney and Deputy Secretary of Defense Paul Wolfowitz, among others. It was the President's personal desire to take out Saddam Hussein and his sons because of their assassination attempt on his father. But that whole WMD rationale? That was all propaganda."

Allard was silent again, looking as if he wanted to say something in response but had decided against it.

Feeling the need to steer the conversation in a more positive direction, and realizing that now was not the time to get up on my soapbox, I said, "On the other hand, there's no disputing that Saddam was a bad actor. Even though there are no WMDs, he was responsible for serious human rights violations. The intervention of the Coalition forces stopped the genocide of the Yazidis, the Marsh Arabs, and the Kurds, not to mention atrocities against untold numbers of Iraqi citizens. That's what I like to focus on."

Allard nodded, still looking a little troubled about what he had previously said, so I assured him, "Don't worry, Lieutenant. I won't say a word about this conversation to the President when I speak to him again."

We walked on in silence, the air now so hot and musty that it was becoming difficult to breathe, much less converse. Again it struck me that being in these overcrowded cells under these conditions could be a death sentence itself. I thought, *I can never again complain about my own problems.* Like most people who have similar thoughts when witnessing the extreme misfortune of others, I knew that I most likely *would* complain again, but at this moment my troubles seemed trivial in comparison with those of the prisoners in this hellhole.

I stopped walking, and reached into my backpack to get a drink of water and try to catch my breath. My team mates halted too and also took drinks. The heat was stifling, and it was really starting to get to me as well as the others, but we needed to continue in our search for the seven brothers. I was hoping that this brief break would give us our second wind.

When we resumed walking, we were all quiet for what seemed like a long time as we moved through the corridor. Finally I broke the silence. I said, "You know, I really miss the operating room. I love the OR. I love teaching the residents and the students, preparing a new generation to take my place. And I love the drama, the pressure of a difficult case, the excitement. I was comfortable there. I did a lot of good there."

"Well, Doc, you are doing a lot of good here, too," Aziz said.

"Thanks," I replied, smiling. "But my years in the OR actually helped prepare me for what I'm doing here. When you walk into the OR, no matter how challenging the procedure might be, you can't allow yourself to be intimidated. And sometimes, you have to be completely oblivious to what other people might say about you. It gives you a level of self-confidence that I think few other jobs do, at least in the civilian world. And it's even more of a confidence-builder when you're providing medical services not in some ultra-modern hospital in the U.S., but in some godforsaken part of the world, in a makeshift OR. Serving the poorest of the poor, the people no one else wants."

"So you're saying that the OR helped prep you for taking out insurgents, or kicking obnoxious OGA guys to the curb, or closing down a prison whorehouse," Lieutenant Allard said. I thought for a moment that he was being sarcastic, until he added, "Yeah, I guess I can see how that might work."

This was followed by another long moment of silence as we continued at an increasingly sluggish pace. I could feel the beads of sweat running down my face and the salt burning my eyes, and my underclothes were already soaked. I stopped again for a moment, taking a deep breath before continuing.

"You all right, Doc?" Allard asked.

"I'm okay," I said. "Just not a big fan of this heat and general airlessness." I knew I had to get my mind solely focused on finding the seven brothers, rather than on my own physical discomfort, but it was getting more difficult. It was also becoming harder to maintain my self-assured demeanor, what with my stomach churning and my heart racing.

Finally Aziz said, "That wall in front of us marks the far end of the prison on this side. We need to find a connecting corridor and begin our search at the far end, then make our way back to where we began."

"The fun just never stops, does it?" I said wryly. That long journey some of us had taken to the subterranean video library had just been a dress rehearsal for the journey we were taking now. But we had come this far…

Aziz immediately took the lead, and I simply nodded and followed, as did Allard and the MP. I narrowed my eyes, blinking and squinting to keep the salt of my sweat from burning them further, but it wasn't doing much good. I wondered how much longer I was going to be able to endure this never-ending trek down one of the corridors of Hell.

CHAPTER 24

JUST WHEN YOU'RE
ABOUT TO GIVE UP...

A s we continued on our chosen path, we finally came to a cul-de-sac of sorts with some metal gates that could close off the passageway, but were only partially drawn down. Beyond the gates was an iron door leading to an adjacent passage, which appeared to be our only choice. I wasn't sure what I was searching for at this point, but I believed I would know it when I saw it.

We ducked under the middle gate and pushed open the iron door, and as we passed through the next set of narrow corridors my doubts came flooding back. I was beginning to worry again that what we were searching for couldn't be found here. These corridors seemed to go on forever, and I wondered for a moment if Aziz had accidentally steered us wrong and was as lost as I was.

Then we heard some noise up ahead; incredibly, there were still some detainees in some of these remote prison cells. I turned my head sharply from one end of this narrow alley to the other, scrutinizing each of the cells and the prisoners as we walked by. I caught bits and pieces of a handful of languages, and though I understood a few words I wondered what they were talking about. I was beginning to feel a little paranoid, as if I were prey being circled by a pack of hungry wild dogs.

But as we continued walking from cell to cell, the detainees seemed relatively benevolent, more inquisitive than threatening, even though I wondered if some of them might be harboring a gun or knife. It was too dark to see very much of the interior of the cells. We could, however, see well enough to ascertain that there was no sign of the seven brothers in any of the cells.

What I could see was that Lieutenant Allard and Aziz were clearly as miserable as I was. The MP didn't seem to be suffering quite as much, but it was apparent that he was not enjoying our expedition. For the rest of us, the oppressive heat, and our tired sore muscles from miles of walking, were visibly cutting into our resolve. And then there was the torment being inflicted by the merciless biting sand flies. I felt as if I had been waging a bloody war of attrition against these little monsters for the last several hours, but the flies were winning. I wasn't quite ready to wave a white flag, but I was close.

Finally we came to another wall, which, to my mingled relief and dismay, had no doors leading anywhere. "This is it," Aziz said sadly as we halted. "This is the end of the line."

"Are you sure?" I asked, though I already knew the answer. "No secret passageways that appear if we push against the right spot on the wall? No trap door leading deeper into the bowels of this god-awful place?"

"I am absolutely certain," Aziz said, and the MP nodded in agreement.

"But don't give up, Doc," Aziz added. "The other corridor that Mr. North's team went down is structured exactly the same way. Maybe they had better luck than we did."

But he didn't sound at all convinced, and I didn't feel convinced. All we could do now was turn around and go back the way we had come. *Where,* I thought to myself, *is that white flag when I need it?*

Feeling more discouraged than I had felt in a long time, not to mention more exhausted and dehydrated, I emerged with Lieutenant Allard, Aziz, and our MP escort back into the main corridor where our two teams had originally parted. We had no idea at this point how Don's team had fared, but I wasn't at all optimistic. The area was empty, with the exception of a lone prison guard; there was no sign of Don, Lieutenant Heineg, Hussein, and their MP, and there was no message to us from them. Obviously we were the first team back. I wanted nothing more than to return to my quarters for a shower and a nap, but we had promised to wait for the others for an hour, so wait we would.

There wasn't any place to sit except on the floor, so all of us except for our steadfast MP and the prison guard sank down, resting our backs against the hard stone wall. Nobody seemed to be in a conversational mood, which was fine with me. I took a long swig from one of my water bottles, then leaned my head back and shut my eyes for a moment, vowing not to fall asleep. Apparently I broke my vow, because the next thing I remember was being startled awake by a commotion that seemed to be coming from the entrance to the south corridor.

As Aziz, Lieutenant Allard, and I scrambled to our feet, a weary-looking but visibly gleeful Don North came striding out, accompanied by Lieutenant Heineg, Hussein, and their MP escort. But they weren't alone; with them was an Iraqi man, obviously one of the prisoners – who, I immediately noticed, was missing his right hand. A bandage covered the stump where his hand had been, and he had a big ugly "X" tattooed on his forehead. My heart must have skipped a couple of beats. I was about to say something when another couple of detainees emerged, and then another one, and then three more.

All seven were missing their right hands. All bore that big "X" on their foreheads.

The seven men gathered in a silent group around Don and his team. As for Don, he said nothing for a long moment, just gave us all a big grin and a two-thumbs-up sign. Then he walked right up to me and said, "We did it, Doc!" He grabbed me and gave me a big hug. I won't lie to you; there might have been a couple of tears in my eyes. Or maybe it was just my own sweat dripping into them.

Then Don said to the Iraqi man who had initially come out of the corridor with his team, "Baasim, come here and meet my friend, Doctor Agris, The Crazy Texan." Baasim approached me, a little shyly, and said, in accented but perfect English, "It is an honor to meet you, Doctor." Shaking hands would understandably have been awkward, but that awkwardness was averted when Baasim dropped to one knee and slapped the bandaged stump of his right hand across his chest in the sign of a friendly greeting. I returned the gesture, my exhaustion completely forgotten.

After we stood up, Baasim turned back to his fellow prisoners and gestured for them to step forward. They did so, some of them a little hesitant until Baasim and Hussein spoke words of encouragement to them. Then suddenly everyone seemed to be talking at once, in a multilingual jumble of words that needed no translation.

Once the initial excitement abated, Don and I and the lieutenants agreed that it was time to take the return walk through the main corridor. Our first task would be to report to the C.O. to let him know that we had located the seven brothers at last, and to introduce them to him. "But while we're walking," I said to Don, "I want to hear all about what just happened."

"You bet," Don said. "Let's go; I don't want to spend any more time in this place than I have to."

After Aziz, Hussein, and Baasim made our immediate plans clear to the brothers who didn't understand English very well, we all began the trek back. As we walked, Don began telling us the story of his team's discovery.

"Actually, we can't take all that much credit for it," he said. "It was Baasim and his brothers who discovered *us,* not the other way around."

Don went on to briefly describe the long walk through the stifling passageways, in many ways echoing the experiences of my team. "Tell you the truth, I was on the verge of giving up," he said. "I'm not proud of it, but I was about to the point of thinking, *to hell with this place, I'm getting out of here while we still can."*

"Believe me, I know exactly what you mean," I said, and Aziz and Lieutenant Allard nodded.

"And then, just like that, it happened," Don continued. "A prisoner came running toward us, waving, and it was clear that he was missing his right hand. I shifted slightly to my right and waved at the man to continue moving forward towards us – not that I probably could have stopped him if I'd wanted to. Our MP here was now on full alert; there was no telling what was going through his head. But I told him to stand down."

Don's MP escort nodded slightly but said nothing as Don resumed his narrative. "Still, I was glad we had backup, because I couldn't be certain whether this guy was going to be a real problem or the breakthrough we'd all been looking for," he said, turning to Baasim and grinning. Baasim, after a moment's hesitation, smiled back.

"The man's arms were raised, and he was waving back to us," Don said. "We couldn't understand what he was shouting, but you can bet that all of us were keeping a close watch on him."

Don said that when the man was only a few feet away from the team, he dropped to one knee and performed the same greeting that he had just performed with me. "Of course, I responded in kind," Don said. "Then I gave Hussein a gentle push forward, suspecting I'd need his skills as interpreter. He didn't panic, just kept a very calm tone as he spoke to the man, which helped me focus on what was happening.

"At that point, all I could do was stand there with my mouth open, but no words were coming out. I stared straight ahead at the man and the otherwise empty corridor. Then I walked the short distance to where he was – he was still kneeling – and gestured for him to stand up. My mind was racing and I was kind of in shock, seeing this guy with an amputated right hand right there in front of me."

"And to think that I missed it," I said.

"Yeah, I wish you'd been there," Don replied, "but you're here now, and that's what counts. Anyway, as I finally emerged somewhat from my confused state, it occurred to me that I had to let things take their course. I was grateful to have Hussein with me, and I told him to ask the man his name. I decided to let this stranger talk without interrupting him, relying on Hussein to translate.

"Then more people appeared. A small group started forming around us, consisting of staff and other men who appeared to be detainees, but I hardly noticed them. After speaking with the man for a few moments, Hussein told me, 'His name is Baasim Al Fadhly,' at which point Baasim stepped forward and said in perfect English that he was pleased to meet me. So much for my assumption that he didn't speak English. You can imagine how I was feeling after I heard his name."

"Of course!" I said. As I mentioned earlier, Don and I each had what we believed to be an accurate list of the brothers' names. Operating on the assumption that the list was valid, Don was certain that he had finally found one of the men.

"So that was one down, six to go," Don continued. "I was on the verge of asking Baasim if he could take me to the other six men as quickly as possible, but that turned out not to be necessary." Don said that as more detainees began to gather around them and the MP stepped forward to try to move the crowd back, Baasim, with a single gesture, got a half dozen of the men to step away from the group. Don noticed they all had their right hand missing and that most of them were wearing crude bandages on their stumps. He also noticed that they all had the "X" mark tattooed on their foreheads. He quickly signaled to the MP that it was okay.

"As each of the six men stepped forward, Baasim introduced him to me. I was still somewhat in disbelief, and I was just standing there with my mouth open again, no doubt looking like an idiot. Then suddenly Baasim threw his arms around me in a big hug. He said there were rumors in the prison that two Westerners had arrived and were looking for the seven brothers. According to the rumor, one of the Westerners was a doctor and the other was a newsman, both sent there to bring the seven brothers back to the United States to get new hands. The rumor also implied that we were there to look into the medical treatment and interrogation techniques to which the detainees in the prison were subjected."

Don had assured Baasim that the rumors were true, explaining that he was the newsman and telling him that it was now time for the seven brothers to meet the doctor who was going to help provide them with new hands. "So… here we are," Don said.

As we continued walking, Baasim, with some urging from both Don and me, began to tell us the story of how he and the six others had formed a bond within the prison walls. His story echoed some of what we had been hearing, but now we were getting it straight from the source. "There was an open courtyard in a far corner of the prison," Baasim said . "We worked as a team to survive. Cooking our meals was one example. We cooked most of our own meals with the provisions that we were able to acquire, thanks to a couple of the prison guards who were sympathetic to our plight. One man would hold the food and chop it up as needed, and another man would hold the pot, while another man placed the food in the pot to be cooked."

The men washed their clothes in a similar manner, Baasim explained. "Ala'a was usually the one to carry the heavy jug with water. Another man would place the clothes out over a big rock, and another would beat the clothes while another man, usually Ala'a, would add the water. When that was finished, another man would pick up the clothes and hang them on a string line to dry. And remember, we did all of these tasks with only one hand, our left hand. It took a lot of practice, but we got pretty good at it."

The men worked so well together that they soon became inseparable. "By forming our brotherhood, we survived Abu Ghraib prison," Baasim said. "We had our own little society, and for the most part nobody bothered us. We did not know when or if we would ever be released, but we were determined to survive as long as possible. When we began hearing rumors that someone was searching for us so we could be released and perhaps even get medical treatment, that gave us extra encouragement. It kept us going on bad days. And there were a lot of bad days."

By this time, we were approaching the C.O.'s office. "Are you all ready to meet Colonel Robert Stevens, the commanding officer of Abu Ghraib?" I asked Baasim, and he turned to the others and translated my question for those who needed it. The men looked a little uncertain at first, but then smiled and nodded their heads. Baasim turned back to me and said, "I think we are as ready as we will ever be."

"Good, because this is his office," I told Baasim. "He should still be in at this time of day, but if he isn't, we'll find him." I was hoping that Stevens would be in, because I really didn't feel like embarking on another search. My exhaustion was beginning to catch up with me again.

I knocked on Stevens' door, and was relieved when he called out, in a cheery voice, "Come on in!" I opened the door just a little and poked my head in. "Colonel Stevens, Don and I have some gentlemen here that we want you to meet." Then before Stevens could say anything, I opened the door all the way and walked in, gesturing for the seven brothers and our team members to follow suit.

I wish I could have captured on camera the expression on Stevens' face as everyone filed in and the team members stepped away from the seven men, allowing the C.O. to get a good look at them and observe that they were all missing their right hand. He broke out into a big grin and stood up, saying, "You found them! Congratulations! And gentlemen, I am very glad to meet all of you." He rushed from behind his desk with his hand out, until he realized the awkwardness of the situation. He knew enough about cultural and religious traditions in the region to know that the men would never offer their left hands for a handshake, so he withdrew his hand and said, "Welcome to... well, to freedom!" Next he turned to Don and me and our team members and said, "Good work, guys."

The next few minutes were filled with introductions, and while a few things may have been lost in translation, the overall mood was one of good will and celebration. The C.O. invited us to bring the men to the officers' mess for dinner that night. "But first," he said, "we'll take them to their new quarters so they can have a chance to clean up and rest."

"Good," I said. "And that will give me a chance to do preliminary medical examinations, and Don and I can brief them about what's coming next." Baasim turned to the other brothers and let them know what was going on, and they all smiled and nodded.

"Lieutenant Allard will take you to the men's quarters," the C.O. said, and he repeated, "I am very glad to meet all of you, and I look forward to seeing you tonight at dinner."

As Lieutenant Allard led us to the brothers' quarters, Don and I filled Baasim in on what was next, and he in turn informed the others. We told them that they would be flown to the United States, to Houston, Texas, and would be staying at my home and some of my close neighbors' homes in the Houston area. They were very excited when they heard this. I explained that many generous donors in Houston had contributed the money to pay for the brothers' surgery, for their new myoelectric hands, and for their care and rehabilitation following the surgery.

"We have a famous rehabilitation center in Houston, called the Texas Institute for Rehabilitation and Research, or TIRR for short," I told them. "After you are trained at this center, you will be able to use your new hands for everything, just like a normal hand. You'll be able to use all types of tools, and even do delicate work such as tying a shoelace." They were especially excited about this.

"And then," I continued, "once your surgery and rehabilitation are complete, you will go on a tour of Texas, and possibly other parts of the U.S., but the big plan is to take you to our nation's capital, Washington, D.C., so you can meet and visit with President Bush. We are not certain yet if or when this will happen, but we have people working on it. In total, you'll probably be in the U.S. for about three months, perhaps a little longer." As Baasim continued to relay this information, the men grew more enthusiastic, apparently undaunted by the prospect of being away from home for an extended period. Given their circumstances, that was understandable.

We reached the quarters that had been prepared for the seven brothers, and they smiled broadly as we showed them their new accommodations. "It's not a luxury hotel," Don said, "but I imagine it's at least a little better than what you had before." Baasim translated that to the other brothers, and they all laughed.

As the men began to settle in, I took the time to examine the stumps of their amputated right hands. Although they had become more or less adjusted to life without a right hand, the healing from the brutal mutilations had been far from complete. The men all had multiple tumors, some the size of golf balls, at the end of their amputated wounds. These tumors, known as neuromas, were quite painful even to the slightest touch. That explained the bandages, which buffered them from the worst of the pain.

Following the examinations, we told the brothers that we were going to leave them so they could rest and clean up, and that we would be back for them at 7:00 that evening. True to our word, we showed up at their quarters at 7:00, and they were ready. We led them to the mess hall, where a special table had been set up for the seven guests of honor. Don and I were seated at the table with them, as were the C.O. and his two trusty lieutenants, Allard and Heineg. I was pleased to see that Aziz and Hussein were also at our table.

The seven brothers were still flush with excitement; in fact, they were so excited throughout dinner that they could scarcely eat. But they were quite talkative, and it became apparent that several of the others besides Baasim were at least conversant in English, though not as fluent as he was. They all attempted some conversation in English, but talked so fast it was difficult at times to understand exactly what they were saying. What *was* understandable was their joy at being rescued and their excitement about their prospects for a brighter future.

The C.O. made a special effort to converse with the brothers, and he and I explained the travel plans to them. Even though Marvin Zindler and I and Marvin's crew, along with several others, had made most of the preliminary arrangements before I left for Iraq, those arrangements now had to be verified and finalized.

I said to the brothers, "There is a lot that still has to be done, since you don't have passports or any type of travel papers. But be assured that in Houston, people are working on several important details, such as your flight arrangements. And Colonel Stevens, Don North, and I will be working on other details here, to ensure that everything goes as smoothly as possible." I told the men a little bit about Marvin Zindler, explaining that both he and I had originally come to be involved in this mission thanks to Don North, and telling them that Marvin was considered a hero by many because he had helped people in need all over the world. I added that Marvin and his crew were planning several major TV news stories to let the world know about the plight of the seven brothers, and to shed light on the suffering of the Iraqi people.

Stevens explained to the brothers that when the time came for them to depart, he would arrange to transfer them in armored Humvees from Abu Ghraib prison to Baghdad. Then from Baghdad, they would travel on a military aircraft to Frankfurt, Germany, and it would all be done in such a way that their lack of passports or travel papers would pose no problem.

"We will be in contact with the German embassy and the Ambassador to make sure that you have no problems landing or staying in Germany," I said. "The plan is for you to be placed in an isolation area within the Frankfurt airport, where there will be comfortable seating and food and drink provided until your flight is ready to leave for the United States."

The men listened intently as I continued, "Mr. Zindler has said he will arrange for limousines to pick you up at Houston's Intercontinental Airport, and take you to the television station in Houston where he works. You will be treated like royalty all along the way. And even though this is all being done without the official support of the United States government, the entire plan is backed by a private agreement between myself and President George W. Bush. He looks forward to meeting all of you."

I may have been exaggerating a little about the private agreement, and the trip to D.C. was still uncertain, but I felt sure that it would all work out. In light of my previous conversations with him, I was pretty sure that the President would not pass up an opportunity to shine a positive light on the narrative about Iraq.

My statement about President Bush was a tough act to follow, and the seven brothers were silent for a while, picking at their dinner. But before long they were all talking excitedly again, and the rest of the evening passed in a joyous buzz of celebration.

Then, at some point towards the end of the evening, I had an epiphany. It suddenly hit me that with the seven brothers having finally been found, and the wheels having been set in motion for their transport to Houston, my primary mission here at Abu Ghraib had been accomplished. Don had already indicated that he would stay on for a few more days to help the C.O. finalize arrangements from this end. I had also done everything I felt was within my power to carry out the secondary mission of addressing the interrogation and abuse problems; the rest was up to the C.O. and the powers that be. There was no reason I couldn't begin my own journey home immediately.

I pulled my chair over so that I was sitting next to the C.O., and I told him that I was finally ready to return home. Was it my imagination that a look of relief washed over his face for a moment? Probably not, but that didn't faze me. I explained to Stevens that Don was willing and able to help him with the rest of the arrangements for the seven brothers, and that I was eager to get back home to Terry.

Stevens responded, "That's perfectly understandable, Doc, and you're in luck. There's going to be a troop transport caravan from Abu Ghraib to Baghdad tomorrow morning. They're leaving at 07:00. Think you can be ready?"

"Do you even have to ask?" I said, with a huge grin. And suddenly my exhaustion was gone again. I stood up and announced to the table at large, "Folks, I'm going to be leaving tomorrow morning to go back home. I'll see some of you in Houston, Texas very soon. As for the rest of you, it has truly been an honor and a pleasure working with you. Now if you'll excuse me, I'm going to go back to my quarters, get packed, and get some rest. I've got an early day tomorrow."

What followed was a flurry of handshakes and hugs all around, including big bear hugs and a kiss on the cheek from Baasim and a couple of the other brothers. Aziz and Hussein, my faithful friends and interpreters, also gave me big hugs, with tears in their eyes.

Then Don came up to me and started to shake my hand, but changed his mind and pulled me into a hug. "See ya soon, buddy," he said to me. His current plan was to accompany the brothers to Baghdad and then on to Frankfurt, and possibly to continue with them all the way to Houston. "Those plans could change," he said, "but either way you and I will see each other soon. Keep in touch, Doc."

It was with a little sadness that I left the mess hall and returned to my quarters to pack and get ready for bed. I would never have believed that I could feel nostalgic for this awful place, but there was no denying that at some level, I would miss it.

After packing, I showered and shaved, set my alarm, and fell into bed. But sleep eluded me, not only because of my excitement about finally going home and seeing Terry again, but also because I couldn't help dwelling on the fact that the troop transport on which I would be riding tomorrow would be passing through the infamous "Ambush Alley" – the very place where that previous caravan I'd been on had been attacked by the white Toyota truck that seemed to come out of nowhere from the desert. I was dreading a repeat performance.

After tossing and turning awhile, I got up, dressed, and walked to the Abu Ghraib communications center. I asked the operator on duty to put a call through to the United States, to the White House switchboard. He was a new guy, or at least I hadn't seen him before, and he looked at me questioningly but didn't move to make a call. Again I said, "Can you please put a call through to the U.S.?"

He immediately said, "Yes, sir. Yes, sir." I gave him the number and instructed him, "As soon as the call goes through, give me the line." It took a few minutes, but finally the operator handed me the phone. There was considerable static, but the phone was ringing, and after several rings a chipper young lady said, "This is the White House."

"This is Dr. Joseph Agris, Retired Lieutenant Commander, calling from Abu Ghraib prison in Iraq. I need to speak to the Deputy Chief of Staff."

"One moment, please," she replied. This was followed by several minutes of silence, and I feared we had been disconnected. But I was prepared to wait as long as it took, and to place the call again if necessary. Finally the Deputy Chief of Staff came on the line, and I explained who and where I was, informing him that Don North and I had located the seven brothers. I told him that final arrangements were being made both here and in Houston for their safe transport from Abu Ghraib to Baghdad, and from there to Frankfurt and on to Houston. I added that the commanding officer at Abu Ghraib would be in touch with the appropriate officials at the White House within the next few days, but that at the moment, I wanted the message conveyed to President Bush, who, I assumed, was anxiously awaiting the information.

"This message is top priority," I said. "Did you get all of it?"

The Deputy Chief of Staff replied, a little sharply, it seemed to me. "Yes, Commander. He will have that information on his desk first thing in the morning."

"That will be satisfactory," I said. "Thank you for your assistance." Then I hung up, only to see that not only the young operator but a few others who had come into the communications room were staring at me. Ignoring their stares and implied questions, I simply said, "Thank you for your help," and then I saluted and left the room.

You may be wondering why I didn't take the time to also call Terry to tell her I was on my way home. I had thought about doing so, but then decided that I was going to surprise her and wait until I got to Houston. I smiled as I walked back to my quarters, imagining her delighted response when I finally made that phone call. Approaching my quarters, I felt that I would finally be able to get some much-needed sleep. And so I did; when the alarm woke me at 06:00 the following morning, I jumped out of bed, feeling ready for whatever would come next.

CHAPTER 25

GOODBYE TO IRAQ

At precisely 07:00 I was standing at the front entrance to the prison with my duffel bag slung over my shoulder and my large backpack sitting on the ground beside me. Although I had taken another shower that morning, I was already sweating through my clothing, and the light breeze was blowing sand into every crevice.

A lightly armored Humvee suddenly pulled up, kicking up even more sand. I was glad to see that my driver that day was Sergeant Major Justin Roberts, who had befriended me at Camp Cropper and had greeted me when I first arrived at Abu Ghraib prison, but whom I hadn't seen since then. He seemed equally glad to see me, shouting as he got out of the vehicle, "Hi, Doc! I get to drive you to Baghdad for your flight to Germany!" He told me that we needed to wait for the other vehicles in our convoy to arrive, which should happen at any minute now. "We're also going to have a few other men join us in the Humvee," he said. He was clearly in a jovial mood.

"You're very cheerful this morning, Sergeant Major," I said. "Matter of fact, I've noticed that everybody seems a little *too* cheerful now that I'm leaving."

"You could say that, I guess," he admitted, grinning. "At any rate, the tensions around Abu Ghraib seem to have decreased substantially already. It's funny; we had learned to live with the occasional mortar rounds each night, but you and that letter of yours... that was like a battery of big guns that kept pounding away."

"Do you think it really made that big a difference?" I asked. "Was it really that bad?" I was pretty sure that I knew the answer already, but I wanted the satisfaction of hearing it.

"Let me put it this way," he said. "The fact that even the C.O.'s attitude towards you and your buddy North seemed to be affected by that letter... that's what really got everyone's attention. I think the scariest

293

part for them was that so few of them knew exactly what was in that letter."

"Not knowing is both a scary and powerful thing," I said.

"Well, at any rate, even though you and North were toasted by everyone at dinner the other night after that second trip to the desert, I'm pretty sure that almost everyone is glad to see The Crazy Texan leaving." I looked at him with a slightly amused but questioning expression on my face, which prompted him to elaborate.

"I think it was your generally undisciplined behavior, and your raving against the Rules of Engagement, that got on their nerves the most. But it was that letter that made everyone up the chain of command a little afraid of you and North. I've been instructed that if anything happened to you before you got on that plane to Germany, they would put me in front of a firing squad." He began to laugh.

I laughed myself, but then said, "What are we laughing at? That's probably true!"

Roberts, suddenly all business, said, "There's a flak jacket and a helmet in there, and unless there are countermanding orders in your precious letter, you have to wear them for the trip. So go around to the other side of the Humvee, put them on, and as soon as everyone else shows up, let's get the hell out of here."

As I donned my protective gear, Roberts continued, reassuring me, "They checked the road last night and told me it was clear, and I know there haven't been any problems the last several days. They didn't even insist on flak jackets and helmets when they had a general come here to make an inspection tour with the Red Cross and a human rights group."

"It's nice to know they love me," I said.

After I'd donned my flak jacket and helmet, I stood by the vehicle with Roberts to wait for the others. Within five minutes, three other Humvees had pulled up behind us, full to capacity with troops and gear. At about the same time, three men in full combat gear came striding out of the front entrance to the prison. I had seen them around the premises at various times, but we hadn't formally met. These were the men who would be joining Roberts and me in our vehicle. Seeing them up close, with their body armor and weapons, made me a little anxious again, reminding me of my previous experience in Ambush Alley. I tried to quell my anxiety and focus on the fact that I was, at last, on my way home.

Roberts introduced me to the three men as a retired Lieutenant Commander. I added, "But my friends just call me 'Doc,' or 'The Crazy

Texan.' At the mention of the second nickname, a couple of the men raised their eyebrows. "Oh, so you're *that* guy," one of them said.

But one by one, they came up and shook my hand. One of the men, Corporal Paul Jenkins, had an especially firm grip that left my hand and arm slightly the worse for wear. "Easy there," I said to him. "I need this hand to operate, you know."

Jenkins smiled and said, "Sorry, Doc." Then he looked at Roberts and said, "I'm glad we're getting an early start, sir. Lately, most of the attacks along the road we'll be taking had been occurring at sundown or later in the evening." Then Jenkins looked at me again, as if sensing that I needed further reassurance.

"Hey, don't worry, Doc," he said. "It's pretty likely we'll be safe and that there won't be any unpleasant surprises. But we're trained to deal with surprises – most of them, anyway. And we've heard about what you did a few weeks ago in Ambush Alley, so if there's anything we can't handle, hey, we figure you've got it covered."

"Gee, was that supposed to make me feel better?" I asked. "Well, nice try, it almost worked."

Everyone laughed, and we all climbed aboard the Humvee with our bags. Roberts honked to the other vehicles in the convoy to signal that we were ready to roll, and then we were off on our half-hour ride from the prison to the airport. I had been told the aircraft would take off at 08:00, so we had plenty of time and did not need to rush. Even at this early hour, the sun was already hammering the desert sands, and the temperature was about 120 degrees.

As we drove, it was clear that Roberts was in a chatty mood, and he directed his conversation at me. "I've been curious, Doc. Why did you go into this line of work?" he asked me. "I hear you've been in more than 70 countries. Some Marines I was talking to told me that during the Reagan administration, around the time of the Contra-Sandinista conflict, you were in Nicaragua with a big medical team."

I really didn't want to talk about myself, but then I noticed that the three other men in the car with us were looking at me as if they were genuinely interested in my answer, so I decided to indulge Roberts for a while.

"What you heard is true," I said. "And I'm pretty proud of what that big team and I were able to accomplish. The doctors, nurses, and support personnel I worked with were amazing." If it had been in existence at that time, I would have mentioned my book about my

Nicaragua missions, *Miracles In Bedlam: A Doctor's Adventures in a War Zone.* Those who know me know that I've never been shy about promoting my books.

Right now, however, I wanted to divert the attention from past accomplishments and focus on the present mission, which wasn't yet over. I also wanted the conversation to center on something besides me. I started to turn to one of the other men and ask him a question, but before I could get it out, Roberts said again that he thought I'd shown a lot of bravery here in Iraq.

I responded, "Actually, Don North has been the brave one in this adventure. He's not only smart, he's fearless. And this isn't the first time he's risked his life. He's been embedded with troops all over the world, reporting the news from some really scary places."

Roberts said, "It sounds like a hero's life to me."

"I couldn't agree more," I replied.

"But I'd like to know more about you and your work. What do you like best about it?" Roberts said. *So much for diverting the conversation from myself,* I thought. But the other men seemed amenable to hearing more of my life story, so I might as well play along.

I told Roberts what I had told so many others: that I loved my work in the hospitals at the Texas Medical Center, especially teaching the students and the residents. I said that I have always felt that the teacher was someone whose job it was to not only pass on the information to the next generation, but also to stimulate their minds, get them thinking, encourage them to develop empathy and compassion, and stress to them the importance of living up to the Hippocratic Oath.

"The operating room can be really hard work," I said, "eighteen hours a day and frequent work on weekends. I've never minded long days, and helping to create good results for patients brings me real joy. But I always wanted to see the real world outside the classrooms and operating rooms. When I started taking trips for something more than the tourist experience, I learned that there were thousands upon thousands of people – especially children – who needed medical care and surgical treatments. I fell in love with the children of the world."

I said that this had led to the formation of Marvin Zindler's and my charity, The Children's Foundation, and that with our teams of medical students, residents, and interns, we traveled the world, taking care of the poorest of the poor. "I think such trips were some of the most valuable parts of their education, not to mention my own," I said. "After all, at home in a modern hospital with the latest equipment, we had all of the luxuries. On these trips to Third World countries, my residents and medical students had to learn to improvise and do the best they could with what they had.

"But I'll tell you: those students and the residents could do more in a few weeks on one of these trips than they would get to do in six months or even a year at the Houston Medical Center hospitals. I always found it interesting that at The Methodist Hospital, we routinely worked them too hard for far too many hours, and they often complained about that – but on these trips the hardest thing for me to do was get them to *stop* working and get a few hours rest."

Roberts turned and looked at me, as if he were trying to find words to respond. Noticing that he seemed to be losing focus on his driving, I admonished him, "Keep your eyes on the road. You're drifting into the sand dunes! Remember what they told you – if something happens to me, you're going to be in front of a firing squad." Everyone in the Humvee broke into laughter.

Turning his attention back to the road ahead, Roberts said, "I want to hear more. I've always been fascinated by people who are really committed to their work, people who love what they do so much that they'd work 24/7 if that were possible."

Intrigued by what I thought Roberts was after, I took my response to another level and dug deeply into layers of memories that I hadn't thought about for many years. I told Roberts that I was sure that many of the people who worked with me thought I was an obsessive-compulsive. He looked a little puzzled by my words, so I went on to explain that when I took on a project, I ran it from beginning to end, and was relentless. I would not allow myself to get sidetracked, and I always brought it to a conclusion, good or bad.

"And my obsessive-compulsive nature fit right in with Don North and Marvin Zindler," I said, grinning. I told Roberts that I had enthusiastically agreed to participate in this mission to Iraq due to the involvement of Don and Marvin, because each of them in his own way was meticulous about addressing every detail, no matter how insignificant or grand. They left nothing to chance in their writings or in their TV broadcasts, and Marvin had always brought that same attention to detail to our medical mission trips. "He's always been there for the underdog; he's one of the kindest and most compassionate human beings you could ever hope to meet. He lives for his work and for his family," I added.

"Iraq really wasn't an end point for any of us – not for me, not for Marvin, not for Don," I continued. "But we were drawn to the project here because we all felt that with the increasing number of American casualties, it was like the war was just beginning again. Tension and violence were increasing and getting worse – and not just in Iraq but also in the States. Political divisions in America were becoming wider and deeper. Don and Marvin and I had an ominous feeling. We all believed that what was taking place at Abu Ghraib prison, and had now become public information, had at least something to do with the increase in violence in the U.S."

"So, in a sense, you guys have been on a peacekeeping – or peacemaking – mission," Roberts said.

"You could say that," I replied. "But I've got to confess that for me, there's something else at work too. I always describe myself as an adrenaline junkie, and as you probably know all too well, when you're in a war zone, the adrenaline flows like crazy. Well, I *like* that feeling. Don't get me wrong; I don't deliberately take risks just to get it, but… well, as I said, I like the feeling." Roberts and the others all smiled, nodding in understanding.

I continued, "Also, for some reason I've always been interested in prisons and the treatment of those held behind bars. I've visited lots of prisons throughout the world and have seem some pretty awful things. I've seen forty men in a tiny prison cell, all sitting on a concrete floor with a hole in the rear of the cell to serve as a toilet, and a metal pipe that would drip water. A lot of these prisons were so overcrowded that the inmates had to take turns to lie down to sleep. In some – many – food had to be brought into the prisons by relatives or friends from the outside, or the inmates would literally starve to death."

I went on to tell my small audience that I had actually spent time as a physician at Terminal Island Prison in California. Some members of the Bonanno crime family, one of whom was the inspiration for Michael Corleone in Mario Puzo's book *The Godfather*, had been imprisoned there. The infamous serial killer and cult leader Charles Manson also did time at the prison. "Lots of other famous folks have been housed there," I added. "But what I think is even more interesting is that during the time I was there, Terminal Island was, as far I knew, the only co-ed federal prison in the U.S." Noticing Roberts' eyes widen, I quickly added, grinning, "But as far as I know, the two genders did not mix. Sorry to disappoint you."

"No BS, you were really there?" Roberts asked.

"Yes, for two years. Maybe one day I'll write a book about my experiences there."

"Go for it!" Roberts said. Then, after a moment's silence, he said that my lust for adventure reminded him of when he was out on a mission with the Marines and a detachment of SEALS. He said he'd been on some tough ones, and had looked forward to working anywhere in the world under any conditions, but his attitude had changed when he came to Abu Ghraib prison. After that first visit, he said, he was ready to go home and stay home. Fortunately, he didn't have much time left in the military.

Roberts wanted to know more about my own military service, so I told him about my experience during the Vietnam War in 1969-71, when I rose to the rank of Lieutenant Commander. "I worked with the Navy," I said, "but they were short of surgeons, and I was officially under the auspices of the United States Public Health Service. They based me at the Naval Base in Los Angeles, where I was the physician in charge of both medical and dental clinics, since I was trained and qualified in both fields. I think they figured they got a twofer; a physician and a dentist, all for one salary."

Then Terence, one of the other men, spoke up. "Did you enjoy it, apart from being underpaid?" he asked.

"I'll be honest with you," I said. "It was both a good time and a bad time for me. I would never trade my military experience with those I met and those I cared for, but as a result, I lost a year at the residency program at the University of Pennsylvania that I would have to make up after my two-year stint in the military was over.

"Also, as you probably know, Vietnam had been a very unpopular war, where a lot of people had been seriously injured or killed. We were losing our corpsmen, medics, and physicians faster than we could replace them, and the American public was growing increasingly disillusioned. I had no grand illusion about the war, whether it was just, whether it was right, and even whether it was winnable. I just volunteered to fill a need."

"Totally understandable," said Roberts. "You have to go where you're needed."

To my immense relief, and, I'm willing to bet, the relief of everyone else in the Humvee, we passed through Ambush Alley with no problems. But the road to Baghdad was rough, to say the least, and I was beginning to get a headache and some back pain from being jostled about so much.

As we drove through the outskirts of Baghdad, we passed a few goats meandering alongside the road, looking for anything they could eat. A few moments later, we spotted some herders' small mud huts, one of which had a donkey tethered to a stake in front of it. Our impending approach to the American military base and airstrip left me with the same set of conflicting emotions that I had experienced the night before regarding Abu Ghraib prison. On the one hand, I was sad to leave Iraq, but my sadness was overwhelmed by the feeling of relief that washed over me. I really wanted to be home, possibly more so than on any of my previous trips.

To distract myself from the mixed emotions that were rising to the surface again, I began talking to Roberts and the other men about the project with the seven brothers. I told them that my good friend Bob Dows, Marvin Zindler's cameraman, would have really enjoyed this trip. He would have loved taking some of the live footage we had gotten at Abu Ghraib prison. "Bob is the kind of guy who will rush to the front line of any riot, demonstration, or military op to get the footage that will bring reality home to the viewers. He's an experienced videographer who would have been perfect for this kind of assignment, and I know that he would have signed on enthusiastically if we'd asked him.

"But Don North is also an experienced camera man, and of course he was already here and embedded with the troops. I think his camera work and reporting are top-notch. Plus he's super smart, fearless to a fault, and damned honorable in everything he does."

"Definitely one of the good guys," Roberts said.

I went on to say that my experience working with both Don and Bob – and of course Marvin Zindler – was made all the more rewarding for me and for their viewers thanks to all three men's professional integrity and the depth of detail that were common elements in all of the news stories they produced. I added that even the smaller stories that Marvin and Bob covered in Houston were riveting to watch, and that no small part of that was because of Marvin's writer and director, Lori Reingold.

"People always tease Marvin and his crew that if there is ever any disaster in the world, they'll find a way to get there regardless of the risks," I said. "And even though this one was primarily Don North's story, at least the Iraq part of it, we're all pulling together and working as a team. Bob's going to take over the camera work and Lori Reingold will handle the production and scheduling when we get the seven brothers to Houston."

Now we were approaching the military base and the airport, and after only a few minutes, we came to the main gate. Roberts lowered his window and answered a few questions for the guard on duty, and we were given permission to proceed. I couldn't believe I was probably just minutes from boarding the military transport that would take me to the Air Force air base in Frankfurt, which was located on the south side of the Frankfurt airport. From there we would continue on to Houston and home, compliments of Continental Airlines and its CEO, Gordon Bethune. Miraculously, I was still all in one piece.

Once again, my assumptions about a smooth process proved to be overly optimistic. Upon disembarking from the Humvee, we were informed that there would be a slight delay and that we still had nearly an hour before flight time. But I didn't let it get to me, at least not at this moment. In fact, although I was a little disappointed I was also relieved because the delay gave us a chance to stretch our legs and get something to eat before the long flight from Baghdad to Frankfurt. I looked forward to a relaxing interval, grateful that I had made it this far with no significant problems to speak of.

But that was soon to change. An unexpected obstacle popped up for me as we were finally preparing to board the aircraft. The other passengers in my Humvee and those who had been in the other vehicles in our convoy boarded with no problem, but I was unceremoniously stopped by a Lieutenant Calhoun, who informed me that I was not authorized to board.

Many civilians are probably unaware of the Space Available flight program, also known as Space A or military hops. Under this program, passengers can fill unused seats on aircraft that are owned or controlled by the United States Department of Defense once all the space-required (duty) passengers and cargo have been accommodated. Eligible passengers can fly for free or at deeply discounted fares. There are several categories of eligibility, but generally speaking, eligible people include active duty military personnel and their friends and family, as well as reservists and retirees, and various specialist categories. I fit into more than one of those categories and had no reason to believe that I would have any problem boarding the plane, particularly since the arrangements had presumably been made for me to do so.

Apparently, however, there had been a glitch in communications between the C.O. at Abu Ghraib and the military personnel at the airport. I took Lieutenant Calhoun aside and said to him very quietly that I was traveling at the request of the President of the United States. The lieutenant looked at me with what I can only describe as an expression of profound skepticism, as if he had heard similar excuses before from people who wanted to take advantage of the Space Available program.

I felt a twinge of resentment at his response, but I quickly pushed that feeling back and decided to look at the situation from his perspective. More than likely I would have responded the same way had I been in his position. I said, "Lieutenant, I realize this is a last-minute request. I had assumed that the arrangements for my travel had been finalized by the commanding officer at Abu Ghraib prison, where I've been stationed for the past few weeks, but I only decided last night that I was going to leave today to go back to the States. It's possible that Colonel Stevens didn't have a chance to finalize the arrangements. I trust you can make it work now."

Lieutenant Calhoun still did not look convinced, so – you guessed it – I pulled out The Letter. I hoped that this would be the last time I would need to use it on this trip.

I motioned for the lieutenant to join me a short distance from the military personnel who were boarding the aircraft, and then I handed him The Letter, with my usual warning that he was not to make a copy of the document and was to return it to me immediately upon reading it.

He looked a little startled, but dutifully took The Letter, his eyes widening when he saw the heading from the White House. Once he had read it and re-read it, he said, "So this is for real?" Now, where had I heard that question before?

"Lieutenant," I replied, "I can give you a phone number directly to the White House to confirm it, but I wouldn't advise that at this point." Then I repeated, "So I trust you can make this work?"

He handed The Letter back to me, then came to attention, and saluted. I returned the salute.

"We do have room for you, sir," Lieutenant Calhoun said. "I'll take care of the manifest and I'll vouch for your identification and your luggage."

"Thank you, Lieutenant," I said. "And so there won't be any further misunderstandings, I want to verify that this aircraft is in fact flying into the Air Force air base in Frankfurt, Germany, am I correct?"

"Yes, sir," Calhoun replied.

"Good, because that's also my destination," I said. "I'll then be going to the civilian section of the airport to catch a Continental flight to Houston, Texas."

"I'll be sure to verify that, and I'll make any necessary arrangements," Calhoun assured me.

"Thank you," I said. Then, noticing that he looked as if he wanted to say something else, I asked, "Any questions, Lieutenant?"

I am sure that the lieutenant had a dozen or more questions to ask me, but that he knew enough to keep those questions to himself and just salute smartly once again, which he did. He then said, "No, Commander, no questions. I've got this for you."

"Good," I said. "And I thank you for the way you're dealing with this. May I board?"

The lieutenant said, "Just give me a few minutes, sir. If you could wait here, I'll be back as soon as I can." He then vanished into what appeared to be a tiny makeshift office. I stood there and waited, and waited, and waited. Meanwhile, the line of military personnel continued steadily up the steps, looking like a group of men playing follow the leader. When the last man in the line had boarded, Lieutenant Calhoun still had not returned, and I was afraid that the plane might take off without me.

I had only waited about fifteen minutes, but it seemed like an hour. Finally the lieutenant returned, then reached out and took my large backpack, saying he would see to it that it was properly stored, and that I could now board the aircraft. So with my duffel bag slung over my shoulder, I climbed the steps and made my way towards the front of the plane.

Although the temperature outside the plane had been starting to grow uncomfortably hot, as was normal out here in the desert, it was nothing compared to the blast of heat that hit me as I entered the hull of this oversized aircraft. It felt like a preheated oven, which was no wonder, since it had been sitting out in the sun most of yesterday and all of today so far, with little relief having been provided overnight.

This being a military transport plane, passenger comfort was clearly not the objective. There was red webbed seating running along each side of the fuselage – actually a series of hard metal chairs strapped into a web sling – and in the center was a flat metal deck with metal rings to hold down pallets and equipment. But I had no complaints. I hadn't been expecting luxury; I just wanted to get to Frankfurt and then get home. So I dutifully took my seat and placed my duffel underneath it.

No sooner had I sat down than the pilot emerged from the cockpit and moved across the flat metal deck, an annoyed expression on his face. I wondered what was wrong, but soon found out. He stopped in front of me, his arms folded against his chest as he looked down his nose at me and said, "So you're the last-minute VIP passenger responsible for the additional delay in takeoff. Nice of you to join us." The sarcasm in his voice was not lost on me. I looked up at him, studying his close-cropped military crewcut and his red face. He was wearing a uniform that was so tight he looked as if were about to burst out of it.

I can guarantee that every eye in the plane was on us – especially on me, as my fellow passengers waited for my response. There being no in-flight movies on planes like this, perhaps they were counting on the pilot and me to provide some entertainment.

But I said nothing for a few moments as I fastened myself in, wondering why the hell the pilot would be so upset about an extra fifteen-minute delay. Then I forced myself to smile as I said, "I am truly sorry for the disruption, Captain. I'd thought that the arrangements had been made for me to be on this flight, but apparently that wasn't the case. It was a last minute decision so that's understandable. But Lieutenant Calhoun was kind enough to help me straighten it out, and that's what took the extra time. I need to get back home to Texas as soon as possible, and I appreciate this more than you will ever know."

That changed everything. The pilot's expression softened, and he said, "Glad to be of service, sir." This time there was no sarcasm. I smiled at him again, and then he promptly turned and strode back to the cockpit.

Moments later, a man who identified himself as the technical sergeant appeared at the front of the plane and shouted out orders through a microphone, telling everyone to make sure they were buckled up for takeoff. The troops who hadn't buckled up did so now, and I laughed to myself to see one of the young men strapping himself in with one hand while playing a video game with the other. The technical sergeant began the obligatory safety briefing, warning everyone about possible air disturbances as we departed the Baghdad airport. "These disturbances are usually pretty mild," he said, "but even if they're not so mild they are generally nothing to worry about."

I listened with my eyes half-closed, exhausted and overheated from the trip across the desert in the Humvee, and feeling as if my skin had been rubbed raw from all of the bouncing. Once the technical sergeant had completed his briefing, I said to him, "This is a long-ass flight, isn't it? Will we have to stop and re-fuel?"

"Negative," the sergeant said. "It's actually less than six hours nonstop, and while that's not what you would call a short flight, we should be good all the way. We're well under gross weight and we're not carrying any heavy equipment, just you guys and fuel. That gives us an extended range with this aircraft – more than we need for this flight."

"Thank you," I said, and he nodded, then moved on down the length of the aircraft to do his last minute preflight checks. I closed my eyes, hoping for a smooth flight and, notwithstanding the uncomfortable seating, several hours of sleep to recharge my depleted batteries.

The aircraft began to pick up speed as it rumbled along the taxiway. I couldn't help smiling as I thought of being home, cuddled up with the love of my life, Terry. In fact, that was just about all I could think about right now. Various physical discomforts prevented this interlude from being a completely blissful experience, however. I had to keep coughing to clear my throat, and even though I had been drinking water fairly steadily, I still felt dehydrated. Not to mention that I was jammed with dozens of other men like a sardine in a hot metal can – and a very noisy metal can to boot. The engine noise was so overbearing that I found myself reaching for my ear plugs. They muffled the noise somewhat, but by no means eliminated it. I might as well grin and bear it, because this was the only way I was going to be able to get to Frankfurt so that I could get home.

After a minute or so I opened my eyes, thoughts of a nap pushed aside for now as the plane moved even faster down the runway, its speed pushing my fellow passengers and me back into the webbed seating. It was a rough takeoff, and I was glad to be strapped in. As the plane arched its way upward and the wheels were retracted with a loud clacking sound, my back was jammed up against the hard metal plate that served as a seatback.

Then we were airborne. And suddenly I was filled with nervous energy, my adrenaline pumping, although it failed to counteract the underlying exhaustion very much. I instinctively checked my watch, but didn't remember which time zone I'd set it for, so I contented myself with looking around me.

There was a young Marine sitting directly across from me, and I could see that he was nervous. He was rubbing his hands together faster and faster, almost fanatically. I shouted at the top of my voice to him, since he never would have heard me had I spoken in a normal tone, "We're in the air now! We're going to level off very soon. All is okay, so calm down."

That seemed to help him a little, so I turned back to my own thoughts as I suppressed a yawn. It had already been a brutally long day for me, and there was no end in sight. We didn't have the luxury of windows in the passenger/cargo area, but as I glanced through the open cockpit door, I could see that the sun was up high in the sky. Not a cloud was visible. I yawned and closed my eyes again, but my adrenal glands and my exhaustion were still locked in battle with each other, and the adrenaline seemed to be winning for the moment.

But as the plane leveled off, I decided to try to relax as much as I could under the circumstances. My thoughts returned to Terry, and I thought about our ranchette and our beloved menagerie, and about how wonderful it would be to finally get home again and fill up on iced tea. For that matter, maybe I wouldn't have to wait till I got to Texas for the tea, which I was suddenly craving; surely I would be able to get some at the Frankfurt airport. Then I thought about the seven brothers, and the plans to help restore them to wholeness, and about how proud I was to be part of those plans.

And somehow, sitting in this deeply uncomfortable sling high above the Earth, I could feel my energy coming through to me again. I took a deep relaxing breath, rubbed the sweat from my face and the salt from my eyes… and finally drifted off to sleep.

The next thing I knew I was feeling the wheels touching down on the tarmac. My eyes flew open, and I raised my arms high over my head in a long, shuddering stretch. Only two things were on my mind: one, that I was alive and in one piece after a bloody few weeks in Iraq, and two, that I had just landed in Frankfurt, Germany.

Before long, the doors to the plane were opening up to a radiant blue sky, with the sun producing constantly changing shadows whose abstract patterns lent an air of surrealism as we disembarked. I stepped out into those surreal surroundings, re-energized once again, and ready for the next stage of my adventure.

CHAPTER 26

WELCOME TO AMERICA, WELCOME TO HOUSTON

O nce I was safely back home, and had taken a couple of delightful days to make up for lost time with my beloved Terry, I rejoined the hometown team in preparation for the arrival of the seven brothers. After the complex arrangements for their trip to the United States were finalized, the men left Baghdad Airport on a C-17 military transport to Frankfurt. Since they had no passports or visas, they would not be going through immigration. They were escorted across the tarmac to a private, enclosed area, so in theory, they never touched German soil, as per the final arrangements that Lori Reingold had worked out with the German Consulate and Ambassador.

It was a relief to all involved that the men were able to make their long international journey without encountering any trouble, despite having no passports, visas, or ID papers. As I noted at the beginning of this book, such arrangements were unheard of in the post-9/11 world, and would have been impossible were it not for the cooperation of so many people, from Iraqi citizens to the President of the United States.

I was pleased to hear from the men that they treated very respectfully, even though they were isolated from the public and basically hidden in the Frankfort Air terminal. While they awaited the arrival of their flight they were given something to eat and provided with drinks to make the time pass more quickly. They told me that they were amazed by the kindness of everyone they encountered, both before and during the flight.

The C-17 was a large aircraft, and there were more than adequate seats available for the seven brothers. To them, it was like being in the lap of luxury. As they boarded the aircraft, a call was made from Germany to Lori in Houston, updating her on their status and giving her the estimated time for their arrival in the Bayou City. Lori in turn called me at my medical office. The plan was for me to accompany Marvin, Lori, and Bob to the airport to meet the brothers, and from there we would proceed to the Channel 13 studios.

Naturally, everyone was very excited. After many months of effort on the part of everyone, including numerous volunteers, it was all coming together.

Marvin, who had also been contacted by the airport authorities in Houston, told me we would be met by some airport security officers, who would be taking us through the secure gates at the back of the airport. From there we would drive out onto the runways to meet our guests; once again, they would not be going through passport control or immigration, but rather departing directly from the tarmac, as we had done. They would never set foot in the terminal building at Bush Intercontinental Airport.

Back at my practice, I was so filled with a mix of anxiety and joy that it was difficult getting through the morning, making rounds and seeing my patients. Finally it was time to join Marvin, Lori, and Bob at the Channel 13 studio, where I helped Bob get his camera, extra batteries, and equipment into the back of the van that had "Channel 13 ABC" emblazoned on both sides. Not everyone would be able to fit in the van, so Lori had already arranged for an SUV to accommodate some of the men and their luggage. The SUV driver would follow us through the airport and the security gates when we got there.

The usual hour ride to Bush Intercontinental Airport took only about 30 minutes. We were then directed to the airport security office, where several security patrolmen told us to meet them in the passenger pickup area and follow them. I appreciated that airport security was well organized, and was glad to have been thoroughly briefed on the "special" handling that would be followed upon our arrival. We left the inner sanctum of the airport and terminals and followed the security vans on a road paralleling a 16-foot-high chain link fence with barbed wire on top that ran the length of the airport-controlled periphery road.

Our little caravan came to a stop at a secured entrance on the far side of the airport, where the security guards used their pass codes and opened the gates. They said they were in contact by radio with the airport tower, and we would be told on which runways we could take the vehicles. The security patrol people told us to stay close behind their van and to drive slowly. Aircraft were landing, and even though we were in the big Channel 13 van, we were heavily buffeted by the thrust of the jets as each of the aircraft landed.

When there was a break in the incoming traffic, the guards in the security van waved for us to follow them across the runway. We followed them to the far end of the incoming runway to a turnoff just before the terminal, then halted again.

In the van, everyone was very excited. We looked at our watches and knew the plane should touch down any minute; it could be the next one. Two more aircraft landed and taxied to their gates, and then we saw the big Continental plane, with the emblem of the world on its tail, make a perfect landing not too far from us. The aircraft taxied almost to where we were parked, then slowly pulled onto a side tarmac. But it did not continue to the International Terminal. A few minutes later, a tractor-pulled stairway was driven up to the aircraft, and a few men jumped out and put the stairs in place. With this, we all got out of the news van, and Bob Dows started the camera rolling.

The door of the aircraft at the top of the stairs opened. I couldn't wait. I just ran right up to the top of the stairs, introducing myself to the flight attendant, who invited me aboard. Another flight attendant was on the intercom system telling the passengers that there would be a few minutes delay and they would soon be going to the International Terminal. I think she was surprised when I just took the microphone out of her hands, introduced myself to everyone on the plane, and told them that there was no emergency, but some V.I.P.s were disembarking at this point. I told them it wouldn't be any fun if I let them in on what was happening, but that if they watched ABC Channel 13 News at six or ten that night, they would see the story in which they now played a part.

I then started to call out the names of the seven brothers – Baasim, Ala'a, and the others – one by one. As he approached me, Baasim told me that they each had just a small traveling bag, and the bags were in the overhead compartment. I told him to instruct the other men to get their belongings and come forward quickly. As they started down the stairs to the tarmac, I again picked up the microphone and thanked everybody for their patience, then told them that as soon as they removed the stairs, the aircraft would continue onto the terminal where they could deplane.

I said, "I again remind you that you are part of something interesting and unusual. Turn on your TV to ABC Channel 13 at six and ten tonight, and you'll see what this was all about."

Someone in the back said, "Tell us more." I replied, "That would ruin the surprise! Besides, the plane needs to get to the International Terminal and you need to disembark. Have a good evening." I thanked the flight attendants and exited the aircraft just as the stairs were about to be removed.

Bob Dows had moved further down the tarmac into a safe area and was filming some of the other flights coming in, as well as shooting film of the seven brothers as they were deplaning. We had room for one of the Iraqi men in the van with us, and I selected Baasim because his English was good, and because of his background as a TV anchorman on Al Jazeera in Iraq during the Saddam Hussein regime. The others went into the waiting SUV, and after the plane had departed for the terminal, we again followed the security van, with its red lights blinking on top, back to the gate. One of the officers in the security vehicle got out, put in the code, and waved us through. We lowered the window for a moment to thank them, and were then on our way to the Channel 13 TV station. Lori had called ahead and ordered a half-dozen large pizzas and some soft drinks to be delivered to the conference room at the station.

In the van I was sitting next to Baasim, who had his nose and forehead pressed up against the window, unable to take his eyes off of our freeways. As we moved along at 70 mph with six wide traffic lanes heading in our direction, and six more equally wide lanes heading in the opposite direction, Baasim was mesmerized. He told me that he had never seen anything like it in his life. The freeway then seemed to climb into the sky as we elevated up and above on Loop 610 and back down again. He turned and looked at me when this occurred, then looked down again at the cars speeding by underneath as we passed over the U.S. 59 Highway. I tapped him on the shoulder and pointed to the front window, where the Houston skyline was now coming into view. He said, "This is truly the country where the streets are paved with gold."

I said, "Houston is not quite there yet, but I'm sure we're working on it."

I thought to myself what the excitement of seeing these things must have been like to the other six Iraqis in the SUV, having just come from a country where they still use donkey carts and camel wagons, and where the majority of all labor is still done by hand. After we exited the freeway and began driving through a tree-lined suburban area, Baasim asked, "What kind of businesses are in those beautiful buildings?"

I answered, "Those buildings do not house businesses. They are private homes of middle class Americans." Baasim was clearly astonished, which I could easily understand.

As we approached the TV station's headquarters, I pointed out a shopping center, a supermarket, and a myriad of small businesses. At long last, we were approaching the gate at the Channel 13 building. The gate code was entered, and the gate slid slowly aside. There were at least a dozen giant dishes the size of an automobile, and multiple towers sending and transmitting signals to and from the television station. Baasim told me that in his years of working in television in Iraq, he had never seen transmission dishes of this size, nor had he seen so many dishes in a single location.

"Welcome to America," I said.

Once we were inside, the aroma of the fresh, hot pizzas wafted from the conference room and into the hallways. Since none of us had eaten in hours, we all gathered around the savory spread that almost covered the large conference table, and we literally attacked the pizza and soft drinks. We also began answering the many questions that our guests of honor had for us. Bob Dows stood to one side of the room with his big 40-pound TV camera filming the event. No one was paying much attention to Bob; everyone was excited, and the conversation was rapid and brisk. There were translations in several different languages crisscrossing the table. Looking back on the scene, I found myself surprised that I didn't ask our guests if they had ever eaten pizza, as I had a difficult time recalling whether I had ever seen a pizza restaurant in Iraq.

I excused myself from the group and called Tom DiBello, president of Dynamic Orthotics & Prosthetics, who would be fitting the prostheses to the men's amputated right forearms. I wanted to let Tom know that the businessmen had arrived safely, and that I would follow up with him and keep him in the loop as our joint efforts progressed. I then called hand surgeon Dr. Fred Kestler to schedule appointments at his office with some of the men. And lastly, I called my office to clear the schedule so we would have time for examinations and pre-op photos with the men. My office staff informed me that there had been an outpouring of hospitality from their neighbors and friends, with many offering to open their homes to these men. I appreciated their kindness, of course, but I felt that it would be more comfortable and convenient for the men to stay in my home and surrounding homes so they could visit each other within easy walking distance.

Don North was expected to arrive from Iraq within a few days, and once he got here we could all rest a little easier. I knew that these next few days would be busy ones, consisting of preliminary examinations of the seven men by myself and Dr. Kestler. Then there would be X-rays of the amputated limbs, EKGs and, of course, a battery of blood tests.

In my travels around the world on medical missions, I have seen people suffering from numerous diseases and conditions that are either uncommon or virtually nonexistent in the United States. I have also had many patients who have come to the Texas Medical Center from foreign countries. I've always considered it a privilege for my students, interns, and residents to see these foreign guests, as they often present with medical problems that are not normally seen in Stateside practices. I enjoy quizzing my students on their examinations, findings, and diagnoses, but almost invariably, even the residents miss one very important thing.

The examination results are in front of them, and their challenge is to make a diagnosis, but they all seem to miss the hidden unseen factors. They fail to consider the basic fact that these patients are not from the United States, but at times, that can be the single most important factor in taking their medical history and evaluating their problem.

Depending upon where the patient is from, healthcare professionals need to consider diseases that are common in that patient's country but are rarely if ever seen in the U.S. The practitioners need to think about and rule out diseases such as malaria, tuberculosis, or schistosomiasis, the latter being a disease caused by freshwater parasitic worms. Most U.S. physicians never see schistosomiasis in their normal practice, but it is second only to malaria in the dangers it poses to afflicted patients.

I will also have some of my colleagues from the international infectious disease service talk with these foreign patients and order the laboratory tests they feel are appropriate for their care as well as for the safety of their caregivers. Care and safety are so intertwined that the failure to take appropriate measures in either can, and often does, result in the continued suffering of the afflicted, their communities, and the healthcare providers who treat such disorders.

Just before I left on this trip to Iraq, I'd had a patient visit from Nicaragua who had come for laser treatment of a hemangioma, a noncancerous blood vessel tumor. My senior resident conducted his examination and correctly diagnosed the hemangioma, but when I went through his notes on the patient's medical history and the physical examination, I saw that there was a statement about recurrent fevers on a daily basis, as well as a loss of weight. Knowing the patient was from Nicaragua, I told the resident to get a few drops of blood, make a blood smear on a glass slide, and have it looked at. The resident looked at me with a strange expression on his face and asked, "Do you think he has leukemia? I didn't know of any relationships between leukemia and hemangiomas!"

I said to my resident, "No! He has malaria. You need to begin treatment for malaria and dehydration immediately. The hemangioma will be treated, but not for several days until his malaria is treated." The resident still looked doubtful.

I'm afraid I lost my temper a bit, and I really tore into him. "We're here to treat the entire patient," I reminded him. "I trust you performed a good history and physical exam. Your own personal observation is also very important. Eighty to ninety percent of your diagnosis can be based on the patient history and your own personal observation of the patient. I've told you that again and again. You may be studying to be a plastic and reconstructive surgeon, but you're *here* to observe and treat the entire patient.

"Do finger sticks on this patient. Get the smear of the blood on the glass slide. Take it to the lab and find a pathologist there who is familiar with looking at blood smears for malaria. If that pathologist agrees with my diagnosis and the blood smear is positive, then I want him or her to tell me what type of malaria we are dealing with."

My response may have been a little harsh, but by this point in his training, the resident should have known what to do. Anyway, I'm pretty sure that he took the lesson to heart.

It's understandable, then, that while I was in Iraq, I had actually been more concerned about contagious diseases that we do not see in the United States than I was about the mortar fire and the many other risks. And now that our patients were in Houston, it was paramount for them to undergo full medical exams, blood tests, X-rays, and laboratory studies. If all tests came back negative, then the revision surgery, and the subsequent application of the right-hand myoelectric prostheses, would be relatively simple and straightforward procedures.

I told my assistant, "We know what their obvious physical problem is – their right hands were amputated. But keep in mind that because they come from Iraq, we also have to check them for any endemic diseases that aren't as apparent as an amputated hand. Be sure they all get a Tine test as well, because tuberculosis is rampant in Iraq." (We would also take chest x-rays, of course.)

On the evening of the seven men's arrival, Marvin Zindler introduced what he called the "Band of Brothers" on Channel 13's evening newscasts, and we all listened to their stories. Notwithstanding my enthusiastic and impulsive performance on the plane as the seven men were disembarking, I personally would have preferred to wait a few days before going public, given the many things we had to accomplish before the revision surgery that was necessary for the application of the prostheses. But I also knew that I wasn't calling the shots on the publicity part of the mission, so of course I went along with it.

Immediately following Marvin's broadcast, the phones at the television studio were ringing almost non-stop. The operators at the station couldn't keep up with calls. Everybody seemed to want to participate and do something to help these men. My office phone and home phone were in no better shape, with even my electronic voice mailboxes filled to capacity. Over the next several days, reporters throughout the state of Texas and across the U.S. started calling Marvin and asking if they could get permission to interview these men as well. The story of the seven brothers had gone viral. A few days later, we were getting calls from the U.S. State Department and the White House. It was all happening so fast.

Because of the crude and inhumane manner in which the seven brothers' right hands were removed, revision amputation, which would require weeks of recovery, was needed on all seven men before they could be fitted with their prosthetic hands. The amputated part was very painful because the median, ulnar, and radial nerves had neuromas – some of which were very large – due to the nerves not being properly treated at the time the right hands were amputated.

A neuroma is a jumbled growth of nerve cells, sometimes caused by biomechanical deformities such as a high-arched or flat foot, but more commonly the result of trauma to a nerve bundle – in the case of the seven brothers, a botched amputation. Their neuromas were a combination of nerve cells and scar tissue that had formed a shape much like a ball of yarn. Within this ball were thousands of strands of nerve cells, which caused excruciating pain even from the slightest touch.

The myoelectric prostheses could not be fitted until the brothers' neuromas were removed. Since there were seven patients who needed this surgery, and we wanted to get all of the procedures completed in as short a time as possible, I couldn't do it all myself. That's why I was grateful for the help of my colleague Dr. Fred Kestler and his department of hand surgery. Dr. Kestler and I divided the patients into two groups of four and three so that all of the surgeries could be conducted in a day. That way they should all heal sufficiently, at approximately the same point on the timeline, for the fitting of the prostheses.

The seven brothers were individually brought to my office at Scurlock Tower at The Methodist Hospital in Houston's Texas Medical Center, where Dr. Kestler and I took a medical history and conducted a physical exam of each man. Then the men were sent for x-rays at Methodist's department of radiology. When we received the radiographs, a second consultation was held for each patient, including another physical exam and review of the x-rays in order for us to properly assess what needed to be done. We always had an interpreter present for the men so they would understand what was happening every step of the way.

The examinations and radiographs were completed for all seven men within two days, and then their surgeries were scheduled in The Methodist Hospital OR. I would be assisted by the senior plastic surgery resident, and Dr. Kestler would be assisted by his colleagues at the department of hand surgery.

The patients received a general anesthetic for their procedures. First, the existing surface scars were excised and the wounds were opened, revealing the large neuromas almost immediately. Dissection continued around the neuromas for the median nerve, ulnar nerve, and the radial nerve, and the neuromas were then excised. This would eliminate the pain the men had been having, which meant that they would now be able to tolerate the fitting of the myoelectric prosthetic hands without pain. Then the ends of the nerves were treated in such a manner that the neuromas would not reoccur. Next the bone ends were tapered so the prosthetic sleeve could easily be placed on and removed as needed.

The surgery was performed with a tourniquet in place so there was no bleeding into the surgical site. This made it possible to quickly and easily locate the neuromas, cut the nerves, and treat the nerve endings to prevent the reoccurrence of the neuromas. What followed would be nearly six weeks of recovery, as well as several fittings for their prosthetic hands. Recovery would consist of changing the dressings periodically and removing the sutures, then wrapping the site with elastic bandages to prevent swelling and prepare the stump for the application of the prosthesis.

There was one other procedure necessary for the brothers to finally live a normal life in Iraq: the removal of the disgraceful "X" tattoos from their foreheads. During their surgical procedures, while they were asleep, I used a laser to remove these marks of shame.

The men tolerated their surgeries well, and within a few days all were comfortable and did not require any pain medication. After a second week, the dressings were changed and the wounds all looked excellent. And the seven brothers were feeling great. They were growing restless and were eager to begin sightseeing in Houston, as well as other parts of Texas.

So naturally, we accommodated them.

CHAPTER 27

CELEBRITIES ON TOUR

T here is a lot to see and enjoy in and around Houston, the largest city in Texas and the American South, and the fourth-largest in the United States. Our only problem was narrowing down the list of attractions, and then deciding where to go first. Naturally, the brothers were given a guided tour of the Channel 13 studios early on, where they were presented with an insider's view of what it takes to produce news and local programming in a major market. Baasim, the newsman, was particularly interested in this.

We also took the men to Houston's famous and lovely Hermann Park, near the Texas Medical Center and the Museum District, and of course we visited the Houston Zoo, which is located in the park. The brothers thoroughly enjoyed their trip to the Downtown Aquarium, which had just opened the year before. But they were really impressed when we took them to NASA's Johnson Space Center, the hub of human space flight activity and research for more than five decades.

Sporting events were on the itinerary as well. The men were taken to the (now-shuttered) Gulf Greyhound Park in LaMarque, Texas, about 40 miles from Houston, to see the dog races. They also attended a Houston Astros baseball game, where they enjoyed the game from the lofty perspective of the owner's box. All of this was televised on Houston's ABC-13.

Seeing the sights in and around Houston was only the beginning of the seven brothers' adventures. We took a trip to the Texas Hill Country and visited the famous Y.O. Ranch in the beautiful town of Kerrville, where the brothers put on cowboy outfits and attended a big Texas barbecue. They were fascinated by the Y.O. Ranch's animals, which included a vast number of exotic and native species, and by the rich and colorful Texas and Old West history that the Ranch represents. With this visit, the brothers became not only Houston TV celebrities, but Texas TV celebrities as well.

No tour of Texas would be complete without a visit to San Antonio to see the Alamo, which for millions of Texans is an enduring symbol of perseverance and courage. Originally known as the *Misión San Antonio de Valero*, and now officially named The Alamo Mission (Spanish: *Misión de Álamo*), the Alamo is a historic Spanish mission and fortress compound. Founded in the eighteenth century by Roman Catholic missionaries in what is now San Antonio, the Alamo was the site of the famous Battle of the Alamo in 1836, where American folk heroes James Bowie and Davy Crockett were killed. These days it is a museum in the Alamo Plaza Historic District and is part of the San Antonio Missions World Heritage Site.

Because of the battle that took place in 1836, every proud Texan is familiar with the slogan, "Remember the Alamo!" And every school child in Texas learns about the fabled history of this Texas landmark at some point in his or her schooling, generally in Texas history classes in the fourth and seventh grades. When the John Wayne movie *The Alamo* was released in 1960, many elementary and junior high school classes were taken on field trips to large movie theaters to see the film.

In recent years, however, teaching about the Alamo has become increasingly controversial. Historians and advocacy organizations alike have stepped up efforts to separate entrenched myth from unpleasant reality, while traditionalists express indignation about "revisionist history" and "cancel culture."

I'm not going to go into all of that here. I'll just acknowledge that any history is full of nuances and complexities. Information about the history of the Alamo, including the associated controversies, is freely available elsewhere, both online and in books. Suffice to say that the seven brothers, who against terrible odds had demonstrated incredible perseverance and courage of their own during their years-long ordeal, were eager to see this beloved tourist attraction. And as a proud Texan myself, if not by birth then by long years of residence in the Lone Star State, I was glad to be along for the trip.

The day of our visit was a hot one, and one by one each of the seven brothers removed the wrappings from their surgical sites. And then, sitting together on a bench facing the Alamo, they draped their amputated limbs over the shoulders of their fellow amputees. They sat there for a while, just staring in awe at the façade of the beloved Texas shrine.

At one point, a photographer from one of the major San Antonio newspapers came up behind us and took a photograph as they sat there. It was not staged; it just happened. It is one of the photos that I have always treasured from the visit of the seven brothers.

We took a tour inside the Alamo, and then it was time for lunch. Following lunch, there was a press conference in the Alamo plaza, in which reporters from major San Antonio media interviewed the seven men. The resulting stories – and the photos – were picked up by the wire services and went across the country within 24 hours. Subsequently they were even seen in newspapers in Europe and the Middle East.

After the Alamo and the interviews with the press, it was time to tour the beautiful city of San Antonio, including its famous River Walk. We took a boat ride on the river, which was a wonderful experience for all of us. If you are ever anywhere near San Antonio, I urge you to pay a visit to the River City (also fondly known, of course, as the Alamo City). It will be well worth your time.

Once the brothers had sufficiently recovered from their surgeries, it was time for the next phase of their restoration. They underwent hours of practice on prototypes of the artificial hands, and, as mentioned above, several fittings for the final product. Finally the day came to attach the prosthetic hands. The prostheses had been carefully matched to the skin tones and arm size of each patient, and were as close as medical technology could get to the men's real hands. Though it was plain to see, particularly upon close scrutiny, that the hands were artificial, they were able to perform many of the tasks of a human hand. Certainly they were a massive improvement over a chronically painful stump.

They were a great improvement over older technology as well. Myoelectrics is an electrical-impulse based technology that, at the time of the seven brothers' operation, had been utilized in prostheses for over a decade and a half. It works through detection of small electric pulses from muscle movements on either side of the forearm, which in turn trigger motors to open and close the thumb, the forefinger, and the middle finger. Prior to this significant breakthrough, a prosthetic hand required the use of a harness stretched across the shoulder of the wearer. Moving the shoulder in one direction would pull on a cable to open the hand, while tightening the shoulder would close it. Not only was this quite awkward, but it required conspicuous body movements.

The artificial hands provided for the seven brothers had been available for only a few years at the time of their procedures, and contained several additional upgrades from previous generations of myoelectric devices. For instance, they had sensors that would detect when an object was in danger of slipping from the hand, and would automatically tighten the grip. They also had proportional control, which allowed an experienced user to flex the forearm muscles somewhat in order to open and close the hand either more quickly or more slowly. They even included "smart" electrodes to prevent cell phone towers and anti-theft devices (such as those found at the entrance to retail stores), from unintentionally opening and closing the hands, which had been a problem with the older technology.

As soon as their new prostheses were in place, the brothers, with big smiles on their faces, immediately began shaking hands with and hugging the specialists at Dynamic Orthotics & Prosthetics who had made the limbs. One of the men tied his shoes, then untied them and tied them again, just to show that he could do it. Others grabbed a pen from the front desk and wrote their names with their new hands. And one of them removed a silver ring – a symbol of his Islamic faith – from his left hand and placed it in its proper place on his new right hand.

The hours of practice the men had had with the prototypes were paying off. Even so, there was a period of adjustment as they became accustomed to their new prostheses. It was truly a joy for all of us to watch their progress, to see them re-learn how to master the myriad everyday functions that those of us with intact hands all too often take for granted.

During their extended stay in Texas, I spent a lot of quality time with the seven brothers apart from the medical procedures. I came to know them not merely as patients, but as people. Besides the tours we took together, I had many enjoyable visits with them at my home. I even hosted a big cookout in their honor, with many of my friends and neighbors in attendance.

But Houston and the Lone Star State were only the beginning for our seven honored guests. The nation's capital was calling.

The seven brothers had become American celebrities, thanks to several hundred newspaper and magazine articles and multiple television interviews over the past few months. It wasn't really an exaggeration to say that they had become American heroes.

In addition, the flow of detrimental photos from Abu Ghraib prison had stopped. The practices of enhanced interrogation at the prison had apparently been ended at last, and there had been no further stories from that facility to embarrass President Bush or the U.S. military.

As the story of these seven brave businessmen continued to spread throughout American news media, a formal invitation was extended from President Bush to visit him at the White House. We had expected this to happen, and the brothers had been eagerly awaiting confirmation ever since they had been told that they might get to travel to Washington and even meet the President. But now it was official. In addition, the Pentagon and State Department requested interviews with the seven men for information and insight about what had been taking place in Iraq before and since the war.

"We are all going to the White House!" That was the giddy response, shouted almost in unison, when I told the seven businessmen that we would indeed be making a trip to Washington, D.C. and would be guests at the White House. Their excitement was almost palpable, and suddenly they had a barrage of questions for me.

Ala'a asked, "Will we really get to meet the president? Will I be able to shake the President's hand? Will I actually walk through the White House?"

Baasim said he had heard about the wonderful museums in Washington, D.C. and asked if he could take a day and go through the Smithsonian. I told him that the Smithsonian is actually several museums in one, and that it would take far more than a day to take it all in, but I would see what could be arranged.

Nazaar was jubilant and jumping up and down. He said, "I want to go inside that tall needle and climb to the top and look out over all of Washington."

I said, "You mean the Washington Monument?"

"Yes, your Washington Monument. I want to climb all the way to the top," he said again.

I told him, "That will all be possible. There is also an elevator if you don't want to climb the stairs." At that, they all started laughing.

Qaasim was the serious one in the group, and it was obvious from his expression that he was contemplating everything that was being said. He cried, "We are nothing. We are ordinary businessmen. We are guests in your country. We are being invited to the White House? We are meeting with the President of the United States, the most powerful man in the world? We are simple businessmen. What will we say to him?"

"I suggest you let President Bush do the talking, and just answer any questions the President asks. You will all be just fine."

Hassan seemed very pensive as he looked at me and said, "So when do we leave?"

Everyone else joined in, asking excitedly, "When do we leave?"

"We will fly to Washington, D.C. in two days," I replied. "Lori Reingold, the ABC Channel 13 producer and writer, whom you've met, will help me make the arrangements." They smiled eagerly, and their smiles grew even broader when I added, "Now I have another surprise for you. Tomorrow we are going to the famous Houston Galleria shopping center, and we are going to get you fitted with appropriate suits, shirts, and ties to make this visit."

The group's excitement was almost impossible to contain. I immediately called Don North and told him about our invitation, adding that since he was part of the group, he should meet us in Washington in two days. We would all stay at the famous Hay-Adams Hotel. I then called Lori Reingold and we worked out the transportation and hotel logistics.

Ala'a said, "When we get home no one will believe us."

"You will have photos," I said, smiling. "And our time in Washington will be covered by international news. I expect your families will see you on television long before you return to Iraq."

The next day we went to the Houston Galleria, the iconic two-million-plus-square-foot retail and luxury residential complex in Uptown Houston. The men were visibly stunned as we entered, and they repeatedly said they had never seen anything like it. They said that even in Baghdad, there was nothing to even remotely compare with the huge, opulent mall. The lights, the music, the stores, the restaurants, and the hundreds of people freely and casually walking through and shopping amazed them. Where the men grew up, they were used to open markets and small private shops – nothing at all like they were now seeing.

They were very concerned about the proper clothing for the trip. I took them to stores that I knew would appeal to their taste, and yet be appropriate for a meeting with the President of the United States.

As we walked through the Galleria, my friends received a surprising amount of attention from the other shoppers. What with the many news articles, photos, and TV appearances, they were recognized and treated like Hollywood celebrities as they strolled the length of the corridors and wandered through numerous shops in the complex.

Quite a few people stopped and wanted to speak with them. Others wanted to shake their new prosthetic hands. Several strangers even asked to see how these intricate hands worked. The men took it all in stride and were very polite and amicable, even to the point of signing autographs when requested.

That night they packed their new duds, except for the outfits they planned to wear on the plane, and in the morning we left for Bush Intercontinental Airport, where we boarded a non-stop Continental flight to Washington, D.C.

The White House had arranged our transportation from the airport, and when our group arrived in Washington, we were greeted by members of the White House staff. We were each handed a twenty-page schedule for the next several weeks. None of us had expected this attention to detail, not even me, but I suppose it made sense, given the importance of the occasion. I didn't know if we were being escorted and driven by the Secret Service or the FBI, but clearly we were in good hands, as the trip from the airport to our hotel – complete with lights flashing – was quick and uneventful.

Reviewing the program that I was handed, I could see that the first day in D.C. was dedicated to touring the city and some of the museums, which the seven businessmen had requested. This would give us time to orient and acclimate ourselves. The second day we were to be guests at the White House. The programs said there would be an afternoon "meet and greet" in the Rose Garden. The President expected three to four hundred news persons to attend, and both live and taped interviews were planned.

The program I was handed said that I would do the introductions with President Bush, after which the men would engage in individual interviews where they would be given time to tell their stories. I looked through the program and could see that there would be another press conference and photo session with the President in the Oval office on the following day.

I was later handed a program that listed other scheduled events, including visits to the Tomb of the Unknown Soldier at Arlington National Cemetery, the then-new World War II monument, and other D.C. attractions. Following all of that, there would be meetings at the Pentagon and possibly the State Department. This was going to be an unforgettable trip for me as well as for the seven Iraqis.

We took the proverbial whirlwind tour of the nation's capital that first day, as scheduled, and it was almost too much to take in at once. We didn't get to visit all of the museums the brothers wanted to see, but nobody was complaining. (Handy traveler's tip: Don't even *think* of visiting the Smithsonian Institution unless you have a few days set aside for just that.) By the end of the day we were all exhausted, but we thoroughly enjoyed ourselves nonetheless. We managed to get a good night's rest so that we would be fresh and ready for our first visit to the White House the following day.

Early the next morning we had breakfast at the Hay-Adams Hotel, and then several black SUVs arrived to take us to the White House. With lights flashing, the drivers wove through the notorious D.C. traffic. It was a typical late-spring day in Washington, feeling like summer was already upon us. The temperature must have been in the 90s and the humidity the same. Unfortunately the conference and the interviews were to be outside in the Rose Garden, and I was not looking forward to being outdoors in this heat in a suit and tie.

Throughout the Rose Garden, shade covers had been put up, under which the interviews with various TV and news stations would be held with each of the seven brothers. To my dismay, however, the central area of the Rose Garden was uncovered. There was a podium with more microphones than I had ever seen in my life, and other mikes on big booms hanging over the area where the speaker would stand. It was clear to me that this was going to be a major news event in the U.S. and worldwide.

Bob Dows, Marvin Zindler's camera man, had a reserved front row spot with Lori Reingold and, of course, with Marvin himself, working as always for KTRK-TV 13 in Houston. Don North was there with his camera as well. The rest of the press was behind a roped-off area facing the podium. It was pure pandemonium, with press members jockeying for the best location.

The seven brothers and I were offered cold drinks, and then a very serious looking young man said I was to follow him to the Oval Office. When we got there, President Bush and his press secretary were waiting for me. I was told the President would leave the Oval Office through the side exit and come directly to the podium to make some remarks. I was to stand to the President's right, and, since I knew the men intimately, I would be asked to introduce them one by one to the press corps. Following those introductions, President Bush would make further remarks.

Notwithstanding the nearly stifling heat and the humidity, the program went smoothly. After President Bush completed his remarks, he put an arm around my shoulder and introduced me again to the several hundred representatives of the press who filled the Rose Garden.

President Bush then whispered in my ear, "It's hot as hell out here, so I'm going back into the Oval Office. This is now your program. Give a short introductory story about what took place in Abu Ghraib prison, and then start taking questions from the press." I nodded.

The President added, "Set a time limit on the questions. Also, pick a woman from the press corps to ask the first question. When the time is up, *cut it off*. Tell the press corps they can interview each of these Iraqi gentlemen for the afternoon. Then come back into the White House and visit with me in the Oval."

With that President Bush said, "Good luck, Doctor," and retreated to the cool interior of the Oval Office.

I re-introduced myself, then introduced Marvin Zindler, Bob Dows, Lori Reingold, and my good friend, Don North. I proceeded to give a short history of what had taken place in Iraq and at Abu Ghraib prison, then told how Don North and I had located the seven brothers at Abu Ghraib prison.

I said that I would take questions from the press, and I pointed to a lady in a bright yellow summer skirt and blouse that seemed to just pop out of the hundreds of press corps personnel. I was thinking to myself that she had most likely chosen this colorful outfit so she would stand out enough to get the opportunity to ask her questions first. If so, her plan had obviously worked.

I took questions for the Iraqi businessmen for about a half hour, then quieted the crowd of reporters and said that there would be no more questions. "But," I added, "the seven brothers will be available for individual interviews and photos in designated shaded areas throughout the Rose Garden. All of the men will be accompanied by interpreters. Interviews with the seven men and their interpreters will begin as soon as the men are escorted to their designated areas."

I then directed Hassan to the first covered area on my right, Salaah to the second one, and Laith to the next interview area, giving each name loudly and clearly to the reporters and other attendees. Then I continued to the other side of the Rose Garden, assigning covered areas to Qaasim, Baasim, Nazaar, and Ala'a, and saying their names to the people gathered at their respective kiosks.

I ended by telling the press corps that most of the men spoke adequate English, but it would still be necessary to speak slowly and clearly. I reminded them that there were interpreters in the individual areas to help out if necessary.

With that I thanked the reporters and camera persons for coming and left the central podium to walk back to the White House, where a Secret Service agent escorted me directly to the Oval Office. He knocked and we opened the door; President Bush was at the desk and asked me to come in.

"You look like hell, Dr. Agris," said the President.

He had a point, no doubt. I could feel the sweat dripping down my forehead, and the salt was burning my eyes. My new shirt was very visibly soaked through in the front.

There were several other people in the room; the President pointed to one and said, "Get this man an iced tea and take his jacket."

The President then motioned for me to sit down. We spoke for a few minutes about his family and mine. I was very friendly with his dad, George Herbert Walker Bush, and his mom, Barbara. I had visited with them on regular occasions at Houston Astros baseball games, where I was one of the Methodist Hospital doctors for the Astros team. We were all baseball fans. I had also been presented the Points of Light Award by the elder Bush a few years earlier for the medical care that the Children's Foundation provided in Houston, throughout the U.S., and across the world.

The iced tea arrived, and sipping it gratefully while sitting in the air-conditioned Oval Office, I felt revitalized. President Bush and I spoke for a few more minutes about family and friends. Then he had a few questions about the seven brothers. Finally, he reassured me that things would be a lot more comfortable tomorrow, because the press corps was invited here into the Oval Office, where we would be seated with the

President for the next interview session.

I finished my iced tea and told President Bush that I felt I needed to get back to the Rose Garden to help out with the interviews with the seven brothers. I asked if I could be excused.

President Bush said yes, and added that he felt my getting back out there was a good idea. "But if it gets too hot outside, please return here for some more iced tea," he added.

I got up, and the President and I shook hands. Then I left to rejoin the seven businessmen and the crowd of reporters. I walked from kiosk to kiosk to see if my friends were having any problems with the interviews, and to fill in the press with any additional clarification and information they might need.

I stopped for a while at Nazaar Joudi's kiosk and chatted for a while with the press who were gathered there. To Nazaar I said, "These interviews will go worldwide. Your family and friends will be seeing you at the White House and with the President. You told me that you thought they wouldn't believe you. Well, now you will have your proof."

Nazaar said, "I still don't believe that I am here at the White House with you."

I then went to the kiosk where Don North was with Baasim Al Fadhly. Baasim's English was excellent and, probably because of his experience as a leading commentator with Al Jazeera, he seemed very much at home at this press conference. I leaned over and whispered in his ear, "You're doing very well here today. All of you are. But I will be honest with you; I am a little worried. I'm concerned about you and your family when you go home, because of this publicity."

Baasim replied, "I feel we'll be okay, but you are right. There could be trouble for us, once we get home with this type of publicity and our new hands!"

The reporter who was interviewing Baasim at the time heard part of our conversation, and continued with a series of questions regarding the dangers he and his family might expect upon his return to Baghdad. Baasim replied, "I have been a TV newsman and I have always reported honestly, which put my life in danger anyway. My life was always in danger in Abu Ghraib prison as well. I do not like that my family may be in danger too because of me, but under Saddam Hussein, everyone was in danger, and with all that is going on now, that is still the case. It is part of the reality of living in Iraq." Questions then continued about

Baasim's family and whether he would be returning to his position as a newsman.

He replied, "Dr. Agris and his colleagues gave me this new American right hand so I can hold a microphone again and tell the truth to the Iraqi people and the world. I am not afraid. With each of my broadcasts, I will hold my microphone high and show my new prosthetic hand to all of Iraq."

I was taken aback by his statement, but also impressed, because I knew that he meant every word.

The sun would soon be setting over the Rose Garden, and I looked at my watch. I couldn't believe that we had been here all day. As Baasim continued talking to members of the press, I couldn't help but be impressed by his understated and yet infectious passion. The depth of his comments, and his easy command of the English language, transformed what could have been merely a political diatribe into a logical and indisputable argument against Saddam Hussein and the Ba'athist party. And it was all accomplished with a charm and charisma that seemed to captivate the many reporters who stood around him.

Baasim told them, "I am a reporter just like you, but I was in the wrong place at the wrong time. I was sought after for the wrong reasons, and as a consequence, under Saddam Hussein's orders my right hand was cut off."

He continued, "Dr. Agris here represents causes bigger than ourselves, and reminds us that there are struggles everywhere that require us to give up part of ourselves." He held up his right hand and added, "I, my family, and my countrymen were under constant attack by Saddam Hussein and his sons, Qusay and Uday. Generations of Iraqis to come would have been under attack as well had Saddam and his sons not been removed. For us, it was never a question of weapons of mass destruction. It was always about people and their desire to live free."

After hesitating for a few moments he went on to say, "As a newsman for Al Jazeera, I was under the constant dread of being caught, and killed, and of bringing danger to those I love. But it was worthwhile and absolutely necessary. For this they took my right hand and also scarred my forehead with a tattoo indicating I was a prisoner at Abu Ghraib. The doctors in Houston not only gave me a new hand, but also removed this tattoo with a laser."

This speech by Baasim to the news reporters brought several of them almost to tears in a way I could not have anticipated. I hope that if he hears how proud I am, to this day, of him and his six "brothers" he will know that my pride is heartfelt.

Baasim repeated, "There are causes bigger than ourselves, and struggles that require us to give up our own fears in order to take on something greater."

The sun had nearly set by now. Baasim drew his left hand across his forehead and wiped away the drops of sweat. It had been a long day, and he and the others were obviously exhausted. Yet all of them smiled at me, making it clear that they were still enjoying their notoriety and their day at the White House Rose Garden.

Across from us was Nazaar, who was in the process of dabbing sweat off his cheek with the corner of the cuff on his new jacket. As we walked around the kiosk, Laith was telling a group of reporters that there were many good reasons to change the direction of Iraq's political party, and that it needed to be done very quickly.

I nodded at him and smiled. He grimaced slightly and began to massage his neck.

"You okay?" I asked him.

"Just a stiff neck," he said. "But if you don't mind me asking, how long do you think we have to remain here?"

I glanced to either side, seeing that the crowd of news reporters was thinning out. "I think a few more minutes will be enough. I am going to return to the Oval Office in the White House and speak to the President or his press secretary so we can wrap this up."

As I was moving away I could hear one of the newsmen ask Laith who I was, and he replied, "Dr. Agris has become a good friend. He is one of the men who made this all possible. He operated on me. He helped to provide me with my prosthesis."

Passing Nazaar Joudi again, I heard him telling reporters that he was a jeweler and a craftsman, and he was good at his craft. He said he loved what he did, and that he had also been dealing in silver and gold. But he was dealing in American dollars as well and therefore had been charged with a crime; in fact, because of his involvement with American currency, he was the only one of the seven brothers who had actually been "guilty" of anything. But, he explained to the reporters, that was not the real reason he was imprisoned and disfigured. He had also criticized the regime.

"The truth is that I was a political prisoner," he said. "By cutting off my hand and tattooing my forehead they were sending a message to everyone in my town." I had already heard his story several times before, of course, but it never got old for me. And I felt that it was important for him to tell it to as many people as possible.

I continued on toward the White House side entrance, where the Secret Service gentlemen saluted me, opened the door, and allowed me to pass. I continued down the hallway and asked for the press secretary or the President. Without hesitation I was again taken to the Oval Office.

As I entered the Oval Office, President Bush looked up at me in surprise and said, "Are you all still here?"

"Yes, Mr. President."

"Go home. I will see you tomorrow!"

"I would not leave without your permission, sir."

"You are our guests, and you do not need my permission."

"Thank you. We will be leaving shortly."

But "shortly" is a relative term. I had a feeling that the day wasn't quite over.

CHAPTER 28

MEDIA STARS

When I walked back out to the Rose Garden, there were still about sixty reporters at the various kiosks interviewing the Iraqi businessmen. As I passed Ala'a I heard him heaping praise on my team and me. Of course, I had to stop to listen.

But Ala'a also wanted to talk about how terrible life in Iraq had been under Saddam Hussein. Like so many of his fellow countrymen, Ala'a was firmly convinced that had Saddam Hussein not been forcibly removed, decades would have passed and hundreds of thousands more people would have been slaughtered under his rule. "Look at the Marsh Arabs; they have almost been eliminated, as well as the Yazidi people," he said emphatically. "And those are just two of the groups that suffered under Saddam and the Ba'athist party. President Bush and the American soldiers saved all of us from the worst demons and gave Iraq and the world a last-minute reprieve."

And then Ala'a returned to what was clearly one of his favorite subjects: his benefactors and his gratitude for a chance at a new life.

"Dr. Agris and Mr. North, with the help of Mr. Zindler, made it all possible," he said. "With my new right hand, I will again be respected when I return home to Iraq. I will be able to sit at the dinner table with my family. I will be able to visit friends and neighbors. I will no longer be shunned because I have no right hand." Then he raised a single finger on his new right hand to emphasize his point.

Walking past each of the kiosks, I let the reporters know they had five minutes to wrap things up. As I was finishing my rounds, one of the newswomen, who obviously had been deeply moved by the men's stories, took me aside and said, "Nothing justifies fanatical extremism. Nothing. Never!" There was a deep seriousness in both her voice and her facial expression. I could tell that she was expecting something more than a perfunctory response from me, so I climbed back up on my figurative soapbox.

I responded, "You are absolutely right. I couldn't agree more. Saddam Hussein, like Osama bin Laden, is nothing more than a terrorist. Every terrorist thinks his cause justifies his actions. But no one has the right to cut off a man's right hand. No one has the right to spill innocent blood. No one has the right to take the law into their own hands. These men who have participated in the maiming and killing of their fellow countrymen are not unique and they're certainly not heroic. They are modern day terrorists." She nodded as I spoke, and I saw that she was taking notes.

I then excused myself, telling her that it had been a long day, and that we all needed to return to the hotel and refresh ourselves before dinner. I told her there would be a press conference in the Oval Office tomorrow afternoon, and that she should check with the President's press secretary and see if she was on the invitation list. The reporter thanked me and I continued on.

I waved at Baasim and told him it was time to leave. He beamed and said, "This experience has rocked my world."

I said, "Please reach out to the others, and tell them to meet me under the portico at the side entrance of the White House."

Even in his lightweight summer suit, and with the hottest part of the day over, I could see that Baasim was still sweating profusely. It was past time to wrap this up. I looked for Marvin Zindler and Lori Reingold, and learned that they had already left. Then I checked my watch and realized why my stomach was growling: it was time for dinner.

We had been surrounded by security in the Rose Garden for most of the day – a very long time for such a hot day. It was time to go back to the hotel, get a cool shower, change clothes, and take everyone to dinner. It occurred to me that they might prefer to take a nap first and get dinner later. I would ask them as soon as we arrived at the hotel.

Now some of the seven brothers were sitting, slumped over, their exhaustion even more apparent than it had been earlier. But they were real troupers. Even as I was waving them away from their respective kiosks, I could hear Qaasim saying, "We are here because we need to lead by example. We have already made tough choices. Because of those tough choices our right hands were chopped off. Our struggle has entered a critical phase. President Bush and Dr. Agris and Mr. North will see to it that our story will go worldwide. We are not kept down by what has happened to us. What is important is what we present now to the world." Fatigue notwithstanding, the other men seemed buoyed by his words.

At that time, I cut the few remaining reporters off, saying that it was past time for us to leave. Then at long last we returned to the hotel for the evening, pleased with the way the day had gone. I felt certain that President Bush had also been very satisfied with the way it went. But we still had another event ahead of us the next day.

After dinner at the hotel, I was completely exhausted, and I was asleep within minutes after hitting the bed. Alas, it was not to be an uninterrupted slumber.

Sometime in the wee hours, the telephone rang, and I really don't know how many times it had rung before I finally realized that it *was* the phone and that it probably needed answering. I was initially disoriented; I knew that this was not my bedroom at home, but it took me a few moments to realize I was at the Hay-Adams Hotel in D.C. I finally got my hands on the telephone receiver, lifted it to my ear, and listened.

A deep voice said, "The President of the United States is calling and will be on the phone in a few minutes."

I looked over at the clock on the night table. It said it was a little past 1:00 A.M.

My response was a little less than polite. "I don't know which of you is playing the prank, but I'm too tired to care, and I'm going to hang up."

The deep voice on the telephone said, "Don't hang up, the President will be on the phone in a minute. He needs to speak with you. He said that he has some questions that have been bothering him regarding the Oval Office press conference tomorrow."

A few minutes later I could hear other voices, and then someone said to me, "I'm sorry to have disturbed your sleep, Doctor. This is President Bush."

I recognized the voice and realized it was no prank. "Yes, Mr. President, how can I help you?"

President Bush said, "I'm a little concerned about shaking hands with the seven businessmen in the Oval Office in front of the press tomorrow morning."

"Mr. President, that should not be a problem. The artificial hands that you will be shaking feel almost like skin. The main difference is that because they do not have a blood supply, they will be cool or even cold to touch. But you will notice that they look almost like real hands; the skin tone even matches each man individually."

President Bush said, "What will the grip be like when we shake hands?"

"Other than the fact that the hand will feel cool, the grip should be pretty much the same as if you were shaking anyone else's hand – except that it might be a little stronger than you anticipate."

President Bush continued, "Will all the men be able to do this adequately? The press will be filming the entire time."

"Mr. President, the only reservation that I have is that some of the men might get anxious, nervous, or tense. Closing the bionic hand will be no problem. But the opening of the hand, and the release, take more thought and effort. When you shake hands with the seven brothers, they may not immediately release your hand. I think it would be helpful if you would talk to them or ask them a question that will take their mind off the fact that they are shaking hands with the President of the United States. This should relieve their tension and relax their muscles so they can open their artificial hand without any trouble." He was silent for a moment, and I felt he needed further reassurance.

"I really think that it will all go well. But just to be sure, I will coach them prior to your meeting with them in the Oval Office. For your part, all you need to do is to guide them through this by seeing that they are relaxed. Talk to them, or ask them a question, perhaps about their family. I'm pretty sure that they will be able to concentrate on releasing your hand from their bionic grasp."

The President finally responded, "Well, I was concerned. I do want to shake each of their hands. And of course I want this question and answer period with the press to go well."

"Mr. President, I'm sure it will go well, and I will not only coach them in the morning, but we'll practice, so there should be no worries."

"Doctor, I really am sorry to wake you at this hour of the morning, but like I said, this had been troubling me – and I wanted to have a better idea of what to expect when I shake hands with these men in front of the cameras."

"Mr. President, your questions are very appropriate and your concern is understandable. As I said, we'll have a practice run before we get to the White House."

"Okay. Good night."

"Good night, and we will see you on time in the morning, Mr. President."

Now I was the one who was fully awake. I fluffed my pillows and stared up at the ceiling, hoping that the seven men would not be too intimidated shaking hands with the President of the United States with the whole world watching. In my mind, I could just see them locking onto his hand to the point of inflicting pain, and not being able to release their grip. Having a Secret Service agent coming over and physically removing one of them would really take the glory out of what was supposed to be a great photo op.

I kept telling myself I was being foolish. After all, these men could turn a key in a lock and tie their shoelaces, so they surely could perform a handshake without any problems.

I fluffed the pillow again, rolled over, and finally went back to sleep.

I awakened early, at a little after 6:00 A.M. After showering and shaving, I began calling each of the men's rooms to make sure they were awake and properly dressed to go to the Oval Office and meet with the President. I told them we would all meet downstairs in the lobby, where we would get breakfast, adding that once everyone was finished eating, we had a special task to perform.

After we were all gathered around the breakfast table, I stood up and said to the group, "Remember when you wanted to go to Washington D.C., see the city, and visit the President? You have gotten to do more of that than most people ever will. And Ala'a and Nazaar said they wanted to shake hands with the President. Well, each of you will get to shake hands with the President in front of several hundred newsmen and photographers with their cameras running. It has to go perfectly. But there's no need to get nervous. This will be a wonderful opportunity for all of you. And if you have a question or wish to say something to President Bush, this is the time for you to do that."

As each one finished his breakfast, I walked around the table, and we practiced shaking hands. As I had expected, the muscle reflexes for closing the hand were easily and swiftly done. But as I had explained to President Bush, it was the extension – the opening of the hand – that took more thought and effort. A different set of muscles was involved to work the myoelectric fingers.

Even so, everyone did well with the practice run except Hassan Gereawy, who had already seemed particularly anxious about shaking hands with the President of the United States. But after a little more coaching and encouragement from me, he seemed to be more at ease. He appeared to be confident that he had mastered the procedures to open the hand at the right time, and I felt certain that with a little conversation he would relax his muscles and the fingers would open without any problem.

I also reminded the group that we would not be outside in the uncomfortable heat and humidity as we had been yesterday, but inside the Oval Office for a meet and greet with President Bush and the American press corps. They all looked relieved.

On the whole, they all seemed to be quite relaxed, or at least as relaxed as possible under the circumstances. I thought to myself, *It's being sure that the little things work that make the difference.* Even so, I couldn't help being a little nervous myself. I knew that a great deal was riding on this meeting and photo op, and I prayed that all would go well.

I needn't have worried. The meeting – and the photo op – went very well, resulting in the desired positive coverage in the national and international media. Shaking the prosthetic hand of one of the brothers, President Bush famously said, "I'm honored to shake the hand of a brave Iraqi citizen who had his hand cut off by Saddam Hussein with six other Iraqi citizens as well who suffered the same fate. They are examples of the brutality of the tyrant." Some critics laughed at Bush's declaration about shaking the hand of a man who'd had his hand cut off. They framed his statement as yet another "Bush-ism" by a President who had become notorious for his gaffes. But the President's meaning and his message were clear, and his heart was definitely in the right place. So I think we should give him a pass on this one.

The seven brothers' photo session in which they shook hands with the President seemed like a tough act to follow, but more adventures awaited them on this trip. The day after that photo op, our group had another exhausting but fun day of sightseeing. After dinner that evening, I had just arrived back to my room at The Hay-Adams Hotel when the telephone rang. Sitting on the edge of the bed as I picked up the phone, I heard the operator say, "The White House is calling, sir. Will you accept the call?"

"Yes, please put them through." A couple of moments later, another voice came on the line. "This is Charles O'Brian. I'm on the President's staff at the White House."

"What can I do for you, Mr. O'Brian?"

He replied, "The itinerary you were given when you first arrived in D.C. indicates that you and the seven Iraqi men are scheduled to visit the Tomb of the Unknown Soldier at Arlington National Cemetery on Memorial Day."

"That's right," I said. "We're all looking forward to it."

"Well, Doctor, the President is extending an invitation to you and the seven brothers to participate in a special ceremony at the Tomb a few days before Memorial Day as well."

I was momentarily taken aback. Another special invite from the President hadn't been in our plans, but obviously it was an invitation we wouldn't refuse.

After a few moments O'Brian said, "Are you still on the line, sir?"

"Yes, yes, sorry about that. Please tell me more about this ceremony."

"Even though it won't actually be *on* Memorial Day," he said, "it will be part of the official observance of the holiday, and will include the laying of a wreath on the Tomb of the Unknown Soldier. It will also be a special ceremony to honor U.S. service members who were killed during Operation Iraqi Freedom and are buried at Arlington. That's why the President wants the Iraqi men to participate. He wants them to be the ones to lay the wreath on the Tomb."

"Okay," I said, my thoughts whirling as O'Brian added, "I apologize for the short notice about the ceremony."

"That's quite all right," I said. "We've learned to be flexible on this trip. We're ready for just about anything. At least none of it will be happening tonight; we've already had a long day."

O'Brian chuckled, then went on to say that everyone was required to wear a white shirt, tie, and sports jacket or suit. "Have your breakfast, and the limos will pick you up at 10 A.M. in front of The Hay-Adams Hotel. They will be driven by a Secret Service Security Detail. And don't worry; we'll have people instructing the Iraqi men on exactly what to do tomorrow. I'm sure they'll do fine; they seem to be at ease with the public and the press."

"Yes, I've been pleased with our experiences so far," I replied. I thought for a moment and then added, "As you probably know, we're here with ABC-TV reporter Marvin Zindler, his cameramen Bob Dows, and his producer Lori Reingold. They're staying with us at the hotel, and..."

Before I could even finish, he said, "Of course. We will have a car for them too, and I'll arrange for them to be in the front row to view the ceremony. They can photograph and film it as they wish."

I thanked him and said, "I don't know if the President was planning to have me participate in the ceremony too, but I don't wish to do so. I'd just like to be positioned in the front row too so I can take my own photos."

"That's no problem at all," he replied. "I'll make arrangements as you've requested."

"Thank you very much, Mr. O'Brian, and have a good night."

After we hung up, I immediately called the hotel operator to connect me with the rooms in which the seven men were staying. I explained to them what would take place tomorrow, including how they were to dress. I told them that we were all expected to be ready and waiting in front of the hotel at 10:00 A.M., where we would be picked up by the United States Secret Service.

When those calls were completed, I called the hotel operator back and requested a 7:00 A.M. wakeup call for all of us. Then I tried to call Marvin's room, but nobody answered. He was probably sleeping and had his hearing aids out. So I called Lori Reingold, who immediately answered, and I explained to her what was going on. She was delighted, and said that she would make sure she got the message to both Marvin and Bob Dows. I knew I could count on Lori.

Now, finally, I could get some sleep.

At 10:00 sharp the next morning our little group assembled at the front of the Hay-Adams Hotel, where three long black limos were already waiting for us. The area in front of the hotel was completely blocked off. The drivers stood there holding the doors open for us to enter the cars. Everyone was quickly seated and then we were on our way.

Before long I realized that we were not going in the direction of Arlington National Cemetery. I figured out what was happening when the White House came into view. As we reached the front entrance the gate opened, and our little caravan drove directly up to the front of the White House and stopped. It was then that we spotted President Bush. The limousine windows rolled down, and the President stopped at each of the cars to say hello to all of us. He told me that he would be joining our procession to the cemetery.

After the exchange of greetings, the President was escorted to his car. Then, with half a dozen police motorcycles leading the way and another six cycles bringing up the rear, we were off. The Presidential limo was directly behind the first group of motorcycles and several other black SUVs containing Secret Service personnel, and our three cars followed. Red and white lights flashed from the motorcycles as well as each of the cars, and there was the occasional whistle or car horn. The motorcycle cops had cleared the lane for us, so our motorcade was able to proceed quickly.

Upon our arrival at Arlington, we were driven to the hill where the Tomb of the Unknown Soldier is located. The hill overlooks D.C., and the view is impressive. A large crowd had already gathered, and the members of our group were taken to our respective stations, from which we would either view or participate in the ceremony. A separate section had been set aside for the press, and as Mr. O'Brian had promised, front row seats had been reserved for Marvin, Lori, and Bob. The seven brothers were taken to an area facing the Tomb, directly in front of the large crowd, and were given instructions. I was positioned in an ideal spot facing the seven men and the Tomb, with my camera and telephoto lens at the ready.

The sense of anticipation and excitement among the crowd was almost palpable. It became audible as well when President Bush and his entourage were led to the front row, near the seven brothers, and were seated. The crowd cheered and clapped, but grew silent soon after the President sat down.

I think I can accurately state that every person who was there was profoundly aware of the significance of this moment, including and perhaps especially the seven brothers. It had been explained to them that Arlington National Cemetery is hallowed ground, that the service members buried there had sacrificed their lives for the United States, and in many cases for the freedom of people in other nations as well. When they learned that Arlington was the final resting place of 65 American service members who had given their lives in the fight to free Iraq from Saddam's brutal reign, and that these Americans were to be honored at this ceremony, the brothers were eager to be part of the event.

The crowd sat in silence now while the ceremony known as the Changing of the Guard began. Since July of 1937, the Tomb of the

Unknown Soldier – which is sometimes called the Tomb of the Unknown Soldiers or the Tomb of the Unknowns, as more than one unidentified service member is buried in the area – has been perpetually guarded 24/7, every day of the year, regardless of the weather. The Tomb Guards, also called Sentinels, are volunteers from the 3rd U.S. Infantry Regiment, the famous division that is also known by its two nicknames, "The Old Guard" and "Official Escort to the President." This is the oldest active-duty infantry unit in the Army, having served the U.S. since 1784.

While historically almost all of the Sentinels have been men, there are a few female Sentinels as well. In October of 2021, the Changing of the Guard was carried out by an all-female cast for the first time in history.

Being a Tomb Guard or Sentinel is a prestigious and highly selective post that requires intensive training and a rigorous series of tests. To say that it also takes a high level of dedication would be an understatement. Currently the Guards work in 24-hour shifts, and during any given shift, when they aren't on active guard duty they are living in quarters in an area beneath the Tomb. This is not "down time" for them, though. Instead, they participate in physical training, Tomb Guard training, and preparation of their uniforms for the next day. Believe it or not, uniform prep takes the average Sentinel about eight hours.

The Sentinel on duty carries a rifle over the shoulder and follows an intricate routine, marching 21 steps southward down the 63-foot-long black mat laid over the Tomb, then turning left and facing east, towards the Tomb, for 21 seconds. The Sentinel then turns left and faces north, changing the weapon to the outside shoulder, and waits 21 seconds, then marches 21 steps down the mat, turns east, and begins the entire routine anew, repeating it until the end of his or her shift. At each turn, the Guard executes precise movements that include a sharp "shoulder-arms" movement to place the weapon on the shoulder that is closest to visitors. This signifies that the soldier stands between the Tomb and any potential outside threat. In other words, don't even think of coming between a Guard and the Tomb. (In case you're wondering, the number 21 was chosen because it symbolizes the highest military honor, the 21-gun salute.)

Given all of the above, it's easy to understand why being a Sentinel requires such extensive training and testing. Fortunately, no individual is required to walk the mat for many hours without relief, as the Changing of the Guard occurs every half-hour during daylight in the summer, every hour during daylight in the winter, and every two hours at night, when the cemetery is closed to the public. Again, this is regardless of weather conditions. In fact, according to the Society of the Honor Guard, it's considered an honor to "walk the mat" in bad weather.

On or near Memorial Day, Veterans Day, and other special occasions, the President of the United States or the President's designee places a wreath at the Tomb. I'm sure that many folks in the crowd were expecting President Bush to do the honors today, but a surprise was in store for them.

Following the Changing of the Guard, the seven brothers were asked to stand, and were guided by several soldiers who served as Tomb Guards to an area front and center. All eyes were on the Iraqis as they were handed a large wreath on a tripod, and, still under the direction of the Guards, were given the honor of carrying the wreath and placing it in position in front of the Tomb.

The brothers moved in almost perfect unison, as if they had rehearsed for days. Then they stood in solemn silence as they regarded the wreath and the Tomb itself, on which is the famous inscription:

**HERE RESTS IN HONORED GLORY
AN AMERICAN SOLDIER
KNOWN BUT TO GOD**

To my knowledge, this was the first time that citizens of a country with which we were at war had placed a wreath at the Tomb of the Unknown Soldier. The momentousness of the occasion was not lost on the crowd, particularly the press, and the flashes from cameras in the press section were almost blinding. After a few minutes the Iraqi men were led back to their sitting area near the President. President Bush then stood up and was escorted to the Tomb, where he placed a smaller wreath, and then said a few words in praise of the Americans who had given their lives in the war to liberate Iraq. As the ceremony concluded I looked around at the crowd and saw that quite a few people were wiping their eyes, having been profoundly moved by what they had just witnessed. I confess that I was one of those people.

The event at Arlington, like nearly everything else that the seven brothers had done since their arrival in the U.S., received favorable coverage in the media. Reporters highlighted the sincere gratitude the Iraqi men had expressed for the tremendous sacrifices of American servicemen and women, without whom, in the words of one of the brothers, Nazaar Joudi, "we would never have had a new beginning and a new Iraq." Another brother, Laith Aggaar, said, "Life is the most precious thing for a human being, and these people have made the ultimate sacrifice. They came to Iraq and died for Iraq and for all humanity. We will never forget the contribution these heroes have made."

If you ask me, there are quite a few Americans who could take a page from the seven brothers' book of gratitude and appreciation. It seems to me that far too many of our fellow Americans don't fully grasp the sacrifices that our fighting men and women have made and continue to make on our behalf.

With the ceremony completed, the crowd began to disperse, and I walked the short distance to where President Bush and his entourage were still seated. The seven brothers were standing a respectful distance away from the President, waiting for a cue about what to do next. President Bush spotted me and said, "Dr. Agris, I know that you and our Iraqi guests are scheduled to take a tour of Arlington National Cemetery and some of the other famous monuments in the area. I wish I could join you, but… well, you know, duty calls. But I've left special instructions with your tour guides that you all are to be given star treatment. Anything you want, just ask. Of course you'll have a Secret Service escort as well. I hope you enjoy your tour."

"Thank you, Mr. President," I said, "for everything you've done to make this visit one that we'll all remember for the rest of our lives."

"Glad to do it," President Bush said, smiling. He turned to several people who were in his group and gave them instructions. As he waved goodbye to all of us and was escorted away, a couple of the Secret Service agents remained behind.

The seven brothers were eager to begin the tour, as was I. Accompanied not only by the Secret Service personnel but also by several of the Tomb Guards who were in full dress uniform, our little group was taken around the hill to a plain and almost hidden door on the other side. This, we were informed, was the entrance to the Tomb Quarters where the Guards stay during their 24-hour shifts. We learned that very few civilians ever get to see these Quarters. Needless to say, we felt honored.

One of our guides rang the doorbell, and it was opened by another Tomb Guard, who was more casually dressed than the guides. We were warmly welcomed as we entered an absolutely spotless area that a writer for the *Washington Post* described a few years ago as looking like "the world's neatest dorm common area."

As we were led through a series of small but equally immaculate rooms, which included bedrooms, bathrooms, and a lounge area, I spotted a young man sitting on the side of his bed polishing his brass. I introduced myself, and he smiled and nodded but kept polishing his buckle for a few more seconds. Then he set it aside and turned his attention fully to me, apologizing and signaling that he was open to conversation.

"How long have you been a Tomb Guard?" I asked.

He replied, "This is my second year. I feel very honored to be part of this program."

"As well you should," I said, smiling.

He continued, "You know, over the years quite a few 'Unknowns' have been added to the original Tomb. But in the future there won't be any more, because of DNA matching. In fact, I bet that if they wanted to, they could do pretty good matches of all of the unidentified soldiers who are buried here now. Then I guess they'd have to change the name of the Tomb, as well as the inscription."

"That's a good point," I replied. "DNA identification of both the living and the dead has really changed the world, hasn't it?"

"You got that right, Doctor," he said.

We talked a little while longer, and then our group completed its tour of the Guard Quarters and we were escorted back outside by our guides. As we began our walking tour of Arlington National Cemetery, one of the guides gave us a brief history of the cemetery. He explained that it is located on the confiscated estate of Confederate General Robert E. Lee, and includes the mansion in which Lee formerly resided, now known as Arlington House. He added that Arlington National Cemetery had hosted the first national Memorial Day commemoration in 1868.

We were taken to see the graves of several notable people who had been buried there over the years, including President John F. Kennedy, his wife Jacqueline Kennedy Onassis, and two of their children – one who was stillborn and one who was born prematurely and died a few days later.

Then we were escorted to the graves of three World War II prisoners: two Italians and one German prisoner. Although they were enemy combatants, they had died in captivity in the D.C. area, and the Geneva Conventions required proper burials. As Arlington was the closest national cemetery, it was there that the men were buried. Our guide told us that there are approximately 60 foreign nationals buried in Arlington, most of them allied servicemen who had died in air disasters that included American soldiers.

As we continued our walk, another one of our guides mentioned that Arlington is also the burial place of nearly 4,000 emancipated, freed, and fugitive American slaves. The federal government had originally set aside acreage after seizing Robert E. Lee's estate, intending the land to be a model community for these former slaves. It was called Freedman's Village, and not only did it have farmland and homes, but also a hospital, school, and mess hall. It was shut down in 1900, but Black people who lived in Freedman's Village were buried on the property. Their graves were incorporated into Section 27 of the cemetery, and their headstones are inscribed with either "Citizen" or "Civilian."

Walking a little further, we came to a tombstone that had a bronze plaque, in the center of which was a spaceship. This was the monument to the seven crew members who had died when the Space Shuttle Challenger exploded shortly after takeoff on January 28, 1986. Visiting this lovely monument was especially moving to me since several of the deceased astronauts had been patients of mine at the Texas Medical Center in Houston. In addition, the reason for the explosion was determined by a group of engineers, one of whom was related to me, so I was on the inside track almost from the beginning. I was one of the few who knew the cause of the explosion within 48 hours of its occurrence, considerably before the results of the investigation were made public. I took a few extra moments to pay my respects at this very special memorial, and then caught up with the rest of the group as we concluded our tour with the Tomb Guards and our Secret Service escorts.

After thanking and saying our farewells to our guides, we were taken back to our waiting cars, and were driven to the newly constructed World War II Memorial. This also had a special meaning for me, as several members of my family had fought in World War II, among them, my beloved stepfather, Leonard Rokaw. Every day I thank God because he is still alive and living well at the age of 101.

We went on to visit the Vietnam Veterans Memorial. Viewing this monument is a poignant and even cathartic experience for millions of visitors every year. As I've mentioned elsewhere in this book, I served as a Lieutenant Commander during the Vietnam conflict, and although I did not fight there, I saw firsthand many of the devastating results of this unwinnable war.

We also visited other statuary representing various branches of the military service. I was getting tired by now, but the Iraqi men were still clamoring to visit the Washington Monument. I told them that we would certainly do that, and it would be the next and last stop before returning to the hotel and dinner.

It had been an exciting and informative day for all of us, but I was grateful that it was drawing to a close.

Later on, as I lay down in bed resting my exhausted body, I found it surprisingly and frustratingly difficult to get to sleep. It wasn't the residual excitement of the day that was keeping me awake. Instead, all I could think of were my experiences in and around Abu Ghraib prison, particularly the mass unmarked graves in the desert outside the walls of the prison. As I replayed in my mind the violent battles and the near-misses, as well as the horrors within the prison, I was reminded once again that it was going to take me years to recover from the trauma.

Thinking about all of this as I tossed and turned, I found it remarkable that I had been able to retain my usual composure during this entire trip to Washington, especially in meetings at the White House. I had been genial to all, and, I thought, as helpful as possible to President Bush. This was despite my growing conviction that our engagement in Iraq had been a terrible mistake, that we were in the wrong place at the wrong time with the wrong enemies. Notwithstanding the humanitarian element of this war, an element of which I was reminded every day by the seven brothers, it was looking more and more as if the war was ultimately one that America could not win, even with the most powerful military in the world.

Yet in spite of all of the above, my love for my country, and my fond regard for the elder and younger Presidents Bush and their families, had not changed. As frustrated as I was by the decisions that had been made regarding Iraq, I believed that the current President Bush was doing his best under the circumstances. Politics is a rough business, to say the least, and foreign policy is complex and riddled with unintended consequences. And yes, "W" was probably in over his head. How he will be remembered by historians for his role in the Iraq war is still an open question even now, two decades later. But I liked the guy, and I was rooting for him.

As well, I couldn't overlook the flood of positive press coverage that the seven brothers had generated ever since landing on American soil. Then there were the brothers themselves, with their constant and sincere expressions of gratitude for having been made whole again thanks to the goodness of so many Westerners.

In short, there were good things happening. I had to cling to these realities, which were every bit as genuine as the many events that were preventing me from falling into a restful night's sleep.

At some point in the wee hours, I finally did fall asleep, with my last conscious thought before slumber being about a long-ago incident in the operating room. As I've mentioned elsewhere, the OR is the one place where I always feel relaxed and completely in control. I remember standing at the operating table one day when a young medical student said, "This sure seems to be an awful lot of blood."

I looked at him and said, "Do you feel any blood dripping onto your shoes?"

"No, Doctor," he replied, looking puzzled.

"Then we have nothing to worry about, do we?" I responded.

That's the way I look at life. And it is this perspective that finally relaxed me enough to get some sleep on that night in D.C., and that has carried me through countless challenging times before and since.

CHAPTER 29

PENTAGON MEETINGS
AND FOND FAREWELLS

A few days after the seven brothers participated in the special
ceremony at Arlington National Cemetery, we all attended the
Memorial Day ceremony there. In between, we did more touring. But we
had known since our arrival in D.C. that our Washington trip was to be
more than just tours and photo ops. After the fun and fanfare, the time
finally came for the more serious business: our debriefings at the
Pentagon, which would take place over a period of about two weeks.

The Bush administration had been in the process of gathering as
much information as possible about what life had been like for Iraqis
under Saddam Hussein's brutal regime. They surmised, correctly, that the
seven brothers would be rich sources of information and insight. I found
these sessions to be a very interesting experience, and at the time
anyway, a productive one as well. The meetings certainly gave me hope
that the administration was prepared to help calm the chaos that had
ensued after Saddam was taken down.

Constructed during World War II in Arlington County, Virginia – just
across the Potomac River from Washington, D.C. – the Pentagon is the
headquarters building of the United States Department of Defense. It also
happens to be the largest office building on Earth, with about 6.5 million
square feet, or 150 acres, of floor space, of which 3.7 million square feet
(85 acres) are used as offices. You've probably heard facetious remarks
about something (or, if one is being unkind, some*one*) being so oversized
that they have their own ZIP code, but in the case of the Pentagon, that's
no exaggeration. In fact the Pentagon has not one, not two, but *six*
unique Washington, D.C. ZIP codes, notwithstanding its physical location

in the state of Virginia. The Secretary of Defense, the Joint Chiefs of Staff, and the four service branches each have their own ZIP code.

You no doubt remember what happened to the Pentagon on September 11, 2001, which coincidentally was the 60th anniversary of the building's groundbreaking. An American Airlines jumbo jet, Flight 77, was hijacked by five al-Qaeda affiliated Saudis, who deliberately crashed the Boeing 757 plane into the western side of the Pentagon at 9:37 A.M. EDT. Not only the hijackers but all 59 passengers and crew on the jet died, and 125 people in the Pentagon, who were just doing their jobs, also perished. The number of casualties on the ground would have been much higher had the Pentagon not been under renovation at the time, which meant that many offices were unoccupied. In addition, the area hit was the section best prepared for an attack, as the renovations there had nearly been completed.

The damage to the Pentagon was quickly repaired, and a small indoor memorial and chapel were added at the point where the jet had impacted the building. Later, in 2008, an outdoor memorial dedicated to the Pentagon victims of 9/11 was opened.

Upon our arrival at the Pentagon, our group was cleared through security and escorted by armed guards. We walked through a seemingly endless labyrinth of corridors in which we would have been hopelessly lost without our escorts. And no wonder: the Pentagon has nearly 18 miles of hallways, composed of concentric rings that are designated, from the inside out, as "A" through "E." (As if that weren't enough, there are additional "F" and "G" rings in the basement.) "E" Ring offices are the only ones with outside views, and, as is usually the case in the civilian world as well, those rooms with a view are generally occupied by senior personnel. The office numbering system takes a little getting used to: office numbers go clockwise around each ring, and each office number has two parts – a nearest-corridor number from 1 to 10, followed by a bay number from 00 to 99. Hence office numbers on each ring range from 100 to 1099. Are you confused? If so, I'm glad to know I'm not the only one.

Indeed, I could see myself working here and still getting lost in this labyrinth every day. I have never lost my bearings in Iraq, Afghanistan, Pakistan, or any of the myriad other places I've visited over the decades, but in the Pentagon I felt hopelessly lost. I was grateful for the presence of armed-guard escorts who knew their way around the place.

When we finally arrived at our destination, one of the guards opened the door, and our group entered an office suite. We stood in a spacious anteroom whose walls were decorated with an impressive display of flags. Soon another door opened, and we were greeted by a military officer, at which time our escorts were dismissed.

The seven men and I were led into an interior conference room, one entire wall of which was covered with an array of photos of high-ranking military officers, and, of course, the President and Vice President. A long, highly polished conference table filled the center of the room, surrounded by large comfortable leather chairs. There was state-of-the-art electronic equipment for translating and recording, as well as a big-screen monitor at one end of the table. It was all quite impressive, not to mention a little intimidating.

As we stood there looking around the room and wondering what would happen next, Vice President Dick Cheney entered, followed by President Bush's Secretary of Defense, Donald Rumsfeld, and the Deputy Secretary of Defense, Paul Wolfowitz. I was very surprised by this, and I'm sure my face showed it. Cheney, Rumsfeld, and Wolfowitz were followed by several interpreters and administrative personnel, as well as a few people who, we learned, were from the State Department. Introductions were made all around, and then we all took our seats at the conference table.

The Vice President spoke first, making some general remarks about the purpose of this and future debriefings that were planned. I nodded slowly as he spoke, maintaining a somber and, I hoped, neutral expression. I confess that my mind wandered a bit during his spiel. But when I heard Secretary Rumsfeld say, "Now let's get down to business," my attention returned fully to the room.

Rumsfeld cleared his throat and took a few moments to compose himself, then said, "We are investigating crimes committed by Saddam Hussein and his Ba'athist party." That was no big surprise, but I wondered where he was going with this. He looked around at the seven men and told them that he wanted to know as much as possible about what life was like in their towns under Ba'athist rule and Saddam's control. "Let's hear first from the newscaster, Baasim Al Fadhly," he said. "And please relate your remarks specifically to you and your family, and your village or town."

Baasim, and the other six brothers in turn, did their best to provide the information Rumsfeld requested. Beyond the men's own suffering while in Abu Ghraib prison, life in Iraq under Saddam had been very hard for decades for them and for their families and friends. What Baasim and the other brothers did not know at this time was that some of their and their families' worst experiences were still ahead of them, thanks to the insurrectionists who remained a deadly force in Iraq, and would be a threat for years to come.

Testimony from the seven brothers continued all morning, with a short lunch break in the afternoon before reconvening. I had considered myself to be well-informed about the men's stories and about life in general in Iraq, but I learned a lot from listening to them in that hidden office in the Pentagon. Looking at the faces of those around the table who were supposed to be our leaders, I could see that this was an eye-opening experience for them as well. They seemed to be as perplexed as anyone else about how to resolve the issues that the brothers' testimony addressed. It pained me to know that most of the problems would probably not be resolved any time soon. I was right: to this day, many of those problems remain. That wasn't acceptable to me then, and it isn't now.

At around 6:00 P.M., a halt to the proceedings was declared. Wrapping it up, Wolfowitz said to the men, "Thank you for your time. We intend to pursue any leads and evidence you men present to us, as we have every right to do. Therefore we want you to be open with us in every way. But we also wish to assure you that there will be no repercussions, and nobody, either in the military or civilian world, and certainly nobody in the government or on this committee, will contradict or block your testimony. I want to make that message very clear." As the interpreters conveyed his words to those who needed help understanding, all of the men nodded their heads, and they appeared to be relieved.

"Again, we appreciate your being here," Wolfowitz concluded. "We will follow up on your comments when we continue tomorrow, and we'll be asking for more information in the meetings to come. Cars are waiting to take you to your hotel. Thank you again, and enjoy your evening."

I stood up then, and so did the seven men. There were handshakes all around, and we were shown back to the anteroom, where our armed escorts met us and took us back out to the real world.

Outside, I gazed back at the sprawling building in which we had just spent most of the day. It struck me then, as it never had before, that the Pentagon is synonymous with the power and might of the U.S. military; even the attack on 9/11 had failed to destroy it. Nobody who is sane wants war, least of all me – but if and when it comes to that, America needs a bulwark such as this.

It had been quite a day, and we knew that it was only the beginning. Every day over the next two weeks, from morning until evening, we met in that office in the Pentagon. We also met with officials at the State Department. In that time the seven brothers were able to provide key members of the Bush administration with a detailed and graphic picture of life in Iraq under Saddam Hussein, as well as giving them insights about Iraqis' hopes and dreams for their country's future. In retrospect, I wish that there had been much more focus by the Bush administration on addressing the unintended consequences of ousting Saddam, and on coming up with realistic programs to help the Iraqis rebuild their country – but that was not within my power to decide.

All good things must come to an end, and after their unforgettable extended stay in the United States, it was finally time for the seven brothers to go back to Iraq. The men had thoroughly enjoyed their visit to America, having done more in this relatively short period than many people do in a lifetime. They had toured Houston and several other parts of Texas, had visited our nation's capital and had been honored guests at the White House, and had been the subject of more than 1,200 reports in print publications, on TV and radio, and on the Internet.

But now the seven brothers were eager to get back home and resume their lives. As remarkable as their experiences had been in the States, it was clear that they were homesick. While those of us who had come to know them empathized with their feelings, and had taken for granted from the beginning of this project that they would eventually have to go back home, we were still worried about problems they might encounter upon their return. We had no delusions that their lives would be a "happily ever after" fairy tale once they received their new hands.

To the contrary, we knew it was possible that their myoelectric hands had the potential to create as many problems as they solved. After all, the men could have only received their new hands through the efforts of many good-hearted Americans (and assorted other Westerners), with the assistance of the less publicized, but certainly not unknown, efforts of the U.S. government. We had known from the outset that this could present a real problem for the men, and we worried that when they returned to Iraq they would be targeted by ISIS or Al-Qaeda, or even just some random anti-American thug.

It was a legitimate concern, as other Iraqis who had associated with the American forces had been identified as pro-American, and as a result they and their families at home in Iraq had been targeted. We had talked about these concerns with the men on several occasions, and as I mentioned earlier, the issue was even addressed at some length during their public appearance at the White House Rose Garden. But overall they seemed less worried than we were.

During one of our private conversations about this matter, Baasim said, "I speak for the group. We are all proud of what the Americans have done for us."

Ala'a added, "I am more than just proud. You have given me my life back."

Their responses were similar every time we had the conversation.

On the up side, the war had seemed to have calmed down in Iraq. Though a cloud still hung over everyone's head, life was slowly returning to normal in most places. Trying to make a decent living and put food on the table was still quite difficult for many if not most Iraqis, but overall the country seemed to be on a path towards its own version of normality.

And despite its many serious challenges, Iraq was home for the seven brothers. It was time for them to go back.

The brothers' enthusiasm about returning home with their new hands was contagious, and in spite of my worries I couldn't help but be happy for them. At the same time, I also couldn't help feeling sad to see them go. I had come to know them well as individuals, and to like, respect, and even love these men. I was going to miss them.

I thought about the fun we'd had together and about some of their adventures – and misadventures – after they had received their new hands and were getting accustomed to using them. One memory that stuck out involved Ala'a Abdul Hassein. Ala'a was a trained engineer, but he was very fun-loving, personable, and outgoing, contrary to the well-known Western stereotype of engineers as shy, nerdy, socially awkward types. Ala'a always seemed to have a song in his heart, as the old saying goes. He had a perpetual smile on his face, and he made everyone around him feel good to be alive. It was he who had kept the brothers' spirits high during some of their most grueling times at Abu Ghraib prison.

But sometimes his sense of fun really tested the limits. One afternoon during the brothers' rehab period, Ala'a used his bionic hand to borrow the keys to my new Jaguar, but he apparently "forgot" to tell me. When we went out looking for him, we found him doing donuts in the parking lot at TIRR. If it had been anybody else, I would have been outraged, but I just couldn't be mad at Ala'a. (Fortunately, no damage was done to either my car or to Ala'a and his new hand.)

This was just one of countless memories that I cherished. But now was not the time to focus on the past; we needed instead to concentrate on the future.

There was only so much we could do to prepare the seven men for any social or political issues they might encounter once they got back to Iraq, but at least we had some control over their medical issues. We provided each of the brothers with two extra batteries for his new hand. Each battery should last over a year, and we made arrangements so that if any of them ever had a problem with the electronics or physical function of the limbs, they could travel to any of the U.S. military bases and would then be sent to Houston for necessary repairs or adjustments.

After many emotional goodbyes, with promises from us and from the seven brothers to keep in touch via email and phone, the men boarded the aircraft that would take them to Frankfurt and ultimately back home to Iraq. And life went on: my busy life in Houston, the lives of my many colleagues and friends who had helped the brothers during their stay in America, and the brothers' lives in Iraq. But that's not the end of the story – not quite.

CHAPTER 30

BACK TO REALITY IN IRAQ

We kept our promise to stay in touch with the seven men. In email communications during the weeks and months following their return to Iraq, we learned that they were using their myoelectric hands every day in their daily life and their respective businesses. This of course had been the goal all along, and we were very pleased that things were working out as intended.

Ala'a, as I mentioned previously, was a trained engineer. When he returned to Iraq he resumed his work in that capacity, and he operated a textile store in Baghdad with his family as well. He told friends, family, and pretty much everyone he met that his life had improved dramatically with his bionic hand. He even became an unofficial ambassador for the country that had hosted him, telling people that he had found American girls "friendly" and that "Americans are not a bad lot."

And when elections were held in Iraq in 2005, Ala'a proudly emailed us about how he went into the polling booth and used his new American right hand to stuff his ballot into the ballot box. Several of the seven brothers went with him and did the same thing.

Nazaar Joudi returned to his hometown in Iraq, where he reopened his jewelry shop and began trading in gold and U.S dollars. Several months later, however, Nazaar's shop was broken into, and everything of value in the shop was stolen. Family members and friends helped him to reestablish his shop, and for the next year or so everything went well, for the most part, even though his jewelry shop was robbed again, and, alarmingly, some private guards who patrolled his neighborhood were killed by the insurgents.

There was no question in my mind that he was being targeted because of the time that he and his brothers had spent in the United States. Nevertheless, Nazaar said that he'd had the photo of him shaking hands with President Bush during the White House visit laminated, and he showed it to everyone every place he went, as well as to customers at his shop. He said he was well aware that he and the others were all at risk, but he didn't feel that showing the picture of him shaking hands with President Bush made it any worse.

He also told us that the people he'd met in Houston had made a lasting impression on him and the other men, and that their entire time in Houston was a peak experience in all of their lives. Nazaar said that all of the Iraqi businessmen were impressed by the work ethics of the people he met in Houston and at The Methodist Hospital.

Baasim Al Fadhly was again working with the TV news station Al Jazeera, and his sign-off on every program was the same. Wielding his microphone with his myoelectric hand, he declared, "I am able to return to my work because the Americans gave me this hand so I can hold a microphone and I can report to you the truth."

He was particularly pleased to report on the capture and arrest, made public in February of 2005, of a general named Sabawi Ibrahim al-Tikriti, who was in charge of the very feared domestic intelligence agency in Iraq – and was Saddam Hussein's half-brother. It was actually General Sabawi who had brought about the arrest of the seven men, and who saw to it that their right hands were amputated. In Baasim's broadcast on Al Jazeera about the arrest, you could hear the joy in his voice over the fact that the evil General Sabawi had finally been caught and would be punished for what he had done to the seven brothers and so many others.

On his Al Jazeera broadcasts, Baasim expressed cautious optimism about the progress taking place in Iraq, and especially about the improved local security. He also commented regarding an increased and uninterrupted supply of electricity in Iraq's cities, and an increased supply of gasoline. Overall, his pro-American broadcasts were optimistic.

Laith Aggaar returned to his hometown outside of Baghdad and opened a successful household appliance and electronics store, selling items such as TV sets and satellite dishes. He couldn't order them fast enough to keep up with the demand. Indeed, when I was in Iraq you could go up to any rooftop and look out over the city, and you would see a satellite dish on the roof of virtually every home, and multiple dishes on the roofs of businesses.

Laith also sold the usual major appliances, such as refrigerators, stoves, and other items that most people desired for their homes. He and his family did quite well at their business, at least for a while.

Salaah Zinaad returned to his hometown too, and resumed a

relatively quiet and peaceful life, grateful every day for the new beginning that had been made possible by his myoelectric hand. Salaah would be one of my gracious hosts when I returned to Iraq in the year following the men's surgeries.

Qaasim, now living and working in Baghdad again, was very proud of his four sons. He told us that he and his sons played basketball together, and he was able to use both hands in the game.

If I worried about anyone, it was Hassan, who was now living with his family in Holland, where he had initially found employment at a furniture factory. For some reason he wanted to return to Baghdad, though his wife and children were opposed to that. They were understandably in fear of what might happen if they returned to Iraq.

To add to his stress, Hassan lost his job in the furniture factory and was looking for new employment. This may have been a factor in his desire to go back to Iraq. Ultimately he understood that in order to stay safe, he needed to stay in Holland with his family, at least for the time being.

The seven brothers still faced many difficulties in war-torn Iraq, but overall they told us that their lives had changed in a positive way. They were all confident in their attitudes and showed off their new American-made prosthetic hands wherever they went.

Still, the fact remained that this only added increased danger to an already difficult life in their home country. While Hassan was using his new prosthetic hand to place his vote in the ballot box, the first Iraqi election of his lifetime, insurgents fired mortar rounds at his home because Hassan was seen by the radicals as an American supporter.

I finally decided that email and phone communications weren't sufficient for me. I wanted to visit the seven brothers in person and see for myself how they were doing, and for that matter how their country was faring. So in 2005, I went back to Iraq.

The first of the brothers I visited was Salaah, and he and his family could not have given me a warmer and more sincere welcome. They made me feel right at home. I was delighted to see Ala'a there too. Sitting in Salaah's front room with Ala'a, Salaah, and Salaah's family, we got into a discussion about the Iraqi economy, and how challenging it remained for many Iraqis to make a decent living. "A lot of people here live on the barter system," Salaah told me. "It's the only way that many can survive. But it works out well."

I nodded enthusiastically. I had seen firsthand, in my own country, how the barter system could and did work – well, once upon a time, anyway. I was a child at the end of World War II and throughout the 1940s and early 1950s, but I remember people trading goods and services. As I mentioned elsewhere in this book, my father was a dentist and his brother was a physician, and they shared a common office in Brooklyn, New York. They were very familiar with the barter system, often using it with patients who came in for treatment when times were hard. In lieu of cash, the butcher brought meat, the grocer brought vegetables, the man who had the confectionery store brought cookies and chocolate, and the man who would fix a leaking faucet in the sink would trade his services for medical care. Dollars were not exchanged.

My father and his brother never charged a police officer or firefighter or any of those to whom we refer today as first responders. There was a big Catholic church and a seminary in the neighborhood, and they were never asked for money either during World War II.

The United States government issued ration booklets during the war; these booklets had small blue-green stamps inside that were torn out by the holder and were used to purchase certain items at the grocery store. Stamps were also used to obtain tires and gasoline for your car, and I remember that we always had good tires on the car and a tank full of gas. The stamps had become yet another form of currency in the barter system and were traded for medical and dental services, as well as other goods and services.

I continued the same tradition in my fifty years of medical practice when circumstances called for it. This was my way of giving back, or perhaps more accurately, paying it forward. Unfortunately, most of the newer generation of practitioners seem not to have learned this lesson. Today we have so many different types of insurance that you need a computer to keep up with the different insurance plans. We have an overwhelming variety of co-pays, payment plans, and so forth... but the old unwritten but long adhered-to rule that *doctors do not charge other doctors* seems to have been forgotten.

That's not all that has changed. In many medical schools upon graduation, the Hippocratic Oath is not even taken anymore by graduating physicians. Medicine is simply not the calling that it was fifty or more years ago. Instead it's a huge money-making business controlled by big corporations, and most physicians today are just salaried employees. The private practice of medicine has all but been abandoned, to the detriment of medical care and patients' health.

The point is that I have considerable knowledge of the barter economy and how it functions. Even so, I had never experienced it to the extremes that were taking place in Iraq. Pondering on these matters now, I was suddenly startled back to the reality of where I was and who I was visiting here.

Everyone was talking, but I had remained quiet for several minutes, and I saw some of the folks in the room looking at me, as if wondering why I wasn't my usual loquacious self. I smiled at them, sitting back in my chair and running my hand through my hair, but still I said nothing. I crossed and uncrossed my legs, and then tried to sit up a bit straighter, but my lower back pain had been bothering me and was getting worse, and changing position didn't seem to help. I rose from the chair and stretched my back, then stood, leaning against a wall, which often helped in relieving my discomfort.

Ala'a looked me in the eye, the expression on his round face turning darkly intense, and his lips were compressed in a tight line. I could see he was worried about me. I said to him, "I have an old back problem, and sometimes it gets uncomfortable sitting for very long, so I just needed to stand and stretch."

He took my arm and walked me towards the kitchen, which was dark and smoky and filled with the wonderful smell of frying meat. Ala'a turned the overhead kitchen fan on to clear the haze, but the fan merely pushed the smoke around. I didn't really mind because the smell was heavenly.

A young woman dressed in the typical garb of the region was busy at the old stove, and she nodded to me to come forward. With a wooden ladle, she removed some of what she was cooking and handed it to me. An overwhelmingly wonderful aroma reached my nostrils as I brought the ladle to my lips. The young woman drummed her fingers against the side of the old stove, waiting for my response. I was nearly overcome by the superb smell and flavor, and I am sure that my eyes lit up as a smile literally filled my face.

She let out her breath in a big sigh. It was as if a deep concern had been lifted, and her own face lit up with a glorious smile. I just stood there in front her, smiling and thinking, *How can I properly express my thanks to her in my far less than fluent Arabic?* I was the one to be surprised as she said, in perfect English, "It's good? Yes? You like it?" I nodded and she added, "It's almost ready. We will have this later. My

English is good? I studied English in school."

"Your English is wonderful. You must have been a good student. My Arabic is not very good."

She gave a smile and then began to giggle. Salaah entered the room then, putting a hand on my shoulder and saying, "I'm afraid we must get moving. We will return later in the afternoon and have lunch here."

"She is a good cook. I just had a taste, and it was excellent."

"You can enjoy her cooking and spend more time here with my family and me later today. Right now, we are going to visit with Nazaar. I know you want to see him, and he is anxious and expecting us. My neighbor, Muhammad, drives a taxi, and he is waiting outside for us." We walked back through the room where we had been visiting, and I said my farewells to the others, then followed Salaah outside.

Even though it was early evening, the oppressive summer heat refused to abate. A light breeze stirred as it does on most evenings, and peppered us with fine grains of sand, but the temperature held rather constant, and to say that it was hot didn't really do it justice. When it is this hot, dehydration can kill you very quickly. You never feel it coming until you pass out, and by then it is too late.

I was already uncertain about being in Iraq again, and for several reasons I was concerned about the upcoming visit with Nazaar. I tried to relax but could feel my pulse rate increasing, and seeing the taxi that awaited us did nothing to calm my nerves. As I stood there looking at the vehicle, I tried to imagine what make and model it was, and came to the conclusion that it was actually a patchwork of salvaged parts with an undetermined chassis and motor. Clearly this car had also been through the war.

It took several pulls to get the vehicle's door open. There was a colorful quilt-like blanket covering the backseat; I slid over and Salaah followed me in. He spoke with the driver, Muhammad, for a moment, and then the car accelerated quite noisily, which only added to my anxiety. Though it was only a short distance to Nazaar's home, I was wondering if we were going to make it in this contraption, this laughable excuse for a taxi.

I was hot and sweating, and as we rode I kept telling myself, as I always did when visiting faraway places during their most sweltering seasons, that this was not much different from Houston in mid-summer. But I stubbornly refused to embrace my own attempt at logic; this was clearly not Texas, and each intake of air made me sweat more, as if I were biting into a hot pepper at my favorite Mexican restaurant. No matter where you travel or where you live, it seems that Mother Nature always gets the upper hand. I was just going to have to grin and bear it as I always do.

Muhammad was a heavyset man, probably more than 300 pounds. He had broad shoulders and long dark hair that curled over his ears; his brows were thick and heavy and his eyes deeply set. He had a full beard and mustache, both of which I thought could have used a little trimming, but I was aware that the Islamist extremist factions that were a growing force in the area did not allow this.

He did speak good English, and I asked him where he had learned it. He said he'd learned some in school, and after the American coalition troops arrived in Iraq, he worked as a driver, and his English improved greatly.

I asked Muhammad how he would compare the Iraq of today against when Saddam Hussein was in charge of the country. He replied that he now worked freely and could earn a satisfactory living so he could put food on the table for his family, and they might have a little money left over at the end of the year to make a trip to visit his cousin. He said he didn't require much, and that most people here didn't.

"We are all good neighbors and work together," he said. "What happened to Salaah and his 'brothers' – the amputation of their right hands – was terrible. The amputations and the torture that so many of our countrymen suffered under Saddam was terrible. It is something that all of us will carry with us every day of our lives."

As we drove, I noticed that many shops that had been closed down the last time I'd been in Iraq had been rebuilt and opened, and the merchants seemed to be doing a thriving business. As we continued past the open market, it appeared that the vendors had more than an adequate supply of fresh vegetables and meat for the shoppers. This was a significant change since my previous visit, which seemed like far longer than a year ago. Then again, a lot can happen in a year, or even a few months.

Muhammad was very talkative, and began providing me with a narration of what we were seeing, along with a history lesson. He said, "Al-Kadhimiya is a city within a city." His reference was to the famous neighborhood in northern Baghdad, through which we were driving. "Al-Kadhimiya is a holy city founded by Musa ibn Ja'far al-Kadhim. Al-

Kadhim was the son of Ja'far al-Sadiq. This family's pedigree goes all the way back to the prophet Mohammed." He paused to let me take this in, then continued, "I know the man you are going to visit, Nazaar Joudi. I also knew Nazaar's father and grandfather; they were all from Al-Kadhimiya." After another pause he added, "Muslims and others from all over the world come to visit Al-Kadhimiya."

"What is special about this city, besides it being a holy place?" I asked.

"It is also a tourist attraction," he replied. "But in my eyes it is important because it is a place of trade too. Because of these three things – the fact that it is a religious center, a tourist attraction, and a center of trade – Al-Kadhimiya has a special ranking among Iraqi cities."

As we traveled I saw a few automobiles, but mopeds seemed to dominate. A young group passed us by on bicycles, but most shoppers seemed to be walking and carrying the goods they had purchased.

A few minutes later we arrived at our destination. I thanked Muhammad and handed him some dollars. All of the Iraqis I'd encountered seemed to appreciate and want dollars, but Muhammad pushed them back at me and said, "You've done too much already. Have Nazaar call me when you two are ready to leave, and it will be my pleasure to pick you up and bring you back. No charge, of course."

Nazaar Joudi and his family were waiting for us. They were all dressed in their best clothing; Nazaar was wearing some loose black cotton trousers and a light blue cotton shirt with an open collar. He enthusiastically extended his American-made trademark, the myoelectric hand, to me. Then he embraced me in a bear hug and kissed me on both cheeks. I shook hands with the other men who were there, but merely bowed respectfully towards each of the women. Unless they chose to extend their hands it would have been improper for me to extend mine.

I was ushered into a room where the table was already set. Almost as soon as we sat down, hot tea was served, and then we were served those little sugar cakes that I loved so much.

I had originally thought I was going to lose some weight on this trip, what with being in this sauna-like climate and lacking easy access to clean water to drink. However, with these sugar cakes at every stop, the best I could hope for was to break even: *calories in, water out.*

I couldn't have been happier to see Nazaar, and apparently the feeling was mutual. I asked him if he was still working with gold and jewelry. He replied that he was, and that he had been doing well. He had opened shops in Mosul, Najaf, Hillah, and other cities in the country.

He took a sip of tea, and I could see that he and his guests were waiting for me to take the first sweet cake; only then would they help themselves.

Well, as I mentioned, I really love those little cakes, so I took two. With that, others began to help themselves, and the conversation around the table picked up.

Everybody had questions. They wanted to know about my animals – the horses, burros, llamas, deer, and the swans on my lake at my little ranchette. Nazaar asked about the animals at the Y.O. Ranch in Kerrville, Texas; clearly that visit had been one of the highlights of his Texas trip. I can well understand why, as I have always enjoyed my visits to the Y.O. Ranch.

We talked about President Bush, politics, and other topics that a few years ago could never have been discussed openly in Iraq. I said, "It seems that the dollar is not only accepted now but favored in most transactions; is that right?"

Nazaar said, "Yes! And, just think a few years ago, I was criminally charged with working in dollars... and ended up losing my hand as a result." He held up his prosthetic hand for emphasis.

"The Iraqi government hated even hearing the word 'dollar,'" Nazaar continued. "Saddam Hussein passed an ordinance forbidding the Iraqi people to use the American dollar – even though the Iraqi government and its officials used the dollar for themselves. Such hypocrites! The people didn't realize until it was too late that something as simple and harmless as using the dollar could have such terrible consequences. But the Ba'athist ranking party members and the secret police were making tape recordings of conversations that merchants were having while they were doing their ordinary business. These recordings prompted security officers to come to their place of business or their homes, and ultimately resulted in long prison terms under terrible conditions, and..." Again he held up his myoelectric hand. "And it was all supposedly for using dollars, pounds, or other foreign currency in their business transactions!"

Of course, I already knew the basics of this background story, as well as many of the details, but I figured that Nazaar needed to vent. After all that he'd been through, the least I could do was to allow him that. Besides, I had never had an in-depth discussion with him about his personal experiences, and I was glad to learn more about what he had endured. I nodded sympathetically as he continued, "I did not know about the tape recordings being made by the secret police. They tape recorded every single word I said over the phone to other persons with whom I was doing business. I had several telephone lines to my different stores, and they were all illegally monitored. Every time I picked up the receiver, the secret police were recording my voice from the first word to the last, even the telephone as it rang. The secret police came to my establishment, and I was very frightened. They took me away to an interrogation room, where they asked the same two questions over and over again: 'How much did you sell?' and 'How much did you buy?'"

Nazaar's story was interrupted by knocking at the door. When one of the young men went to open the door, there stood a man whom they referred to as the Sheikh. We all stood up from the table as he entered. For my benefit Nazaar explained, "The Sheikh is a religious man with a good reputation amongst the people in Al-Kadhimiya, and he is a good friend of ours." I nodded and smiled.

"I want you to see with your own eyes that this religious man has come to welcome you," Nazaar continued. "He and all the people, both young and old, like me and trust me. That's why they do business with me."

Nazaar gave the Sheikh his own seat at the head of the table and poured tea for his honored guest. The Sheikh was well educated and spoke fluent English. He had many questions about America and about my interest in the seven brothers. Some of the Sheikh's questions were political in nature, others religious, but always with friendly overtones. The Sheikh had never been to the United States and just wanted answers; he seemed to be more motivated by curiosity than by anything else.

After an hour or so, the Sheikh left, and I wanted to get back to Nazaar's story. I felt that he still needed to talk about it, and I also knew that there were more details that he hadn't really had a chance to share in our previous conversations. I wanted to find out more about what had happened after the secret police had taken him away for interrogation, and about his "trial."

Nazaar said, "That trial was a sham! It wasn't even the proper court. The trial was held in the same place where I was interrogated. The secret police did not assign me an attorney. There was no opportunity for an appeal. The court was a façade all done within the secrecy of the security department.

"Right there, I was sentenced to have my right hand cut off at the wrist. I was told that it was for disobedience of the leadership council decision regarding the use of dollars and gold. I remember asking the leadership council if I really had caused such a big problem, and if I was really a criminal, and whether the interrogations and sentencing and everything they were doing to me were just because I was working with dollars. Everyone was using dollars!" He paused, as if trying to calm down a little, and took a sip of tea. Then he continued.

"But I still didn't believe these people were actually going to cut off hands. I just *couldn't* believe it. I realized they were serious when I experienced the most agonizing pain I'd ever felt, and suddenly my hand wasn't there anymore."

I could see the emotion in his face and tears in his eyes.

"Then the Ba'athist party was finally no more," Nazaar said. "Saddam Hussein was gone, as were his two sons, Qusay and Uday. The Americans and coalition forces had liberated Iraq. We were all hopeful and looking for change, even those of us who were locked away in Abu Ghraib prison.

"Since I have come back from America, our house has been open from morning to evening. People have been visiting me from all over Iraq. Many have expressed disbelief that I had lost my right hand – that I would have to suffer such pain and humiliation – because of my work with gold and multiple currencies. And it is shocking, but it is also true that almost everyone who has visited me told me that they either know, or know about, other people who suffered similar fates, or worse, under Saddam. So even though these things are shocking and unbelievable, they have also been an everyday reality for too many of us who live here."

Then he suddenly smiled at me, and the contrast between that smile and his demeanor of just a few moments ago was remarkable. "But now... now I show them my new hand! And actually there are some people now who don't even realize I've had my hand cut off. The American prosthetic hand is so realistic that at first, unless they look closely enough, they do not realize it is a prosthesis. I feel whole again. I feel good. Now I can work in my shops and take care of my family, thanks to you and the other Americans who made this possible."

Due to numerous commitments at home, I could only stay in Iraq for a short time. That time flew by, and almost before I knew it, my Iraqi friends and I were going through another round of emotional farewells. But as I boarded the plane to leave Iraq, I felt better than I had in a long time. Most if not all of the seven brothers still faced a rocky future, and I had no illusions of a happily ever after scenario for any of them. And make no mistake: I was still worried about them. But at the same time I felt confident that they would be able to face and overcome any challenge that came their way. I knew that I would do everything in my power to help them in any way I could.

I was right to be worried about my friends, as it turned out. Iraq continued to make limited progress towards normalcy, but it was like constantly taking one step forward and two steps back. The insurgency was a force that would not go away. The situation for the brothers, as well as for many others all over Iraq, deteriorated in the years that followed. Despite the optimism and bravado that the seven men had expressed in the months immediately following their surgeries, their homeland was increasingly becoming a place of danger and despair.

Ala'a had a frightening series of near misses, and he ended up having to give up his textile store. Customers feared being caught in the kill zone should he be targeted by insurgents who knew about his American ties. Ala'a and his family moved to Beirut, Lebanon, for a while.

After nearly a year of respite from trouble, Nazaar was hit with several robbery attempts at his shop, and, even more frightening, he was personally attacked. He had no doubt that these attacks were politically motivated, and while he believed in standing his ground, he was also worried – not just for himself, but also for his wife and children. He felt obligated to confine himself and his family to their home, which is far from an ideal situation for a family with growing children, as many Americans learned the hard way during the recent pandemic lockdowns. It finally got to the point where Iraq no longer felt like home to Nazaar and his family. He turned to the American government for help, but it was actually through the efforts of some of us private citizens that he was able to obtain a U.S. visa and other papers that were needed for him and his family to come to the United States and apply for citizenship.

Trouble caught up with Baasim as well. His bold positions regarding free speech prompted several attacks on his life. One day armed gunmen came to his door looking for him, and although he wasn't home, his brother Talal was shot and killed. In the autumn of 2006, his sister was gunned down on a Baghdad street, and later on, a nephew was slain. "They were killed because they had the same name as me," Baasim later told a newspaper reporter.

He became progressively more afraid for his life and the lives of his family, and even though he remained steadfast in his convictions about telling the truth, he knew he had to take precautions. Baasim and his family were moved for a while to an undisclosed location near Dubai. He continued to work at various radio and TV stations doing the news, and his reports were sent electronically throughout the Arab world, including Iraq. Today Baasim is safe, and living a quiet life with his family in the United Arab Emirates.

Laith Aggaar encountered trouble too as Iraq's situation grew more volatile. He took his family to live in Dubai.

It saddens me to say that the United States government dropped the ball for a while where these seven men were concerned. Their story had been excellent PR for President Bush and America, and during one of the men's White House visits, Bush had expressed a bright shining vision of the future that he believed Iraq faced as a result of American intervention. It all made for good press in those early weeks and months after the men's surgeries. In the years that followed, however, as life in Iraq became more dangerous for them, Baasim and several of the others contacted various American officials, but were frustrated by the lack of help. Some of them felt they had been abandoned by the United States.

Their plight was part of a larger problem: escaping Iraq had become very difficult, particularly for friends of the United States. Bordering countries such as Syria and Jordan had all but closed their doors to Iraqi refugees, and since 2003 the U.S. State Department had severely limited the number of Iraqis to whom political asylum was granted. In 2007, under mounting international pressure to help Iraqis who had fled their homes, the Bush administration said it would allow 7,000 Iraqis to come to the U.S., and would immediately contribute millions of dollars for a worldwide settlement and relief program.

But the seven brothers persisted in their efforts to obtain help for themselves and their families. Ultimately, five of the seven men came to the United Sates. It was not an easy process, but they are presently living in the Washington, D.C. area and nearby cities such as Bethesda, Maryland. Marvin Zindler's producer, Lori Reingold, helped expedite some of these arrangements.

To this day, when I think about the medical aspects of my experience with the seven brothers, I am still amazed and grateful that everything went so well, from the pre-op procedures to the surgeries to the post-surgical care and rehab. The entire process exceeded our most optimistic expectations, due in no small part to the seven patients' remarkable strength and determination. Still, since there had been so much to accomplish, and we'd only had a short time together, the process had been much more demanding than any of us had thought it would be. But in light of the satisfying medical outcomes, I would definitely do it again.

And from a deeper personal perspective? Yes... I would do it all again. Though the traumas of two decades ago have faded, my experiences in Iraq left an indelible mark on me. It was sobering to witness what was taking place in that war-ravaged country, and to see what the seven brave men lived through and endured. But it was gratifying to be an instrument in improving their lives. The brothers in turn carried the message to Iraq that Americans are basically good people. They had all vowed that when they returned home, they would be sharing their positive American experiences with as many people as possible. And they did. They paid the price for that, of course, but even so, several of them said that they still had warm feelings for America – particularly Houston, I am pleased to say.

I can close my eyes now and see the face of each man: Baasim, Nazaar, Hassan, Ala'a, Qaasim, Salaah, and Laith. I can feel their love and gratitude at being made whole again. And I feel thankful all over again that I had the privilege of being part of their story.

America is facing more challenges than ever before, including (or especially!) a deep divisiveness within our own borders, and there are still plenty of people in other parts of the world who don't like us. In some cases, we've earned their dislike. But I think that we have also done a lot to earn admiration for, or at least acknowledgment of, the good things America has accomplished, as well as for our aspirations to live up to our highest ideals. America is still a work in progress, and our story is far from over.

The saga of the seven brothers is only one small chapter in a large, ongoing, and very mixed narrative. I have never believed in sugar-coating or whitewashing that narrative. But I also think it is appropriate, and necessary, to highlight the good parts of the American story. I hope I've done that in these pages.

AFTERWORD

The story of every war, from isolated conflicts to world wars, is a narrative not only about winners and losers, but also about lessons we learned and those we failed to learn. To reference a well-known adage, the result of our chronic failure to learn from our folly is that history repeats itself, over and over and over, and yet we either don't grasp the lessons or we choose to ignore them.

My late friend Don North dedicated his life to presenting clear and often brutally honest narratives about the horror and ultimate futility of war. He and I had several conversations about these matters, and the two of us were, for the most part, on the same page regarding our opinions about war and human nature.

I was probably a little more cynical than Don, however, my general feeling being that humans are simply a bellicose species and that war is something we're stuck with, come what may. I would love to believe otherwise. And as I expressed earlier in this book, part of me still has hope that eventually the human race will move on from its seemingly insatiable hunger for war, but I have serious doubts. Don, on the other hand, never gave up on his hope that documenting the atrocities of war, and making that documentation accessible to as many people as possible, could inspire more folks to work harder for peace and might even help bring an end to war. He was not as convinced as I that warfare is an inevitable part of the human experience.

While I'm on the subject of our differences, I'll add that although I respected and admired Don and his work, I was in some ways more critical than he of the overall role that journalists have played in influencing public opinion and even foreign policy. For instance, I felt that some of the negative or sensationalist press coverage about the invasion of Iraq might have made an already difficult and dangerous situation even more so for our military and allies who were stationed there, while making our leaders' jobs harder as well.

On more than one occasion I also complained about the priority that the newsgathering industry continually gives to sensational or violent stories – not just regarding war coverage, but as a general practice. We've all heard the old colloquialism, "If it bleeds, it leads." That's particularly true of television news, but the phenomenon exists in all news media. I have never believed in glossing over bad news – that would be journalistic malpractice at best and a mark of tyranny at worst – but like many other people, I do sometimes get tired of the constant flow of negativity from our news outlets. And while producers, station managers, and editors are ultimately in charge of the content that gets aired or printed, journalists and reporters also bear some responsibility for the focus on bad news.

Understandably, Don was more sympathetic to journalists and the news industry than I, declaring at one of our press conferences in Washington, D.C. that journalists often do good work in very dangerous situations. He believed in journalism in its purest form, however, without spin, and felt that the job of a journalist covering war was neither to be PR for the military or government nor to be a critic, but simply to report what was happening, and let the chips fall where they may.

But it seems clear to me that Don also believed that this mandate to report objectively does not preclude journalists taking a moral or even a political stance on occasion. In fact, as I mentioned in my tribute to him at the beginning of this book, a few years after that press conference he did admit that he felt the Western allies were poorly served by journalists who failed to seriously question the wisdom of attacking Iraq. Even so, he was for the most part a staunch defender of his profession, and he always held himself to the highest standards of journalism.

I said previously that every war is a narrative about lessons learned and not learned. The story of America's intervention in Iraq in 2003 is no exception, and certainly there were several lessons to be taken from this war. To this day we still seem to be sorting out those lessons, as well as dealing with the consequences of the Western allies' invasion of that country. For example, the ultimate revelation that there were not and never had been weapons of mass destruction in Iraq made many Americans skeptical of our own government's "intelligence" – a skepticism that has only grown, rightly or wrongly, in the years since Saddam was ousted. We have also witnessed the unintended consequences of toppling a brutal tyrant but subsequently creating instability and "endless war" in an already volatile region.

The bottom line is that our involvement in Iraq, and to a greater extent in the twenty-year war in Afghanistan, has led to a wider and deeper skepticism about American involvement in *any* war. That skepticism is behind the growing objections to continued aid for Ukraine to help that small brave country stand up to Vladimir Putin's brutal and unjustified attack in February of 2022. (On the other hand, a reluctance to get involved in an overseas war is nothing new. Consider the longstanding policy of neutrality that prevented the United States from entering World War I, egregiously misnamed "The War To End All Wars," until Germany forced the issue in 1917; and think about how long America resisted getting involved in World War II, until Japan attacked Pearl Harbor on December 7, 1941.)

When American voters of all political stripes, or politicians on either side of the aisle, protest the aid that is being sent to this or that country to help fund their wars, the rationale is generally that the money would be much better directed towards helping Americans in need, particularly our veterans. It's an old argument, and not wholly without merit. Yet even when we're not actively funding some overseas war, our legislators all too often continue to neglect the needs of Americans at home, including and especially veterans. The rich continue to get richer, while the poor and middle class continue to struggle. Meanwhile, our defense budget continues to grow, and grow, and grow, regardless of which political party is in power. I don't think that's going to change any time soon.

Notwithstanding the chronic bellicosity of our species over the millennia, recent research, such as a 2018 Rutgers University-Newark study, indicates that humans may not actually be hardwired for warfare. It's interesting research, but it doesn't do much to lessen my cynicism on this issue. And let's face it: even the most meticulous and credible study is of little help when some soulless autocrat wages genocide on an innocent population, or when some obscure tribal conflict explodes into a region-wide war that threatens to destabilize the world economy. The possibility that war is not in our hardwiring certainly didn't help the seven brothers, or millions of other innocent Iraqi citizens, when they were being brutally maimed (or worse) by Saddam Hussein's henchmen.

In short, and with all due respect to the Rutgers researchers, I don't think I would go broke if I were to bet against the possibility of an end to war in our lifetime.

As individuals, we don't have the power to halt war. All that any of us can do is try to work for peace, and/or to help heal the wounds of war, by any means we have, large or small. In our own respective ways, Don North and I spent decades trying to do just that: Don through his intrepid reporting and his teaching, and I through my global medical missions and my Children's Foundation.

You may be wondering, "What can I do?" The answer is: "Plenty." I'll give you the same advice I shared in my previous book, *Mission Divided*. Perhaps you aren't in a position to donate money, or you don't have the ability or means to provide medical care or other humanitarian aid directly to affected areas in the U.S.A. or abroad. But there are still things you can do.

The best place to start – and it won't cost you anything – is to educate yourself as to what is really going on, both in other countries and right here at home. When you begin to see past the diet of artificially-sweetened, or conversely, exaggeratedly dire, news that we are being routinely fed, raise your voice. Point out the falsehoods wherever you see them, no matter where those falsehoods originate or are being disseminated. Demand the truth, not only from your elected officials, but from the press as well. Call, write, send emails or texts, and sign and share petitions that address issues that you know to be important. And never, ever be silent when you see abuse, cruelty, or dishonesty. By adding your voice to the truth, you will make it available to more people, and help to make deception ineffective for those whose success depends upon it. In whatever way you can, take action. Let me know how it goes; I would love to hear from you.

I thank you for taking this journey with me.

~ Doc Joe

PHOTOS

President George W. Bush, who helped make it all possible.
Above: Official Presidential portrait (public domain).
Below: President Bush meeting with the seven brothers
and Dr. Joseph Agris in the Oval Office, May 2004.

Journalist and videographer Don North on the day the seven brothers arrived in Houston via Continental Airlines

Dr. Joseph Agris meets the seven Iraqi brothers on the tarmac at Houston Intercontinental Airport. Left to right Nazaar Joudi, Dr. Joe, and Qaasim Kaadhim.

Left: Don North photographing the arrival of the seven brothers. Right: Terry Bodkin Agris.

The seven brothers celebrating their arrival in Houston with Doc Joe Agris and Don North.

Arrival at ABC Channel 13 TV (KTRK) in Houston, Texas. Pizza lunch for everyone.

Don North with Marvin Zindler of ABC-TV Channel 13.

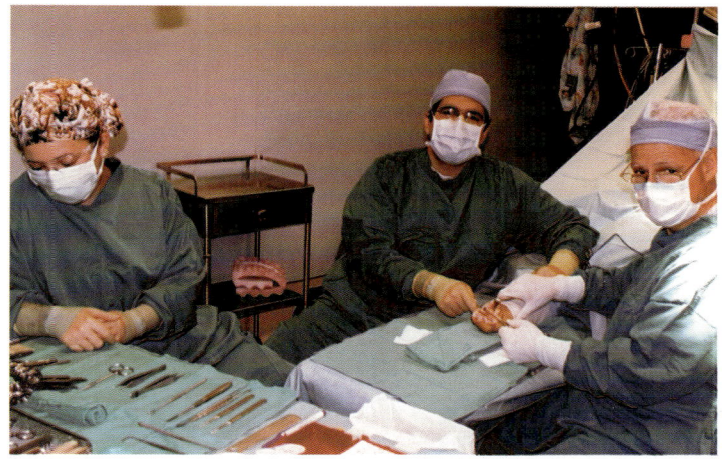

At The Methodist Hospital, preparing for the procedure to correct the hand amputation. Dr. Joe Agris in the foreground.

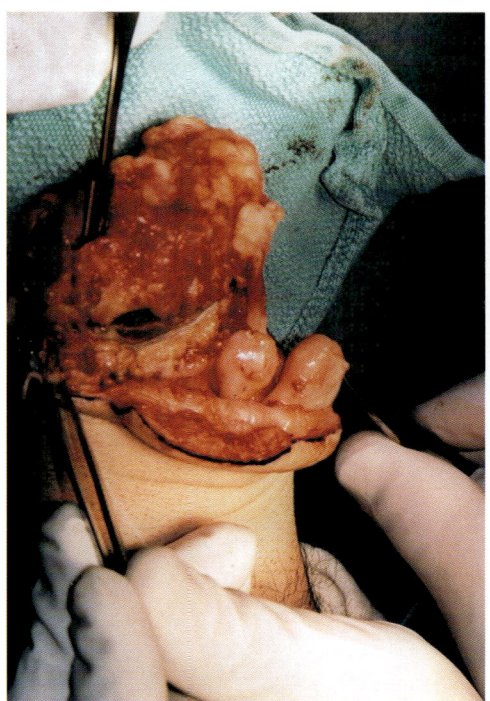

On the operating room table: Very painful tumors (neuromas) were removed during the revision amputation in preparation for the fitting of the prostheses.

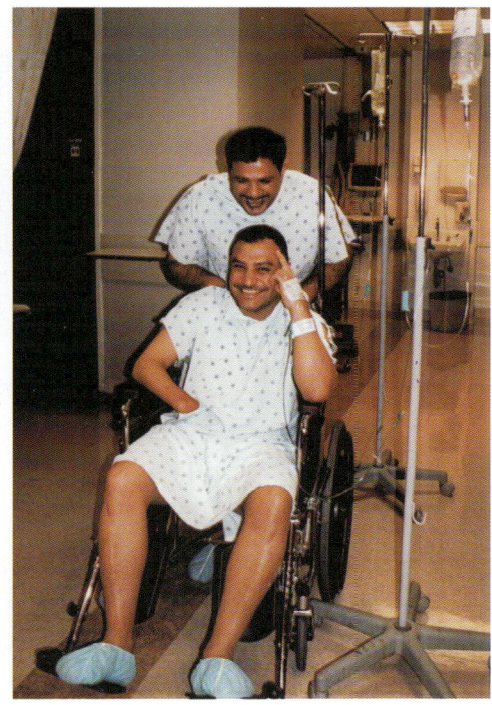

Boys will be boys! Salaah Zinaad pushes Ala'a Hassein down the halls of the hospital.

The Methodist Hospital post-op with Ala'a Hassein, Don North, Dr. Joe Agris, and Marvin Zindler.

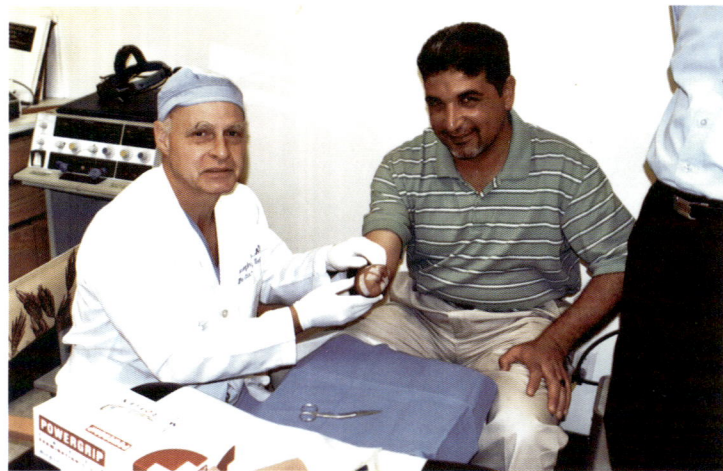

Dr. Joseph Agris at the Texas Medical Center, changing the dressing for Laith Aggaar.

ABC-TV cameramen Bob Dows, producer Lori Reingold, journalist Don North, Dr. Joe Agris, and Marvin Zindler visiting post-op with Baasim Al Fadhly.

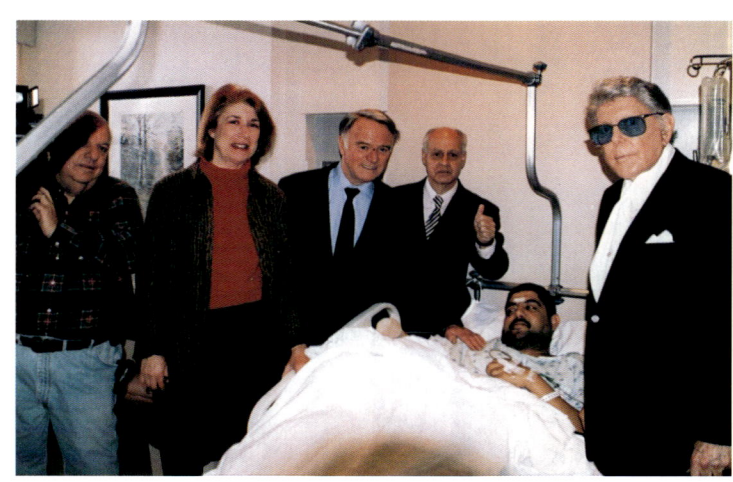

The seven brothers at Dynamic Orthotics and Prosthetics in Houston, ready to be fitted with their new prosthetic hands. With orthotist David Baty and Dr. Joe Agris.

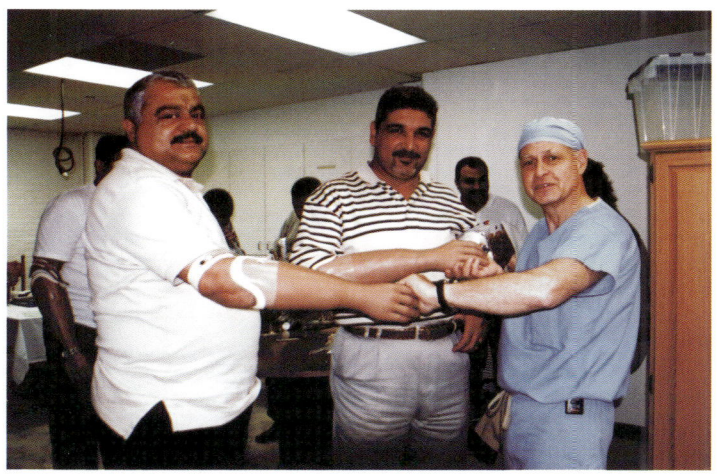

At the Texas Institute for Rehabilitation and Research (TIRR): Qaasim Kaadhim, Laith Aggaar, and Dr. Joe Agris as the men learn to use their new myoelectric hands.

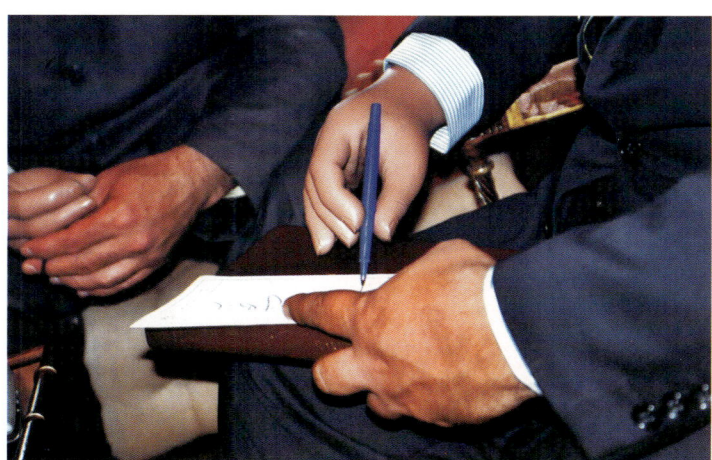

One of the seven brothers demonstrates his ability to write with his new myoelectric hand.

Right: Unknown to Dr. Agris and the group, Ala'a Hassein "borrowed" the keys Dr. Agris' Jaguar. Ala'a was later found doing donuts in the parking lot of TIRR.

Below: Nazaar Joudi holds a new video camera, hoping to document what the Americans did for him and the other six brothers, so he can show everyone back home.

Bob Dows and Hassan al Gereawy, who is proud and grateful to be in America (and out of Abu Ghraib prison).

Ala'a Hassein lakeside at Dr. Agris' ranchette, "Eden," in Bellaire, Texas. Left, with Lady Liberty and right, with Doc Joe.

Laith Aggaar, Dr. Joe Agris, Terry Bodkin Agris, Baasim Al Fadhly, Nazaar Joudi, and Qaasim Kaadhim, at the Agris home in Bellaire, Texas.

At a car show in Houston. Don North, Dr. Joe Agris, interpreter, and Ala'a Hassein.

As guests at the Houston World Affairs Council, Don North (standing) and Dr. Joe Agris (not shown) conducted a presentation along with the seven brothers.

You can't come to Houston without seeing an Astros baseball game.

Houston Astros owner Drayton McLane invited the seven brothers to watch an Astros baseball game in a private box. Terry Bodkin Agris with Mr. McLane.

The group in front of the Ferris wheel in downtown Houston, fronting the Aquarium Restaurant.

Visit to the Aquarium Restaurant in downtown Houston, as guests of owner Tilman Fertitta. Shown here: Laith Aggaar, Baasim Al Fadhly.

The seven brothers visit NASA as special guests. Here, the entire group poses in front of a rocket.

Dr. Agris and some of the seven brothers on their visit to NASA inside the control room of the rocket, post-op. Some of the brothers are still in their slings.

The entire group enjoy lunch in Galveston, Texas on the Gulf.

About 2 weeks post-surgery, the group visited the famous Y.O. Ranch in Kerrville, Texas. Top left: the brothers went on a hay ride (that's ranch co-owner Byron Sadler at the far left of the photo). Bottom left: They also got in some horseback riding. But it's not all horses and cattle at the Y.O. Above right: Qaasim Kaadhim and Doc Joe feed the giraffes.

Group picture at the Y.O. Ranch.

During their post-op Texas tour, the seven brothers visited the famous Alamo in San Antonio, Texas.

Group photo with several sailors in front of the Alamo.

Laith Aggaar poses in front of the Alamo.

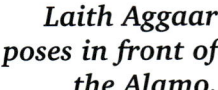

Dr Joe Agris, Ala'a Hassein, Don North in Washington, D.C.
The Washington Monument is in the background.

Dr. Agris lecturing at the
National Press Club in D.C.

Doc Joe and Ala'a Hassein
at Kennedy Center in D.C.;
They couldn't be happier.

Dr. Agris, standing with the group of Iraqi men in the Rose Garden at the White House, addresses the press.

Dr. Joseph Agris' beautiful wife Terry and ABC-TV writer, reporter, and news producer Lori Reingold pose with a military guard at the Rose Garden entrance to the White House.

One of the seven brothers (second from left) shows his myoelectric right hand to a service member who also lost his right hand. To the right: US Deputy Secretary of Defense Paul Wolfowitz and Dr. Agris.

At Walter Reed Hospital in Washington, D.C. Dr. Joseph Agris presenting photos of the seven brothers from Iraq to Paul Wolfowitz, the U.S. Deputy Secretary of Defense.

Senator Bill Frist (R-TN, fourth from right) poses with the seven brothers.

At a special ceremony in Washington D.C., the seven brothers place a wreath on the Tomb of the Unknown Soldier.

Dr. Agris at the World War II Memorial in Washington D.C.

Dr. Agris with two of the brothers in front of the river entrance to the Pentagon.

A meeting at the State Department. Over a period of two weeks, at both the Pentagon and the State Department, the Iraqi men provided information on the status of Iraq as a country and on their individual cities and towns.

*Doc Joe sitting across from the
United States Capitol Building
with his first book,
White Knight in Blue Shades.*

*Nazaar Joudi and family. After
returning to Iraq following his
surgery, Nazaar reopened his
jewelry shop, but faced continual
threats from insurgents.*

*A Show of Hats: On the back porch of Dr. Agris' home
in Bellaire, Texas. Everyone now has a Texas hat.
They may not all be Stetsons, but it's the thought that counts.*

Doc Joe, "The Crazy Texan" at the Houston Livestock Show and Rodeo (where his outfit blends in much better than it did during his travels to Iraq and many other countries across the globe).

ABOUT THE AUTHOR

Besides having been one of Houston's premier cosmetic, plastic, and reconstructive surgeons for many years, with a bustling practice in the world-famous Texas Medical Center, Dr. Joseph Agris (now retired from medical practice) is an activist and philanthropist, especially when it comes to children's health problems and education issues.

In recent years he became more involved with fighting the effects of the horrible abuses to which women in countries such as Pakistan and Afghanistan are subjected. He has helped repair and restore the faces and bodies of many victims who have suffered the devastating results of acid burning and kerosene burning. At the same time, he has continued his commitment to children and adults in need in many parts of the world, including the United States.

Years ago, Doc Joe and the late journalist, consumer advocate, and philanthropist Marvin Zindler formed The Agris-Zindler Children's Foundation to deliver needed medical care to kids all over the globe. The Children's Foundation remains one of Doc Joe's passions.

A true Renaissance man, well read in the arts and sciences, Doc Joe is a world traveler and an accomplished photographer who has exhibited his spectacular photos on several occasions. When he's not traveling to some remote corner of the planet, Doc Joe is in Houston, Texas, enjoying time with his lovely wife Terry and their menagerie of animals on their ranchette they call "Eden," planning his next project or mission, and working on his next book.

IN GRATITUDE

This book would not have been produced so professionally, nor indeed, would it have even been possible, without the patience, persistence, and generosity of Ron Kaye and Connie Schmidt of Schmidt Kaye & Company, my long-time collaborators, who have donated so much of their time and expertise to help craft my story. My former transcriptionist and assistant Beverly Winter, as well as my current transcriptionist Mirele Guillen, also deserve my profound thanks for making all of our jobs easier.

More than anyone else, I owe my thanks to my wife Terry, who has humored the often extreme passions of a husband who can't quite seem to sit still and let things be. She has supported me in my endeavors, rejoiced with me in my successes, and comforted me in those times when I fell short of living up to my aspirations. Every man should be so lucky as to have a muse as remarkable as she has been for me.

THE CHILDREN'S FOUNDATION

Every two minutes, a child is born with a birth defect. Cleft palates, disfiguring birthmarks, and other defects are "silent catastrophes" that can ravage any child. Even if the condition does not threaten a child's health and is "merely" cosmetic, it can be psychologically and emotionally devastating. These children need special attention, yet a heartbreaking number of them fall between the cracks of the system.

The Children's Foundation, founded in 1981 by Joseph Agris, M.D., and the late Marvin Zindler, exists to help these forgotten children. With your help, we have been able to deliver badly needed care to children (and adults) in some of the poorest areas on the planet, including Central America, the Middle East, the former Soviet bloc, China, and many other places. We have also helped many children and their families in the United States.

The Children's Foundation is dedicated to identifying the problems, bringing about solutions, and mobilizing resources for the implementation of needed care and support services. This encompasses medical care, surgery, medications, and prostheses, as well as family support. And while these clinical applications are certainly needed, research leading to cure or prevention is also paramount.

We owe to children the best that we can give. Every child has a right to necessary medical care. But not all children are born equal; the world is full of desperately poor children whose families can scarcely afford food and shelter, much less medical care.

Even though medical care is often costly, however, it is an affordable cost... if we all give something. Give a child a chance, by giving your tax-deductible gift to the Children's Foundation today. Send your check or money order, made payable to THE CHILDREN'S FUND, to:

The Children's Foundation
400 Mulberry Lane
Bellaire, Texas 77401

We also accept Visa, MasterCard, or American Express. To find out how to donate via credit card, please contact Dr. Joseph Agris at 713-705-6625. Or email TerryAgris@Att.net (Subject line: Children's Foundation)

And remember... a portion of the profits from the sales of this book will be donated to the Children's Foundation.

"The kids" and the families who love them thank you!